THE
QUEENS
NOBODY KNOWS

Date: 4/9/21

306.09747 HEL
Helmreich, William B.
The Queens nobody knows :
an urban walking guide /

THE

QUEENS

NOBODY KNOWS

=== AN URBAN WALKING GUIDE ===

WILLIAM B. HELMREICH

PRINCETON UNIVERSITY PRESS
PRINCETON AND OXFORD

Published by Princeton University Press
41 William Street, Princeton, New Jersey 08540
6 Oxford Street, Woodstock, Oxfordshire OX20 1TR

press.princeton.edu

Library of Congress Cataloging-in-Publication Data

Names: Helmreich, William B., author.
Title: The Queens nobody knows : an urban walking guide / William B Helmreich.
Description: Princeton : Princeton University Press, [2020] | Includes bibliographical
    references and index.
Identifiers: LCCN 2019058691 (print) | LCCN 2019058692 (ebook) |
    ISBN 9780691166889 (paperback) | ISBN 9780691200026 (ebook)
Subjects: LCSH: New York (N.Y.)—Social conditions—21st century. | New York
    (N.Y.)—Social life and customs—21st century. | New York (N.Y.)—Civilization—
    21st century. | Queens (New York, N.Y.)—History. | Neighborhoods—New York
    (State)—New York. | Community life—New York (State)—New York.
Classification: LCC HN80.N5 H453 2020 (print) | LCC HN80.N5 (ebook) | DDC
    306.09747/1—dc23
LC record available at https://lccn.loc.gov/2019058691
LC ebook record available at https://lccn.loc.gov/2019058692

British Library Cataloging-in-Publication Data is available

Editorial: Meagan Levinson and Jacqueline Delaney
Production Editorial: Mark Bellis
Production: Erin Suydam
Publicity: Maria Whelan and Kathryn Stevens
Cover photographs by Antony Bennett
Interior photographs by Christopher Holewski

This book has been composed in Adobe Caslon Pro, Futura Std
and OL Heavy Metal Grecian

Printed on acid-free paper. ∞

Printed in China

10 9 8 7 6 5 4 3 2 1

For Alan

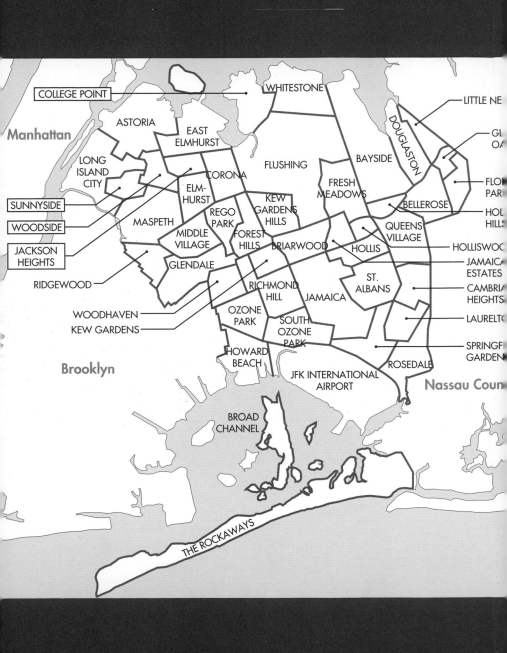

COLLEGE POINT

WHITESTONE

LITTLE NE

Manhattan

ASTORIA

EAST
ELMHURST

DOUGLASTON

GL
OA

LONG
ISLAND
CITY

CORONA

FLUSHING

BAYSIDE

FLO
PAR

ELM-
HURST

KEW
GARDENS
HILLS

FRESH
MEADOWS

BELLEROSE

HOL
HILL

SUNNYSIDE

WOODSIDE

MASPETH

REGO
PARK

QUEENS
VILLAGE

JACKSON
HEIGHTS

MIDDLE
VILLAGE

FOREST
HILLS

BRIARWOOD

HOLLIS

HOLLISWO

RIDGEWOOD

GLENDALE

ST.
ALBANS

JAMAIC
ESTATES

RICHMOND
HILL

JAMAICA

CAMBRI
HEIGHTS

WOODHAVEN

OZONE
PARK

LAURELT

KEW GARDENS

SOUTH
OZONE
PARK

SPRINGF
GARDEN

HOWARD
BEACH

Brooklyn

JFK INTERNATIONAL
AIRPORT

ROSEDALE

Nassau Coun

BROAD
CHANNEL

THE ROCKAWAYS

CONTENTS

INTRODUCTION

OF THE SIXTY-FIVE MILLION OR SO VISITORS to New York City every year, the overwhelming majority spend their time only in Manhattan. Because of Brooklyn's cachet as a destination, a certain number will also include it in their itinerary. Queens remains something of a mystery to most visitors, a place that they know is part of the city, but that might not be of particular interest. Queens was named in 1683 by the British in honor of Queen Catherine, wife of King Charles II. It's ironic, really, that most visitors see Queens as they arrive, albeit from the air, as their plane circles the borough before swooping down to land at Kennedy, LaGuardia, or another nearby airport. But as soon as they land and collect their bags, most head for the nerve center—Manhattan. Manhattanites, too, can see Queens quite easily. From the East Side, they can view communities like Hunters Point and Astoria, and beyond, but rarely think of them as places worth exploring.

This book, which is part of a series whose focus is on the unknown aspects of New York City, is an attempt to change this dynamic, to open up for visitors a place that is endlessly fascinating and has far more to it than most people realize—from its history to its architecture, its communities, and its individuals. Of course, to its 2.3 million or so residents, Queens is very well known. After all, they live there. But their knowledge is often limited to the communities in which they reside rather than to the borough as a whole.

Queens contains some fifty-seven distinct communities spread out over about 109 square miles. It has some very high-quality cultural centers, beautiful parks, and attractive residential neighborhoods. It has a throbbing nightlife, with clubs, restaurants, and entertainment of all sorts. In Astoria, there's Steinway Street with its hookah lounges and ethnic restaurants. In Jackson Heights, restaurants and clubs from more than a dozen Latin American lands line

Roosevelt Avenue, competing for the affections of both Latinos and others interested in Latin cuisine and music. Just off Roosevelt, on Gleane Street, there's the Terraza 7 Jazz Club. They host many world-famous performers from a dozen countries, with affordable prices. Along Thirty-Seventh Avenue and its side streets in the 70s there are eateries serving Indian, Bangladeshi, Nepalese, Afghani, Tibetan, and Filipino food. Other parts of the borough in places like Sunnyside, Forest Hills, and Bayside hum with activity as well, especially on the weekends.

In part because it's so spread out, Queens lacks a clear identity and defies easy categorization. There's astonishing variety in so many areas—art, architecture, nature, entertainment, foods, and more. It also has an incredible array of ethnic and racial groups. Finally, its residents possess a very strong sense of community. One of the borough's essential characteristics is how varied and unique it is in terms of what there is to see. For example, far away from the central core of Queens, which lies within easy reach of Manhattan, in the community of Bellerose, there's a museum within Creedmoor Psychiatric Center devoted exclusively to the art of the mentally ill, the only sizeable one in the United States. Touring the museum I meet a man who creates objects made entirely from coat hangers—a giant sunflower, a detailed guitar, and more. Another paints large murals combining different aspects of the civil rights and antiwar movements of the 1960s.

Further evidence of variety exists in nearby Little Neck, site of the city's only functioning historical farm, a 47-acre plot of land where fruits and vegetables are grown, and where sheep, cows, and some friendly llamas graze. Adjacent Douglaston is home to the city's tallest tree. It's a 450-year-old specimen, a tulip tree that tops out at 133.8 feet. Finding it isn't easy as it's in a densely wooded area. In Springfield Gardens, a good ten miles from here, lies a pristine wilderness, on the edge of a sleepy neighborhood, called Idlewild Park Preserve. It's a wild area of woods, marshes, and fields, filled with chirping birds, small mammals, and fish, a veritable Shangri-la and perhaps the most isolated spot I've ever seen in this city, save for some parts of the Staten Island Greenbelt.

One of the last taxidermists in the city, John Youngaitis, has a storefront located in Middle Village. Close by, there's an opportunity to grab a beer at Gottscheer's German tavern in Ridgewood, a holdover from a century ago, one of the last in the city. And then it's on to the Underpenny Museum, an exquisite space crammed with thousands of items based on the idiosyncratic interests of its creator, a Korean immigrant named John Park Sung. Included are a collection of cast-iron trivets from the nineteenth century; hundreds of eggbeaters; mechanical piggy banks, created to encourage children to save money; shaving mugs; snuff bottles; miniature houses; and much, much more.

I also explore the house in which Madonna lived in Corona, a former synagogue and Jewish school, which still has Stars of David set in bricks. The story of how and why she ended up there is a truly intriguing one. In Astoria, one can view the oldest home in the United States. In Addisleigh Park, a subsection of St. Albans, one can walk by the still-standing homes of great musical artists like Ella Fitzgerald, Lena Horne, and James Brown, as well as sports giants like Joe Louis, Jackie Robinson, and the one white person among them, Babe Ruth. But that's another story, also told here. The former home of the founder of Pan-Africanism, W.E.B. Du-Bois, sits anonymously, on a one-block street, sadly forgotten and neglected.

As to ethnicity, Queens is home to more ethnic groups than any other borough, with residents speaking close to 150 different languages. All in all, it's probably the most diverse urban area in the world. Some of the largest groups are the Chinese, Indians, Koreans, West Indians, Mexicans, Irish, Italians, and Jews. But there are other groups too, like the Tibetans, Filipinos, Paraguayans, Ghanaians, and Nepalese. These groups are most often concentrated in one geographical area, and a visit to where they live often feels like a trip to the country from which they originated.

A walk along Liberty Avenue in Richmond Hill reveals block after block of clothing, furniture, and jewelry stores, all of them catering to the needs of the Indo-Guyanese community. Navigating the side streets, one sees many homes with the traditional clusters of multicolored prayer flags in their front yards. In another part of the same community one comes to the section where the Sikhs live. Entering their temple on a Sunday morning, one can hear the haunting strains of their religious songs as hundreds of men and women sway to the music. For Sikhs it is a religious commandment never to cut one's hair. Doesn't it grow too long? I wonder. A turbaned man tells me, "On my head it stops growing after a time. And my beard, I show you—I roll it up."

A stroll through Flushing's Chinatown is a special experience. It is one of the largest and fastest-growing Chinatowns in the world, with new people constantly arriving. The number of Chinese living there, both legal and undocumented, is estimated at about eighty-five thousand. As I wander through the area, I see almost no one who isn't Asian, and almost everyone is speaking an East Asian language. Street vendors hawk their wares, mostly in Chinese, and crowds on the main avenues make them almost impassable at certain times of the day. I pass by Maple Playground and see four young men kicking, soccer-style, a small butterfly-shaped object. The game is called *jianzi*, and it originated thousands of years ago during the Han dynasty.

In another part of Flushing, the most ethnic community in the borough, I enter, on Bowne Street, the famous Indian temple, dedicated to the elephant deity, Ganesh. Made of granite and intricately carved, it must be seen to be fully appreciated, especially at night when a kaleidoscope of bright colors from large moving searchlights envelops it. Not far away is an Afghan community and another made up of Malaysians. In Astoria, I observe ethnic succession in real time, as the Greek community recedes and is replaced by a Muslim population, many of them Egyptians and Yemenis. One can visit the LGBT community in Jackson Heights and learn about the Rastafarians in

Springfield Gardens. And in one neighborhood over in Cambria Heights it's possible to stand by the grave of the Lubavitcher Rebbe, revered by millions around the world. Those who love magic will find Houdini's grave and the story behind it in the section about Glendale. And music lovers will be delighted by the discussion about the Steinway Piano Factory, still operating after 150 years in Astoria.

What's truly amazing is how well these groups get along with one another, notwithstanding occasional discord. Some of them have long histories of tense relationships between them, like Pakistanis and Indians or Muslims and Jews.

It turns out there isn't one overarching explanation. Rather, it's a combination of factors. First, Americans, as a nation of immigrants, celebrate ethnicity, notwithstanding their apprehensions about certain groups, whereas Europeans want newcomers to assimilate. Second, in New York City, conflicts between nations or religions are seen as something that's happening far away. Those living here are far more interested in problems of unemployment, housing, and crime. As I heard over and over again: "There's no room for hatred here. We're all trying to make it." Most important perhaps, the sheer number of groups tends to reduce conflict because when everyone is "new," then being new is no big deal. In fact, it's almost irrelevant. People also seem to welcome the opportunity to make friends on neutral territory with people they wouldn't ordinarily even meet.

Within the realm of ethnic groups lie some unusual patterns, for lack of a better term. For instance, ethnic succession doesn't always mean whites being replaced by Asians, blacks, or Hispanics. For example, in Bayside, Koreans are "replacing" blacks because they are willing to pay higher prices for homes. In Jamaica, a Bangladeshi woman explains why she has deliberately moved into a Chinese part of Flushing. She doesn't want to be restricted to her own group. In Holliswood, a rigorously Orthodox Jewish family becomes close friends with a lesbian couple, who have a lifestyle that the Orthodox Jews frown on. The Jewish family even takes care of the couple's kids when the couple go away for a weekend.

In addition to ethnicity, Queens has a strong sense of community. New Yorkers of all backgrounds tend to see living with other groups as an opportunity to get to know each other. I remember walking down a street in Woodhaven, a community filled with minorities from Asia and South America, where almost every house had an American flag flying in front of it. In a white working-class community, this wouldn't attract much attention since displaying American flags has become synonymous with a conservative viewpoint of America. But Woodhaven is filled with immigrants, and this block was no exception. Spying two Guyanese men chatting in front of a home, I asked them why they were flying the flag.

"Because," said one, "a man on the block gave us the flags and asked us if we would put them in front of the houses, and we thought it would look nice." That person turned out to be Paul Kazas, a white man who lives on this street. In all, thirty-six homes now fly the flag. Another home owner, a Bangladeshi immigrant, told me that Kazas was so nice he couldn't refuse, especially when the man offered to replace or repair, free of charge, any damaged or missing flags. Kazas is an attorney and a dyed-in-the-wool community activist. He has also been honored by Congress for his volunteer work. He fixes street malls and prunes trees, and this was his way of engendering pride in being an American. In his words, "I tell them the flag unites us all, and they relate to that."

In my walks I witnessed examples of civic pride. Queens residents take tremendous pride in their communities. When they're asked where they're from, their first response is far more likely to indicate Jamaica, Forest Hills, Astoria, or Douglaston than Queens. When they reminisce about having grown up in Queens, they often exhibit great fondness about what that was like for them. They are also active in the local organizations that represent them—neighborhood and block associations, social clubs, houses of worship, and the like. The borough has a steady stream of parades, ranging from the Memorial Day parades in Little Neck and Broad Channel, to the annual Sikh parade in Queens Village, and the gay pride parade in

Jackson Heights. And there are block parties everywhere. This is true of Brooklyn and the other boroughs as well, but here the practice struck me as even stronger and more ubiquitous. The communities are so far away from the central city that they develop a self-image of being a collection of small independent villages.

Another example of strong communal involvement is the hundreds of streets and vest-pocket parks named after residents who gave of themselves to the community, like Bud Haller Way in Glendale, named after a longtime resident. In the aftermath of Hurricane Sandy many people opened their doors to neighbors, even strangers, whose homes were damaged, or donated clothing and food. Scott Lowry, a Brooklyn businessman, delivered hot meals to people living in the Rockaways. Such generosity of spirit often crosses ethnic lines. Ghanwatti Boodram was a nurse from Guyana who died in 2009 when her house in Floral Park exploded because of a gas leak. The Boodrams were involved in neighborhood groups, and their children were enrolled in the local public schools. Hundreds of mourners attended the funeral, and people, many of them white, collected more than a thousand gift cards to help family members rebuild their shattered lives.

What of the future? What will happen to Queens in the next twenty years? The city's failure to come to an agreement with Amazon that would have brought jobs to the borough's residents was a blow in the view of many, but a victory in the opinion of others. It's too early to judge what the long-term effects will be, but it's a reminder of how complex things can get when interests, ideology, and politics collide. As Brooklyn fills up with gentrifiers, Queens begins to look more and more attractive to some members of this varied group of displaced Brooklynites. The prices are lower than in Brooklyn, and the core neighborhoods, those nearer Manhattan, are very accessible via public transportation. And this pattern is becoming clearer with every passing day. Hunters Point is today a forest of glass-and-metal apartment towers resembling elongated spaceships, and Astoria is following suit, as is Ridgewood. But will this extend to the next ring of communities, like Forest Hills, Rego Park, Kew Gardens, and Glendale? To some extent yes, because there are subway lines that reach these areas. But those communities beyond that circle—Douglaston, Bayside, Little Neck, Fresh Meadows, Floral Park, Bellerose, and so on—will attract such people only if transportation improves dramatically.

Then again, it doesn't have to happen. These communities are, so to speak, full. It's a seller's market as largely East and South Asians are snapping up every home on the market in northeastern Queens, most of which belong to retired whites departing for sunnier climes. The same holds true for southeastern Queens, where Caribbean blacks are purchasing homes in predominantly black middle-class areas. There are private homes and garden apartments in these sections, and those who live in them love the relative peace and quiet that prevails. The neighborhoods are quite safe, and affordable housing is available for those who need it. Hispanics are also moving into eastern Queens, but most are still in Jackson Heights, Elmhurst, and Corona, with those who are better off settling on Long Island and in other parts of the metropolitan area.

Regardless of what happens, Queens remains a great place to explore. This borough is one where both natives and immigrants are busily engaged in living in America. This introduction only scratches the surface of what Queens has to offer. To learn more, dive into this book and find out what surprises are in store for the curious and adventurous.

* * *

My love for walking the city can be traced back to a game my father played with me when I was a child, called "Last Stop." On every available weekend, when I was between the ages of nine and fourteen, my dad and I took the subway from the Upper West Side, where we lived, to the last stop on a given line and walked around for a couple of hours. When we ran out of new last stops on the various lines, we did the second to last, and third to last, and so on, always traveling to a new place. In this way, I learned to love and appreciate the city, one that I like to call "the world's greatest outdoor museum." I also developed a very close bond with my father, who gave me the greatest present a kid can have—the gift of time.

In walking, actually rewalking, Queens, my approach was the same as when I did the research for *The New York Nobody Knows: Walking 6,000 Miles in the City*, a comprehensive analysis of all five boroughs. I walked and observed what was going on around me, all the while informally interviewing hundreds of people. New Yorkers are a remarkably open group if approached in a friendly and respectful manner; no one refused to talk to me. Sometimes I told them I was writing a book, but much of the time I didn't need to, and I simply engaged them in casual conversation. I often taped what they were saying, using my iPhone function in front of them. Hardly anyone asked why, and if their attention lingered on the phone, I explained why I was recording. No one minded. Perhaps that's a statement about what we've become—a society accustomed to cameras and recorders, and one that assumes that few things are really private anymore. Clearly, this is a great boon for researchers. Greater tolerance in general and an abiding belief that the city is safe are also contributors to this state of affairs.

I walked in the daytime, at night, during the week, on weekends, and in all seasons, in rain, snow, or shine, from mid-October 2016 through February 2018. I averaged about 72 miles a month. I attended parades, block parties, and other events and also hung out on the streets, in bars and restaurants, and in parks. Most of the time I walked alone, but sometimes, my wife, Helaine, and, on occasion, our dog, Heidi, accompanied me. I began in Little Neck and finished in Astoria, walking through every community for a total of 1,012 miles, as measured by my pedometer. I had, of course, walked almost every block in the borough for the first book, and probably sixteen times before that, albeit more selectively. I wore Rockports, in my view the world's most comfortable and durable shoe.

Although I'd already walked nearly every block in Queens, the findings here are almost all new because the city is constantly changing. New stores, murals, and buildings go up, parks change, and there are different events every year, like concerts, comedy shows, protests, parades, feasts, and town hall meetings. Everyone with whom I spoke was new, and the conversations often led in different directions. Walking is, for my money, the best way to explore a city. It slows you down so that you can see and absorb things and literally experience the environment as you talk to those who know it best, the residents. And the more you walk, the greater the chance you'll get really good material. You just can't know whether you'll meet that special person or see an exquisitely beautiful private garden in the first or the fifth hour of your trip on any given day. Bicycling is the next best option.

This book is intended to be a guidebook for those wishing to explore Queens. Because the intended audience here consists mostly of tourists, curious residents of these neighborhoods, nostalgia seekers who grew up in or lived in these areas, and New Yorkers looking for interesting local trips, the book discusses in detail every single neighborhood in Queens. In order to make it a book that could be easily carried around it was necessary to limit the discussion to what I saw as the most interesting points, but there's much more to see.

The focus is on the unusual and unknown aspects of these neighborhoods. The book is largely a combination of quotes from conversations with residents and reflections on life in general, plus many anecdotes about all manner of things. And its focus on sociological explanations of why things are the way they are combine with all the rest to make it what I believe is a rather unique guidebook.

There's a street map for each community, and you can walk it in any order you'd like, searching out whatever moves you.[1] What was chosen is meant to whet your appetite, to entice you into wandering these streets on your own, where you're also likely to make new discoveries. Most of the borough is quite safe, with crime rates way down, though you might want to exercise caution in some areas.

They're identified in appendix A in the back of the book, along with some tips on how to safely explore them.

The areas are divided into ten groups of communities and are arranged in this book according to contiguous sections of Queens. You can, nonetheless, walk the borough in any order you choose. There's some historical information in the sections, but it is admittedly brief. This is, after all, a book about the present. Queens has many famous residents, past and present, a few of whom are noted here. If that's your area of interest, I suggest looking them up on various sites by Googling "famous residents of Queens, NY," or going directly to https://en.wikipedia.org/wiki/Queens. Some sites actually provide addresses and other details. And if you're interested in specific topics like parks, the Italian community, or bars, you should definitely consult the comprehensive index at the end of this book.

The vignettes, interviews, and descriptions have one overall goal—to capture the heart, pulse, and soul of this magnificent borough. Naturally, whether or not this has been accomplished is for you, the reader, to judge.

LONG
ISLAND
CITY

ASTORIA

SUNNYSIDE

WOODSIDE

LONG ISLAND CITY

A) Colbar Art
B) MoMA-PS1
C) Manducati's Restaurant
D) Pet Memorial
E) The Comedy Show
F) New York Irish Center
G) Sacred Waters
H) MONA COAL-ICE company
I) Underpenny Museum
J) Gantry Plaza State Park

LONG ISLAND CITY, THE LARGEST COMMUNITY IN QUEENS, is an irregularly shaped area and therefore a bit hard to delineate. Its borders are, generally, Broadway, plus Thirty-Fourth and Thirty-Sixth Avenues on the north; Woodside Avenue, Van Dam Street, and Laurel Hill Boulevard on the east; Review and Borden Avenues, plus Fifty-Third and Fifty-Fourth Avenues on the south; and the parks running along the East River on the west.

Historically, in the early to mid-nineteenth century Long Island City was mostly farmland. In 1861, the Long Island Railroad (LIRR) began providing service, and in 1909, the Queensboro Bridge was completed, followed shortly thereafter by the elevated train. Around this time, it became a popular place for Irish and Italian immigrants to settle. The year 1954 marked the completion of the Pulaski Bridge, which connected Brooklyn with Queens. Large portions of it were rezoned for industrial use only in 1960, discouraging residents from moving there since

3

they couldn't get loans and mortgages in these areas. The largest racial and ethnic groups living here today are Hispanics from various lands, African Americans, and Asians, augmented by a burgeoning population of gentrifiers who are predominantly white.

With this mélange of populations and structures, it's clear that the area has a little bit of everything. Residential and commercial towers loom over the area, a tall forest made of steel and glass silhouetted against the sky. The twenty-six buildings of Queensbridge Houses make it the city's largest public housing development. Most poignantly perhaps, one can see, from the entrance to the Queens Midtown Tunnel, built in 1940, several small, old walkups, one or two of them very pretty, clinging to life on the outer edge of the toll plaza. They symbolize a tough, gritty, and even, at times, charming neighborhood, determined to survive, one that looks to the influx of young people who work in Manhattan law firms and banks as its best chance for a new life. The commercial thoroughfares are 21st and 11th Streets, Vernon and Jackson Avenues, Queens Plaza, Northern Boulevard, and Broadway.

There are also some well-known places in Long Island City that are well worth a visit, like the MoMA-PS1 (Museum of Modern Art); the Isamu Noguchi Garden Museum, with its gorgeous sculptures; and Silvercup Studios at 42-22 22nd Street. Behind it, on Forty-Third Avenue, is a block-long building whose walls are filled with artists' renderings of immigrants who came to the United States from early on until today. It was commissioned by the owner to attract tourists and, hopefully, renters. If you're interested in parks, you have Gantry Plaza State Park, Rainey Park, and Socrates Sculpture Park.

My trip begins on Bradley Avenue, in the small, unknown neighborhood of Blissville, in the extreme southeastern portion of the community, east of the Long Island Expressway (LIE). It owes its name to Neziah Bliss, who purchased a large farm that encompassed this section and neighboring Hunters Point. With the establishment of Calvary Cemetery in 1848, people began visiting nearby lodging houses and taverns, and monument stores opened up as well. The cemetery is divided into four sections, stretching across several communities, and there are approximately three million people interred here, making it the largest cemetery in the country. The area became both industrial and residential soon thereafter, propelled in part by transportation lines that were built to accommodate the increase in population. The houses built then were plain, and most houses still are, many of them very old, some in good condition, others quite dilapidated.

Today, the streets are lined with small businesses and manufacturing plants, and only about five hundred residents remain, feeling somewhat isolated in a sea of mostly light industry. If you're into Statue of Liberty replicas made from acrylic, stop in at Colbar Art at 3503 Bradley. They are the largest makers of these statues in the world, and they also produce replicas of other famous structures like the Empire State Building. The company was founded by Ovidiu Colea, who immigrated to the United States in 1978. While labor costs would be cheaper elsewhere, he insists on producing his molds, castings, and models here. He feels he should give back something to a country he loves. Colea was an avid listener to Radio Free Europe and grew up hearing many stories from his father about the Statue of Liberty. In his view it's not appropriate to produce such statues in a country where there's no liberty and where there's no statue celebrating it.

Leaving Blissville, I walk north on adjacent Van Dam Street and hang a left on Forty-Ninth Avenue. Here the entire vicinity from Van Dam on the east to Jackson Avenue on the west, and from Forty-Ninth on the south to Skillman Avenue on the north, is almost completely industrial. When I cross Jackson, however, the area shifts dramatically to both small and large apartment buildings along with a small number of private older houses. I've now entered the Hunters Point area. Hunters Point, first settled by the Dutch in the 1600s, is named after George Hunter, who owned property there in 1825. In 1989, Citi Group built a fifty-story building, to date the tallest in Queens and one that dominates the skyline. The forty-eight-floor City Lights residential tower opened in 1996, and several more large condo/co-op/rental buildings have followed, all gleaming high-rises situated on or adjacent to the waterfront. They are the future of the area—one that appeals to younger professionals looking for nice apartments within easy commuting distance to Manhattan.

In many ways Hunters Point is a condensed version of New York City. It has lots of old-style brownstones and, scattered through the old streets, many plain, clapboard houses, plus nondescript three- and four-story structures that alternate with supply companies; small manufacturing plants; taxi paraphernalia stores and taxi garages, run mostly by South Asians; plain-looking taverns; and auto repair shops. A good number of the limo companies have signs proclaiming proudly: "We specialize in black cars." These are plain-looking sedans, usually Lincolns and Chryslers, favored by businesspeople.

As I turn right on Jackson Avenue, it's clear that the avenue is beginning to resemble a forest of tall new apartment residences. Three blocks up however, where Davis and 23rd Streets intersect with Jackson, I meet the elevated 7 train. As I turn right onto Davis I hear all sorts of grinding, squealing, and grumbling noises, best known to regular subway riders, as the 7 slowly winds its way through the Hunters Point community, past the Citi Group building, and the Sunnyside Yards as it heads toward the city. The new towers on the East River's shore nearby, not to mention the Empire State and Chrysler Buildings across the river, are metaphorically far removed from where I am walking.

When I first visited this part of Long Island City in 2010, this was the home of 5Pointz, a famous graffiti art center that attracted people from all over the world. They came because it was an opportunity to put up their creations in a place minutes from Manhattan that had become a major tourist venue with buses transporting gawking visitors amazed at the vitality and richness of these murals. These included monsters, superheroes, stick figures, and clowns. In fact, the building that displayed the art on its walls housed many art studios, open to the public.

Alas, 5Pointz is no more. The landlord, Jerry Wolkoff, decided to replace the old warehouse with condominiums and had the building's walls whitewashed at night, when hardly anyone was around to protest. Just a year later, when Wolkoff received the building permits, the structure was razed to the ground, and today, the high-rise residences are being completed. The artists, feeling insulted and degraded, sued Wolkoff and won a large judgment in court. To everyone's amazement, the judge, Frederic Block, ruling in federal court, awarded the twenty-one artists $6.7 million. That worked out to $150,000 for each artist, an unprecedented decision for graffiti enthusiasts. The jury found that Wolkoff had violated the Visual Arts Rights Act, which protects art. "Hell hath no fury," as they say, "like an artist scorned!" Moreover, graffiti became enshrined as art, just as if it had been hung in a museum.[2]

Nothing can bring back 5Pointz. But art is not forgotten in these parts. It has been reincarnated across the street at 22-25 Jackson Avenue in the form of MoMA-PS1. Affiliated with the Museum of Modern Art, it has the goal to promote contemporary art in the form of art exhibitions and musical performances, and it attracts about two hundred thousand people a year. Obviously, it's well known, but any book about exploring Queens cannot ignore it.

I turn around on Davis, make a left on Jackson Avenue, and soon come to Manducati's, on the corner of Jackson and Forty-Seventh Avenue. Located at number 13-27, it's one of a fading breed of old-style Italian eateries that were very popular forty years ago. The outside is totally nondescript. There's no fancy lighting, no large advertising, just the words in simple neon letters, "Manducati's: Fine Foods." The inside is cozy. There are several warmly furnished dining rooms, all flowing into another one, which results in a feeling of both spaciousness and intimacy. The rooms are very traditional—cherrywood chairs, upholstered in a floral pattern; early American simple brass chandeliers, with individual lampshades; exposed red-brick walls; and several fireplaces, and old-world paintings hanging next to nooks in the walls, each containing several wine bottles.

The owner, Vincenzo, is sitting at a table, reviewing some papers, perhaps bills. He's dressed in the way older Italian men are often attired—dark suit, white shirt, and a conservative tie—even though it's midday and the restaurant is officially closed.

"How are you doing? Are people coming in?" I ask.

"Well, it's okay, but not so much as before. We're from the village of Nusco, in Italy, and the people from Nusco settled here. But now many of those people have died or moved away."

"Are you getting the young people?"

"Not so much because they live near the water and their tastes are different. But we get the people who work here every day, and our old customers still come from other parts of New York." In truth, I've seen this place several times in the last five years at night, and most of the tables are filled. It's just not what it once was. Most people feel the food is delicious, with large portions and reasonable prices.

On the west side of Jackson Avenue, where it crosses 11th Street, I see a waist-high wall made of small cement blocks that look like bricks with names on them—Rufus, Thor, Monkey, Elvis, Buddha, Smokey, Peanut, Zoey, Spikey. This is the brainchild of Steve, who lives two doors down. He invited local folks to memorialize the names of their dogs. It's nothing elaborate, but it's the kind of thing that enables people to remember their loved pets in a public way that also connects residents with each other. Also, as anyone who has ever had a pet they loved knows, this fulfills the need to show some appreciation to the years of devoted love and loyalty pets show their owners.

Next door is a storefront at number 10-93, housing "The Comedy Show: Freak in the Cave," and offering up "surreal comedy"

The wall of cement blocks where locals memorialize the names of their dogs.

every third Friday night. They're also featuring Grant Lindahl, "a famous artist whose show was banned from the Museum of Modern Art (MoMA) in Queens." The comedians performing here are described as "New York's up and coming weirdos." When you're a tiny place and not on a busy Manhattan or Brooklyn street, you have to be creative to attract attention.

At 10-40 Jackson I discover the New York Irish Center. This is an entertainment venue, offering music, theater, and dancing, serving the community and focusing on seniors, although they also have dance classes for youngsters, an evening talk about North Brooklyn history, card games, and free help with taxes; and they even offer Irish pancakes on Shrove Tuesday, the last day of the pre-Lenten season. The making of pancakes comes from the custom of using up all the milk, eggs, and butter that are left in the house. These are foods that many strictly observant Catholics refrain from during Lent. I speak with Jane, a young woman with an Irish brogue. "The center was founded by an Irish priest from Belfast, Ireland," she tells me. "And a generous businessman funded it. The Irish community was aging here and in nearby Woodside, Sunnyside, and in the Rockaways. Every Wednesday we have a huge lunch for about eighty seniors. It's very important because many of the seniors don't have family. And the younger people come to our concerts, plays, and such."

Crossing Jackson Avenue, I head down Fifty-First Avenue and see almost immediately, on my right, a place called Sacred Waters. It's a new age holistic wellness center offering various therapeutic treatments, including reflexology, sensory deprivation, tribal body art, and Reiki. I walk into a very well appointed large room with exquisite décor—exotic-looking potted plants, a small tree, modern wooden end tables, and colorful paintings along the wall. A woman seated at a desk greets me warmly, and I ask her what these therapies are all about.

"First, we have the one and only sensory deprivation floating facility in all of Queens. Come, I'll show it to you." She takes me to a darkened room in the back where I see a water tank filled to the top. I ask her what the benefits to this are.

"People lie down on top of the water. It's filled with salt like that found in the Dead Sea, 850 pounds of Epsom salt so you feel like you're free-floating. The room is totally dark and soundproof. So essentially, you're going from a place that's filled with noise and bright lights. Here, you feel totally at peace because you're neither sending nor receiving any messages. As you immerse yourself the toxins in your body are drawn out, the blood flow improves, and you feel like you've entered a world of peace and quiet. We're only two years old, and most of our business comes from word of mouth, but we're starting to market our own products."

"What's Reiki [pronounced "Rayki"]?"

"Simply put, it's a Japanese energy-balancing treatment where we use our hands to direct life force energy to your body." Tara explains some of their other methods to me, and I can see that these approaches are likely to appeal to a younger generation that's constantly on the go, and in that sense Hunters Point is the perfect market for it.

As I walk down the block, I notice a constant stream of people walking by. This was a much quieter community ten years ago, but with all the new apartment buildings, especially on the upcoming block between 5th and 2nd Streets, it has become a very lively place. The towers, while nice enough, lack the character of the old small houses that have been here for a century. It's not seen as a positive development by the old-timers, who complain vigorously, but it's great for the young professionals with young children, who are saving, on the average, $1,000 a month in rent compared to, say, Manhattan's Upper East Side. Here's what Craig, a finance person in his thirties, with two children, had to say about all this.

"Some of these buildings have affordable housing, which is nice. I've been here about four years. We moved here from the Flatiron district in Manhattan because we had a dog and a baby and we wanted more room. It's kind of the natural progression in this community."

"Do some of the people who are paying full market rate resent those who pay affordable housing rates?" I ask.

"Not really. I mean, some of them have better views than I do, but so what?" True, but until the practice was banned, some developers had separate entrances in such buildings for affordable housing residents.

This discussion is one of the favorite topics of New Yorkers, the ins and outs of housing. I bid Craig a good day and walk up Fiftieth Avenue back to Vernon Boulevard. There, I hang a left, and midway up the block on the left side at number 69 I stop in front of a stunning wooden door with a gleaming golden handle. A gold-lettered sign tells me it was once the home of "MONA COAL-ICE," a company established in 1897. Beneath it is an ancient seven-digit phone number from the days when telephone exchanges in every borough had names, for example, MOnument, followed by five numbers for Manhattan's Upper West Side, with the first two letters of the word listed, followed by five numbers. Thus, HU corresponded to 48, because any of the letters GHI corresponded to the number 4; and any of the letters TUV corresponded to 8.

This one begins with HUnterspoint, followed by the numbers. Antonio Mona immigrated to the United States in the nineteenth century, and this was where he set up his company. Both coal and ice were in great demand then. The dedication on a plaque is courtesy of his great-grandchildren. Clearly, this business has been gone for decades, but history lives for as long as people remember and honor it. Knowing what once was is essential for understanding what now is and how we evolved. To me, this is also an excellent example of filial piety. On a personal level and generations later, these descendants want to ensure that Antonio Mona will not be forgotten.

Returning to Fiftieth Avenue I continue walking east and see, just before I return to Jackson Avenue, a store on the left at number 10-13 called the Underpenny Museum. Outside, at street level, I read the story of this establishment. A man named John Park Sung spent thirty plus years in business, first operating a Dunkin Donuts in Freeport, Long Island, then, for thirty years, as the proprietor of a Hunters Point juice bar. In midlife, he found his calling and started a museum in 2008, which also sells antiques.

John gives me a friendly greeting as I tell him I'm writing a book. A middle-aged man, he has black, silvery hair and twinkling eyes. It's not a large place at all, but the displays are neatly arranged. The most prominent collection is his cast-iron trivets, circa nineteenth-century America, arranged in a long row along a shelf. At first, they all appear to be similar, but upon closer examination I see that the designs in the center of the trivets are quite different from each other. They can be anything conjured up by the imagination—flowers, letters in cursive style, dates, profiles of people's heads as one would find on a coin, animals, scrollwork, swastikas, American eagles, pentacles. Round trivets are used when you take pots off a hot stove and need to put them somewhere that won't burn a surface like a table or tablecloth, and triangular ones are for resting a hot iron. Why did he collect

The Underpenny Museum, a fantasyland of antiques.

trivets? How and why did he become a collector? What's for sale, and what's not? Classical music is playing softly in the background as I'm pondering these questions, and John, who immigrated to the United States from South Korea, interrupts my reverie.

"I also have a collection of eggbeaters, hundreds of them," he tells me. "I started thinking about doing this, maybe in 1996. I went to a local history education center to learn about the trivets. I have over one thousand trivets, but not all are shown here. I began traveling through New York, Watertown, other places, wherever they had antique shops." I can't help but notice that when he speaks about his collection there's a certain lilt reflecting joy as he talks about what he has here.

"But you don't sell these, right?" I ask.

"If someone fall in love, I let him have it, maybe. If he don't fall in love, I say 'not for sale.'" In short, he will not sell to a casual buyer. A buyer must share his passion.

"And what about these things?" There are many of them on another shelf.

"These are mechanical piggy banks." Like the trivets, they came into vogue in the nineteenth century and were made from cast iron. The various figurines, baseball players, dolls, and so on were aimed at encouraging children to save money. When they put money into the banks by pulling a lever, they performed "a trick," one could say. They would move a certain way, for example. Today, they are collectibles.

"Tell me John . . . at the end of the day, are you a more a businessman or more a collector?"

"It's really 50/50. I sell on e-bay to different parts of the country, but not a lot. I'm a small guy, and don't make much money doing this. I'm much more interested in the collections. This is my love, my passion."

Of course, he's a salesman by trade. He ran businesses, but how many trivets, carpentry planes, or piggy banks can you sell? He bought one thousand trivets; they have a very limited market. The same is true for his astonishing collection of tiny delicate figurines, vases, old radios, animal-shaped pens, unusual antique jewelry, ducks, miniature houses, noisemakers that one shakes, people riding on motorcycles, snuff bottles, shaving mugs, owls of all shapes, sizes, and materials, and so much more. To wit, he hasn't sold them, nor does he seem to care. "I love looking at them, even all day. What makes me happy is that artists have gotten ideas from looking at my collections. That's more important to me than selling."

One could spend an entire day, maybe more, in this fantasyland, and one could write twenty pages about Underpenny. It's a joy to visit here.

At Forty-Ninth Avenue I head back to the waterfront to explore the park. On my way there I pause and glance at some old houses that are not necessarily shining examples of the homes of yesteryear. Those would be the ones on the historical-landmarked block on Forty-Fifth Avenue between 23rd and 21st Streets. These houses on Forty-Ninth, which run from number 521 to number 539, are rather plain two-story brick rowhouses, and they're not in very good shape. They provide a more well-rounded picture of how much of the community once looked. The Forty-Fifth Avenue homes, on the other hand, show us how the well-to-do lived in their brownstones and townhouses made of Westchester stone, which is very durable, one reason why they're still in such good condition after 150 years.

I enter Gantry Plaza State Park, which runs from about Fifty-First to Forty-Fifth Avenues. It's a warm, sunny afternoon in February, and I'm not surprised to see that the park is filled with mothers, nannies, small children, seniors, and, I suspect, some adolescent hooky players, all of whom are enjoying this rare spring-like weather. The views of the Manhattan skyline are fantastic. It's not surprising that people will pay to have such panoramas, playgrounds, sports facilities, dog parks, and ferry service twenty minutes from the city. I pass the red, truly iconic nine-story-high Pepsi Cola sign in script, with an old-fashioned, swirl-shaped Pepsi bottle next to it. The sign sits right behind 46-10 Center Boulevard inside the park. The seagulls are in attendance, hoping for a free meal of human food; Frisbees are flying, and a game of volleyball is in progress. A new modernistic sustainable library is going up on Center near Forty-Eighth Avenue, which will also boast views of Manhattan, a reading garden, and a performance space.

Walking east on 47th Road, I turn left on Vernon Boulevard and take it to Queens Plaza, the main commercial street that begins at the base of the Edward Koch Bridge, which becomes Queens Boulevard as it crosses Jackson Avenue. The northern side of Queens Boulevard all the way to Broadway, where Astoria begins, consists mostly of light industry and commerce, for example, taxicab companies, auto repair places, and inexpensive hotels, as well as residential areas. One can walk it of course, but it's not nearly as interesting as the southern side.

ASTORIA

(A) Rikers Island Bridge
(B) Oldest home in the
United States
(C) Steinway Piano Factory
(D) Steinway Mansion
(E) Site of *General Slocum*
Disaster
(F) Interesting murals of Rev.
Dr. Martin Luther King
and Mahatma Gandhi
(G) Welling Court
(H) Former home Sohmer
Piano Factory

ASTORIA'S BOUNDARIES, ROUGHLY, are Twentieth Avenue and Berrian Boulevard on the north; 81st Street and the Brooklyn-Queens Expressway West on the east; Northern Boulevard, Thirty-Sixth Avenue, and Broadway on the south; and Vernon and Shore Boulevards on the west. The first Europeans to settle in Astoria were Dutch farmers who came here in the 1600s. The land was then populated by Native American tribes. Large numbers of them perished during a 1662 smallpox epidemic. The European settlers purchased land from the tribes; in the case of Astoria, the land was purchased from the Canarsie tribe.

Astoria's modern history goes back to the 1830s, when it was called Halletts Cove, after a European landowner who bought land from the Canarsie in 1652. The name was changed to Astoria in 1839, after John Jacob Astor, who purchased land in the area. Henry Steinway, who built the Steinway Piano Factory, moved the factory from Manhattan to Astoria and established a community in the 1870s for its workers. Many were German immigrants who began arriving in the United States in the nineteenth century. It is said that

Steinway wanted to avoid the labor strife that prevailed in Manhattan. In the years that followed, the development of transportation in the area, which was just across the East River from Manhattan, attracted thousands of people to Astoria, and builders began construction here to accommodate them. Czechs and Slovaks arrived in the early twentieth century after the Germans and Irish. Italians and Jews began moving to Astoria in significant numbers after World War II, and in the 1960s Astoria became home to large numbers of Greeks.

Astoria's diversity has since been augmented by the many new groups of Hispanics, African Americans, Middle Eastern immigrants, and Asians who now reside here. These include Brazilians, Egyptians, Bosnians, Japanese, Lebanese, and Ecuadorians, to name just a few. They have contributed to making Astoria one of the most ethnically varied places in the country. Astoria is also home to a substantial LGBT community, further cementing its reputation as a tolerant and accepting community for all. Like its neighbor to the south, Long Island City, Astoria has had thousands of young professionals move here in recent years, attracted in part by its vibrant nightlife, its closeness to Manhattan, and the construction of new housing, which continues unabated. Ferry service to Manhattan is yet another incentive.

While the fact is well known, it would seem appropriate to note that Bohemian Hall, the most famous and oldest outdoor beer hall in New York City, is in the Ditmars section of Astoria, at 29-19 Twenty-Fourth Avenue. It was founded by Czech and Slovak immigrants. Also deserving of mention is Kaufman Studios and the Museum of the Moving Image, continuing a tradition of film centers in Astoria from the industry's early days. Finally, there's a small piece of Socrates Sculpture Park, the northern portion, that's in Astoria, but most of it is in Long Island City.

The main commercial thoroughfares are Steinway Street, 31st and 21st Streets, Ditmars Boulevard, Astoria Boulevard South, Thirtieth Avenue, and Broadway. Because of its population density,

Astoria also has numerous other streets that have shopping strips for one to three blocks. The area is quite safe and has several parks, the largest of which is Astoria Park.

My walking excursion begins at the intersection of 81st and Hazen Streets. Standing there I glance at a large billboard that proclaims: "Rikers Island, Home of New York's Boldest," referring to the correction officers who work there. The island, which is home to New York City's primary jail, was purchased in 1664 by a Dutchman, Henry Rycken. Beneath the billboard are forty-two wax candles in a variety of colors. Could this be the number of officers who have been killed at the prison over the years? I turn right onto Hazen Street, which leads directly, via a bridge, to the prison. Here I ask a guard, stationed on the street in a booth adjacent to the shuttle parking lot for visitors, if that's what the candles are for.

"No. These candles have to do with a vigil for an officer a few weeks ago. He was attacked and seriously injured by four inmates, and he's recovering in the hospital." I've learned over time that it's important to ask questions when in doubt. I often find myself thinking if I might have mistakenly described something incorrectly by not asking when I could have. Astoria today is known as a happening place, one attracting thousands of young New Yorkers looking for affordable living. But communities are complex places, and there can be great variation within a community. Hazen Street emphasizes that reality. Astoria is also home to quite a few Rikers Island employees, one of many diverse groups who reside in this northwestern Queens community. Rikers Island itself is actually in the Bronx, but the only way to get there is from Queens.

I walk one block south on Hazen and turn left onto a short street, 19th Road. In two minutes, I see, on my left, at 78-03, a large Cape Cod house with yellow siding and green shutters, three dormers on the second floor, and a sloping roof. Here, in this quiet, unassuming neighborhood, with many attached Tudor homes, single and multifamily, lies the oldest home in the entire country that's still privately

Behind this fence is the Riker-Lent Homestead, built in 1655.

owned and inhabited. Known as the Riker-Lent homestead, it was built in 1655 and belonged to the same Abraham Riker who owned nearby Rikers Island.

Peering through the white picket fence, covered with vines, I can clearly discern the historic landmark sign next to the small entranceway. Off to the left of the house I see a very large garden that stretches all the way back to Nineteenth Avenue, which is the property's rear border. A high wooden fence along that more heavily traveled street shields it from any real view for passersby. On the grass are chairs, benches, trellises, and a children's play area. An ancient-looking cobblestone wall runs along the side of the home. There are also two large statues on the lawn of painted cows, one gold, with a fake-pearl necklace around its neck, the other off-white. A standard sign warns: "Premises guarded by my pit bull." Anyone's pit bull should deter trespassers, but on the blustery cold March day of my visit, there's no sign of any canine present.

The owner, Marion D. Smith, who has lived here for over forty years, offers group and individual tours by appointment, which includes the historic graveyard on the property. The interior has antique collections and has beautifully restored polished wooden floors, walls, and staircase. A charming small gingerbread-style house outside served for many years as a workshop for Marion's handyman.

Returning to Hazen, I swing left and head one block over to Twentieth Avenue, where I have another brief encounter with history. On the left, between 42nd and 41st Streets, there's a collection of two-story red-brick rowhouses, with decorative cornices, continuing at the corner onto 41st Street for a short distance. Still occupied, these federal-style structures served as modest but clearly durable residences for workers at the Steinway Piano Factory. As two concrete markers indicate, 41st was known as Albert Street, and Twentieth Avenue was called Winthrop Avenue in earlier times. I'm always grateful when history is respected and preserved in this manner in a city where such things matter.

Continuing down Twentieth Avenue past a mixed industrial/residential area, it's only fitting that I soon come to Steinway Place and the world-famous Steinway Piano Factory, which has been located in Astoria since the 1870s. It was founded in Manhattan, by Henry Steinway (originally Steinweg) in 1853, who immigrated to the United States from Germany, eventually moving to Queens. One of the major commercial thoroughfares, Steinway Street, is named after this company, which employed many people over the years in its manufacturing plant. The Steinways also created a streetcar line and a sawmill. To learn more about the piano factory's inner workings I speak with Jana Helmrich, the human resources director. She has been here for only a few years, but her knowledge,

It takes a year to produce each of the handcrafted pianos that come from the Steinway & Sons piano factory.

enthusiasm for the company, and love for her job comes through very clearly, as I soon find out.

"What would you say is special about this company?" I ask.

"One of the things is that it's a real family. There are people who've been here their entire adult lives and also grew up in Astoria. In some instances, their parents worked here as well. Quite a few of our employees are talented musicians, yet they work in business positions in our marketing, sales, and corporate departments. They're modest about their abilities. And they may have been interested in a career in music, but when they realized a high position as a professional musician was not in their future they came here because they wanted to be around music and top-quality instruments, which a Steinway is. In fact, the president of our company went to Juilliard."

"What's so special about a Steinway?"

"There's so much; there are over 135 patents developed by Steinway, but additionally it's the high-quality wood and the workmanship. It takes a year to produce a Steinway, and we handcraft every piano that comes out of our factory—even the uprights. The action and sound is really unique; each piano has a rich, powerful tone, a wide dynamic range, and a keyboard touch that is extremely responsive. Steinways aren't cheap by any means and can cost $70,000 or more, even $2 million, for very special pianos that are part of our Art Case Collection. And there are all sorts of special orders, like the purple-colored piano we made for someone because the décor in their room was purple. There are over eighteen hundred performers around the world, known as Steinway Artists, who own Steinways and use them exclusively. We also have high-quality but more affordable pianos that we designed, called 'Boston' and 'Essex.'"

"Are you facing challenges from others?"

"Yes, but the Steinway name is always going to be there. For many people there's a certain status in having one. It's even been the piano for the White House. The one hundred thousandth piano was presented to Theodore Roosevelt in 1903. In 1938, the three hundred thousandth piano was given to President Franklin D. Roosevelt. You can see it in the White House entrance hall, and we're very proud of its presence there."

"What are some of the most unusual pianos you have produced?"

"Well, there was the Victory Vertical, an upright, made during World War II. It was parachuted in from cargo planes for the armed forces who were fighting and used to entertain them by people like Bob Hope. There was a copper shortage then, so they used soft iron for some of the strings."

"Anything more recent?"

"We've tried to respond to technological advances. We are now selling the digitalized Spirio player piano. It's the same concept as what you saw in the old movies, but it's high resolution, controlled by an iPad, and has various types of music—jazz, classical, and pop—that we capture from live performances by Steinway Artists in our studios on a daily basis. Come, I'll show you upstairs." We walk up a flight of stairs into a large room, where the player piano is situated. It's gorgeous. I listen to world-renowned Vladimir Horowitz, now deceased, playing a composition. A video of him comes up on a screen, and the piano is playing with no one seated. The effect is both soothing and surreal because he's not there, but as the keys move, it feels like a real performance. It turns out that the piano has particular appeal to purchasers of Steinways who want a great Steinway piano but also want to be able to hear live piano music from a variety of genres. I meet Michael Mohr, director of manufacturing, who tells me, "I grew up on Steinway in my house because my father worked here on the pianos themselves, as a piano technician to well-known pianists. We always talked about the company in the house. So, it was natural that I would end up here, though I'm focused on the piano-building aspect."

Next, I speak with Robert Berger, who was raised in Astoria and is director of customer satisfaction and concert services. He tells me something about the history of the company during World War II. "Many companies contributed to the war effort, and we were one of them. Of greatest importance was that we produced glider planes for the American army. These gliders were assembled in kit form at the Astoria factory and delivered to the Army Air Corps. They were eventually used during the invasion of Italy." This place, despite its modern office building, has an old-world charm about it, highlighted by the tasteful chandeliers, the spiral staircase, and the stunning pianos located at strategic spots. Public tours of the factory are given on Tuesdays, but there is a very long waiting list.

At 18-33, I come to the Steinway mansion, where the family resided in the nineteenth century. It's impossible to miss from Nineteenth Avenue or from anywhere else in the area. Situated high on a hill, a towering majestic building, it offers unparalleled views on all sides of Queens and Manhattan. The style is Italianate, and the house is made of bluestone and dark-gray granite, rough-hewn blocks, with cast-iron decorations on the exterior, namely two lampposts that flank an elaborate gate with many curlicues that curve into each other forming a complex design. A tall multiwindowed tower rises above the lower floors, topped with a slate roof. Built in 1858 by the entrepreneur and inventor Benjamin Pike Jr., it was part of a 440-acre site that was purchased by the Steinways in 1870. I speak with Sal, a businessman who bought the mansion in 2014.

"What can you tell me about the mansion?"

"It belonged to the Steinways, and I'm refurbishing it now with the intention of using it as offices for my company. It's very beautiful on the inside. There's woodwork and chandeliers, marble fireplaces. There's also a really nice-looking breezeway with three stone arches. Right now, it's not open to see because it's under reconstruction. We're adding and fixing lots of things, and it should be even more beautiful when it's done." Efforts were made by a private group, Friends of Steinway, to purchase and open the house to the public, but they were unsuccessful. Hopefully, the present owner, who lives in Astoria, will at least make it available to visitors on a limited basis.

The rest of this area comprises unremarkable, low-slung industrial buildings. I leave the Steinway neighborhood of Astoria and walk along 41st Street to the Ditmars neighborhood, turning right on Ditmars Boulevard. Here's what's left of the Greek population. I say "left" because the Greeks are declining in number as they age or are priced out. Thus, it's no surprise when I speak with the owner of a Greek restaurant who tells me: "I don't like the hipsters or yuppies because they're not friendly and they think they know everything. People who think they know everything don't really know anything."

"Do they eat in your place?"

"Yes, some of them. But the problem is also that when they come into this neighborhood, the rents go up, and the Greeks who are the main steady customers are moving out. I do like the tourists. The tourists are usually nicer."

"Where are the Greeks going?"

"Different places, like New Jersey or Long Island to be near their kids. Some move to Sunnyside, Woodside, or Elmhurst, but they're not going to come back here that much because they're old and it's hard for them to travel, even a short distance." He's right. It's a sad story for what was once a thriving Greek community. Those who hang on miss their friends, and the lifestyles of the young aren't necessarily compatible with those of the older generation—in terms of noise, barhopping, friendship circles, shopping choices, and so on.

Continuing on Ditmars, I turn left on Steinway Street. It's more or less residential until Twenty-Fifth Avenue. The long block between Twenty-Fifth and Twenty-Eighth Avenues changes abruptly into a section dominated by Muslim-owned businesses—restaurants, travel agencies, medical offices, and clothing stores emphasizing modest clothing for women. Most striking however, is the proliferation of hookah lounges, an incredible twenty-one of them on this one block by my count. Of course, Steinway (and Broadway) are represented by other ethnic groups besides Muslims—Hispanics, Japanese, Brazilians, and others. I speak to one elderly shopkeeper who isn't Muslim and ask him how he gets along with his Muslim neighbors.

"The block is mostly Muslim," he says. "I have very little to do with them other than hello, goodbye. I don't bother them, and they don't bother me." Others on the block with whom I chat express similar sentiments. It's coexistence, but very little interaction. There is here a strong sense of boundaries, of lines not crossed, conversations not had. He knows very little about his newer neighbors and doesn't want to know more. The neighborhood was once very different ethnically, and these store owners are old-timers from the days when it was Jewish, Greek, and Italian. After Twenty-Eighth, heading south, Steinway becomes a shopping emporium, with local delis, eateries, and bakeries; 99¢ enterprises; and chain stores like T-Mobile.

Returning to Ditmars, I continue eastward until it dead-ends into Shore Boulevard about a mile later, and I turn left. Here Astoria Park runs south along Shore Boulevard to about a block before 25th Road. It's a beautiful place that is situated under both the Hell Gate and the Robert F. Kennedy Bridges. Its bucolic appearance belies the once-raging waters beneath Hell Gate Bridge, where hundreds of ships were lost through the centuries. The passageway became considerably safer with the massive dynamiting of the dangerous area in 1876. But when I look at the water under the bridge, I can still see the waters swirling angrily beneath the span. A plaque beneath it by the East River tells the infamous and heartbreaking tale of the *General Slocum*, about which more will be said later, in the Middle Village section of this book. Here's the basic story:

In 1904, on a Wednesday morning in mid-June, the *General Slocum* set out on an all-day excursion. Aboard were some 1,358 women and children, German Americans who lived in what was called Kleindeutschland, a German community on the Lower East Side. As the vessel approached the Hell Gate Bridge near Astoria, Queens, the ship caught fire, causing panic among those on board as they raced toward the lifeboats, only to discover that they had been painted onto the decks and could not be pried loose. There were other egregious code violations, including useless life preservers that had turned from once-buoyant cork into dust, thereby weighing the preservers down, causing those flailing about, many of them children, to sink and drown. The thirty-five-member crew lacked experience, having never even conducted a fire drill.

Meanwhile, people were screaming for help and waving their hands frantically in the air. Those on the shore, hearing the music, thought that everyone was having a good time and waved back, not realizing the tragedy that was unfolding. Over one hundred vessels joined in the rescue, some catching fire when they came too close to the *General Slocum*. It all happened very quickly. Within fifteen minutes the ship had burned down to the waterline. When it was all over, 1,021 souls had perished, making the disaster the largest loss of human life in New York City until 9/11.

As I enter Astoria Park, I see that the name of the playground near the bridge is Charybdis. The name isn't a coincidence, for in *The Odyssey*, Odysseus and his crew must navigate the straits between Scylla and Charybdis. Charybdis is a dangerous whirlpool and Scylla a monster. The latter's relevance is that there were stories about strange apparitions, not to mention rapists, who were rumored to frequent the Hell Gate Bridge.

Notwithstanding all this, the 60-acre park is very pretty, overlooking the river, with many amenities, including a track, sports facilities, and trails, as well as the largest and perhaps nicest public swimming pool in the city. For city kids, many of them from low-income families, this is a real bonanza. On this cold day, a lone man is playing with his dog, who is frolicking in the grass.

Immediately south of the park is Halletts Cove, a small old section of Astoria. I begin exploring it by turning left off of Shore Boulevard onto 9th Street, then right onto Twenty-Seventh Avenue, followed by an immediate left onto 8th Street, and then, finally, a right onto Astoria Boulevard. I soon arrive at Astoria Houses, a twenty-two-building New York City Housing Authority (NYCHA) project constructed in 1951 and in better condition than many other NYCHA structures. The buildings are six or seven stories in height, and they sit right on or adjacent to the waters of the East River. The residents have beautiful views of the water.

Continuing west into the development, I soon arrive at an unusual mural at 4-03 Astoria Boulevard, near a senior citizens' center commemorating and honoring the black civil rights movement of the 1960s. On the left a black man stands, back to me, on the

Washington, DC, mall wearing a ministerial blue robe, his arms outstretched, addressing a huge crowd. It's only when I come close to the mural that I see countless small faces standing in front of the man, who, I assume, is Reverend Dr. Martin Luther King. On the right is another drawing of King that portrays him hugging a small child. There's also a drawing of a bus in flames, with plumes of dark smoke rising into the blue sky. It may well represent the Freedom Riders, who went south in the early 1960s to support black people, asserting their right to live with dignity. Almost but not quite invisible against the light-colored brick is a portrait of Mahatma Gandhi. Donald, a twenty-five-year-old black man wearing a windbreaker and passing by, confirms my general description. When I point out Gandhi, he looks surprised and says, "You know, I've lived here twenty years, and I pass this mural just about every day. But I never noticed Gandhi was in the picture." I ask Donald if it's safe to live here.

"Oh yes. Definitely, much more than in the nineties because now there's all this money coming in here, and there are thousands of new jobs because of the private developments being built here. Used to be it was all drug dealers. But now there's all these training programs for jobs, working on the construction sites, doing the Citi Bikes that they're putting up."

"Are you in one?"

"Of course. I wouldn't pass this up." His voice rises with excitement as he continues. "There's a ferry already operating here taking folks from Manhattan [to Queens]." It's true, and the ferry drops people off right in front of the projects. People might resent seeing these well-heeled people disembarking and heading off along a walkway to their much nicer digs. But it may be offset by the fact that this has brought jobs for the unemployed. Donald agrees, saying, "This is the best thing that's ever happened here. Everybody's happy."

These jobs are critical for those residing here. In the wake of Amazon's decision not to proceed, people in the New York City

Housing Authority (NYCHA) houses in the immediate area expressed great disappointment because Amazon had indicated that it would employ people from here. A number of tenants' association presidents from public housing complexes expressed their dismay at a press conference, saying that they had very much wanted the project to thrive. On the other hand, many advocates for the poor in the city were very opposed to it, saying that Amazon had refused to make adequate concessions to the city. I returned to this housing complex after the decision and spoke with a number of residents. The predominant view was that jobs that could have helped them were lost.[3]

I head east on Astoria and continue along Main Avenue, which intersects Astoria at an angle. There are many "Main Streets" in America, but a "Main Avenue" is unusual. I had not thought about it until now, and I wonder why? I take a right onto 12th Street and then a quick right on Welling Court, a curving lane, filled, to date, with some 150 graffiti art murals on the walls, many of which emphasize social and political messages. On my immediate right is a shiny mosaic tile of, again, Mahatma Gandhi. His message of unity and peace seems to have resonated in Astoria for rich and poor. Another mural is made up of bee honeycombs, proclaiming: "Bees. We can't live without them!" A third implores people, "Stop staring at the screen," meaning, I presume, stop looking at your iPhone or iPad or computer, get out, and see what's happening around you. Finally, Welling Court is home to a new building filled with young people who have decided to become part of the graffiti world, by putting graffiti art in their elevator shaft, on their walls on each floor, in the parking garage, in the fitness gym, and in other places. Called "Graffiti House," at 11-07 Welling Court, it's a one-of-a-kind house in every sense of the term.

Turning left off Welling onto Main, I immediately go left onto Vernon Boulevard. Shortly after Main dead-ends into Vernon Boulevard, I come to a handsome, red-brick Romanesque revival converted apartment house at 31-01 between Thirty-First Avenue and

A shiny mosaic of Mahatma Gandhi.

31st Drive, with a large clock tower, featuring gold-painted Roman numerals against a dark background. Atop the tower is a copper-trimmed mansard roof and a curved dome. The time is incorrect, but the clock and tower are really neat looking, as is fitting, for this building was once the home of the Sohmer Piano Factory, built in 1886, and that year appears on the tower in large numbers just beneath the clock.

The clock hands are intricately designed, and the clock itself is literally encircled by red bricks. These clock towers on buildings were very common in New England mill towns, and this was a factory. In the late nineteenth century inexpensive watches were not yet available to the masses. Yet the industrial age made adhering to strict schedules a critical part of daily and communal life. Thus, the clock became an essential way in which New Yorkers and people in general organized their lives. The pioneer sociologist Georg Simmel took note of this in his seminal essay on modern urban life 120 years ago, writing that life in the city is so varied and complex that "without the strictest punctuality in promises and services the whole structure would break down into an inextricable chaos. . . . If all clocks and watches in Berlin would suddenly go wrong in different ways, even if only by one hour, all economic life and communication of the city would be disrupted for a long time."[4] While it looks like a wonderful additional design feature to passersby, it was clearly essential in the nineteenth century when the factory hummed with daily activity. Now that it's a residential building in the twenty-first century, it doesn't matter if the time is correct. After all, just about everyone has a watch, not to mention an iPhone, if they want to know what time it is!

The "big news" in the neighborhood is the construction of thousands of apartments in the immediate area along the shore. But for lovers of New York City history and architecture, this area, Halletts Cove, like the Steinway section, still has charming structures worth seeing. Just a few blocks from the piano factory, I wander past homes from long ago. For example, on 30th Road, there are several preserved stone houses, including the one at 11-55 30th Road that's being refurbished on the inside when I walk by. One can only hope that the proper balance will be struck between what was and what's going up now.

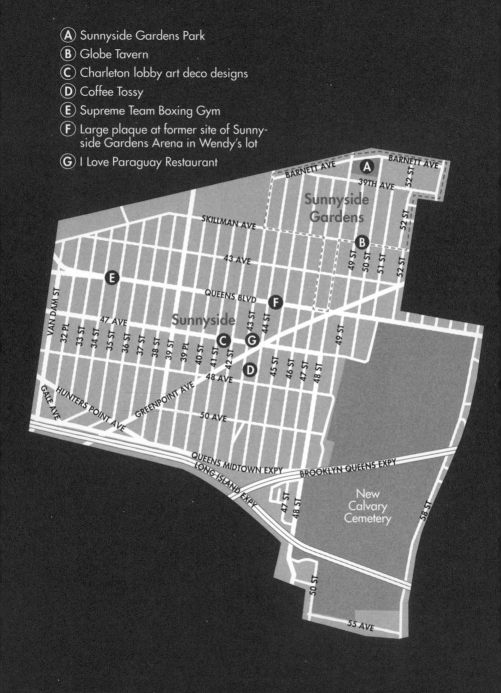

A Sunnyside Gardens Park
B Globe Tavern
C Charleton lobby art deco designs
D Coffee Tossy
E Supreme Team Boxing Gym
F Large plaque at former site of Sunny-
side Gardens Arena in Wendy's lot
G I Love Paraguay Restaurant

SUNNYSIDE

SUNNYSIDE HAS A LONG HISTORY, having been first settled by French Huguenots in the 1700s. They named their rural farming community Sunnyside. Its borders are Skillman and Barnett Avenues on the north, Woodside Avenue and 52nd and 58th Streets on the east, the Long Island Expressway and the Brooklyn Queens Expressway on the south, and Van Dam Street on the west. The area was largely uninhabited until the twentieth century, but once the elevated line was completed in 1917 it grew rapidly. In the 1920s, as part of the garden city movement that originated in England, Sunnyside Gardens was established as part of the community, one with its own distinct borders.

The housing stock is a mix of small homes, mostly brick, and older prewar apartment buildings in varying styles, including art deco. It's a very diverse community with eastern Europeans, many of them Romanian; Hispanics from many lands; Middle Eastern people, especially Turks; and Asians, quite a few of them Koreans. In the last twenty years younger urban pioneers, interested in putting down roots with their young children in a community with easy access to Manhattan, have moved into the area. Scattered throughout are older folks who've been here for decades—Irish, Italians, Germans, and Jews. The main commercial thoroughfares are Skillman and Greenpoint Avenues, and Queens Boulevard. Public parks are scarce; the most popular one, Doughboy Park, is located along Woodside Avenue between 54th and 56th Streets. While rough-and-tumble during the 1980s and 1990s, the area is considered quite safe today.

My trip begins in Sunnyside Gardens, the planned garden neighborhood, built in the mid-1920s between 43rd and 52nd Streets and from Barnett to Skillman Avenues. As noted earlier this was part of a national movement emphasizing green spaces and healthy living, which also included Forest Hills Gardens and nearby Jackson Heights. The brick homes, many of them boasting slate roofs, are mostly one- or two-family attached structures and have gardens behind them as well as enclosed green areas for the residents. Garages for autos away from home are located near the Long Island Railroad Station. Sunnyside Gardens also encompasses the art deco Phipps Gardens Apartments, which can be accessed on Thirty-Ninth Avenue, near 51st Street. This complex has a nicely landscaped interior courtyard with gardens and sitting areas. Past notable residents include the artist Raphael Soyer; the historian Lewis Mumford, author of *The City in History*; and the entertainers Perry Como and Rudy Vallee. While it hasn't retained the luster of the past, it's still a nice place in which to live.

The Landmarks Preservation Committee gave the Gardens historic district status in 2007, but this decision was not well received by everyone. On the one hand, the historical designation confers prestige on a neighborhood, and there are tax abatements for preserving and renovating historic homes. On the other hand, you can repair but rarely replace basic items or designs, and these older homes sometimes have structural issues, often making renovations both challenging and expensive. Plus, expanding these homes within the requirements isn't easy. Views vary on this topic because tastes and priorities differ from one individual to another. One person may want to remove certain interior features, like arched entrances and distinctive moldings, in favor of modernizing, but that isn't always possible.

Tall sycamore and London plane trees flank the twenty-foot-high sign that marks the entrance to Sunnyside Gardens Park, established in 1926. The park entranceway is at the intersection of Thirty-Ninth Avenue, originally called Middleburg Avenue, and 49th Street, once known as Heiser Street. When the Gardens were first built, these streets had names as opposed to numbers. Today, both versions are routinely listed on the signposts. The park is a 3.5-acre site operated by and open only to residents of the Sunnyside

The subway-shaped performance stage in Sunnyside Gardens Park.

Gardens neighborhood. It is one of only two private parks in the city, the other being Manhattan's Gramercy Park. The Sunnyside Park prohibits entry by nonresidents without permission, but this is not enforced, and, unlike Gramercy Park, it doesn't require a key to gain entry. It has ballfields, a grassy playing area, and clay tennis courts. Inside a playground, there's a structure, designed like a pirate ship, with a Jolly Roger. One can easily forget that this is a highly urban area, but for the fact that the Long Island Railroad commuter train, which services the length of Queens, rumbles by every few minutes on elevated tracks behind the park.

There's a gaily painted stage in the shape of a subway here for park events; performers appear as if they're inside a train. Thus, private as the park is, it is, at the same time, very much part of Queens, with the backyards of two-story homes clearly visible from the park entrance. It's a mild day for January, and several mothers are playing with their children.

The surrounding streets are tree lined, and the houses are attached. At 49-10 Skillman Avenue, I enter the Globe Tavern, one of many Irish-type bars in Sunnyside, a reflection of its rich social history. It's a long rectangular place with a fireplace, lithographs of the British Isles hanging on the wall, six televisions, dartboards, and a pool table with a Tiffany-style lamp above it. The wainscoting and the tables where one can sit combine to give the tavern a cozy feeling, especially as board games, like Sorry, Easy Money, Scrabble, and Monopoly, are piled up nearby. There's karaoke and open-mike nights for anyone who wants to play.

"We have a lot here," says the bartender. "Knock yourself out. We've been here forever, an Irish bar with several previous names—McGowan, McGovern, and a couple more names."

Turning left onto 41st Street, I leave the Sunnyside Gardens area, cross Queens Boulevard, and, a block later, make a left onto Forty-Seventh Avenue. I head in to look at the lobby in the Charleton, an art deco building around the corner at 41-16 Forty-Seventh Avenue, between 41st and 42nd Streets. It looks fairly nondescript, and if not for a suggestion by Monica Lynch, a media professional who lives on 41st Street, I would not have gone inside. As she noted, it has an exquisite lobby with a neat marble fireplace. Above the fireplace there's a delicate pink bas-relief of a woman with delicate features and flowing hair. The ceiling's design features include ocean waves, circles, gold-inlaid stars, and flowers in a largely art deco motif in varying colors. There are birds, perhaps storks or cranes, in flight, with an attractive gold chandelier with electric candles. It's a special place, for sure.

One block south, at 42-14 Greenpoint Avenue, I jump into Coffee Tossy. There are young people working on their laptops, drinking coffee. The place resembles a cross between a Starbucks and a Caffé Bene. The women behind the counters are wearing white, hipster-like hats with small brims, and I learn that the employees hail from Ecuador and Colombia. As I look around, it strikes me that the décor is distinctly Latin American. It's a one-of-a-kind place, not part of a chain. There are murals related to coffee production, and burlap sacks for coffee hang from a wall made of wooden planks in a herringbone design. In the back I see shelves lined with books and a display of straw hats, plus an antique, gold-plated telephone that actually works.

I angle right off Greenpoint onto Forty-Eighth Avenue near 40th Street and enter an industrial area that runs from here down to about 33rd Street, where I turn right and head over to Queens Boulevard. As I walk along the boulevard, I see wall murals sponsored by the 7 Train Murals group. This organization is dedicated to showcasing the works of community artists from neighborhoods along the Queens route of the 7 train. The importance of this train for Queens cannot be overstated. The ethnographers and sociologists par excellence Stephane Tonnelat and William Kornblum wrote an entire book about it, *International Express: New Yorkers on the 7 Train*, discussing at length how no other subway in the city traverses such a varied ethnic landscape.[5] And my wife had a four-year-old student in the preschool at which she worked who came to a Halloween party dressed as a 7 train.

At 34-09 I step into the Supreme Team Boxing Gym and speak with one of the employees, a tall, well-built fellow named Nelson, who gives me an impromptu tour.

"How long have you been at this location?" I ask.

"About three years." I mention to him that a major boxing arena, the Sunnyside Gardens, was once in this area, a half mile up Queens Boulevard on 45th Street. I suggest to him that he consider opening a museum in his place with photographs of the arena during its heyday, along with artifacts like boxing gloves.

"That's a great idea," he says. "We have a lot of space here too. I'm going to pursue it."

"Do you have any name fighters who train here?"

"Oh yeah. We have Shannon Briggs. He was world heavyweight champion twice. And we also have Sullivan Barrera, a Cuban boxer who won the World Boxing Association Light Heavy

Championship title." This is the kind of cred that attracts people to a gym. As we're talking, rap music is playing in the background, and people are pounding the leather punching bags.

"You have classes for kids, but aren't parents afraid to send their kids? I mean boxing can be pretty violent."

"True, but we emphasize defensive boxing with no real contact. We have little kids as young as four who come here."

"How did you end up working here?"

"I was a big kid at twelve, but I had problems. I grew up in Alphabet City in the East Village. You know what they say about Alphabet City—Avenue A, okay; B, beware; C, caution; D, death. I'm Puerto Rican, and we lived in the projects on Avenue D. My brother got shot in the head. It was very bad in the 1980s when I grew up. Boxing saved me, gave me a reason to live, and taught me discipline. Milton La Croix took an interest in me. He was the founder of this company. We have a location in Manhattan too. And I've been here ever since."

"What's the most rewarding thing you get out of being here?"

"Oh man! Just looking at these kids' eyes when they learn something new and when they stay out of trouble."

"I see you have a picture of Bruce Lee."

"Yeah, he was only 135 pounds, but he proved that speed is power, and we believe that." We kid around for a couple of minutes, and I bid him good day, continuing on my way. Next door is a taxi school teaching "defensive driving." How appropriate having two places next to each other that teach people to be defensive, one on the road, the other in the ring.

On 45th Street and Queens Boulevard, I stand in front of a Wendy's. There are thousands of Wendy's, but this one's special because in front of it near the boulevard there's a large plaque dedicated to those who fought in the amateur and professional bouts held at the Sunnyside Garden Arena from 1945 to 1977. While no Madison Square Garden, it did seat twenty-five hundred people who avidly watched both boxing and wrestling matches. Those who competed there included Floyd Patterson, Tony Canzoneri, Bruno Sammartino, and Haystacks Calhoun. Political figures, including John and Robert Kennedy, made campaign appearances at the arena, too.

My foray into Sunnyside ends at an eatery with an unusual name, "I Love Paraguay," at 43-16 Greenpoint Avenue. It's a very well appointed, spotless place. Large photographs of Paraguay line the wall, among them forested areas with stunning waterfalls. Lemons meant to evoke the locally grown variety hang from the walls and are arrayed on the countertops, which contain a wide selection of pastries, including a traditional favorite, honey cake made with black honey. I meet Jaime, a waiter from Paraguay who speaks lovingly of his country, telling me that he came here a year ago seeking economic opportunity.

Paraguayans are the smallest Hispanic community in the United States, numbering only about twenty thousand. The New York metropolitan area has about nine thousand residents, mostly in Queens; Westchester County; and Somerset, New Jersey. I have a lengthy conversation with Natalia, a mother of two, who manages "I love Paraguay" and works together with the owners, her parents.

"My parents and I, as well as my brother, run these restaurants," she tells me. "We all came here starting ten years ago. Although we were doing very well in our restaurant back home, the economy wasn't very good. I always wanted to come here because here, if you work hard, you can make it. Also, in this country, if you want something, you follow the rules, and it mostly works out. If I want to get a driver's license, I do the six things, and I come down, and I get it. In Paraguay, you have to bribe people a lot because it's often corrupt. You have to know someone. Even if you have all the papers, they try to find the one thing you don't have so they can get some money from you."

"I understand what you're saying. But if this is what's wrong with Paraguay, along with the corruption, why did you name your place "I Love Paraguay?"

New York's nine thousand Paraguayan residents can get a taste of home at I Love Paraguay.

"Because we love the country itself. It's beautiful. That's why we decided to open the restaurant. And we love our food. I used to take my native food to school to eat it there. We feel like we're in heaven when we eat it. Many years ago, we were a big country, but we lost most of our land through wars."

In many ways this is a typical story. An ambitious individual comes here, works hard, and makes it. She finishes college, and her family business succeeds. Underlying it is a strong desire to leave her own community and enter the successful life that being an American represents. But her personal ambitions are always at the forefront.

(A) Emerald Isle Immigration Center
(B) Saints and Sinners
(C) Maguire's Public House
(D) P.S. 361
(E) Jollibee
(F) Solar clock on schoolyard wall

WOODSIDE

WOODSIDE IS AN ETHNICALLY DIVERSE middle- and working-class community with a rich history. Its boundaries are Thirty-First Avenue on the north; the Brooklyn Queens Expressway, 69th Street, and 74th Street on the east; Queens Boulevard on the south; and 52nd Street, Woodside Avenue, and 49th Street on the west. It was first settled in the 1850s as a place where the wealthy built large homes. In 1867, small lots were built by developers, most notably Benjamin Hitchcock, who also built up Ozone Park and Corona. To attract customers, he gave them free lunches and hired bands to play for them as they considered moving to Woodside. Most of those who came there then were Irish. Today, new Irish immigrants still gravitate to this community. The turn of the twentieth century brought railroad, trolley, and subway service, making the area even more accessible. Employment opportunities nearby also were an attraction—foundries, chemical plants, and the Bulova Watch Company and the Steinway Piano Factory, both of which are still there today. For entertainment and relaxation, there were hotels, dance halls, and beer gardens.

Woodside today is quite different from those days. It's home to an increasingly diverse population, with Asians making up 30 percent of the residents. This includes Chinese, Koreans, Filipinos (about 15 percent of the community), Tibetans, Thais, and Nepalese. There are also a number of Hispanic groups like Mexicans, Puerto Ricans, Dominicans, Colombians, Guatemalans, and Peruvians; smaller groups of Italians and Jews; and a steady stream of recent Irish immigrants. These groups live together in relative harmony and make the local public schools look like a permanent model UN. And there are Catholic, Protestant, Jewish, Buddhist, Muslim, and Hindu houses of worship. There's quite a bit of industry north of Northern Boulevard and along Queens Boulevard, but the area is still devoted mostly to small businesses. The main commercial thoroughfares are Roosevelt Avenue, Queens and Northern Boulevards, Woodside Avenue, and Broadway.

My journey begins on Woodside Avenue and 63rd Street, where I head south toward Queens Boulevard. About two-thirds of the way down the block, on the right side, I gape at a really giant tree. A beech tree whose origins may go back all the way to the Revolutionary War—according to local lore—sits next to a five-story apartment house, dwarfing the building with its huge spreading branches on all sides. Retracing my steps, I return to Woodside Avenue and go left. This area was once heavily Irish. To learn if the Irish still find Woodside to be a popular destination, I speak with Siobhan (pronounced shiw-vawn) in the Emerald Isle Immigration Center, located at 59-26 Woodside Avenue. As the executive director of many years, she is a fount of knowledge on the subject.

"I know that the Irish have had a long presence in this community," I say, "but didn't that end as they moved out and new groups, Hispanics and Asians, came in?"

"How long is your book going to be?" she responds with a laugh. "Seriously though, one wave led to another, starting with the Irish famine in 1845 and continuing until today. This is also a fantastic place. As a transportation hub, Woodside's always been excellent with its subway and rail connections and its closeness to the city, twelve minutes away by train. There's still a strong Irish representation here. In 1965, with the changes in immigration laws, another wave began, also including other groups, and we've had more waves in the past twenty years. Plus, we help immigrants from other lands."

"Do the Irish immigrants make contact with Irish people here before they come?"

"Yes, and the first thing they do when they come is they look up their Irish relatives and friends who live here. And they do integrate rather well. They know people here, speak the language, and many find their accents rather charming. All in all, it's a good fit."

It's important to understand that there were differences between the Irish waves that were not as openly shared with outsiders. One study of the community found that the Irish of Woodside who settled here before the later groups came did not necessarily mix with the newcomers. One woman who came in the 1980s summed up the complexity of it. In many ways it was typical of so many ethnic groups.

"Snobs they were to us. Because we didn't have the papers like their parents did. We were just trying to get out of Ireland and find a job . . . same as their parents and grandparents. And some of them even come from up north as I did. But the ones who were already here weren't all bad. There was the Emerald Isle Center, of course, which helped us a lot. And some who had lived here for a while liked to hear our accents. But many of them thought we was beneath them. Because we couldn't always get proper jobs on account of not having papers. What's wrong with being a waitress? I ask you."[6]

I leave the center, which sits where Woodside and Roosevelt Avenue intersect. On Roosevelt, I notice almost immediately that there are still a number of Irish bars here despite the fact that there's only a small number of Irish left in Woodside. The nearest one is Saints and Sinners, at 59-21 Roosevelt Avenue. In a nod to the changing demographics, they offer quesadillas, chicken curry, and Italian lasagna, topped with cheddar cheese, but also the standard Irish fare of shepherd's pie and other dishes. The Irish waitress cheerfully informs me: "Oh, the Irish love this exotic kind of stuff. This weekend we have Irish music. Actually, the singer's mother is Irish, and his father is Polish, so it's a mix. Everyone's happy."

Farther down, there's yet another place, Maguire's Public House, at 54-20 Roosevelt, that specializes in music and has Irish singers on a regular basis. The bright red awning with its drawing of a banjo on the left and a violin on the right tells it all—it's a place where serious music lovers, especially Irish music lovers, and drinkers come together, as no meals are served here. I remember how I used to take my kids to see and listen to Tommy Makem and the Clancy brothers on a regular basis. My wife and I also listened to Irish bands at a Hicksville, Long Island, pub, Stack o' Barley. There was no conscious connection. We just loved the music and the words to the ballads. Today, they are no more, but there are clearly plenty of replacements still entertaining the faithful.

Walking up 57th Street I hang a left and a block later happen on P.S. 361 at 39-07. It's a brand-new elementary school with a really modern design, colorfully decorated, with a spacious dining room and large brightly lit classrooms. As I stand in the lobby, I notice, halfway down a stairwell, an interesting piece of artwork hanging on a wall. Approaching it, I see it's made of hundreds of small and variegated pieces of wood. It turns out to be, of all things, a scale model of every street in Woodside, plus some streets just outside the community. In a way, it might be reflecting the strong sense of community that pervades this borough.

I return to Roosevelt via 57th and turn left, picking up my pace until I arrive at 62-29 Roosevelt, the location of Jollibee, a well-designed, attractive-looking Filipino fast-food joint that, according to many, is the real deal, serving inexpensive but fresh, delicious Filipino food. It's spotless inside, and the employees are very friendly. They have a six-piece fried chicken portion served in a red-and-white cardboard bucket that looks like KFC's, and spaghetti dishes, in addition to traditional Filipino favorites like palabok fiesta, a garlic-flavored noodle dish with pork rind, shrimp, and egg; and peach mango pie. Currently it's one of only two Jollibees in New York, but they have eighteen hundred stores worldwide. Most of the Jollibees in the United States are on the West Coast, especially the Los Angeles area.

The Filipino businesses are concentrated in an area known as Little Manila that stretches from about 63rd to 74th Streets along Roosevelt. There are about fifty-five thousand Filipinos in the city, with most of them living in Woodside and the surrounding communities. About 90 percent are Catholic, but a significant number of them are also followers of Felix Manalo, a religious leader who

Jollibee serves up inexpensive and delicious Filipino cuisine.

founded a movement in 1916, called Iglesia Ni Cristo (Church of Christ), promoting Evangelical Protestantism. Today the group has three million followers worldwide, and it has two large churches in Queens, one in Forest Hills and another in Long Island City.

I walk over to Woodside Avenue back to where Woodside crosses Roosevelt. Near 71st Street, I pass a public school, P.S. 12, and see a curious design attached to the wall of a building adjoining the schoolyard. It appears to be made up of long, raised lines in many directions, a fascinating geometric display. These are accompanied by a square piece of what looks like wood about six feet long that juts out from the wall. I cannot tell from where I'm standing what materials were used to construct this. The lines come together sometimes,

The time is right at the solar clock at P.S. 12.

but not always. At the end of some of these lines are numbers, going from one through five. I walk around the block and into the school lobby to inquire what this is all about. The guard has no idea, but an after-school program volunteer named Melanie explains it to me. It's a solar clock. I thank her and return to see if it works, and indeed it's perfect. My watch reads 3:30 p.m., and the sun's shadow is exactly between the three and four lines. As I take a last look at the schoolyard, I'm impressed by the number of different groups playing together in this yard, children of different races and nationalities, in hijabs, Sikh turbans, traditional Indian dress—a microcosm of Queens.

ELMHURST

JACKSON HEIGHTS

EAST ELMHURST

CORONA

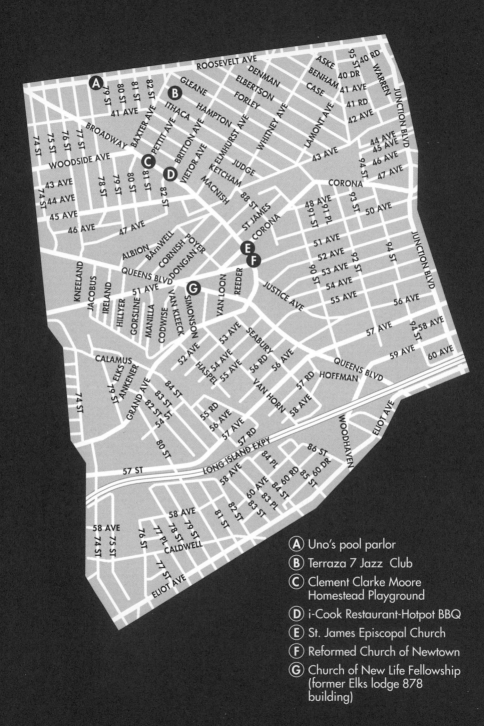

(A) Uno's pool parlor

(B) Terraza 7 Jazz Club

(C) Clement Clarke Moore Homestead Playground

(D) i-Cook Restaurant-Hotpot BBQ

(E) St. James Episcopal Church

(F) Reformed Church of Newtown

(G) Church of New Life Fellowship (former Elks lodge 878 building)

ELMHURST

ELMHURST, AN OLD COMMUNITY, was first established by the Dutch in 1652. Its earliest settlers were fleeing neighboring Maspeth because of attacks by the Maspat (also known as Maspeth Indian tribe). When the British took control of the area in 1664, they renamed it Newtown. That designation lasted for 250 years but was changed back to Elmhurst in 1897, in part to recognize the beautiful elm trees that grew there, but also because developers didn't want buyers to think of the befouled Newtown Creek when considering the community for their families.

Elmhurst's boundaries are Roosevelt Avenue on the north, Junction Boulevard on the east, Eliot Avenue and a bit of the Long Island Expressway (LIE) on the south, and 74th Street on the west. By the 1930s, the residents were overwhelmingly Italian, Jewish, Irish, and German, most of them seeking to escape crowded Manhattan. The trend accelerated with the completion of the IND subway line in 1936. Through the 1960s this was a typical white middle-class Queens community.

Beginning in the 1970s, immigrants, largely from South America, began arriving, a pattern that has continued to this very day. Their numbers have been augmented by Chinese, as well as Koreans, Malaysians, Indonesians, Thais, and Vietnamese. Smaller populations include Nepalese, Tibetans, and Filipinos, most of whom are concentrated in the area around Roosevelt Avenue. One indicator of how the demographics have changed is that whites today are probably 2 percent of the total population. Elmhurst is an ideal location for newcomers for several reasons. There are many apartment buildings for those unable to afford private homes, as well as attached and semi-attached dwellings. Moreover, transportation is abundant and provides quick access to Manhattan, and there is ample shopping, what with the many commercial streets, the Queens Center mall, and Queens Place, another shopping emporium.

Geographically, Elmhurst can be divided into three fairly distinct areas. The first, largest, and most densely inhabited begins at the northern perimeter, along Roosevelt Avenue, and meanders in a southeasterly direction to Queens Boulevard. It encompasses both the Hispanic and the Asian parts of Elmhurst, and the major shopping centers. It has older residential housing, predominantly apartment buildings and attached homes. The second area, continuing south from Queens Boulevard to the LIE, also has a significant Chinese presence. There's a mix of apartment houses, and small homes of various types. The third and smallest part runs between the LIE and Eliot Avenue, which straddles the Middle Village section, and just east of Maspeth. This part features many more private, mostly brick homes. Its streets are much quieter. There are some small shops for basic needs available on Eliot.

The main commercial thoroughfares in Elmhurst are Roosevelt, Junction, and Grand Avenues; Queens Boulevard; and portions of Elmhurst, Baxter, Woodside, and Eliot Avenues. For recreation there's Clement Clarke Moore Homestead Park, named after the man who wrote the famous song *A Visit from St. Nicholas*, which begins with "Twas the night before Christmas." Elmhurst Park, situated where the gas tanks of Elmhurst once sat, is the other major park in this very urbanized area. Near the LIE, the gas tanks were an essential part of daily traffic reports on the radio, which clocked progress on the LIE, telling millions of listeners: "Traffic is very slow as you approach the Elmhurst gas tanks." Thus, while not an official city landmark, it was most definitely a local one.

Elmhurst, completed in 2011, with entrances on 74th Street and on Grand Avenue, includes a fairly steep hill used for sledding in the winter and has a futuristic restroom facility with a brick-and-glass-block exterior that cost $2 million to build. The curved brick wall has a space so people can enter the facility, but it is deliberately designed to be at different heights on each side, or, if you will, asymmetrical. Similarly, the two small windows, one on each side of the wall, are in different places, with one lower, the other higher. The inside of this two-story-high wall is lined with glass blocks in the art moderne style. Inside the bathrooms are green, orange, and white tiles in an unusual geometric pattern. One civic leader called it an obscene waste of money, arguing that resources spent on it should have been used for park maintenance or police patrols.

My visit to this multiethnic community begins with a stop in the 75 Laundry shop at 75-10 Roosevelt Avenue. I'm intrigued by two very plain-looking Styrofoam heads of people in the window. The male head is covered with small straw, hipster-like hats in various colors—orange, pale blue, and beige. The lone female head is wearing a broad-brimmed floppy hat.

I enter and meet two friendly Hispanic ladies who wash, dry, and fold huge amounts of laundry every week. I ask them about the hats and am told that they're for sale at $8 each. It's a good price; I bet they would fetch much more in North Williamsburg. They tell me they are new to the country.

"How do you like America?" I ask.

"Very much. We love our own country too, but there's no money there, so we came here. I have two children. One is starting college and wants to be a systems analyst." She is proud of his accomplishments to date. Maria travels two hours from the farthest reaches of Long Island to get here. She'd rather work closer to home but needs to be in New York City to do her immigration paperwork, which turns out to be pretty complicated—lots of forms and other requests.

My next stop on this constantly busy boulevard is Uno's pool parlor at 78-01 Roosevelt. I climb the steps and discover a very nice pool hall, one that's been here for over twenty years. There are old tables, with leather or plastic pockets, covered in traditional green felt, used for the traditional games—straight pool, eight- or nine-ball, Chicago, or rotation. And then there are newer blue-felt tables for billiards. There are many lockers available for those wishing to store their own cues. Those playing are all men. On the walls, there are large, well-made drawings of famous soccer players representing various Latin American nations. All the players are Hispanic as far as I can tell, and no women are present. I'm ignored, which suits me just fine, allowing me to look around in peace.

Uno's also has an attractive bar with a rectangular, rounded-off counter and a large selection of drinks. I approach the manager and begin a conversation with him.

"Who are most of your customers?" I ask.

"Most are Spanish, and almost all are men."

"And where are you from?"

"Korea."

"Do Asian people play this game in, say, Flushing?"

"They do, but not so much, and they don't drink when they do, so no bar. But I'm not interested in this game at all. I just work here, and I don't know Spanish, just a few words." I'm a lifelong pool player who played pool for money in the past to help pay my college tuition—mostly eight-ball, straight, and Chicago (also known as money-balls, or rotation). I still play sometimes at the Cue Bar in Bayside, an establishment with a mostly Asian clientele. But overall, the sport is much more popular in the Hispanic community.

Roosevelt Avenue has many nightclubs, and I ask a young female Hispanic college student standing outside one what that scene is like.

"Very unpleasant if you're a woman who is unattached," she tells me. "My friends and I went in one night, I was twenty-one, and we were accosted by some men right away. They were making kissing noises, asking us to dance with them, and one or two started groping us. We ran away, and the five of us just took a taxi. It was my first experience, but other people told me the same thing happened to them."

As I walk these streets, I see clear evidence of cultural intermingling. In a Colombian restaurant that typically shows news from back home, the TV is tuned to the New York City Marathon, being run that day. Across the street a Mexican fruit-and-vegetable store calls itself Cinco de Mayo, that nation's national holiday, one that the newcomers presumably wish to remember and even celebrate here. Of course, this popular holiday is also familiar to Americans, as evidenced by their presence at the annual Cinco de Mayo parades in East Harlem. And a city fire hydrant outside the Copacabana Brazilian Grill on Roosevelt and 81st Street is painted red, blue, and yellow, the colors of Colombia.

I come to the Terraza 7 Jazz Club at 40-19 Gleane Street, close to the forty-five-degree intersection off Roosevelt near 82nd Street. With a bar, and a terrific reputation for live jazz and singers, it's open every day from 5:00 p.m. to 4:00 a.m. There's room for people both downstairs and in a balcony, where the audience sits on benches in front of the stage. Perhaps fifty people can be seated here, and another eighty, mostly standing room, can be accommodated downstairs, where the bar is. The jazz represents many countries, each with its own music, songs, and combinations of instruments. Many of the performers are world renowned, and at affordable prices, Terraza 7 makes a long trip into Manhattan unnecessary. I speak with Freddy Castiblanco, the creator of this special space.

"How long have you been here?" I ask.

"About sixteen years. We have Latin jazz, Peruvian and Cuban jazz with flamenco inferences. We also have music from the Atlantic and Pacific coasts of Colombia. And the different strains of music sometimes have to do with the slave trade, which emphasized African influences." Freddy is a very friendly man. Initially, most of the clientele was local and Latino, but now they come from all over the metropolitan area.

"We have the only weekly commercial jam session in Queens," he tells me, "led by a five-time Grammy-award-winning musician, and we show movies too. On Sundays we have classical music jazz. At 8:00 p.m. we have musical theater. Right now, we're running a monologue based on Gabriel García Márquez's book *The Autumn of the Patriarch*. The music we're playing with the actor and the accordionist is great. And the bass player plays with Yo-Yo Ma. Flamenco is crazy now, so many people come to see the dancers perform."

"I'm curious," I tell him, "as to whether or not people who come here from the different countries, but similar regions, are more likely to be friendly with each other. For example, Ecuadorians, Peruvians, and Bolivians, all of whom come from the Andes Mountains, as opposed to say, Mexicans, Hondurans, or Argentinians."

"It's really different. There are actually some tendencies to self-isolate among certain groups. For example, Ecuadorians are one of the most nationalistic peoples. And Medellin is very different from Bogota, both of them in Colombia. It's so different that each town has its own music. And language too. There are over two hundred indigenous languages in Colombia and in the other countries too. It normally depends more on how one relates to the individual." It's a fascinating point because it illustrates the dangers of generalizing and also the complexity and diversity of the Hispanic community as a whole.

Turning around on Gleane I walk to the corner and turn left onto Baxter Avenue, taking it a short distance to where it ends on Broadway. This is the Chinatown of Elmhurst, also referred to by locals as Little Flushing. Its geographical center runs from about Forty-First to Forty-Fifth Avenues along Broadway, including many of the side streets. The elderly Chinese men hang out in Clement Clarke Moore Homestead Park on Broadway between 82nd Street and Forty-Fifth Avenue. This park reminds me of Columbia Park on Bayard Street in Manhattan's Chinatown, where, like here, knots of men watch and talk as others play various card games. This population is growing rapidly, and its influence in Elmhurst will continue to increase. To my right in the park I see a multiethnic group playing basketball—South and East Asians and Hispanics, mirroring the area's ethnic makeup. As the park is undergoing a reconstruction, things may be a bit different once it's completed.

Elmhurst is certainly one of the most diverse communities in the city, with well over 120 nationalities living here.[7] Of course, this doesn't necessarily mean that members of these groups become friends. But even their limited contact in business or physical

Clement Clarke Moore Homestead Park is a gathering place for residents of all ages.

proximity means that they develop an awareness of cultures other than their own. In the future, their children may extend the boundaries of social contact. Current research has demonstrated that this is happening, not only here but elsewhere in the country.

Continuing on Broadway, I stop in front of the i-COOK Restaurant at 81-17, whose sign also says Hotpot BBQ. What has caught my attention is a most intriguing color video above the restaurant windows that look out onto the street. It shows all manner of delicious dishes being thrown into sizzling pans and pots and prepared with various combinations of pork, beef, chicken, rice and noodles, and vegetables, with sauces. You can see them being stirred and fried, and the effect of this five-minute presentation is mouthwatering. But is it really so irresistible? I walk in and try to find out, asking a young Korean fellow, "Tell me, do you think that video outside of the food cooking attracts customers?"

"No."

"How do you know?"

"They don't say so."

Regardless, I don't recall ever seeing a video with such variety and movement quite like this. Inside the restaurant are beautiful paintings and sculptures that definitely add to its allure, and silkscreens painted with tree and flowers. The food served is both Chinese and Korean.

In the past few years, Asians have extended their presence from Forty-Fifth Avenue, beyond Fifty-First Avenue and to the other side of Queens Boulevard along the many side streets on either side of Grand Avenue, which begins on the southern side of Queens Boulevard. In the midst of this Asian neighborhood, on Broadway, lie the remnants of a much earlier era in the form of some of the oldest churches in Queens. First, there's St. James Episcopal Church on Broadway near St. James Place. Next to it is the Reformed Church of Newtown, founded in 1731. Today, all that's left of the original is the 1735 cornerstone. A bit farther is the original, much smaller site of St. James Church, a rather modest affair. But, as the oldest existing building in Elmhurst, it's a real piece of history, having been constructed in 1734.

Crossing Queens Boulevard, I wander along Grand Avenue and see that many of the shops are now Chinese owned, a dramatic change from ten years ago. I turn right on Van Kleeck Street and find myself at Queens Boulevard, where I turn right again and soon am face to face with a large, majestic bronze statue of an elk in front of a limestone, granite, and brick palazzo-style structure that once housed the Benevolent and Protective Order of Elks lodge 878, at 82-10 Queens Boulevard. In their heyday, which lasted from the 1920s until the 1960s, the Elks were a powerful group, the place where important business and political deals were made in Queens. The organization was also very charitable, donating millions of dollars to Queens charities. Among its amenities were a barbershop, a bar, a restaurant, and even a bowling alley, all of which are now gone. Today, it's home to the local nondenominational church of New Life Fellowship, which has been there since 1992. Its congregation, whose multiethnic members I meet on a Sunday morning, is a reflection of how much things have changed. Yet even as new groups move here, a respect for history remains among both local residents and preservationists. And so, the beautiful exterior with its intricately carved designs, and the interior, with its giant remarkable coffered ceiling, remain for all who wish to see them.

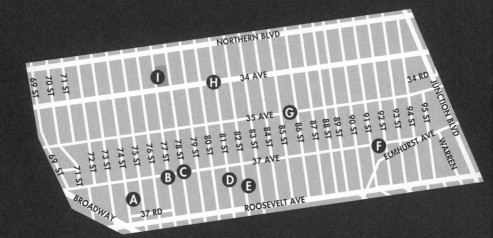

(A) Jackson Diner
(B) Jackson Heights Jewish Center
(C) Julio Rivera Corner
(D) Jahn's Restaurant
(E) $5.00 Shoe Warehouse
(F) KIKE Barber Shop
(G) Original home of SCRABBLE
(H) Towers apartment building
(I) Travers Park

JACKSON HEIGHTS

JACKSON HEIGHTS WAS BUILT AS A PLANNED COMMUNITY beginning in 1916, on what was primarily farmland. It was part of the English garden city movement of the nineteenth century, which combined urban residential, industrial, and green areas. The community is named after John Jackson, who built Northern Boulevard, the main road that ran through the area. It was designed to attract middle- and upper-middle-class residents, and it did not allow anyone except white, Anglo-Saxon Protestants to live in its buildings, which were constructed by the Queensboro Corporation. Its boundaries are Northern Boulevard on the north, Junction Boulevard on the east, Roosevelt Avenue on the south, and 69th Street on the west.

The apartment buildings, many of which have beautiful interior gardens, make up the bulk of the community. They are concentrated from Thirty-Seventh to Thirty-Fourth Avenues, running from the western to the eastern borders. There are also some pretty one- and two-family homes, located mostly between Thirty-Fourth Avenue and Northern Boulevard. The major commercial thoroughfares are Roosevelt Avenue, Northern Boulevard, Thirty-Seventh Avenue, and parts of 73rd, 74th, and 82nd Streets, as well as Junction Boulevard. Access to Manhattan, a twenty-minute trip, is available via various subway lines, including the 7, F, and E trains.

After the restrictive covenants were declared illegal, Jackson Heights saw an influx of Jews and Catholics, who lived here until the lure of the suburbs became too strong. Many wanted to live in private homes with their own backyard. When the United States began relaxing its immigration quotas in 1965, Asians and Hispanics began coming to the United States. Today, the community is home to people from many lands in Central and South America and from South Asia, especially Indians and Bangladeshis, but also people from Tibet, Nepal, and Afghanistan, in addition to Chinese and Korean immigrants. Finally, a thriving gay community has existed here since the 1970s and hosts an annual parade on Thirty-Seventh Avenue, which attracts thousands of people.

My stroll through this area begins at 73rd Street between Thirty-Seventh and Roosevelt. This is a commercial center for the Bangladeshi community, with restaurants, supermarkets, mosques, and clothing shops. Around the corner on 74th, again between Roosevelt and Thirty-Seventh, is the long-established Indian commercial hub, anchored by the Jackson Diner. Despite its American-sounding name, it's actually a large cafeteria featuring Indian food, sitting among a host of Indian jewelry and bridal shops, plus the gigantic Patel Brothers supermarket. It has also been a political stop on the campaign trail, and visitors have included Hillary Clinton and Michael Bloomberg.[8]

Turning right on Thirty-Seventh Avenue, I come to the Jackson Heights Jewish Center at 77th Street. It was once home to a large Jewish community, which began to dwindle in the 1970s as the older generation either passed or moved to retirement communities. I discover that the center has adapted to changes in the community's composition. A Hispanic Evangelical church rents the center out on Sundays for services. As a Conservative Jewish and therefore more liberal congregation, it can more easily accommodate their presence. A Hispanic duo, Hector and Miguel, are scheduled to perform on Thursday night. The center also rents out space or allows it to be used free of charge during the week for community meetings and other events such as book review meetings, discussions about local community issues, concerts, and the like.

The Center for LGBT Seniors is also located in the Jewish Center building here. Jackson Heights has been a popular community for gay New Yorkers for many years, and the existence of an organization for LGBT seniors of varying backgrounds is itself proof of how established they are here. There's the annual gay pride parade, too, and, given the community's strong overall Hispanic presence, it is unsurprising that many Hispanic gays live here as well. The parade

Julio Rivera, who was brutally beaten to death in 1990, is memorialized at this intersection.

takes place in June and runs from 89th to 75th Streets. The highlight event is the festival, held on Thirty-Seventh Avenue and 75th Street, featuring singers, drag acts, comedians, and dance groups. This is in stark contrast to a darker period, thirty years ago, when there was far more prejudice against gays. In July 1990, Julio Rivera, a twenty-nine-year-old gay bartender in the community, was brutally beaten to death by three skinheads. The intersection at 78th Street and Thirty-Seventh, where the murder took place, has been named Julio Rivera Corner in his memory.

Not far away, at 81-04 is Jahn's Restaurant. I remember Jahn's as a hugely popular ice cream parlor that also served some regular coffee-shop food on the side as well. The first Jahn's opened on Alexander Avenue in the Bronx in 1897. Jahn's once had about thirty locations throughout the Big Apple, but I learn that this is the only one left in the city. While ice cream is only a small part of the daily fare here, you can still see the classic red, white, and green Tiffany light fixtures, with Jahn's inscribed on them, that date back to that era. Those who remember the "Suicide Frappe" and the thirty-scoop "Kitchen Sink Sundae" from the old days can still indulge in a standard marshmallow sundae.

At 82nd Street, I turn right and soon see a sign for a store, $5.00 Shoe Warehouse, at 37-39, one of many stores that line the block—Gap, Fabco, Ponce de León Bank, Foot Locker, and Children's Place. While there are shoes for $12, $20, and $25, the ones for $5 are in the large back portion of the store. I examine them, and while they appear to be cheaply made, they're certainly passable, especially considering the cost.

Most of the workers speak only Spanish, but one, a young woman in her early twenties, Maria, is fairly fluent in English.

"How are you able to sell these shoes for so little? Do they last for a week?" I ask.

"Two weeks!" she retorts, laughing.

"Right," I respond. "But seriously, do they last?"

"They could last for a year, depending on how much you wear them. They're not going to fall apart in a week or a month. They only cost a buck or so to make in China."

"Are there people who look like they could pay more for shoes, but buy the cheap ones anyway?" I'm thinking of some wealthy people I know who boast that they can buy knock-off Gucci handbags because no one imagines that they would purchase anything but the real Gucci bags. Perhaps these folks wouldn't come here, but Jackson Heights has many middle-class residents who might also appreciate the good deal. If so, Maria isn't aware of it.

"No," she says, "but there are many people who go visiting their families in the Dominican Republic or Mexico, and they buy sometimes many pairs of shoes to give to the really poor people back home." This is a market that I hadn't considered. Maria is now in school getting a GED and plans on going to college. Her dream is to be a teacher of small children.

Returning to Thirty-Seventh, I continue my travels east and eventually come to a jarring sign, "KIKE Barber Shop," at 91-19. The sight of this word surprises me, and I walk into the shop to learn more. There are several chairs, and, as is typical, every barber's name is taped to the wall in front of the chair. Seeing that the first barber's name (usually the boss) reads Kike, I say hello and ask what he charges for a haircut. After some chit-chat I discover that the place has been at this location for seventeen years. I ask him how he pronounces his name, and he says, "'Ki-keh.' That's short for Enrique in Spanish. I'm Dominican." I thank him and leave. If the shop were in a predominantly Jewish community there would probably be an outcry, regardless as to whose name it is. Clearly the store could be called "Enrique's," or something else, even "Kikeh's." But this part of the community is predominantly Hispanic, and its residents are familiar with the nickname and pronunciation. I wonder if anyone ever said anything to him about it. Overall, it's fair to ask how sensitive people must be to the sensitivities of others. As an aside, those who work in the office of the Jackson Heights Jewish Center, just thirteen blocks away, lifelong residents, say they have never seen the sign.

I head north on 89th Street to Thirty-Fifth Avenue and go left, stopping at 81st Street because a street sign has caught my eye. Underneath the Thirty-Fifth sign I see several small numbers. These include "1" beneath the "A" and beneath the "t." The "v" and "h" sport 4's. Most passersby would never notice these small numbers. But those who know understand it. The word game Scrabble was invented by Alfred Mosher Butts, who lived nearby on 79th Street. Why here? Because Butts and his friends regularly gathered at the Community Methodist Church to play the game. The game was rejected for twenty years by game manufacturers before being

Scrabble fans will appreciate this clever street sign in honor of Alfred Mosher Butts.

accepted. It proved to be wildly popular, and more than 150 million sets have been sold to date. Only Monopoly, checkers, and chess sell more. The game is very popular among older people. Butts died in 1993 at age ninety-three.

One nearby building that captures my attention is the Towers, taking up a full city block, from 80th to 81st Streets, between Thirty-Fourth Avenue and Northern Boulevard. It's a perfect example of the numerous apartment developments in Jackson Heights that have interior gardens, surrounded by apartments, many of them between 80th and 87th Streets from Thirty-Seventh to Thirty-Fourth Avenues. All around this huge brick complex are turrets atop the various sections. It's a design inspired by Renaissance and Roman architecture, with columns and a red-tiled roof. It also features ornately carved stone griffins at various outdoor, iron-gated entrances that lead, in turn, to a spacious interior garden for residents. Constructed in 1923 and designed by Andrew J. Thomas, its large and well-built apartments, many with fireplaces, high ceilings, and hardwood floors, make it one of the most desirable buildings in the area.

If there's one aspect lacking in Jackson Heights, it's parks, an irony since it was, as discussed before, the first garden city community in the country. The lone park is Travers Park, a 2-acre area on Thirty-Fourth Avenue, between 77th and 78th Streets, half of which consists of playing fields for soccer, baseball, handball, and basketball. Another third of the park is devoted to children's playgrounds. Here there's some noteworthy artwork. Entering the area on 77th Street, I see, as part of the fence, a tall, blue, metal rendition of what looks like a fanciful tulip with cutouts inside. The sign, made from the same metal, reads "Travers Park." The metalwork continues around the children's playground and includes a cutout area for anything from a photo-op for kids to a puppet show. The shutters around a window in the park attendant's office (walk to the back) have beautiful carvings with oak leaves and acorns. The same is true of the wrought-iron front door. It's divided into squares with a carved leaf inside each one. Travers is due to be renovated and may look better by the time this book appears. Regardless, there's clearly much else going on in Jackson Heights, and its richness and variety definitely make it a place worth seeing.

EAST ELMHURST

Flushing
Bay

Flushing
Bay

AVE
DITMARS BLVD
27 AVE
'SSON
'F
29 AVE
BUTLER
CURTIS
31 AVE
104 ST
103 ST
106 ST
105 ST
31 DR
108 ST
107 ST
110 ST
111 ST
112 ST
112 PL

(A) Mural of Louis Armstrong,
on wall of I.S. 227
(B) Queens Spy Shop

EAST ELMHURST IS ONE OF QUEENS'S SMALLEST COMMUNITIES in terms of population, with about thirty thousand residents. The land boundaries generally are Ditmars Boulevard on the north and east, Northern Boulevard on the south, and the Brooklyn Queens Expressway (BQE) on the west. It was originally the site of the North Beach Bay Gala Amusement Park, which began operating in 1886. People flocked to the park from all over New York City. It thrived until Prohibition. The government closed down the giant beer hall there in 1929, and the place went bankrupt. Also, at the turn of the twentieth century, residential construction, consisting of mostly frame houses, began in East Elmhurst. The homes on the higher elevations, overlooking Flushing Bay, were fancier, with private beaches. Commercial development commenced at the beginning of World War II. In the 1940s, African Americans began moving in, resulting, eventually, in a middle- and working-class, predominantly black, enclave. At the time, it was one of the few communities in the city where African

Americans could purchase homes. The 1990s saw a marked demographic change, with the area becoming much more Hispanic. Today, it's a diverse mix of minorities.[9]

Northern Boulevard, the boundary between Corona and Jackson Heights on the south, and East Elmhurst on the north, is one of the community's main arteries, extending from 102nd Place all the way down to 68th Street. The commercial establishments are unremarkable but highly functional—tire shops and auto supply places; a plethora of restaurants, pizzerias, and delis; nail salons and barber shops; gas stations, sign shops, modest dental and medical facilities, storefront churches, bakeries, taverns, and karate schools. Many of them service the Hispanic population that predominates here. Below 78th Street, auto dealerships occupy a prominent part of the streetscape. Astoria Boulevard South, which cuts through the center of East Elmhurst, has a mix of stores, which is very similar to that of Northern Boulevard, that serve the community's basic needs. Ditmars Boulevard, on the other hand, which runs along the Grand Central Parkway, is both commercial and residential and includes some large homes dating back to the early days of the twentieth century, which are best viewed from the parkway itself. The rest of the community is made up primarily of modern brick and frame homes, most of them attached or semi-attached.

My walk begins on Northern Boulevard and 112th Street, heading west. At Junction Boulevard I turn right and walk one block to Thirty-Second Avenue. On the left-hand corner is the home of Intermediate School 227, also named for the legendary jazz great Louis "Satchmo" Armstrong, who lived not far from here, at 34-56 107th Street, now fully restored, with collections of his recordings, an educational center, and much more. Gracing one of the school's walls is what can best be described as an exuberant mural of the man and his kaleidoscopic aura, fairly bursting with life.

From left to right I see four renditions of Armstrong in various poses, wearing a blue suit. In one he's playing on a trumpet, eyes

An exuberant mural of Louis Armstrong at Intermediate School 227.

bulging from his exertions, with other musicians accompanying him. In another version he's blowing the trumpet, and musical notes are emanating from it, gracefully curling through the mural, which has drawings of unidentified people, mostly children. On the bottom is the title of one of his greatest hits, "What a Wonderful World," released in 1967. The song was first offered to Tony Bennett, who passed on it, and then to Satchmo, who embraced it and made it a big hit.

How inspiring to the students and those who pass by, a great musician from the community who became a household name. The mural is interrupted at various points. For example, there's a sign inside the mural, under Armstrong's suit jacket, that says: "portion of building sprinkled," and there are two standpipes and building entrance doors because they're necessary and were there before the mural was created. Sometimes in a crowded city the artists have to improvise. Here, it in no way detracts from the overall beauty of what's depicted.

From here I head north, turning right at Astoria. At 98-11, I come to one of the most interesting establishments that I've seen in Queens, the Queens Spy Shop. I enter and look around, perusing the offerings. It's replete with all sorts of listening and visual surveillance devices. Several customers are being waited on. The business cards make for provocative reading. One asks, in large block letters: "CHEATING SPOUSE?" Immediately to the right is a photo of luminous lips, seemingly begging to be kissed.

There are books about how to get revenge on people, like *Spite, Malice, and Revenge: The Complete Guide to Getting Even*. Another, on "dirty tricks," features on the cover a photo of a bike hanging at a crazy angle on a lamppost with a sign attached that announces: "THE OWNER OF THIS BIKE IS A THIEF!" There's also a magazine about Amanda Knox, ultimately acquitted of participating in the murder of her roommate in Italy. But most of the displays are of spy equipment. Included are devices recording everything one does while on the internet. Some are tiny, like a spy pen that has a hidden video camera. I speak with an employee.

"What are those items you have in the display case for," I ask, "the Coca-Cola and Canada Dry cans and other products?"

"Come here. I'll show you. The opening's at the bottom of the can, and it only costs $10. You see this Ajax Cleanser can? It has real powder coming out of it, but on the bottom of the can there's a secret space where you can insert a listening device, or a camera, or hide cash." Josh is a college student at CUNY.

"I'll bet this is a fun job for you."

"Oh yeah. You hear a lot of weird stories. Look at this. If you need to pass a drug test you get this. It has liquid that comes out from inside your pants, and it comes with a belt that straps around your waist. It has synthetic urine, and it's already heated up."

The Queens Spy Shop is replete with all sorts of listening and visual surveillance devices.

"Have people gotten away with it?"

"Oh yes. You put it right where your penis is. But they can't see it. Of course, it's not legal to do that, but we're not telling people to do it. We just sell it." A trip to this place is definitely entertaining. There aren't many retail shops like this in the city, and Queens has only two, both under the same ownership. It's both lighthearted and dead serious.

East Elmhurst had over time a particularly high level of stability according to those residents with whom I speak, and census statistics seem to support that notion. According to the Census Bureau, East Elmhurst was for many years first in the city out of more than two thousand census tracts in terms of people who remained in one community for a long period of time, though it began changing in the 1990s as large numbers of Hispanics and some Asians began moving in. The median number of years for people, most of them black, had been a high thirty-six. Some of its best-known residents at one time or another include Willie Mays, Harry Belafonte, Malcolm X, former attorney general Eric Holder, and Dizzy Gillespie.[10] Malcolm X lived at 23-11 97th Street from 1959 until early 1965. A week before his assassination in Manhattan, gasoline bombs were thrown into his home.

East Elmhurst's stability was highly unusual, though there are other communities like Cambria Heights with the same pattern of little turnover in residents. Those with whom I spoke gave various reasons, ranging from the quietness of the community and its good schools, to longtime friendships and an easy commute to Manhattan. But in truth these characteristics apply to many communities that change more frequently. So then, what makes one community gel while another doesn't?

In my view, the answer can be found in W. I. Thomas's famous sociological dictum: "If people define situations as real, they are real in their consequences."[11] Black East Elmhurst residents saw themselves as upwardly mobile pioneers of a sort. Mostly middle- or working-class when they moved into the community, they forged close relationships and ties, emphasizing their heritage at the same time as they sought to fulfill the traditional American dream of a nice home in a safe community in a city where few white communities were open. It was an experience that shaped how they viewed themselves as a group.

Ultimately, what most determines whether a community succeeds are the intangibles. The feeling of unity that emerges has to do with a certain mix of individual personalities, community leadership, family socialization, and group dynamics that is set in motion whenever residents come together as parents at school PTA meetings, in churches, in fraternal orders, at social events, and even at a common school bus stop. The right mix of people and their degree of communal involvement cannot be artificially created, but if it's there, the community flourishes, and that's what probably happened in East Elmhurst.

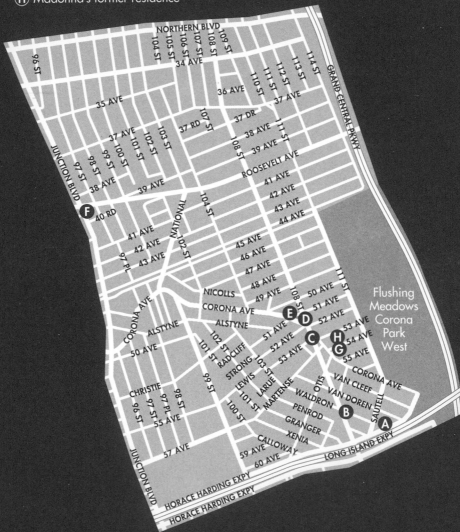

Ⓐ Paris Suites Hotel
Ⓑ Empanadas Café
Ⓒ Lemon Ice King of Corona
Ⓓ William Moore Park/"Spaghetti Park"
Ⓔ Parkside Restaurant
Ⓕ Rincon Criollo
Ⓖ Estée Lauder's former synagogue
Ⓗ Madonna's former residence

CORONA

CORONA IS A DENSELY POPULATED CENTRAL QUEENS COMMUNITY.
Its boundaries are Northern Boulevard on the north, the Grand
Central Parkway on the east, the Long Island Expressway (LIE) on
the south, and Junction Boulevard on the west. Corona's modern beginnings date back to 1872 when many lots were made available for
residential development. Its growth accelerated in 1917, when the
"el" was built above Roosevelt Avenue. It has been there ever since,
and today's subway, the 7 line, has more people from different lands
using it than any other train in the city.[12] The main commercial thoroughfares are 108th Street, Roosevelt Avenue, Northern Boulevard,
Junction Boulevard, and Corona Avenue. The dominant high-rises
besides some NYCHA projects are in the middle-class development
of Lefrak City, along the LIE. The housing stock in Corona is a mix
of many different styles, with more recently built three-to-six-story
brick apartment buildings predominating, as well as thousands of
two-story, multifamily dwellings of literally every type. What they
have in common is that they are overwhelmingly modest, and some
are very old, dating back to the nineteenth century.

The earliest ethnic groups to settle here in modern times were
Italians, Jews, and a small number of African Americans, followed
by Irish, Germans, and eastern Europeans. Today, the area is overwhelmingly Hispanic—with Puerto Ricans, Dominicans, and Mexicans predominating, and augmented by immigrants from many
other Latin American lands. The streets throb, day and night, to
the beat of the Latin music emanating from restaurants, homes,
and passing cars. The signage on the commercial streets is largely in
Spanish. The African American population, which lived at one time
between Roosevelt Avenue and Northern Boulevard, is no longer
there, and today the population is overwhelmingly Hispanic. All
that's left of the black heritage is Louis Armstrong's home, now a

museum, located at 34-56 107th Street. The legendary jazz great resided there from 1943 until 1971, when he passed away.[13] Corona also has a small number of Chinese Americans, a trend that is likely to grow.

Corona is also home to a variety of institutions catering to the city as a whole. These include the National Tennis Center, where the US Open is held; the hands-on New York Hall of Science; the Queens Theatre, in Flushing Meadows Corona Park, another city attraction; and the Queens Museum of Art. The art museum has a permanent exhibit that will interest readers of this book: "The Panorama of New York City." It's a giant architectural model of the city, containing within it virtually every building constructed until 1992. But it's always being updated, with the latest revision occurring in 2009.

I begin my journey through Corona along the western service road of the LIE, where I spy the Paris Suites Hotel at 109-17. It's on the corner of the service road and Saultell Avenue. With its large replica of the Eiffel Tower on the roof, this edifice is literally almost impossible to miss, and I've seen it hundreds of times from the highway, always wondering what sort of place it is. As I walk along, the strength of the Paris theme is reinforced by the presence of nine gold-colored, gilded metal copies of the Eiffel Tower in front of windows along the first floor.

As I enter the small lobby, someone calls out, "Hello." I turn left and, in a few steps, see a clerk behind the counter. A young man, he turns out to be a college student looking to make a couple of extra bucks. It's convenient because it's near the college. He's surrounded on both sides of the opening by an incredible fish tank, with some pretty big fish that I wouldn't want to mess with, like a giant stinging pleco catfish. And that's only the beginning of what there is to see here.

This cramped space is filled with amazing artifacts that include statues of women, one of whom is a scantily clad beauty who looks like Wonder Woman, riding a tiger, as well as several jade statues of Buddha. There's the head of a Zebra above two carved elephant tusks; brown-and-beige ornate Bombe dressers; a silver-colored eagle with every feather carved, poised atop a rock; several enormous painted urns; a coffered ceiling, and a lion's skin affixed to a portion of that same ceiling. There are also a couple of geodes with amethyst rocks inside them. There's nothing here, however, even remotely related to Paris or the Eiffel Tower, and the clerk doesn't know why the French theme was chosen. The lobby also has what looks like some Tiffany-style lamps, but I couldn't verify their authenticity. In an odd way, this is quite appropriate even if the owners don't know it because the Tiffany Factory, which closed after 1930, was located for many years on Forty-Third Avenue near 97th Place. Today, it's home to P.S. 315.

The clerk started out very suspicious of me but became a bit less uncomfortable after I presented my CUNY photo ID. I ask him if these items are for sale.

"I don't believe so, but you'd have to ask management."

"Can I speak to a manager?"

"There's no one here."

"How can that be? It's 5:00 p.m., a busy time for hotels. How do they manage the place?"

"They just check in once in a while," he says, looking and sounding evasive. I've seen only a few people come in, so maybe it's a quiet time.

"Is he or she in this country? Do they live elsewhere?"

"Well, they're not around much."

"Can I see a room?"

"No. Our policy is you rent on the phone and when you come in you see it. But they're nice rooms, and many have Jacuzzis." The clerk gives me a business card, but there's no name on it, and the phone number is only for reservations.

An online search reveals that rooms can be rented for a few hours or for one or more nights. As it happens, I see a police car parked outside and ask the two cops inside it about the place. They are unequivocal and vocal about it.

"This is the sleaziest place you'll ever see," one of them tells me. "It's a terrible place, and sometimes we have trouble here with fights and real characters hanging out here. It's not the kind of place you or any regular person would want to be in. I'm pretty sure it's owned by a Russian guy, a Bukharian. The best way to describe it is to say it's an infidelity hotel." In fact, there are thousands of Bukharian Jews, most of them law-abiding, living in the adjacent communities of Forest Hills and Rego Park. I can't say this house-of-ill-repute idea hadn't occurred to me, but I wasn't sure because the items in the lobby weren't typical of such places. Usually they're bare-bones affairs that make strong efforts to be inconspicuous. And one can't know this by looking at the website, which boasts of its closeness to the US Open, Citi Field, and museums.

Incidentally, the small streets in this vicinity—Van Cleef and Van Doren Streets, and Westside Avenue, are unusual. There are blocks without sidewalks in some places and many ramshackle houses scattered throughout, with junked cars in some of the yards, all very uncommon for an area that is so urbanized.

Next, I visit the Empanadas Café at 56-27 Van Doren Street on the corner of 108th Street, a block from the Paris Suites. Clean and efficient, with low prices, it has quite a following among both locals and young professionals who travel from all over the city to gorge on empanadas with some really interesting and tasty fillings. Two popular varieties are the chocolate-banana-white-flour combination and the corn-flour-chorizo-and-potato version, topped with green sauce. The café has been able to attract business from social events and corporate markets. There are so many ways one can differentiate empanadas, but the main draw is the freshness of everything.

At 52-02 108th, I stand in front of the famous Lemon Ice King of Corona. Communities bond through culinary experiences— bars, restaurants, delis, and so on. When people talk about Corona, Queens, they frequently reminisce about "the Lemon Ice King of

Corona," in the same reverential terms that Los Angeles residents describe Pink's hot dogs, where sixty-seven years ago people began buying frankfurters that tasted great, at least to them.

I order cantaloupe ices and ask one of the bosses, Vinnie, a gray-haired Italian American man in his sixties, with lively eyes and a friendly face, what it is that makes his place so special and how it has survived and remained immensely popular for so long.

"Everything is fresh, fresh," he tells me. "We squeeze the oranges and lemons, and the people just keep coming back. We're here seventy years. Our newest flavor is peanut butter. This used to be an Italian community. This part here around 108th and the fifties, is still called Corona Heights. But there's no Italians left. Go into "Spaghetti Park," that's what it's called, though the real name is William Moore Park, and you'll find a few old guys there, playing bocce; that's all the Italians that are left."

"But I saw younger guys playing there too."

"Yeah, they got some very good Hispanic players too now, Ecuadorians, Dominicans."

Why do some establishments last when most of the others fade away? Often, it's the ones who encapsulate the nostalgia that the old crowd has for what once was. An ices place, located near the park on the main drag, 108th, will do it because those who return want to feel what it was like when they lived here and hung out in certain places. For this reason, the "look" must remain unchanged, and so it has. In short, it's a combination—the right location, maintaining the authentic trappings, a good product, and having Italians still running it. When this happens, travel through time becomes more real. Patrons remember which friends they went here with, how the ices tasted, and the like.

Diagonally across the street is another insider place, the Parkside Restaurant, at 107-01 Corona Avenue. Many in the know consider it to be the finest Italian restaurant in the city, but because it's in Queens, not at all close to a subway, it doesn't get the play that Babbo or Il Mulino in Manhattan do. But when people talk about

It may be less well known, but the Parkside Restaurant is considered by many to be one of the finest Italian restaurants in the city.

restaurants with mob connections like Rao's, Bamonte's, and Don Peppe, the Parkside is always among them. In fact, mobsters have a reputation for favoring only very good restaurants. The Parkside is operated by Anthony "Tough Tony" Federico, a reputedly high-ranking member of the Genovese family. Queens Borough president Helene Marshall and the police have held dinners there. Ed Koch ate there, and so did Rudy Giuliani, not to mention opera great Luciano Pavarotti. Most important, the food and service are outstanding, and the atrium portion of the large dining room is really special. One cautionary observation. Even with a reservation on a Monday night, one is apt to face a wait in the bar before being seated.

From here I head north on 108th Street, a block away from the Parkside. The neighborhood has mostly inexpensive two-family houses and small apartment buildings. At Roosevelt Avenue I turn left and then go left again on Junction Boulevard. Here I see on my left, at 40-09, Rincon Criollo, a Cuban eatery considered by many to be the most authentic Cuban restaurant in the city. Entering, I discover it's a warm and friendly place, with checkered tablecloths, a stucco ceiling, and little lights strung from wall to wall. My friend, a native Cuban, visiting New York from California, raved about the food and the ambience, and it's why we're here. He's right on both counts.

Along the wall are tributes from organizations and great reviews. There's a photo of a famous Cuban singer and bandleader, Benny More. Next to it is a framed photo of the female vocalist Olga Guillot, also known as "the Queen of Bolero." I ask a woman, who owns the Rincon together with her brothers, "What's your signature Cuban dish?"

"Oh, that's easy—the shredded flank steak simmered in tomatoes, onions, and peppers. We use what we call sofrito, onions, peppers, and garlic, for this dish and for pretty much everything we cook." She walks me through the restaurant, commenting on what's on the wall.

"Some of these folks are ex-ballplayers like pitcher Camilio Pascual." I'm suddenly jolted into the past. The first baseball game I ever went to was a doubleheader with my father. I was eleven, and the Yankees were playing the old Washington Senators. It was a marvelous Sunday for me, and I remember that the pitchers for the Senators were Pascual and Pedro Ramos, also a Cuban. Looking at the photo makes me realize that hanging such photos can cause people to connect with the restaurant in unpredictable ways, in this case through my childhood.

"Our family had two restaurants in Cuba, one owned by my grandfather, and here are some pictures of them. But I haven't been back and won't until it becomes a free country." This response is typical of many in the Cuban expatriate community. It's the opposite of people from countries like Mexico, Guatemala, Colombia, or the Dominican Republic. It's the difference between an economic refugee and a political one. The former usually leaves with mixed emotions. For the latter, leaving becomes a matter of principle, with the memories of the homeland deliberately frozen in time, awaiting liberation.

I retrace my steps and head down 108th Street to Fifty-Fourth Avenue and turn left. I soon see on my right a very well-preserved synagogue at 109-18, Congregation Tifereth Israel of Corona. Estée Lauder, then in her teens, was Tifereth Israel's most prominent member. Her parents were members and owned a hardware store nearby. The synagogue also had a yeshiva, located on Fifty-Third Avenue. It ceased operations in the 1970s, and the building became a private house and the temporary residence of someone at least equal in fame to Estée Lauder. Madonna resided there from 1979 to 1981, just two years before her career took off in 1983, with the release of her self-titled album, *Madonna*.

I walk around the corner on 111th Street and turn left on Fifty-Third Avenue, and there I discover the former yeshiva, or Jewish school, where Madonna lived, which was also used as a synagogue. A red-brick building at 108-44, it's a third of the way up the block on the left. Prominently visible are two large Stars of David, one on each side of the residence. I decide to ring the bell to find out more.

It's answered by a man whose name is Ed Gilroy, a tall, lanky, very pleasant fellow in his late sixties, and seemingly in very good shape. We chat on the porch, and as I stand there, I see signs, in the form of Hebrew lettering on some plaques, including one listing the institution's board of directors, A. Stoller, P. Rosenberg, and M. Tanzman. Yet another sign identifies the year in which the school was founded, 1932. It appears to have been used both as a Jewish school, called Hebrew School of Corona, and as a synagogue. He proceeds to tell me about the building's history.

"The place may well date back to 1916, according to an inscription in my home's basement," he tells me. "Madonna came here from Michigan in 1980, hoping to make it as a dancer in New York. She had no place to stay, and she asked me and my brother if she could live here. We were between bands, and we said yes and taught her to play the drums. Then we formed a band together, called the Breakfast Club. We were actually nominated for a Grammy in 1987 for 'Best New Band.'" Madonna Louise Ciccone is probably the

The former yeshiva where Madonna once lived.

all-time top-selling female vocalist in history, having sold over three hundred million records.

"What was she like? Did she have any interest in Judaism at the time? Was this a precursor to her current strong involvement in Kabbalah?"

"No. She was a Catholic. She came here because it was where my brother and her boyfriend, Dan, lived. They met at a party. She moved out in about 1981. In the old days, there was a synagogue on just about every block from here to Roosevelt Avenue." Ed invites me into his home, and I meet his wife, an Indian woman from Gujarat. Both work as nurses. The structure seems to be in its original shape, a one-story interior, but with a very high ceiling. Ed tells me the ceiling was even higher when they bought the house. He shows me photos of Madonna and his own family and comments that after Madonna was playing the drums for a while, she wanted to get out front more as a performer, playing the guitar and singing, which is exactly what she did. He points out a chandelier in the living room that was in the original synagogue as well as a carved wooden bench. But the main item of note is in their bedroom. I follow him inside, and I see, against the wall, a formerly holy ark in which Torahs are normally placed after being read in the synagogue. It's a medium-brown color with intricate carving and Hebrew inscriptions on top memorializing someone who probably donated the money to build it. It feels very strange to be looking at it because I've never seen a holy ark in someone's bedroom.

"Why did you keep it?"

"I don't know for sure, but I guess I just felt that for the sake of history and posterity, it should just stay there. That's why I love the house. My brother, who's an artist, tells me it's probably a great example of how the wood was stained in those days." In truth, such religious objects are highly prized by members of a faith because they're considered holy in and of themselves. There's also a small stained-glass window, and Ed wonders if it could be a genuine Tiffany because Tiffany had its factory in Corona. Ed takes me down a small, winding metal staircase to his basement, where he shows me the musical instruments used by his old band. He points out the drums and guitars, noting, with some pride, that this was a Cariabella acoustic guitar she used, a really good one.

"And you've kept them all these years."

"Well, they're really good drums. They're made of wood. Today, they're all made out of fiberglass."

All in all, it's a surreal experience to see Madonna's instruments, her former boyfriend's brother, an old yeshiva and synagogue, and a possible Tiffany window, all in one location in a Queens community.

RIDGEWOOD

MASPETH

MIDDLE VILLAGE

GLENDALE

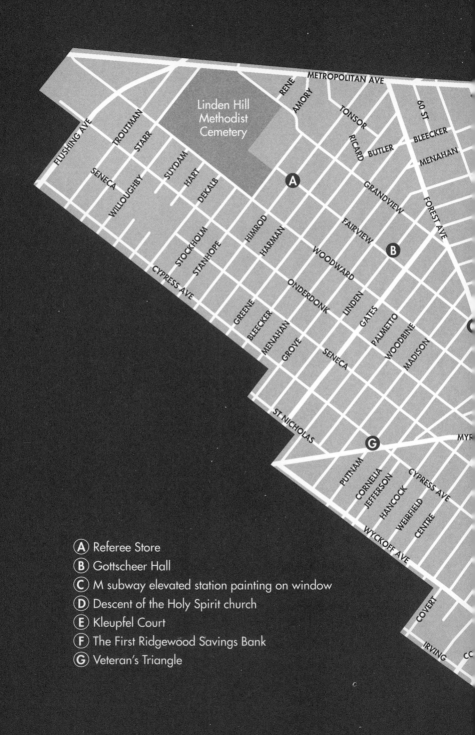

METROPOLITAN AVE

RENE
AMORY

Linden Hill
Methodist
Cemetery

TONSOR

60 ST

BLEECKER

RICARD
BUTLER

MENAHAN

FLUSHING AVE

TROUTMAN

STARR

SUYDAM

HART

DEKALB

GRANDVIEW

FOREST AVE

(A)

FAIRVIEW

SENECA

WILLOUGHBY

STOCKHOLM

STANHOPE

HIMROD

HARMAN

WOODWARD

(B)

CYPRESS AVE

GREENE

BLEECKER

MENAHAN

GROVE

ONDERDONK

SENECA

LINDEN

GATES

PALMETTO

WOODBINE

MADISON

ST. NICHOLAS

(G)

MYR

PUTNAM

CORNELIA

JEFFERSON

HANCOCK

CYPRESS AVE

WEIRFIELD

CENTRE

WYCKOFF AVE

COVERT

IRVING

(A) Referee Store
(B) Gottscheer Hall
(C) M subway elevated station painting on window
(D) Descent of the Holy Spirit church
(E) Kleupfel Court
(F) The First Ridgewood Savings Bank
(G) Veteran's Triangle

RIDGEWOOD

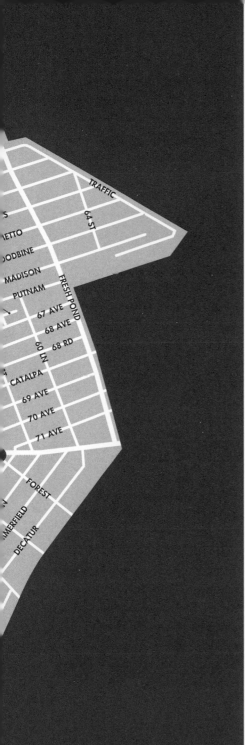

RIDGEWOOD LIES ON THE NORTHERN BORDER of Brooklyn's Bushwick community. It's bounded by Metropolitan Avenue on the north; Traffic Avenue, Fremont Street, Fresh Pond Road, Decatur Street, and Cody Avenue on the east; Wyckoff and Cypress Avenues on the south; and Flushing Avenue on the west. Originally the land of the Mespachtes Indians, it was settled by the Dutch in the seventeenth and eighteenth centuries. The English, who began farming the land in the eighteenth century, called it Ridgewood because of the hilly lay of the land. After trolley and elevated lines were constructed here, German immigrants, many of them middle class, arrived at the turn of the century and built up the community, constructing many brick homes. Breweries, knitting mills, and small businesses predominated. Smaller numbers of eastern Europeans, Italians, and Jews also came here around this time.

Beginning in the 1980s, there was a larger influx of eastern Europeans, especially Romanians and Poles, most of whom moved into the section north of Myrtle Avenue. In the 1990s, the area south of Myrtle experienced a Hispanic influx, mostly Mexicans and

Dominicans, along with small numbers of Asians. Gentrifiers, too, began moving in from neighboring Brooklyn, a pattern that has increased substantially since about 2008. This area, along the Bushwick-Ridgewood border, has been dubbed Bushwood by many of the artists and gentrifiers. Today, Ridgewood is home to all these groups except for the Germans, who have mostly aged out or simply moved away.

The major commercial thoroughfares are Myrtle Avenue, the hub of the community; Metropolitan Avenue; Fresh Pond Road; and Forest and Wyckoff Avenues. Transportation to Manhattan is available via the L and M subway lines. One nice park in the area with good sports facilities is Joseph Mafera Park, located along 65th Place. Another is Grover Cleveland Park, located near Stanhope Street and Grandview Avenue. Overall, the community is quite safe.

Ridgewood is widely known as the most landmarked community in the city, if not the nation. While that section, widely known, is not a subject for a book about the unknown aspects of New York, any walker will want to explore this part of the neighborhood. The landmarking happened, in large part, because of the residents' determination to protect all buildings worthy of historic or landmark designations. In 1975, they created the Greater Ridgewood Restoration Corporation to preserve what had been built here. Information on the four sections of Ridgewood—Central, North, South, and Stockholm Street—that have been landmarked as of 2017 can be found by consulting the NYC Landmarks Preservation Council website. In all, there are currently at least thirteen hundred landmarked buildings or sites built mostly by Germans between 1906 and 1914. Generally, the majority of them will be found in the area north of Myrtle Avenue and bounded by Seneca, Forest, and Fairview Avenues and Stockholm Street. Stockholm, between Woodward and Onderdonk Avenues, with its brick-paved street (which replaced the old deteriorating one) and its Doric-columned porches, is certainly worth a look, as is the landmarked Onderdonk Dutch farmhouse building, now a museum, nearby at 18-20 Flushing Avenue.

The only store in the city devoted almost entirely to the needs of game referees, officials, and umpires.

There are many older buildings not landmarked, especially south of Myrtle and east of Forest, that are worth seeing. Identifying the old buildings of Ridgewood is easy, for they are quite distinctive. Just look for old bay and straight row buildings with beige, yellow, and orange bricks from the brick kilns in Kreischerville, Staten Island, many of them ornamental, plus stonework, terra-cotta friezes, and handsome keystones. The styles are both Renaissance and Romanesque revival, many with rich, polished, often-scalloped wooden doors and gleaming golden doorknobs, highlighting the fact that their owners take great pride in them.

My walk begins on Fairview Avenue, corner of Himrod Street, where I discover what must be the only store in the city devoted almost entirely to the needs of game referees, officials, and umpires. Here you can purchase shorts, hats, whistles, electronic flags, you name it. It's called Referee Store, and the blue sign features a large whistle in the center. I haven't been able to find another place in the city with this emphasis. It reminds me that only in a large city can such specialty enterprises succeed. At the same time, retail businesses are floundering because of the internet, and the referee store does, in fact, have a mail order business. Unlike a restaurant on a busy street, which Fairview isn't, one isn't going to attract too many referees who just happen to be walking by.

At 657 Fairview, just past Linden Street, I stop in and visit Gottscheer Hall, an old and venerable tavern established in 1924. It's Super Bowl night, and the place is rocking, with certain tables reserved for regulars. Everyone's friendly, and I take the opportunity to look at their catering hall, a main source of income for them. Here you can get Radeberger Pilsner, Weihenstephaner Dunkel, Franziskaner Weissbier, Leinenkugel, and of course, all the popular varieties—Budweiser, Coors, Corona. In the old days, when Ridgewood was a very German place, domestic entries might have had a tough time, but times have changed, and Gottscheer must cater to the current population's tastes.

The same is true of the entertainment offered. There are German-themed events like a goulash and spaetzl dinner with music by Emil Schanta. Another event, with dancing, presents music by Heimat Klange Orchestra, with a meal consisting of roast pork and sauerkraut. No doubt these events will also attract other Europeans such as Poles. Indeed, they've had polka nights too. On the other hand, they also advertise doo-wop concerts, one of which I attended several years ago. This time around they're featuring the Tercels, inviting guests to "rock and roll and dance all night." The price? Just $30 a person, including a buffet dinner.

Arriving at the intersection of Fairview and Forest Avenue, I turn right onto Forest and soon come to the elevated M train station. This street is a center of eastern European commerce. There are several Polish-owned food shops, but their products often appeal to other Europeans. There's also a restaurant that announces its "Grand Opening," with the unusual name of "Garlic to the Chicken." The food doesn't seem geared to any ethnic group, and the store informs passersby that all its dishes have garlic. So, if you like garlic, this place is for you.

Standing below the M station I see in the window at the top of the subway stairs some laundry hanging from a line. This seems a bit strange, and I wonder if someone might be renting out a room in the station to do their laundry in. Climbing the stairs and entering the waiting area, I discover, to my surprise, that it's all an optical illusion. As part of the MTA's (Metropolitan Transit Authority's) Transit Arts program, an artist has painted, in color on the inside of the window, different articles of clothing such as socks, a nightgown, a shirt, pants, and so on, all hanging on a clothesline and fastened with yellow clothespins.

Nearby, I find myself in front of a Romanian Orthodox church founded in 1985, called Descent of the Holy Spirit. It can be found at 66-79 Forest Avenue by Putnam Avenue. An old Romanesque-looking building, it has a wraparound porch that offers Orthodox Christian features. There are engraved metal portraits of Mary and Jesus, and only the faces and hands are colored in. I also see arched windows, with what looks like the faces of female saints that I can't discern carved into the keystones. In terms of the engraved metal portraits on the wall and the two-tone colors, its appearance is quite unusual. As luck would have it, an SUV pulls into the driveway. Reverend Father Ionut Preda steps out from it and introduces himself to me, and we start a conversation. He's a youngish, tall, bearded man dressed in black that matches his jet-black hair.

"You started this church in 1985," I say. "Normally a church grows and expands. Is there a reason why it stayed small, so to speak?"

"We're not a very big parish. If we went to a bigger building it would be hard to maintain. Here we have about 150 members, and everyone's happy. We're close with each other." He has a point. Not everyone wants to be big. Some prefer a close-knit, smaller community.

"Father, are the faces on the keystones faces of saints?"

"Well, not saints, I think, because we bought what was a private house. Maybe they could be the faces of angels. On the other side of the coin, as they say, there are faces on the side of the church, on Putnam Avenue, that look like the devil. Come. I'll show you." We walk around to the side, and Father Preda's right. They do look sort of evil, with faces that glare at you fiercely.

"Some people wanted to destroy them, but I told them no. We have to be aware that there's also evil in this world and later on."

"That sounds like a good sermon." He laughs and thanks me for the compliment. I thank Father Preda for his time; he wishes me good luck on my book and says, "May God bless you."

I walk east on Putnam to 60th Place, where I hang a right. In about two minutes I come to a dead-end street on my left, called Kleupfel Court. It's situated almost under the elevated subway tracks of the M train. I enter the block and walk along, under the tracks, past rows of parked cars, for which there is an entrance. In New York City, streets, busy ones most often, run underneath train tracks. This one is used by the Metropolitan Transit Authority (MTA) workers to park their cars. One such worker tells me, "The street actually belongs to the MTA. It used to be an active trolley track. Our bus depot is two blocks away, and the locals don't like it when we take up street space by parking on streets." But the residents have no choice but to cooperate. It's an interesting example of how competing interests must adapt if they are to get along in the same space. People walking by have no idea of this.

Continuing my explorations, I go one short block to Sixty-Seventh Avenue and turn left. This takes me to Fresh Pond Road, so named because it was once the site of a fresh pond, where I again turn right toward Myrtle Avenue. It's a commercial street with the usual assortment of food places, especially Polish delis, and nail salons, barber shops, grocery stores, sneaker shops, and the like. One that stands out is a storefront at 70-01 Fresh Pond Road with a sign, "German-American School." But I also take note of the "For Rent" sign below it. There are few indications here that this was once a thriving community. The school was founded more than a century ago, and the communities of Glendale and Ridgewood were once predominantly German. Today Germans make up less than 10 percent of the total population. When only seven students enrolled for fall 2017 classes, the school called it quits at this branch and offered the students classes at two Long Island locations or one on Manhattan's Upper East Side, which once had a large presence of Germans in Yorkville. The fate of this school is more indicative of what happened to the German community than is the active status of Gottscheer's, which is able to cash in on nostalgia and good eats. Teaching German when no one's here to commit to it is so much harder.

At Myrtle Avenue I turn west and begin my jaunt on what is Ridgewood's most significant commercial thoroughfare. Myrtle also has some houses and three-story apartment buildings made from off-white brick, mixed in with yellow, orange, and brown bricks, some with a concrete diamond in the middle. Sometimes you'll see two-story structures that have castle-type towers and turrets in a Gothic design, usually white-painted precast concrete. The stores are a mix of video shops, hardware stores, nail salons, self-defense schools, delis, barber shops, bakeries, and tattoo shops, the last of which are much more popular today than they were twenty years ago. I see a sign on a bench in front of a 99¢ store that reads: "Please do not seat on the bench." I've learned that when it comes to signage in New York, correct spelling is not a priority.

At the intersection of Myrtle, Forest Avenue, and George Street, I stand in front of Ridgewood Savings Bank of Brooklyn. Looking at the building here feels a bit like visiting the flagship Gucci store in Rome—you're at the source. While the bank has numerous branches elsewhere, it began operations in Ridgewood in 1921. It's a grand-looking limestone building with dark-gray granite surrounding its base and numerous balustrades. The gold-colored metal main entrance features all sorts of intricate carvings of wildlife, including owls, pelicans, storks, rabbits, squirrels, lions, fish, and flowers, even beehives, as well as mythological creatures.

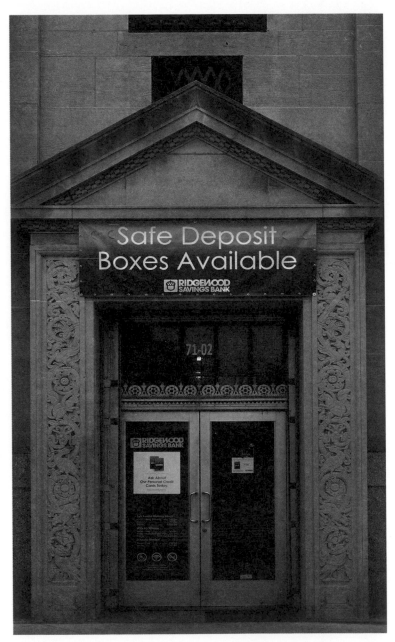

The main entrance of the Ridgewood Savings Bank features intricate carvings of wildlife.

Farther down, where Myrtle intersects with Cypress, I enter a small grassy area called Veterans' Triangle, between Cypress and Myrtle. It was created in 1922 with support from local community organizations and memorializes the armed forces who fought in World War I. Here there's a bronze bas-relief of the sea goddess Neptune standing next to a sailor, commemorating the navy's contribution to defending the United States. On top there's a sphere-like monument where there are names interspersed between several bas-reliefs. Another relief shows an airman wearing goggles and holding binoculars, standing next to a woman and commemorating the air force's contribution to the war effort. A third relief features what seems to be a woman clasping a torch with an army soldier holding a rifle.

One group of employees that has become ubiquitous in New York, certainly during the tax season, has been those who are dressed as Statues of Liberty with Lady Liberty's crown framed around their heads. They work for Liberty Tax, a company with over two hundred offices statewide that helps people file their taxes. As I stroll past one of their locations, I decide to speak with one of these costumed people, a tall, older black man named Walt. He's standing on a sidewalk on a cold and wet Sunday afternoon in February handing out flyers.

"Hey, tell me," I say, "this looks like a hard job. I mean it's cold out here, and you have to stand all the time. And you don't mind wearing that hat, with people saying or thinking, maybe, that it looks kind of silly?"

"No, not at all, bro. After all, I'm getting paid for it. It's better than nothing."

"Is there anything else that's good about the job?"

"Yeah, I talk to you. I talk to other people."

"Is it taxing on you in any way?" He looks at me as if to say, "What kind of question is that?" before responding.

"Taxing? We do taxes. This is tax season."

"Yes, of course. You're right about that. What other kind of work have you done?"

"Different jobs. I worked as a cashier at Yankee Stadium. Not the new one; the old one, the real one."

"If you work as a cashier do you get into the games for free? Do you at least get a discount?"

"No, you have to pay just like a regular customer. The only thing we get discounts on is the food from the concession stands."

"Is that the most interesting job you ever had?"

"Yeah, because I would meet people with all sorts of different jobs—Wall Street, lawyers, pretty women, and whatnot. And I would meet people from different states too."

"Where did you grow up?"

"The Bronx—Tremont, Burnside, the Concourse."

"So you come from far away, traveling all the way from the Bronx to Queens?"

"Oh yeah. I like to move around, go everywhere. I like to travel to all parts of the city, the city I grew up in and love."

"How do you get a job like this?"

"The internet. My daughter found it for me. She's a case manager for child services."

"Now what happens when tax season is over?"

"She's going to find me something else."

"Where did you go to school?"

"Taft High School."

"How many hours a day is this job?"

"Four hours from 11:00 to 3:00, and I get ten bucks an hour."

"Is that really worth it? I mean you're getting forty bucks and that's before taxes, plus two hours of travel time."

"Well, what am I going to do? If I don't do this, then I'll be sitting all day watching TV, which gets boring, and it's a total waste of time. It keeps me out of trouble," he adds, laughing. I thank Walt for his time and insights and move on.

What can be learned here? First, I'm struck by how much Walt actually enjoys his job. I know lots of people with more interesting jobs who complain quite a bit about them. Walt focused on whatever was positive about it—you get paid, you meet interesting people, and you get out of the house. Is this a rationalization? Probably not, since he stated that the alternative, watching TV all day, was worse. It's a choice he gladly makes, but it's presumably not because the forty pretax dollars he earns in a day is so attractive.

Notice, too, how Walt shrugged at my implication that it might be embarrassing to have to wear what some might see as a ludicrous Statue of Liberty outfit. It's probably more a projection of how others, myself included, would feel if we had to wear it. To him it's no big deal. If it were, he wouldn't do it. There are, after all, other jobs out there for the asking. To him, it's just a job.

When Walt talks about his job as a cashier at Yankee Stadium, we see that he has a hierarchy of job preferences. And money isn't mentioned once as an incentive. What he most enjoyed was meeting people at the stadium, just as he does at his current gig. He also took pride in having worked at the original Yankee Stadium, calling it "the real one." He is a sociable fellow who loves interacting with others. It adds meaning to his life. Moreover, he appreciates New York, calling it "the city I grew up in and love."

This man is only one of hundreds of thousands of people engaged in unglamorous yet productive work. They include delivery people, ushers at events, deli-counter clerks, school crossing guards, parking lot attendants, and chair repairers. Without them the city as we know it would cease to exist. This exchange makes clear that they can and do find meaning in what they do and that they value the idea of making an honest dollar. And, at least in this case, they consider themselves New Yorkers as much as anyone else.

Myrtle eventually crosses Wyckoff, and I make a sharp left onto it. This is one of the streets bordering Bushwick, Brooklyn, and it's one of the places where gentrification in Ridgewood began around 2007. It also happened to be home then to many Mexicans and a small outpost of Nepalese. Many of the homes were rather plain and inexpensive, and there were a number of small apartment buildings. Today, twelve years later, some of the older residents remain. But their homes have been joined by apartment buildings of the sleek, boxy, glass-and-metal variety that scream out: "The gentrifiers have arrived." As you walk by you can see the open spaces inside through the windows, the throw pillows, modern track lighting, large TV screens that typify their digs. And on the streets, you'll find internet cafés, wine bars, and trendy breakfast nooks. One can expect that the area between Hancock Street and Cody Avenue, between Wyckoff and Myrtle, will eventually gentrify as well.

Also joining the mix are Poles, Romanians, and other eastern Europeans. The structures attracting many of them are the Kreischer-brick row and bay houses made of orange and yellow brick. New Polish immigrants, priced out of Polish but increasingly gentrified Greenpoint, are buying and renting in Ridgewood, pushing out the Hispanics, and improving the buildings greatly, especially on the northern side of Myrtle Avenue. It seems that besides the area being affordable and near to Polish-dominated Greenpoint, Poles with whom I've chatted have been moving in because there's also a water pollution issue with respect to Newtown Creek in Greenpoint that has made people nervous.

At 1618 Cornelia I meet and speak with Matt Freedman, an artist who hails from Chicago. A thin, spare individual, he greets me in his basement apartment, a mixed-breed, lanky, Shepherd-type brownish dog at his side. The block is a very nice one, with leafy trees providing ample shade for the yellow-orange three-story houses that predominate in Ridgewood, dating back a century or more.

Matt had followed the "river of gentrification along the L line" and bought the old Agudath Israel Congregation between Wyckoff and Cypress Avenues, a half block from Bushwick, in 2003. Agudath Israel had bought the place in 1924 from the German Apostolic Church, which had it for two years prior. The synagogue's heyday was the 1950s and 1960s, when it had five hundred congregants and some one hundred kids in the Talmud Torah. Matt has turned it into an art studio. The locals here think it's really neat to have an old synagogue on the block. And it's nice for the studio to be in a place with these beautiful old stained-glass windows. He explains, "My wife and I use the main sanctuary as our studio. We could have razed the building, but we've chosen not to. We feel it's respectful to those who once prayed here. Jews didn't have it easy here in the 1920s when it was a mostly German area." Matt represents the first stage of gentrification, one that is often a harbinger of a larger influx of more conventional gentrifiers who are looking for convenience, reasonable prices, and a safe community with amenities. And that is what parts of Ridgewood are rapidly becoming.

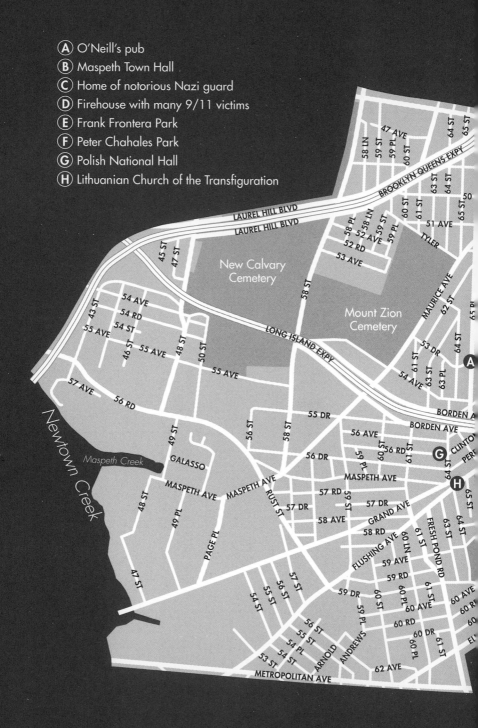

A O'Neill's pub
B Maspeth Town Hall
C Home of notorious Nazi guard
D Firehouse with many 9/11 victims
E Frank Frontera Park
F Peter Chahales Park
G Polish National Hall
H Lithuanian Church of the Transfiguration

MASPETH

MASPETH IS A SMALL, QUIET, WORKING-TO MIDDLE-CLASS COMMUNITY IN WEST-CENTRAL QUEENS. Its general boundaries are Queens Boulevard, the Brooklyn Queens Expressway, and the Long Island Expressway on the north; 74th Street on the east; Eliot and Metropolitan Avenues on the south; and the Kings County, or Brooklyn, line and Laurel Hill Boulevard on the west. Industrial development came to Maspeth in the mid-nineteenth century, and it included the first modern oil refinery. The industries, ranging from lumberyards and rope factories to linoleum and fertilizer manufacturers, were not regulated, resulting in pollution that ultimately poisoned Newtown Creek. This has remained a problem to this very day, though some progress in cleaning it up has been made in recent years.

Geographically, Maspeth is divided into two sections. The eastern portion above Rust Street and 58th Street is residential and quite charming. The other side of these streets to the west is either industrial or home to various cemeteries. The main commercial thoroughfare is Grand Avenue, plus small sections of Metropolitan and

Maurice Avenues, and Queens Boulevard. The housing stock is primarily made up of private homes that are detached, semi-attached, and attached. Despite its proximity to Manhattan, the lack of subways or express buses in the community give it an isolated appearance and feel.

Ethnically, the community is heavily white with the predominant groups consisting of Irish, Italians, Poles, Germans, and some smaller groups from other eastern European nations. The Hispanic, mostly Puerto Rican, population, is growing, as is the Asian community.

Walking up 53rd Drive from Maurice Avenue, I pass by O'Neill's, at 65th Place, an old pub, established in 1933. It opened its doors the day Prohibition ended, December 5, just in time for the Christmas season. Interestingly, there's a sign on the permanent green canopy indicating its availability for business and union meetings. I ask an elderly man seated outside O'Neill's why unions are mentioned. It's an emphasis I've not seen before. His response: "I know. I put it up, and I still work here. The unions have meetings, and I let them use the rooms. I don't charge." This isn't a gimmick. It's a reflection of the working-class population that lives here—white ethnics who belong to and believe strongly in unions. Right now, at noon, they're sitting at the bar watching golf and horse racing.

Next, I speak with Jim, a retired construction worker, and ask him about O'Neill's and the union emphasis.

"Well, this is the makeup of the community," he tells me. "The people are working class and they respect the unions and belong to them, especially the uniformed ones, like the firemen, cops, and sanitation workers." I notice a hand-lettered cardboard sign on the front door of his home about what in the fall of 2017 was a hot-button issue, NFL players taking a knee when the national anthem was played in stadiums around the country.

"I see you've got a sign on your door about respecting the flag and standing for the national anthem."

"Yeah, well, it's crazy. If you have issues, it's not a problem, but you got to express them in the right way and in the right place. Certain things are sacred. When I was a kid, if I was sitting on someone's steps outside, I listened. I got off the steps. It was about respect, and if you didn't, then when you got home you got a little beating. As my father used to say: 'If you weren't there you wouldn't have gotten into trouble.' I had seven brothers, and six of them served in the armed forces, and so did my father." Jim is talking here about respect for the country and the flag. Yet he also feels it's related to respect for individual authority figures, in this case, adults who tell him to get off the steps.

"What do you think is responsible for the change in attitudes about our country?" I ask him.

"You know what it is? It's the phone. Everybody knows what you're doing. Now they trace you with the phone. There's no more privacy anymore. And when respect goes out the window, everything gets lost. Like if these football players want to do something about prejudice, they should go into the community and help the poor people."

Based on my conversations with others about such matters, Jim's views are fairly typical of white, working-class New Yorkers. He's critical of how children are brought up today, arguing that his life as a child was also difficult. His views about loyalty to the flag are grounded very firmly in his background, one where so many in his family were soldiers. He also feels that the players could do a lot of good if they approached and worked with youths in the community. He seems a bit bewildered by how people's values have changed from the way things were when he was young. He tends to simplify things at times, telling me that his parents worked, and he saw little of them, and that he, nevertheless, turned out "all right." More than vilifying or being defensive, he wants to see problems addressed but disagrees mostly with how it's being done. His overall views are in the minority in New York City, yet they are shared by segments of the population here.

Continuing on 53rd Drive I make a left on 72nd Street and almost immediately come to Maspeth town hall. Built in 1897 by a Dutch family, the Brinkerhoffs, it housed, until 1932, a schoolhouse. Subsequently, it became a girls' club, then a local office of the Works Projects Administration, and after that the home of the 112th police precinct. Throughout the years it retained its basic structure, but by the early 1970s it had become somewhat run-down. A local coalition of residents united to restore it, and today, when I pass by, except for some peeling paint, it's a community center that looks pretty good for a place that's over 120 years old.

Two blocks farther, still on 72nd Street, I stop in front of a house, 52-11, that has a notorious past. It's the former residence of Hermine Braunsteiner Ryan, once a Nazi guard at the Ravensbruck and Maidanek concentration camps. Braunsteiner was the first Nazi war criminal to be extradited from the United States to Germany, where she was tried, something that makes her case especially noteworthy. It was followed by other cases of former Nazis living in communities elsewhere in New York, like Mineola, Long Island, and in other parts of the country. When the *New York Times* reporter Joseph Lelyveld showed up at her home in 1964 to confront her about her crimes, she said: "This is the end of everything for me."

Braunsteiner was accused of seizing children by their hair and throwing them on trucks that then took them to the gas chambers and of trampling old women to death with her jackboots. Needless to say, neighbors were horrified by these stories. She was sentenced to two life terms by the German courts and died in Germany in 1999, three years after her early release from prison for health reasons.[14] Today, fifty-five years later, many of the residents near where she lived are Asian or Hispanic and totally unfamiliar with the story. I met only one person who knew about it but only in a very general way. An elderly woman, she said to me, "I remember it was all very hush, hush. The Germans brought her back to Germany and prosecuted her, and boom, she went to jail. But I don't recall the details except that what she did was terrible." Throughout my travels I've emphasized the

Maspeth Town Hall was, until 1932, a schoolhouse.

duality of this city—its hundreds of communities and it's big-city feel. This story highlights the latter. One lives in a place like Maspeth, with its networks of friends, neighbors, schools, and churches. And you think you know your neighbors. Then, suddenly, you discover that you don't, that a quiet family next door has a very large skeleton in their closet, one that emerges into public view only because of events far away from Maspeth. This can shatter the illusion of community and trust that you've held onto through the years.

Rounding the corner, I head back to Grand Avenue via 71st Street, which is one block over and parallel to 72nd Street. I make a right onto Grand, and at 69th Street, I turn right and take a look inside the firehouse. It's a significant historical location as nineteen firefighters, in all, lost their lives on 9/11, more fatalities than any other firehouse experienced. I speak with a firefighter, Tom, who shows me around, pointing out the plaques, and who mentions, almost as an aside, that there were actually twenty victims, something that differs from all the accounts I know of.

"What do you mean, twenty? I thought there were nineteen."

"Well, it's because one of them died a year later, but it's related to it as far as we know. He committed suicide." I thank Tom for his help and step outside into the street. I can't help but notice that it's a crystal-clear day with a cloudless sky, reminding me that the weather was exactly like that on 9/11. Up the block there's a large sign on the wall of the Maspeth Bank, reading: "Maspeth is America." The circumstances of the man's suicide highlight the fact that we will never be sure of exactly how many people died as a result of 9/11. And this extends as well to those who became ill because of 9/11, died or will, perhaps, die, but won't necessarily, in either case, be recorded as 9/11 deaths.

Across the street, in the shadow of the Long Island Expressway, which runs beneath the intersection, is Frank Frontera Park, located at 69th and Fifty-Eighth Avenue. Frontera was an Italian immigrant, a barber in Maspeth and a volunteer for the fire department, serving in that capacity until the age of ninety-one. It has a modern playground with great equipment for kids. For me, having seen so

The firehouse for FDNY Squad 288.

many of these playgrounds, what makes it different are sculptures of three large, almost squat, gray horses. They're not at all the delicate, finely chiseled ones that one sees on a carousel. Their presence here is not surprising, however, for across the street is Brown Place. A pocket park here, Peter Chahales Park, has some iron horse heads memorializing the existence of a horse cart barn here in the old pre-automobile days, and the barn was situated on Brown Place. These carriages, pulled by thousands of horses throughout New York City, generally carried about thirty people and were once a critical form of transportation in the city. In the nineteenth century these horses deposited about 2.5 million pounds of manure and sixty thousand gallons of urine every day.

Three large horse sculptures at Frank Frontera Park.

This community has a strong Polish presence, with a long history of Polish immigrants settling here. At 61-60 56th Road, near 64th Street, there's an old red-and-yellow-brick building from an earlier era with the name still on it—Polish National Hall—founded in 1934 as a community center focused on preserving the Polish heritage of the immigrants. The earliest arrivals came in the 1890s, living in boardinghouses as single men and eventually bringing over their wives. The civic organizations they founded were critical in their adapting to America, and these organizations continue to play this role for those coming here now.

The same is true for other eastern European groups who have made Maspeth their home. For example, the Lithuanians have a large and very impressive-looking church, the Church of the Transfiguration, which I happened to visit on the day the father blessed the animals, most of them dogs, in a special ceremony. Located one block from Polish Hall, at 64-14 Perry Avenue, it was first established in 1908 and has been at its present location since 1962, where it serves the Lithuanian community in Queens and Long Island. It's a fitting end to a stable community that respects its history and the traditions of the various ethnic and religious groups that constitute it.

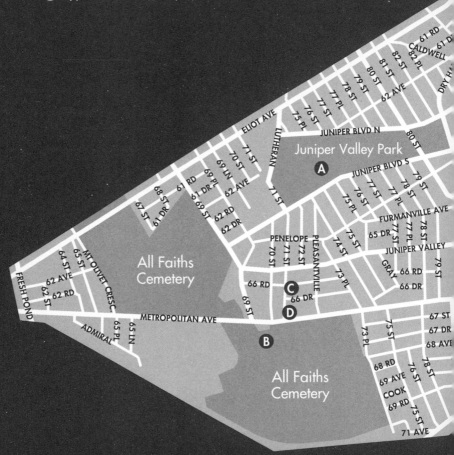

A Juniper Valley Park
B *General Slocum* Memorial
C Architecturally interesting home
D Cypress Hills Taxidermy Studio

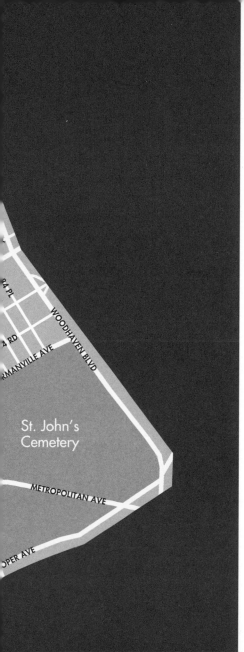

MIDDLE VILLAGE

THIS IS AN OLD, ORIGINALLY ENGLISH COMMUNITY whose modern beginnings started in mid-nineteenth century when it was a farming community and home to various large cemeteries. The latter attracted flower and monument shops, as well as lodging and taverns for those who came to pay their respects to those buried nearby. Its boundaries are Eliot Avenue on the north, Woodhaven Boulevard on the east, Cooper and Metropolitan Avenues on the south, and Fresh Pond Road on the west.

In the early twentieth century, it was largely a German community, but over time it became a popular community for the Irish, Jews, Italians, and people from eastern European lands like Poland and Yugoslavia, as well as Hispanics from various countries. Overwhelmingly residential and largely middle-class, it has one commercial thoroughfare, Metropolitan Avenue. There's only one subway line here, the M train on Metropolitan. Its crown jewel is Juniper Valley Park, one of the most heavily utilized community parks in the city. Not well known at all, Middle Village is likely to remain a tranquil place to live in for the foreseeable future.

My jaunt through Middle Village begins with a stroll into Juniper Valley Park, crossing 80th Street in the process. Here I see middle-aged and younger men off to my right playing paddleball. They smack the ball with shots that are fast, low, and accurate, yelling with glee as their opponents miss, or muttering to themselves as their shots are met with even better returns. On the left and ahead of me are basketball courts where teenagers seem to predominate. And farther down, again on the right, are the bocce courts. As I come near them, I see and hear elderly Italian men, their leathery faces creased from age and sun, talking and gesturing animatedly as they joke, scold, and tease each other in a mixture of Italian and English. They've taken a temporary rest from bocce and are kibitzing as a couple of players are absorbed in a game of pinochle at a concrete table. I approach a younger man who is with an older person and ask him what's going on.

"I'm here with my father," he says, "and I'm introducing him to these old guys. His wife, my mother, passed a few months ago, and it's rough on him. He's at home, lonely, with nothing to do. He's on the shy side, so since I know some of these guys from Middle Village, I thought I'd get him into the game." Charlie tells me that he feels this as an obligation, which he accepts, toward his father, who took care of and loved him when he was a kid. Charlie has also arranged for him to go on trips to his village in Sicily.

As I go deeper into this stunning park, I stop dead in my tracks. Ahead of me there's an incredible vista, seemingly stretching off into the distance, of rolling green grass. As I come closer, I can make out a number of playing fields, mostly for soccer and baseball. On the left, there's a bench occupied by a young couple. I look at them and say, "I had no idea this park was so beautiful."

"You from around here?" a young man asks me.

"No," I say.

"Well, shhh. Don't say nothing. This is one of the best secrets in New York, and we don't want to be discovered." What makes this park so special are the many activities it offers for people of every

The stunning Juniper Valley Park.

age, how busy and active it is, and the fact that it's built to the scale of the community's size and located right in the middle of this vast residential area. Central and Prospect Parks are much larger, but they are not the province of one community. Rather, each of them is surrounded by several communities. This results in a loss of intimacy, one where those using it are often strangers to one another.

Exiting the park on South Juniper Boulevard, I turn left onto Pleasantville Street and, in five blocks, arrive at Metropolitan Avenue, where I go right. In half a mile I come to the main entrance of All Faiths Lutheran Cemetery. At the visitors' desk just inside, I ask the receptionist if she can direct me to the *General Slocum* Memorial. In 1904, on a Wednesday morning in June, a steamship by that name set out on an all-day excursion. Aboard were some 1,358 women and children, German Americans who lived in what was called Kleindeutschland, a German community on the Lower East Side. The boat, as discussed in the Astoria section, caught fire, and 1,021 people died. Wanting to ease the pain of the community's losses, its members picked up and left the Lower East Side, rebuilding in the Yorkville neighborhood of the Upper East Side.

Armed with directions, I cross Metropolitan Avenue to the southern side, where the major portion of the cemetery is located. I walk down a hill on a cobbled street, with Christ the King High School off to my right. Veering sharply left, I make my way along the perimeter fence, beyond which lies Metropolitan. Eventually I reach Slocum Avenue, a cemetery street, and angle right, coming to the memorial after about two blocks.

The memorial was dedicated on June 15, 1905. Translated loosely from the German, it says, simply, "Heartbroken. You did not die in vain." Etched into the surface of the concrete is a rendering of the *General Slocum*, in flames and smoke, with people jumping into the water. On the side are two upside-down torches, burning. On each side of the monument lies a statue of a woman bearing an expression of great sorrow. It has been erected in memory of the sixty-one unidentified victims of the *General Slocum*. The ship and the telling of the story in images of desperate people jumping into the water make everything I've read about how tragic the catastrophe was, resulting in the community relocating elsewhere, come alive again.

Exiting the cemetery, I turn right on Eliot Avenue and then go right again onto Seventy-First Avenue. After six blocks, I hit 66th Road and gaze on a home that's truly unique. It belongs to an electrician who has clearly built his ultimate three-story dream home, and he calls it Bavaria Castle. It's actually an eclectic mix of various styles. It has two tourelles made of stone and stucco, with tan trim around them. The top of one of the tourelles seems to be made of glass, and it has a small roof deck around it. There's a very large bow window on the side of the house, and nearby there's a shield-like ornament on a wall. Part of the house is surrounded by a stockade wall with vines running along it. A neighbor further enlightens me:

"When this fellow first built it, it was just a bungalow. The inside area is two stories high, wide open. There are really nice art murals on the walls inside. As soon as he finished it, he made an open house for the neighbors. It has a great fireplace where the top part turns blue outside where it's all lit up, especially at night. He took his time, and he did it. In the back, he has lots of potted plants."

A man wants an opulent home, but it dwarfs the dwellings of his neighbors. His response is to turn neighbors who might be upset by that into possible friends by inviting them in. No one minds I discover, after talking with others on the block, because he seems like a nice guy. But also, he's one of them. He's an electrician who happened to make good. Actions like this are part of the building blocks of communities.

At Metropolitan, two blocks up Seventy-First, I turn left. Near the corner on Metropolitan, at 71-01, is where I find the Cypress Hills Taxidermy Studio. The owner moved here from Brooklyn a while back and kept the name of Cypress Hills, a nearby Brooklyn community. John Youngaitis is the only, and probably last,

The Cypress Hills Taxidermy Studio where the last taxidermist in New York City works.

taxidermist in New York City. In the window and behind are many specimens of his work. These include, to name but a few, a giant brown bear, a starling, a black bear, an African lion, a housecat, a mallard duck, a giant iguana, a penguin, a cockatiel, various parrots, heads on the wall of various deer, half of a mountain goat, wild boars with all their teeth, a golden tamarin (an endangered species), and many more examples of mammals, reptiles, and birds. It's a display area, representing a lifetime of hard work and fascinating experiences, as it turns out.

I enter and meet John. He's a heavily tattooed man, thin, wiry, with muscles that are rock hard. He has a short, bristly, thin beard that has turned white, but he's only sixty-three years old.

"I'm writing a book about my life in taxidermy, and I work here too," he tells me. "My workshop's in the back. Look at my list."

"What's the biggest challenge in your work?"

"Taking the animal apart is the mechanical part. The creative part is putting it back together again, after you've cleaned it and all. Like the bullets. You don't see the bullet holes, for instance. They're sewn up from the inside. In a way, taxidermy is like reincarnation. We bring them back to life, sort of."

"I see you have the rump of a deer, only the rump. Who wanted that?"

He laughs and says, "It's a gag item. It's for a hunter that misses and never catches anything. Guys buy them and give them to their friends, like, here's what you get for never catching anything. All you saw was the rump going over the hill."

"How'd you get into this profession?"

"Easy. My father was a taxidermist in Brooklyn, and I became interested when I was just five years old. He quit school when he was sixteen and got into it, and now I do it. When I was a kid we lived near a cemetery, and I would bring home garter snakes and stuff. I loved Brooklyn, but I was down there last week. It's all gentrified. They ruined it."

"What have been some of your more interesting experiences?"

"Well, some of these people want their relatives preserved. I had this lady telling me she wanted something preserved. I said: 'You want your shih tzu preserved?' 'Shih tzu? No, my *sister*.' 'This is serious,'" he said, then continued: "I said, 'Lady, it's illegal.' She says, 'I'll pay you anything.' I say, 'In any case, the morgue ain't going to give you the body.' Another guy wanted his grandmother stuffed. You know, half of her body, so he could put her on the table, so she could watch over him, like in the movie, *Psycho*."

"What's that huge long skin on the wall?"

"That's a reticulated python skin."

"And what's that over there, a mountain goat?"

"That's over one hundred years old. My father bought it in the 1960s. See that cat over there? That was somebody's pet. And they never claimed it. I don't know why. It takes me an average of about half a day to create something, depending on what it is.

"I'm going to have to get a part-time job because there's not enough money in it. I wish somebody would give me a million dollars so I could continue. It's my passion, my life. But you see these birds, squirrels? People give me deposits and never come back. So now I'm stuck with them. But after two years they're mine, and I can sell them."

"Why didn't they come back?"

"Aaahh. That's the question of the ages. One problem is that some women aren't taxidermy friendly. Then the guys say: 'Where am I going to put this thing? My wife don't like looking at it.' Or they don't have the money."

"I guess it's not a feeling of 'Now he's in good hands, nicely restored.'"

"Not really. They wanted to put it up in *their* place. As for me, I'm not the Acme Storage Company. I want to sell and make money on it, get paid for my hard work. Saturday's my hardest day because kids come by, and they want to look at the animals, touch them, and so I hardly get anything done. Of course, I can understand it. If I was a kid and saw this, I'd want to be in here too."

"Do you ever rent out the items?"

"Yes, I charge 20 percent of the value of the animal per day. I rent it out to TV stations, movies, parties. But 80 percent of my business is hunters. They shoot it; then they want the meat. And then I get it."

"What kind of other work are you planning to do?"

"I don't know. Something that helps people. Like, me and my biker friends, we built a sun shelter after they made parts of Creedmoor Hospital into assisted living for the mentally disabled. The old people, especially with the medications they take, need to be out of the sun. So, we donated our time."

This interview was illuminating for several reasons First, there's John's disappointment about the fact that a craft that a person dedicated his life to is less and less in demand. He feels passed over and ignored. I experienced this with a piano maker in Queens, an antiques dealer in Manhattan, and an aquarium shop owner in Brooklyn. They know it's nobody's fault, but it's as though they bet on the wrong horse. This is especially true, as is the case here, if they take pride in their work and love doing it. It can also be truly frustrating when you work hard and people don't care enough to come back and pick up what they gave you.

Second, John is altruistic, both in his paid work and in his work in the community. He feels he's helping people become happy by perpetuating the existence of, say, a loved pet or by preserving the memory of the joy someone felt when they killed a bear. That may sound paradoxical, but he sums it up when he says: "I can hunt and still love animals like my cat or parrot." That compassion is a core value for him is clear when he tells me about how he donated his services to help build a shelter. I leave here feeling that human beings are incredibly complex and cannot be judged solely on the basis of one or two actions or beliefs. What's more important is situating their views and behavior within the larger context of their lives.

Ⓐ Yeshiva Gedola Torah Veyirah
Ⓑ Cook's Arts & Crafts Shoppe
Ⓒ Albanian Mosque
Ⓓ Zum Stammtisch Restaurant
Ⓔ St. Pancras Church
Ⓕ Harry Houdini Gravesite - Machpelah Cemetery

GLENDALE

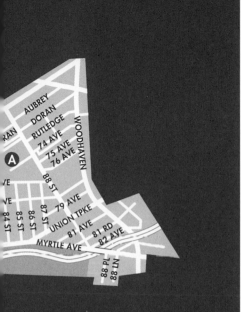

GLENDALE IS A QUIET, MOSTLY RESIDEN-TIAL, AND RECTANGULAR-SHAPED COM-MUNITY IN CENTRAL QUEENS. The major street boundaries are, roughly, Cooper Avenue, the Long Island Railroad tracks, Seventieth Avenue, and a bit of Edsall and Sixty-Seventh Avenues on the north; Woodhaven Boulevard on the east; Myrtle, Cooper, and Cypress Avenues on the south, but also including a portion of Forest Park and the various cemeteries that lie between and beyond these boundaries up to the Jackie Robinson Parkway; and, on the west, Fresh Pond Road, a small section of Central Avenue, and the Kings County line. About half of the community consists of various cemeteries, serving different faiths. It went through several name changes from the seventeenth through nineteenth centuries, when it was populated mostly by German farmers. In the mid-nineteenth century, it acquired the name Glendale, courtesy of a developer who hailed from Glendale, Ohio.

From the 1880s until Prohibition, Glendale was known as an entertainment venue, with taverns, parks, hotels, and a bowling alley. It was also an important manufacturing area, with factories that produced airplanes, ribbons, and textiles, and it was home to several breweries and a silent film studio. The initial population was German, who were joined later in the twentieth century by Irish and Italian residents. Today, besides the long-established groups, there are eastern Europeans, West Indians, and Hispanics, mostly Dominicans, in addition to some Asians.

The eastern part is still a very quiet area, with many detached homes, but also attached and semi-attached houses. These range from Tudor-style brick to frame, but nothing opulent. The community here is a mix of middle- and working-class residents. The western portion is more commercial, starting where Cooper Avenue crosses Myrtle. In this section, the housing shifts to older stock, with frame houses, and the Kreischer-brick structures in various shades of yellow, orange, and beige predominating. The main commercial streets in Glendale are Myrtle; Cooper, which has a new shopping center; Atlas Park; and 88th Street (mostly industrial). Glendale has no subway, with the closest station (the M train) at 62nd Street and Fresh Pond Road in Ridgewood.

My walk begins with a real bang, sociologically. I head down 88th Street from Cooper Avenue. It's a commercial and industrial strip, with many types of enterprises, places to shop, pizzerias and bagel shops, plumbing and heating supply stores, and so on. At 74-10 Seventy-Fourth Avenue, on my right, I pass a nondescript entrance, but what's beyond it and clearly visible through high metal fence is astounding. A huge, distinctively designed, light-beige stucco-and-stone building, with high, Romanesque windows looms out over the large, concrete plaza. It's a yeshiva, or Jewish educational institution. The name is emblazoned in large Hebrew letters: "Yeshiva Gedolah Torah Veyirah," which means "Torah Veyirah Advanced Talmudical Academy." Torah Veyirah (also known as United Talmudical Seminary) is the name of the school system run by the most rigorously Orthodox Hasidic sect, the Satmarer Hasidim. Their New York headquarters are in Williamsburg, Brooklyn. They eschew any kind of social contact with the outside world, including other Orthodox Jews, except when absolutely beneficial or necessary.

This enormous structure, a city block and a half long, contains what turns out to be one of the largest, if not the largest, rabbinical seminaries housed in one building. It accommodates over one thousand students who study the Talmud there for up to sixteen hours a day, from 6:00 a.m. to 10:00 p.m. The students do not live on the premises, as is sometimes the case with other such schools, returning home every evening. But what's really remarkable is that it's in a community that has almost no Jews living in it and certainly not Orthodox ones.

It wasn't easy to build here, where opponents complained at public hearings about the strain on local resources from parking, traffic, noise, and sanitation needs, all for a group that would contribute very little to the community as a whole. After all, the Hasidim wouldn't even shop there since they avoid contact with outsiders and would certainly not patronize restaurants, taverns, and grocery stores that sell nonkosher food. Yet since they complied with zoning laws and building regulations, the city granted them a certificate of occupancy in 2005 but denied them permission to build a dormitory.

I decide to find a person who can tell me more. As luck would have it, I meet someone, who, while wearing a large kippah, isn't Hasidic in his appearance:

"I was wondering, why build a gigantic yeshiva here? This place is in a mostly non-Jewish community. Plus, Orthodox Jews almost always live in a place where there are synagogues, kosher food stores, and others who are like them. This is really out of the way."

"Well, first of all, no one lives here. They all go home at night. Second, you can't find such a large property at a good price in Brooklyn. It's too crowded and expensive in the Orthodox neighborhoods. So, it was worth it to do it here."

Upon entering I see the house of study, called a *beis medrash*, and indeed, it's gigantic. Hundreds of students are sitting at long tables, their heads burrowed inside one of the sixty-three volumes of the

Talmud. The Talmud is an explication of the meaning of the Torah or Old Testament, as discussed by rabbinical sages who lived thousands of years ago. Others are standing, talking in Yiddish in sing-song fashion, gesticulating with their hands to make their points as they debate the meaning of these ancient Aramaic-language books. The study hall is about three stories high and very brightly lit. As I survey the scene, I feel as if I am seeing a world that is a million miles away from the modern society in which we live. As it happens, the home that was the setting for Archie Bunker's in the 1970s sitcom *All in the Family* is only a few blocks away at 89-70 Cooper Avenue.

I continue south down Myrtle until it intersects with Union Turnpike, which ends here. The last block has the subname Frederick A. Haller Way, sponsored by Greenstreets, a program run by the New York City Parks and Transportation Departments, which has also erected a little mall for Haller here, using the familiar name, Frederick T. "Bud" Haller Jr., and offering praise "for his many years of dedication and commitment to the Glendale community." Naming vest-pocket parks and streets after local people who've contributed to a community enhances solidarity, makes people think, even if only momentarily, about what community means, and, most importantly, gives those living there a hope that they or their friends will be remembered by future generations for what they have done voluntarily.

At 80-09, I take a peek inside Cook's Arts and Crafts Shoppe and ask Bill, the owner, if there's anything of interest about his place.

"Well," he tells me, "the building was done in 1899. And you can still see signs of that. Look at the tin ceiling over your head. We also sell three-dimensional puzzles like these wooden cars."

I glance at them and reply, "Yes, but these are in boxes with the names of the manufacturers. So then, they're surely sold elsewhere. But is there anything you have that's unique?"

He thinks for a minute and says, "Well, we have used parts for dolls of every kind. They're in these plastic boxes. If someone's doll loses an arm, a foot, or a head, we can replace it. It may not be exactly what it was, but it's still a replacement. People stopped selling these parts twenty years ago. And we post on the internet and various sites that we have these things." He's right. Having done some research on it, I didn't find any other stores selling used doll parts in Queens.

"How often do people come in for these items?"

"Maybe a couple of times a year. But if you need one and the doll has sentimental value, it's worth everything to you. Or say, a person wants to give a particular doll as a gift to someone they love. One time I had an actor come in, and he bought a bunch of doll heads as a backdrop for a play they were doing." This is a perfect example of how things that seem to have no usefulness can become important to the right customer

It would appear that certain groups would really seem quite incompatible with each other, but that isn't always necessarily the case. For example, a beautiful new Albanian mosque at 72-24 Myrtle coexists peacefully in a community where the residents are a predominantly white, conservative Italian, Irish, and German population, one that would not usually be thought especially welcoming. Queens and Brooklyn have the fewest number of Albanian residents, compared to Manhattan, Bronx, and Staten Island, the last of which has four times as many Albanians as Queens does.

People in the mosque say that most worshipers come here to pray from other areas. One likely explanation for the mosque being here could be economic. There's an available parcel of land at a very good price, and folks buy it. It's also a sign of how much more mobile people are today in terms of travel that they are willing to purchase outside their communities. I've seen this phenomenon of groups creating churches far away from where their constituencies live. In other cases the buyers hope that one day they can move to a place closer to home, so to speak. Incidentally, up the street from the mosque is a large Jewish cemetery, Mount Lebanon, on Myrtle, near 74th Street, and this has never been a Jewish community.

Long after most of the German community has departed from Glendale, a hardy survivor remains. Near where Cooper Avenue crosses diagonally over Myrtle, there is Zum Stammtisch (the Family Table), at 69-46 Myrtle. In fact, it's still flourishing as people come from other parts of New York City, even as far away as Westchester County, for dinner. They may sup themselves or with their parents, who are still tied to what's left of the community from the days when the restaurant was affectionately dubbed "Zummies."

At 68th Street I turn left and soon come to St. Pancras Church on the right at 72-22. The interior is very pleasing aesthetically. It's mostly white, with gold-leaf scrollwork on the walls and in the arches between the Corinthian columns that flank the length of the nave of the church. A domed ceiling above the altar contains religious portraits of Jesus and his apostles. The altar itself has a marble column on each side, and both columns are topped by a statue of an angel. There are stained-glass windows throughout the church, and round pendant chandeliers cast a soft light on the warm wooden pews. Many churches have these features, but what makes this one so outstanding is the way it all comes together because of the brightness and quality of the colors, carvings, and paintings.

On the corner of 68th, I go left down Cooper Avenue, which borders Cypress Hills Cemetery. Among the famous people buried there are Emma Lazarus, Sholem Aleichem, and Jackie Robinson; gangsters like Lucky Luciano, Carlo Gambino, and Vito Genovese; and a man who played gangsters in the movies, Edward G. Robinson. In this sense it's Queens's answer to Brooklyn's Greenwood Cemetery, where many of the rich and famous are also interred. After a few blocks, I turn left onto Cypress Hills Street. In about fifteen minutes I come to the Machpelah Cemetery at 82-30, on the right. It's Friday at noon, the gate is closed but unlocked, and no one else is there. The minute I enter I see the family plot and monument to Harry Houdini, the most famous magician in history.

There are several marble slabs under which lie the remains of Harry Houdini Weiss (1874–1926) and his immediate family. On top of his own grave I see notes, coins, and playing cards with very old-fashioned drawings of kings, queens, and jacks that I've never

Notes, coins, and playing cards left on Harry Houdini's gravestone.

seen before. One of the notes, written on an ace of hearts playing card, and clearly from a fan, reads: "Your awesome. RIP." And it's signed "Luana." There's a lock, perhaps symbolizing his abilities as an escape artist, and some keys.

In front of the graves, there's a structure with a large platform that has three steps leading upward. There's a round bronze memorial put up by what looks like "The Magicians Institute." And on top a handsome bust of the man's head looks out. On the left is a neoclassical statue of a woman bent over with grief and holding her head in her hands. Someone has placed a folded New York Police Department cap directly in front of her. The inscription on the left is dedicated to Harry's mother and reads: "Here, in eternal peace, slumbers our darling mother, Cecilia Weiss, nee Steiner, who entered her everlasting sleep, July 17, 1913, as pure and as sweet as the day she was born on June 16, 1841." Another plaque on the right is dedicated in memory of his father and reads: "Sacred to the memory of our dearly beloved husband and father, Reverend Doctor Mayer Samuel Weiss, rabbi and teacher in Israel, born August 27, 1829;

died, October 5, 1892. Rest in Peace." What's interesting is that there are no security measures such as cameras, fences, and the like in place to ensure that the grave will not be vandalized. Indeed, the items on the grave appear to be undisturbed. But there is a history challenging any such assumptions. Vandals destroyed his bust four times between 1975 and 1993, with a sledgehammer on one occasion, and the police regularly patrol the site on Halloween.

COLLEGE POINT

FLUSHING

REGO PARK

FOREST HILLS

KEW GARDENS HILLS

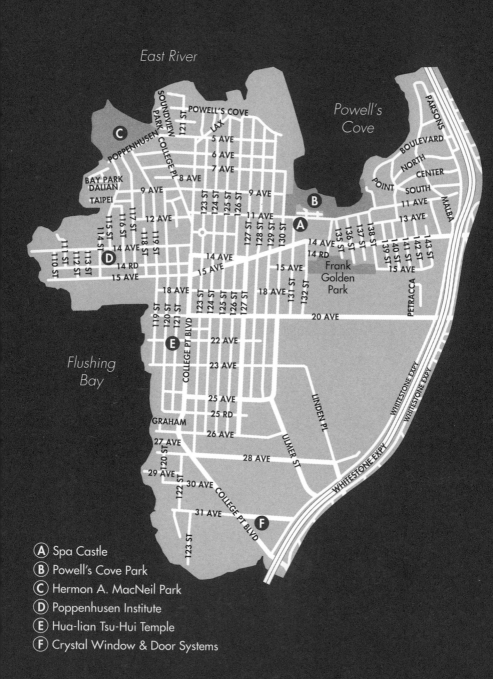

East River

Powell's Cove

SOUNDVIEW PARK
121 ST
POWELL'S COVE
LAX
5 AVE
6 AVE
7 AVE
8 AVE
9 AVE

POPPENHUSEN
COLLEGE PL

C

BAY PARK
DALIAN
TAIPEI
9 AVE

12 AVE

117 ST
116 ST
115 ST
114 ST

111 ST
110 ST
113 ST
112 ST

118 ST
119 ST

D

14 AVE
14 RD
15 AVE

123 ST
124 ST
125 ST
126 ST

127 ST
128 ST
129 ST
130 ST

9 AVE

11 AVE

14 AVE
15 AVE

18 AVE

123 ST
124 ST
125 ST
126 ST
127 ST

131 ST
132 ST

18 AVE

15 AVE

PARSONS

BOULEVARD
NORTH
CENTER
POINT SOUTH

11 AVE

13 AVE

138 ST
137 ST
136 ST
135 ST

14 AVE
14 RD

Frank
Golden
Park

139 ST
140 ST
141 ST
142 ST
143 ST

15 AVE

MALBA

PETRACCA

B

A

20 AVE

119 ST
120 ST
121 ST

E

COLLEGE PT BLVD

22 AVE

23 AVE

25 AVE
25 RD

GRAHAM
26 AVE

27 AVE
120 ST
121 ST

29 AVE

122 ST

30 AVE

31 AVE

123 ST

COLLEGE PT BLVD

28 AVE

ULMER ST

LINDEN PL

WHITESTONE EXPY
WHITESTONE EXPY
WHITESTONE EXPY

F

Flushing
Bay

(A) Spa Castle
(B) Powell's Cove Park
(C) Hermon A. MacNeil Park
(D) Poppenhusen Institute
(E) Hua-lian Tsu-Hui Temple
(F) Crystal Window & Door Systems

COLLEGE POINT

COLLEGE POINT IS REALLY OFF THE BEATEN TRACK because it runs along a portion of the Whitestone Expressway, where cars are speeding by. I feel comfortable saying that most of those who travel along this busy highway to Citi Field, the US Open, JFK Airport, or elsewhere, have never been to this quiet enclave. All they see on the right is a *New York Times* plant, a Toys "R" Us, a giant movie complex, and other commercial properties. The boundaries of the community are the East River on the north, the Whitestone Expressway on the east, Thirty-First Avenue on the south, and Flushing Bay on the west. It was a rural community until the mid-1850s, when Conrad Poppenhusen established a rubber works factory, which employed hundreds of workers. College Point also developed into a resort area in the second half of the nineteenth century with bathhouses, restaurants, and entertainment. Through much of the twentieth century it was a mostly white area, especially for Germans and Irish, but today it's increasingly mixed, with substantial Asian and Hispanic populations.

Much of College Point is industrial and commercial. The main thoroughfares are the service road of the expressway; Twentieth Avenue, where there's a huge shopping center; plus a number of streets immediately north of it, like 130th street and others closer to the water that are home to small manufacturing companies. The main drag is College Point Boulevard, much of it lined with fast-food eateries, delis, beauty salons, and the like. The eastern part of Fourteenth Avenue also has a commercial strip and a shopping complex. The majority of the housing stock is old. Many of the small brick structures commonly found here were built one hundred or more years ago. There are saltbox-type houses, bungalows, brick attached homes, and old three-story apartment buildings. From about 134th to 143rd streets, I see many new homes, some of them quite upscale. More than perhaps any other community in Queens, College Point feels like it's in a time warp, one from the early twentieth century and even before that.

My first stop is Spa Castle at 131-10 Eleventh Avenue. It has seven themed saunas, some with therapeutic minerals, others with multicolored lighting, along with a year-round outdoor water park. Korean-owned, this five-story-high, 100,000-square-foot wonderland attracts both families and singles, and even some Hasidic Jews who come here from Brooklyn. Many show up here on Sunday morning to relax. Those longing for a quiet and peaceful experience should come here in the morning on weekdays. The manager tells me, "We welcome everybody as long as they follow the rules."

At 129th Street and Eleventh Avenue, I come to one of several entrances for Powell's Cove Park, which extends to 138th Street, along Eleventh. I pass through a delicately designed wrought-iron gate with carvings of rabbits, birds, butterflies, and rows of small fish, and a replica of the Whitestone Bridge. An entrance at the other end of the park has the exact same wrought-iron gate. Those wishing to find an isolated and relaxing natural park should try coming here. I meet very few people on a beautiful fall afternoon during a ninety-minute stroll along its leafy paths, one of which includes a very broad tree with five trunks. There isn't much to do here except walk the trails, commune with nature, and enjoy some spectacular views of the Bronx and the Whitestone Bridge. There are no playgrounds or sports facilities, not surprising since the intention was to simply create a wooded area that would protect the tidal areas and marshes.

Many of the homes around the park's eastern border along 138th, 139th, and 140th Streets are elaborate, modern structures, with Spanish-tile roofs, and neatly manicured and extensive lawns. This is one of the nicest residential areas in College Point. I pass by an enormous stucco house with Roman windows, a nicely landscaped garden, and Juliet balconies, and there are others that are equally eye-catching. If one wanted a bucolic place in Queens to relax in,

A delicately designed wrought-iron gate at the entrance to Powell's Cove Park.

this would be the perfect community because College Point is not easily accessible by public transportation, nor is it well known.

Leaving here, I continue up Eleventh Avenue, turning right, at 125th Street, and then going left on Fifth Avenue, looking all the while at the homes and streets, and getting a real feel for this community, with its quaint, old houses and narrow streets seemingly lost in time. In about fifteen minutes I come to my next destination, Hermon A. MacNeil Park, where Fifth becomes Poppenhusen Avenue and meets up with College Place. This park is very picturesque, owing much of its beauty to the many enormous trees, a number of them oaks, that provide ample shade on gentle hills throughout the park. It sits on the shore of the East River, and right by that shore there's a large, well-designed playground filled with many children. It's a wonderful location, so close by the water, and to my left I have a terrific view of the Manhattan skyline, set against one of those gorgeous orange-, pink-, and red-hued sunsets. As I take in the scenery in this urban setting, I find myself thinking that some of the most enjoyable activities in life—in this case, relaxing in a gorgeous park—*are* free.

After a while I head over to 14th Road via 117th Street turning right onto Fourteenth. In three blocks I'm at 114-04, site of the Poppenhusen Institute, built in 1868 by a prominent, wealthy German manufacturing family. It has national historical importance as the home of the first free kindergarten in the United States. The building, a French-inspired structure, now serving as a community center, is being refurbished in an attempt to restore it to its former glory. An elevator has been put in, and the outside will be repainted.

From here I walk one block to my left and take Fourteenth Avenue back to College Point Boulevard, equivalent to 122nd Street, and the community's main thoroughfare.

Just off College Point, at 22-02 121st Street, there's a colorful, artfully designed pagoda-like Taoist house of worship, called the Hua-lian Tsu-Hui Temple. It caters primarily to the émigré Taiwanese community, which is concentrated in nearby Flushing. Taoism, also referred to as Daoism, is a religious system grounded in Chinese

The Hua-lian Tsu-Hui Temple houses an extensive collection of East Asian art and architecture.

philosophy. It differs from Confucianism, which is more of a philosophical approach than a religion, by emphasizing spontaneity and simplicity as opposed to more rigid practices. This temple claims to be the only religious group on the East Coast of the United States that has an extensive collection of East Asian art and architecture. Certainly, the artifacts inside are beautiful, with the main feature a very dignified-looking statue of a supreme Chinese deity known as the Golden Mother of the Jasper Lake.

About a half mile farther I see a large factory called Crystal Window and Door Systems. It's been around for twenty-five years, and its headquarters are here, at 31-10 College Point Boulevard. They also have four other locations, including in Chicago and St. Louis, and, while open to the public, they generally sell to contractors. Impressive as that is, it's not what brought me here. Inside is a remarkable and unique artistic creation by Lin Shih-Pao placed on a wall near the company entrance, which can be reached by first walking through another exhibit of sorts, namely different types of window and door frames. When I ask about the art gallery, the receptionist seems a bit confused, as if she has never heard of this, but when I persist, she directs me to the wall hanging. This isn't surprising since, as I soon find out, the exhibit isn't open to the public, though it can be viewed by invitation and appointment.

A round disk sits in the center of the artwork. There are gold-colored squares scattered throughout the surface, and it consists largely of picture frames of different sizes. Gold- and blue-painted spheres resembling eggs are also attached to it. Beneath the portrait, there's another exhibit by an employee at the plant, Lin Ji Dong, who's in charge of production. He began his work in 2016, and while he isn't primarily an artist, his creations are certainly works of art. Among the items shown are dragons, birds, fish, and baskets, all made from "strappings," a material used to tie together corrugated boxes. In the factory they're discarded, but he has given them a wonderful new life as an art form. Ji Dong's interest in this was a direct result of his work at Crystal.

I meet the president and founder of this company, Thomas Chen, in his office upstairs. He turns out to be a successful Taiwanese entrepreneur who came to this country in 1982 at age twenty-seven and who has always loved art and would have been an artist if he hadn't gone into business. To promote his first love, he created a foundation to support Taiwanese art.

"I love art," he tells me, "and have been collecting it for many years as well as supporting the arts in different ways. So, I created a retreat with mountains, forests, and a lake for artists [in the village of Holmes, which is part of Pawling, a town in Dutchess County, New York], open to all artists who want a place to exhibit their work. I come from a small town in the mountains of Taiwan and have always loved nature. So, we have a preserve in Holmes, of about 200 acres. There artists can enjoy nature and paint." It's clear that art is Chen's passion. In fact, he has made the retreat available to his employees, who also visit it when they want to get away from the city.

What's interesting here is that people tend to think of businesspeople as just that. But they can have surprising and varied interests. And in this case Thomas Chen has found a way to bring together these different worlds, by finding a combination that worked.

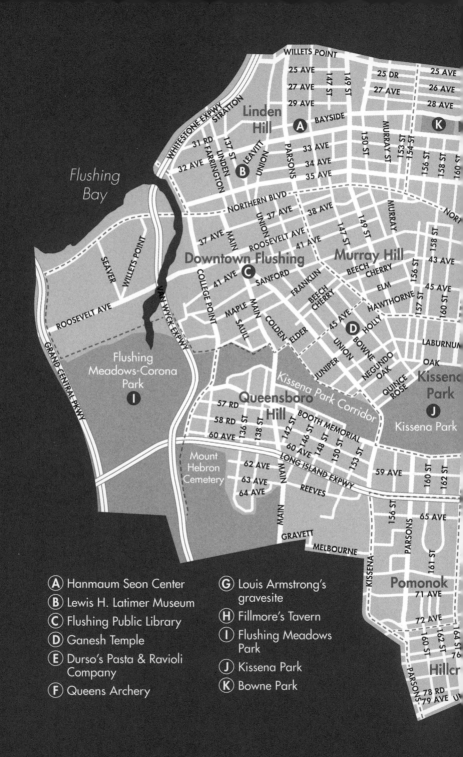

WILLETS POINT

25 AVE
27 AVE
29 AVE

25 DR
27 AVE

25 AVE
26 AVE
28 AVE

Linden Hill

Ⓐ BAYSIDE

Ⓚ

WHITESTONE EXPWY
STRATTON
147 ST
149 ST
150 ST
MURRAY ST
153 ST
154 ST
156 ST
158 ST

31 RD
32 AVE
137 ST
LINDEN
FARRINGTON
BLEAVITT
UNION
PARSONS

33 AVE
34 AVE
35 AVE

NORTHERN BLVD

37 AVE
37 AVE
UNION
ROOSEVELT AVE
41 AVE

38 AVE

NORT

Flushing Bay

SEAVER
WILLETS POINT

Downtown Flushing

Ⓒ

147 ST
149 ST
MURRAY

Murray Hill

BEECH
CHERRY
ELM
HAWTHORNE

156 ST
157 ST
158 ST
160 ST

43 AVE
45 AVE

ROOSEVELT AVE

COLLEGE POINT

41 AVE
SANFORD
FRANKLIN

MAPLE
MAIN
COLDEN
SAUL
ELDER

BEECH
CHERRY

45 AVE Ⓓ HOLLY
BOWNE
UNION

JUNIPER
NEGUNDO
OAK

LABURNUM
OAK

QUINCE
ROSE

Kissena Park

Ⓙ

GRAND CENTRAL PKWY
VAN WYCK EXPWY

Flushing Meadows-Corona Park

Ⓘ

Kissena Park Corridor

Kissena Park

57 RD
58 RD
60 AVE

136 ST
138 ST

Queensboro Hill

142 ST
146 ST
BOOTH MEMORIAL
148 ST
150 ST
153 ST

60 AVE

59 AVE

160 ST
162 ST

Mount Hebron Cemetery

62 AVE
63 AVE
64 AVE

MAIN

LONG ISLAND EXPWY
REEVES

65 AVE

156 ST
PARSONS
161 ST

Pomonok

71 AVE
72 AVE

GRAVETT
MELBOURNE

KISSENA
PARSONS

160 ST
162 ST
76

Hillcr

78 RD
79 AVE

Ⓐ Hanmaum Seon Center

Ⓑ Lewis H. Latimer Museum

Ⓒ Flushing Public Library

Ⓓ Ganesh Temple

Ⓔ Durso's Pasta & Ravioli Company

Ⓕ Queens Archery

Ⓖ Louis Armstrong's gravesite

Ⓗ Fillmore's Tavern

Ⓘ Flushing Meadows Park

Ⓙ Kissena Park

Ⓚ Bowne Park

FLUSHING

THE BOUNDARIES OF THIS LARGE, MULTI-ETHNIC COMMUNITY ARE, GENERALLY, Willets Point Boulevard on the north; Utopia Parkway, Francis Lewis Boulevard, and Fresh Meadow Lane on the east; Union Turnpike, Melbourne Avenue, and Gravett Road on the south; and Parsons Boulevard, Kissena Boulevard, the Van Wyck Expressway, and the Grand Central Parkway on the west. Flushing's history dates back centuries to the Dutch and English periods. It was in Flushing that religious freedom was granted to the Quakers who settled here in 1657, fleeing persecution by Peter Stuyvesant, who headed the New Amsterdam colony. Here, the Quakers signed the Flushing Remonstrance, a document proclaiming religious freedom that preceded the Bill of Rights by a century. For much of the nineteenth century Flushing was a community for the well-to-do who migrated here from Manhattan. In the twentieth century it became a much more urban place as transportation options increased for commuters to the city. It was a largely white ethnic community until the 1970s. The homes and apartment buildings, many of them older, are some of the most varied in the borough. The major commercial thoroughfares are Francis Lewis Boulevard, Main Street, Roosevelt Avenue, Kissena Boulevard, and Northern Boulevard.

The biggest demographic development in northwestern Queens—Flushing, Whitestone, Little Neck, Bayside, and Douglaston—has been the arrival, over the last several decades, of Asians, most of them Chinese, but also substantial numbers from Korea, India, Pakistan, Bangladesh, Afghanistan, Sri Lanka, and even Malaysia, with most of this last group ethnically Chinese. There are still significant numbers of Greeks, Italians, Irish, and Jews, especially in northeast Flushing, but their numbers are decreasing.

The Chinese began coming in the 1970s and were mostly Taiwanese, who spoke Mandarin, unlike the earlier Cantonese population, who had originally settled in Chinatown before moving to Flushing. The Taiwanese have now been augmented by yet another group of, generally, working-class, mainland Chinese speakers of Mandarin. Nowhere are the Chinese more numerous than in Flushing, whose downtown area is their commercial and retail nerve center. It's an extremely crowded and busy place. The MTA subway 7 line ends in Flushing, and the Long Island Railroad (LIRR) stops here as well.[15] Buses are constantly arriving from all parts of the borough, disgorging their passengers onto the main thoroughfares like Roosevelt Avenue. This is, after all, the fourth-biggest business district in New York City. People jostle each other day and night as they try to negotiate Main Street and the narrow side streets that extend eastward from Main, almost like tentacles.

But downtown Flushing is more than commerce. Along Main Street and Kissena Boulevard all the way to the Long Island Expressway (LIE) one can find a variety of apartment buildings, from luxurious to modest and everything in between. As one gets closer to the LIE, there are more Hindu and Muslim establishments, though these are far less common than was the case ten years ago. Today, Chinese residents are replacing the other groups both north and south of Northern Boulevard.

According to Professor Pyong Gap Min of Queens College and CUNY Graduate Center, who has written extensively about Asians in Queens, the Chinese population today is three times the size of the Korean population, who are the second-largest group here. The Chinese own most of the buildings on and around Main Street, but the Koreans, a fairly affluent community, are dominant along parts of Union Street and eastward on Northern Boulevard, from Main Street all the way to the Queens–Nassau County border. A large number of Koreans also live in the Auburndale, Murray Hill, and Broadway sections of Flushing.

Not well known is the existence of a community in Flushing of ethnic Koreans who came to northeastern China in the late nineteenth century for economic reasons and continued immigrating to China until 1949. Known as Korean Chinese, an estimated thirty thousand of them have immigrated from China and have settled in Flushing and in other parts of Queens in the past ten years. They found a niche here in businesses that require knowledge of Korean and Chinese, and their businesses are concentrated along Union Street between Thirty-Fifth Avenue and Northern Boulevard.[16]

Religiously, only a small percentage of Chinese in Flushing are Christian. Among the Koreans, it's the opposite, with perhaps three-quarters of Koreans identifying as Christians. The majority are Protestant Evangelicals.[17] Every winter the Chinese, Taiwanese, Korean, and Vietnamese communities come together to celebrate the Lunar New Year with a giant parade through downtown Flushing.

Some of the neighborhoods in Flushing are quite distinct. They have their own organizations and a distinct identity. As a result they're discussed individually and include Downtown Flushing, Auburndale, and Hillcrest. This generally happens with geographically large communities and reflects the desire of these people to establish a feeling of community within their immediate area.

I begin my exploration of Flushing by walking south down Union Street in the Linden Hill section. Here there are large co-op housing complexes with many Chinese residents, as well as private homes on the side streets. At Bayside Avenue I turn left and soon come to a magnificent Korean Buddhist temple, the Hanmaum Seon Center, at 145-20. It's an imposing pagoda, with an upward-curving roof, that looms over the neighboring homes. Under the eaves are many decorative curved pieces of wood, painted in multicolored designs. Beneath this on the walls are panels depicting various religious and historical scenes. This happens to be the back of the temple, which extends all the way to the next block, Thirty-Second Avenue, where the front entrance is located. While also beautiful, the front is not, in my view, as impressive as the back. The temple is one of twenty-five Seon centers around the world, founded by the Jogye Order of Korean Buddhism. For those interested in visiting the temple, services are held every Sunday morning.

Not far from here, several blocks east of Union, is the Lewis H. Latimer House, the former residence of Latimer from 1903 to 1928, located at 34-41 137th Street. Today, it's also a museum showcasing his life and work. Latimer was an important African American inventor who worked with Thomas Edison on his invention of the electric lightbulb, significantly improving it. He also drew up the patent application for Alexander Graham Bell, inventor of the telephone. One of his own inventions was a carbon filament, which greatly improved the incandescent lightbulb. His life and achievements, not to mention his home, are all on display at the museum. To understand the magnitude of his accomplishments, keep in mind that he lived and worked in the late nineteenth and early twentieth centuries, long before the civil rights movement.

The other side of Northern Boulevard is where what's referred to as "Downtown Flushing" begins. I head west to Main Street, turn left, and find myself in a congested area filled with people walking on sidewalks and spilling over into the streets. Almost all of them are Asian, and I feel as if I'm back in China, where I spent some time visiting Beijing, Harbin, and other major cities. Most people I encounter here speak little or no English.

Despite the American chain stores here, the area has a very distinct Chinese flavor, with many restaurants, butcher shops, and grocery stores that cater to the needs of the Chinese population. Walk down the side streets like 40th Road, where the rents are cheaper than on Main, and most stores are Chinese, save for some Korean shops. South of the railroad, the Main Street shops are predominantly Chinese owned and operated—jewelers, bakeries, pharmacies, shoe emporiums, toy stores, supermarkets.

Where Main Street and Kissena Boulevard meet is the home of the Flushing Public Library. Virtually every language in the borough, of which there are more than 150, is represented on its shelves. It is perhaps the busiest in the United States, with children reading and writing in the quiet sections, but animatedly talking, and enjoying what they see as a serious but welcoming place. I ask one eleven-year-old child, whose family hails from Afghanistan, what she likes about the library.

"Everything!" she exclaims. "They help me with my work, and I can study and play here with my friends."

Walking along Maple Avenue toward Kissena, I pass the Maple Playground. My attention is drawn to a game being played there. Four young men are kicking, with soccer-style foot movements, a small yellow plastic butterfly-shaped object, made of feathers and synthetic materials, that has a circular weight at the bottom. The objective is to not be the one who lets it drop to the ground, like in volleyball. Thus, it's a combination, I would say, of soccer and volleyball that is similar to badminton. One of the men is bare chested; another wears only a t-shirt. It's a cold day in late December with temperatures in the high thirties. They are laughing and clearly enjoying themselves. I ask them about the game, which I refer to as shuttlecock because a bystander called it that.

"In Chinese this game is called *jianzi*," one of them tells me. "Shuttlecock is the name of the object we use. We love it, and we play here almost every day." As it turns out it is, in fact, a Chinese national sport based on the ancient Han dynasty game known as *cuju*. It can be played by up to ten people who stand in a circle. The game is considered great exercise as well as a way of improving foot, hand, and eye coordination. I find myself admiring their dexterity and ability to kick the object in really creative ways. In recent years it has become a more formalized sport with competitive tournaments held regularly in China.

At 45-57 Bowne Street, I enter the famous Hindu temple dedicated to the elephant deity, Ganesh.[18] Called the Hindu Temple Society of North America, it's a truly impressive-looking house of worship, in the style that is typical of South Indian temples. Made of granite, with intricate carvings, on levels that recede gently as it reaches the broad, curved apex, it's truly unique and must be seen to be fully appreciated, especially at night when lights of varying colors illuminate it. It was created by about 150 artisans in Hyderabad, India, and shipped in pieces to New York. A vegetarian restaurant on the premises serves thousands of meals every week. Inside, the temple is a large rectangle, with a marble floor and with shrines for various deities along the walls and in the center. As I stand inside the temple, a group of priests in colorful robes are chanting softly as devotees of Hinduism make offerings to the gods nearby.

Exploring the Auburndale neighborhood of Flushing, I come to Durso's Pasta and Ravioli Company. A long, tiled space, this is one of *the* places to shop if you're into fresh and high-quality Italian food, especially pasta. Located at 189-01 Crocheron Avenue, where it intersects with Utopia Parkway, it's always busy, but especially so on weekends and holidays, when the line can stretch out the door.

A community the size of Flushing cannot be carefully walked in one or even two days. The next day, I continue to walk through Auburndale, a neighborhood known for the hundreds of Tudor-style apartment buildings and semi-attached and private homes that grace its quiet streets. The ones from 190-05 to 190-17 Crocheron Avenue are especially charming. I walk on the blocks north of Crocheron to Twenty-Ninth Avenue, and from Utopia Parkway to 167th Street, and emerge satiated with this distinctive architectural

This impressive building was created by about 150 artisans in Hyderabad, India, and shipped in pieces to New York.

design. Many of the homes feature stones of varying sizes and shapes attached to the stucco walls. Interesting brick patterns are often present along with the traditional slate roofs. Everyone will have their favorites, but, for my money, few can equal 32-64 171st Street at Thirty-Second Avenue. The house was built with great care and beautiful materials, and practically every window has multi-colored leaded glass, even portions of the garage door. The sloping roof and arches are in perfect proportion.

Still in Auburndale, I head south to Thirty-Ninth Avenue, make a left, and see a place, on a block with mostly automotive establishments, called Queens Archery, at 170-20. There are only three such centers in the city, to my knowledge—here, another place in Queens, and near downtown Brooklyn. They have twenty lanes for archers, hunters, and target enthusiasts, with both leagues and private lessons. There are tournaments too, with the motto, "where you need both skill and luck." It's mostly for people who either like competitive events or really don't know much about archery and are intrigued by it. It's also a fun place to take a date according to those who operate it, and I see several young couples there when I visit it. I speak with an earnest and enthusiastic young employee. Andrew sheds more light on the appeal of this sport and who comes here.

"We have a pretty even mix," he tells me. "One range is for beginners, the other for advanced. It's $25 an hour."

"Couldn't beginners accidentally hit someone?"

"It never happens because everyone's standing in the same row. No one's ever shooting past each other. Everyone walks down together. People come from as far away as New Jersey. A lot of places don't have rental equipment. We do. It's a good sport. Children shoot with their parents. Plus, no one has an advantage. The parents and children can both do equally well. A ten-year-old can easily match a twenty-year-old, or vice versa. It's not like basketball where someone's taller or stronger. It doesn't depend on talent. It's mostly technique, concentration, and being a little consistent."

Not far down, Thirty-Ninth Avenue becomes Depot Road and runs along the westbound LIRR tracks, whose trains take commuters through Queens, ending at Penn Station in Manhattan. Walkers looking for the Broadway after which the station is named will come up empty. Generally, station names refer to what's there, but this one doesn't. The station's original name in the nineteenth century was East Flushing. Then it was renamed Broadway, which is what Northern Boulevard (Route 25A) was called from Flushing all the way through Little Neck. In the 1930s, the street name Broadway was dropped so as not to confuse it with another prominent Broadway that runs through Astoria, Woodside, and Elmhurst, Queens. Layers of history sometimes play a role in place names that endure long after their immediate relevance. Who knows? Perhaps city planners will one day change the station from nonexistent Broadway to Depot Road or its original moniker, East Flushing.

From here I take a half-mile walk south on 162nd Street to Flushing Cemetery, wanting to see where Louis "Satchmo" Armstrong is buried. I walk through the gate at 4:15 p.m. and bump into Irene Avellino, who works there. Our meeting is a lucky break for me because she tells me exactly where it is.

"There's a trumpet over his gravestone painted over in white," she tells me. "The first one, which he used to play, was stolen. This is also one of his, but, unlike the first one, it wasn't ever used in his performances. Dizzy Gillespie is also buried here, but it's an unmarked grave, because the family wanted it that way."

"Do you get a lot of visitors to Satchmo's grave?"

"All the time. And they come from all over the world." I stand in front of the black granite gravestone, trying to imagine what this man meant to so many millions of people and how it all ends here. I'm comforted by Irene's words, which remind me that he's still remembered by people who feel his resting place gives them a chance to reminisce and appreciate who he was.

The following day, I begin another trip, this time through the Hillcrest neighborhood, located at the southern end of Flushing. Sometimes considered to be part of the Fresh Meadows community, the mix here is predominantly Asian, Orthodox Jewish, and Muslim.

On Parsons Boulevard, just north of Union Turnpike, I pass the Al Mamoor School for Muslim students at 78-31, which is next door to the Orthodox Congregation Toras Emes at 78-15. Next to it there's the Yeshiva Ketana of Queens. In this city it's not uncommon for groups not known to be friendly with each other to be located in the same small area. Do the people here have any meaningful contact? Are there any conflicts? How are they resolved? Most of the Jews living here are Orthodox, but the flagship institution of the Conservative movement, Solomon Schechter, has its Queens school here too, at 76-16 Parsons. I speak with an administrator at one of the Jewish schools and ask him if there's any meaningful contact. His answer is instructive.

"Frankly, it would seem like a great opportunity to reach out," he says. "Unfortunately, our parents feel that in the current climate it's not appropriate. They feel a sense of danger, especially because the neighborhood has many Muslim residents."

"Have there been any incidents or conflicts?" I ask.

"None that I know of. I hope attitudes will change over time. I certainly don't feel nervous walking around here in my kippah. The only thing I've noticed is that when we celebrate the holiday of Purim and have music outside, the Muslim kids passing by on Parsons will sometimes stop and dance to the music. I look forward to the day when things will improve in the world and we'll able to interact more with our Muslim neighbors." Despite the fact that differing groups at odds with each other often use the city as a testing ground for relationships, there are limits for some. Plus, worldwide events can have an impact on how far people are willing to go.

To many people, the hundreds, if not thousands of low-rise, red-brick garden apartments, a good number of which can be found in this general area, are seen as adequate, even nice, but perhaps short of the ideal American dream. But "American dream" is a relative term depending on one's financial and personal circumstances. To the many immigrant groups who reside in this section of Hillcrest this is indeed what these dwellings are, the fulfillment of a dream—to live in freedom and safety, to reach for the opportunities that America offers, which were absent in their lands of origin—Haiti, Mexico, the Dominican Republic, Bangladesh, Yemen. Moreover, these apartments are interspersed with blocks that contain older, modest private homes, and, in many instances, immigrants are living there too. Previous generations of European immigrants traversed the same path and also appreciated where they ended up when compared to their own modest beginnings. This is what Queens means to so many of its inhabitants. And Flushing epitomizes it.

From here I continue north on Parsons Avenue to Sixty-Fifth Avenue, where I turn right and make my way to an unknown but very important Queens landmark, Fillmore's Tavern, at 166-02, at the corner of Sixty-Fifth and 166th Street. It looks like a dive bar and has a rich history. It was constructed as a tavern way back in 1912, and it's still here, not only functioning, but flourishing. It survived the Prohibition years by posing as a grocery store, though many knew better. Progress came slowly to Fillmore's, but in 1968 women were finally allowed to sit at the bar.

It's a favorite of the locals, who are regulars here. Those gathered are a racially diverse bunch, with the banter among the patrons relaxed, very friendly, and quite boisterous, all of it managed by a cool bartender. The fare's good and not too expensive. The tables and booth benches are wooden, and the pressed-copper ceiling is gorgeous. The walls have wooden wainscoting, with white plaster above them. There are photos of sports teams and their adoring fans. Augmenting this are seven TVs, all showing different sports events.

On the night that I was there, the noise was really loud as a group of first-year law students from St. John's University, located on Union Turnpike, celebrated the beginning of their academic journey. But at 9:00 p.m., most of them departed as a talented mellow band, called Double Dose, featuring two guys on guitars, began playing. They had their own fan club, plus the regulars to cheer them on. It was billed as a tribute to the band known as Hot Tuna. Steve Scianoblo and Daniel Laudman have been at this for a long time, and Steve lives nearby. They clearly love what they're doing. Steve's neighbor was in attendance that evening and said to me, "I've lived here for nine years, and I had no idea there was such a place until tonight."

Queens College is about a half mile away from here, located on Kissena Boulevard, just south of the LIE. I reach it by walking west along Sixty-Fifth Avenue to Kissena, cross the street, and enter the college. As befits its Queens location, it is home to students from over 150 countries and is considered an excellent school and one of the most affordable institutions in the nation. For many immigrants and their children, gaining admission and graduating from there is considered a real accomplishment. Many of its graduates have achieved prominence, even fame, albeit in different areas. They include the comedian Jerry Seinfeld and the singer Paul Simon, both world renowned. There's also Andrew Goodman, who went to Mississippi as part of the black movement of the 1960s, along with James Chaney and Michael Schwerner. All were brutally murdered by the Ku Klux Klan.

The cultural offerings in Queens are perhaps not as well known as some of the other boroughs, and one venue worth visiting is the Queens Theatre, located in Flushing Meadow Park on the site of the 1939 World's Fair. It offers first-class performances, including the renowned Paul Taylor Dance Company, whose performance I attended one Sunday afternoon. A student of the legendary Martha Graham, Taylor has also presented many works at Lincoln Center. Tickets are about half the cost compared to Manhattan, and all the seats are excellent in this comfortable, intimate theater. While some may argue that the offerings are not at the Manhattan level, they're good enough to give people who can't or don't want to travel far the sense that they are still part of that New York City scene that so many people want to experience.

Flushing Meadows Corona Park is Queens's largest park, its answer to Central and Prospect Parks. Portions of the exhibits at the two World's Fairs that were held here in 1939 and 1964 remain for all to see and either reminisce about or simply appreciate. The New York State Pavilion, now closed, still stands. It was built for the 1964 World's Fair. The large terrazzo floor featured a map of New York State, and there were three tall observation towers. Today it's home to the Queens Museum of Art, which includes memorabilia and exhibitions from the fairs. The park has a zoo, a large swimming pool, an enchanting botanical garden, a really cool science museum, and many sports fields. The science museum, known as the New

York Hall of Science, is the city's only hands-on science museum and has over 450 interactive exhibits.

Other parks in this area include Kissena Park, along 164th Street and Booth Memorial Avenue, which has many exotic trees, a nice golf course, and a cycling track; and Bowne Park. The latter is a hidden gem tucked away in northern Flushing, bounded by 155th and 159th Streets and by Twenty-Ninth and Thirty-Second Avenues. One of my favorite activities in the fall is to sit on a bench by the lovely pond and gaze at the mirror image of the weeping willow trees as the geese and ducks float by on the shimmering waters. A piece of heaven in the metropolis!

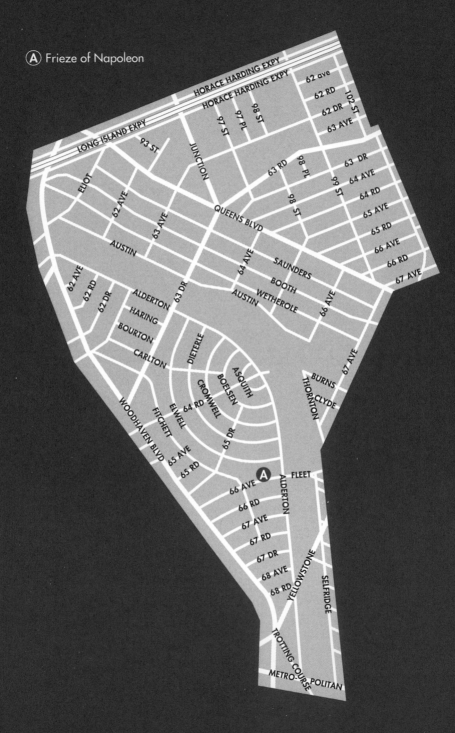

Ⓐ Frieze of Napoleon

REGO PARK

REGO PARK, A SMALL COMMUNITY IN WEST-CENTRAL QUEENS acquired its name from the Real Good Construction Company, which developed the area in the 1920s. The general boundaries are the Long Island Expressway on the north; 102nd Street, Sixty-Seventh Avenue, and Selfridge Street on the east; a sliver of Metropolitan Avenue on the south; and Woodhaven Boulevard on the west. With the expansion of Queens Boulevard and new subway lines, the area drew thousands of new residents by the 1940s, many of them Irish, Italian, Jewish, and German. Besides the red-brick buildings that predominate in Rego Park, there are many smaller homes of various types. These are largely concentrated in the area west of 63rd Drive until Woodhaven Boulevard. Sixty-Third and Sixty-Second Avenues contain many charming attached, Tudor-style homes made of brick. On the whole, they've been well maintained and are definitely worth a leisurely stroll.

The main commercial thoroughfares are 63rd Drive, Queens Boulevard, and Woodhaven Boulevard. Ethnically, the community is heavily Russian with a largely Jewish population hailing from central Russia, especially Bukhara, and from the Moscow and Kiev areas. It also continues to attract South and East Asians, and Hispanics. This is reflected in the many stores that cater to this population. In addition, there's a large shopping mall called the Rego Center that can be accessed from Junction Boulevard and surrounding streets. The area is quite safe and has a busy nightlife, with many restaurants and nightclubs that remain open late, especially on weekends.

I begin my exploration of this community at Sixty-Eighth Avenue and Woodhaven Boulevard. The blocks off Woodhaven— Sixty-Eighth to Sixty-Sixth Avenues—consist of rows of exquisite Tudor-style homes, small colonials, capes, and ranches. It's extremely quiet, even at 5:30 p.m. on a Thursday afternoon, but then again, it's a hot and humid July day with temperatures well into the nineties. As I look at homes like these for the umpteenth time, I take note of the different ways their appearance reveals the priorities and, sometimes, values of their owners.

Some manage to fill up every inch of space in their tiny front yards with shrubs, flowers, and tiny trees, all of it carefully landscaped to achieve the maximum visual effect. As I recall much larger plots of land with only manicured grass, along with perhaps a small section of tended flora, I wonder if, the smaller the plot, the greater the need to fill it to the max, to demonstrate its value. Take 85-60 66th Road, on the corner of Fitchett Street, which has a noteworthy garden of small, blue spruce bushes, hydrangeas, and coleus, much of it sculpted in various shapes. Did the owner do it for those living in the home or for others to appreciate, or both? Nearby, another yard has giant sunflowers standing tall over a small vegetable garden. A third home owner has filled the front yard with small white stones and two potted plants but has also placed small, in some instances, tiny, stone figurines. These include a cupid seated inside a seashell. Next to it are three colorfully painted gnomes and a chicken. The creator of this vignette clearly thought these statuettes were more important or aesthetically pleasing than greenery, what Mother Nature has to offer.

Given the monochromatic colors of those homes here—brown, reddish, and grayish—it's refreshing to see something different—a bright-yellow stucco, bordered by orange lines; a blue door, which captures my attention. Then there's a plain brick colonial at 65-79 Fitchett in which the most outstanding aspect is a giant, two-story glass picture window, which takes up most of the front wall. As the sun hits the glass, making it impossible to see inside, I realize this is done for the owner's benefit, whose priority is bright light and a nice view. Indeed, I've always been struck by how some home owners conceal their windows from passersby with drawn shades or curtains, and how others welcome the natural light and love to display for all what's inside their living and dining rooms. By contrast, the ranch home next to this house has small windows and a manicured garden.

The terra-cotta bas-relief of Napoleon at 85-63 Sixty-Sixth Avenue.

Around the corner, on Sixty-Sixth Avenue, between Fitchett and Alderton Streets, I come across a two-story brick structure, at 85-63, a rather nondescript home except for one outstanding feature. Beneath the raised home, there's a garage, to the left of which is a six-foot-by-six-foot terra-cotta bas-relief of a man riding a galloping steed. He's dressed in battlefield clothing and what's called a bicorn or Napoleon hat. This is a two-cornered hat with a wide brim, with the front and back halves turned up. It was popular in the late eighteenth century, and while it is most commonly associated with Napoleon Bonaparte, it was worn by most senior military officers during this period. In case there's any doubt about this artwork's meaning, BONAPARTE appears on the bottom in block letters. Why would anyone do this? Were they simply admirers of Napoleon? As I'm pondering this, a man wearing a yarmulke emerges from the house, locks the door, and heads toward his small, black SUV.

"Excuse me, can you tell me why there's a statue of Napoleon on the wall?" I ask.

"I have no idea. We just bought the house from someone else, also a Bukharian Jew, like us. But I never asked him why. It just looked nice to me."

"How many rooms does the house have?"

"Well, it's hard to say because the space on the first floor is my office. I'm an accountant. And a lawyer is on the second floor." I would never have guessed the building contained offices and wasn't even a residence.

From here I head left up Alderton to a series of streets shaped like a crescent, each several blocks along—Ellwell, Dieterle, Cromwell, and Boelsen Crescent. Indeed, this section with the curving streets is known locally as "The Crescents." They are fairly typical of what I've been seeing until now. Most of the dwellings are detached, and they're on the small side, but perfectly presentable. At the end of Elwell, I turn left onto Carleton and then hang an immediate right onto 63rd Drive, one of the main shopping streets in the area. It has the usual assortment of stores, many with Russian signage.

Coming to Queens Boulevard, I turn right, and at 96-40 on Queens Boulevard I come across the venerable Ben's Best, a kosher gourmet delicatessen. Inside, it's spotless, with simple, hardbacked, yet comfortable chairs and a chance to appreciate history by looking at all the photos of early and mid-twentieth-century Queens—the streets themselves, communal institutions, and the like. Founded by Ben Parker, it's been in existence in Rego Park since 1945, serving up award-winning dark-red, spicy pastrami, and traditional chicken soup, which is believed by many to have special restorative powers. A survey by Ben's found that 104 out of 110 grandmothers believe that for colds and other minor ailments, chicken soup beats anything sold over the counter. It would be interesting to compare it with a study by pharmacists. There's certainly a showman's instinct at play here. Mickey is a counterman who's worked there for thirty-four years, and I ask him why Ben's is still around when so many others have closed.

"It's very simple," he says. "This is a hands-on place, a family-owned business. We insist on quality. I'm not interested in the cost, just quality. If I don't like the way the meat looks, I reject it. We check every piece. The other thing is, we hire people by their personality, not so much by how they work. If they don't have a good personality they can't work here. I can always teach you how to work, but I can't change the type of person you are."

"You've got lots of Bukharian Jews in Rego Park. Do they eat here?

"No. They only eat in their own restaurants. It's got nothing to do with being kosher. They'll pay $6 more for a prescription in one of their own pharmacies when they could get it much cheaper in a Rite-Aid. You know who we get a lot of? Black Muslims. They come here because it's kosher, and they love our pastrami."

Mickey has loyal customers, and, in the end, that's what counts. It gives those who run the deli the feeling that their way of life is still alive and kicking and that they can enjoy the food they grew up with even if only a few places like this remain. And if young people and those from different cultural backgrounds come in, it's a verification that what they have is desirable to others. Alas, Ben's Best has been closed (over lease issues, I'm told) since 2018, but it's important for readers to learn about this piece of American culinary history. Such restaurants are of a type that people recognize, namely the old-style kosher deli. There are other such delis in Queens, such as Buddy's Deli in Bayside on Seventy-Third Avenue, and Ben's Deli (no relation to the above-discussed Ben's Best; Ben's Deli is part of a chain but still authentic), located in the shopping center on Bell Boulevard, in the Bay Terrace neighborhood of Bayside.[19]

A Iglesia Ni Cristo Church
B Site of notorious murder
C Walking tour of Forest Hills Gardens
D Eddie's Sweet Shop

LONG ISLAND EXPWY

62 AVE
YELLOWSTONE BLVD
62 RD
63 DR
63 AVE
63 RD
63 DR
64 AVE

102 ST

64 RD
65 AVE
65 RD

108 ST
110 ST

66 AVE
66 RD
67 AVE
67 RD
67 DR
68 AVE
68 RD
68 DR
69 AVE
69 RD
JEWEL
70 AVE
70 RD
71 AVE

GRAND CENTRAL PKWY

112 ST
PARKSIDE

67 AVE
67 RD
BOOTH
67 DR
AUSTIN

THORNTON

YELLOWSTONE
BURNS
CLYDE
DARTMOUTH
EXETER
FLEET
GROTON
HARROW
INGRAM

SELFRIDGE

JUNO
KESSEL
LOUBET
MANSE
NANSEN
OLCOTT

QUEENS BLVD

71 RD
72 AVE
72 RD
72 DR

73 AVE
75 AVE

75 RD
76 AVE
76 RD
76 DR
77 AVE
77 RD

113 PL
113 ST
78 AVE

AUSTIN

HERRICK AVE
TENNIS

GREENWAY TERR
OLIVE PL

Forest Hills Gardens

BEECHKNOLL
WINTER
PURITAN
GREENWAY N
GREENWAY S
BURNS

69 AVE
70 AVE

CONTINENTAL AVE
72 AVE

WHITSON
ASCAN
74 AVE
75 AVE
75 RD

WOODHAVEN BLVD

69 AVE
69 RD
70 AVE
70 RD
70 DR
SYBILLA
METROPOLITAN AVE
71 DR
71 RD
72 AVE
72 RD
72 DR

UNION TPKE
JACKIE ROBINSON PKWY

FOREST HILLS

THE GENERAL BOUNDARIES OF FOREST HILLS are the Long Island Expressway on the north; the Grand Central Parkway on the east; Union Turnpike on the south; and Woodhaven Boulevard, Selfridge Street, Sixty-Seventh Avenue, and 102nd Street on the west. Until the twentieth century, the area that became Forest Hills was dotted with farms. Then the Cord Meyer Development Company built single-family homes on the north side of Queens Boulevard, generally from 108th Street to the Grand Central Parkway and from 72nd to 67th Roads. It also sold a sizeable parcel of land south of Queens Boulevard to the Russell Sage Foundation, which established a neighborhood called Forest Hills Gardens, along the lines of the urban theorist Sir Ebenezer Howard's vision. With its cobbled streets, night lamps, and curved lanes, it was similar to what were called England's "garden cities" early in the twentieth century. The idea was to create in Queens a tranquil residential neighborhood within an urban area and near to industry and commerce, one that also included several large apartment complexes and Tudor-style garden apartment buildings. It has not only survived but flourished and is one of the premier neighborhoods in the city. The Gardens was also home to the US Open until 1977, at the West Side Tennis Club, which still exists. There was discrimination against Jews, Italians, blacks, and others that didn't fit the mold, so to speak, in the Gardens in the past, but that largely disappeared in the late 1970s, and today anyone who can afford it is welcome.

The section of Forest Hills from Harrow Street east to Union Turnpike also has hundreds of private homes, but these are far more modest than the homes in the Gardens or the area north of Queens Boulevard. Forest Hills has excellent access to subways and express buses, and the Long Island Railroad has a stop here that can get passengers to Manhattan in about fifteen minutes. Forest Hills is a multiethnic community, including a large number of Bukharian Jews, Israelis, Asians, African Americans, Hispanics, South Indians, and many other groups. It's also quite safe and has remained a highly desirable place in which to live since its inception.

Forest Hills has many large and well-maintained apartment buildings along Queens and Yellowstone Boulevards, 108th Street, small portions of 110th and 112th Streets, and the Grand Central Parkway. There are luxury buildings like the Kennedy House on Queens Boulevard and Birchwood Towers on Yellowstone, but most are just solidly middle class. The commercial thoroughfares are Metropolitan Avenue, Queens Boulevard, 108th Street from Sixty-Fifth to Sixty-Third Avenues, Continental Avenue, and Austin Street from Yellowstone Boulevard to Ascan Avenue.

My trip begins on Queens Boulevard and 72nd Road. Here I stroll through the area of private homes from 72nd Road to Sixty-Seventh Avenue on the northern side of Queens Boulevard stretching east to the Grand Central Parkway. It's made up mostly of colonials, Georgians, and Tudors, many of them pretty and also spacious. In the last fifteen years or so the area has become a favorite choice of many Jews from Bukhara, a region in Uzbekistan. Numbering about thirty-five thousand people in Queens, the community has a broad range of socioeconomic categories. There are a good number of working-class Bukharians, predominantly cab drivers, shoemakers, construction laborers, barbers, and the like. Some have also entered the medical professions and dentistry, and others are wealthy businessmen, especially in the real estate and construction industries and in the wholesale diamond and jewelry lines, headquartered on 47th Street in Manhattan between Fifth and Sixth Avenues. Generally, as they have acclimated to America, the community is becoming more upwardly mobile with a declining working class.

Wherever they have settled, namely Queens, especially Forest Hills and Jamaica Estates, the Bukharians have built large homes that often dwarf the neighboring structures. They are frequently

An elaborately designed home in Forest Hills.

seen as over the top by many longtime residents. Stylistically, the homes combine different materials—brick, stone, and terra-cotta. There are Corinthian columns, elaborate wrought-iron gates, capacious balconies, and increasingly, a porte cochere, which is a large porch-like structure in front of a home's main or side entrance to protect visitors from rain or snow. Often in this neighborhood there are arched windows with orange-tile roofs. Sometimes there's even a throne in front of the entrance. In response to neighbors' complaints, Boris Kandov, president of the Bukharian Jewish Congress of the USA said, "Don't be upset with our people because we like to be large. In Queens most of the houses is old. New people build a new city. It's good for community."[20]

The Bukharians don't care much about front lawns, calling them a "useless land" that requires mowing and hence, "a waste of time." They tend to have large families and want as much indoor space as possible. Also, the house is for them very much a status symbol. One non-Bukharian resident said to me, "I think they're very nice, but others think they're garish, even hideous. They have told me that for them the house is a way of saying: 'I may not be educated, I may not speak English well, but money-wise I made it.'"

A leading rabbi in their community who called for a more modest lifestyle found his message not resonating with the people. "I tell them all the time that our ancestors taught us about being humble. They say: 'Rabbi, this is our home for entertainment, it's our fortress. Now we work, . . . and this is our understanding of America.'"[21]

One of the most intriguing religious groups in the city is the Filipino community who belong to Iglesia Ni Cristo, and a number of them also reside in Forest Hills. Founded in the Philippines, in 1916, by the charismatic leader by Felix Manalo, it's a worldwide Protestant Evangelical movement with millions of members. There are about five thousand branches in the Philippines and hundreds more around the world. About 80 percent of those residing in the Philippines are Catholics. In the United States the Iglesia Ni Cristo churches can be found in all major cities where Filipinos live. New York City has at least one branch in every borough, with Queens having two.

The one in Forest Hills, located between 70th Road and Seventieth Avenue, is the largest in the northeastern United States. It's a truly imposing edifice, ivory colored with two tall, pencil-thin, graceful spires, one on each side of the building, rising high into the sky, with an unusual-looking aqua roof. The inside has a coffered ceiling, with two round crystal chandeliers, and warm-toned wooden pews. I attended services there one Sunday at 11:00 a.m. The service was in English, and men and women sat separately to ensure that services would be seen as "serious." One minister with whom I spoke about this practice answered my question as follows: "Because it's forbidden according to the biblical scriptures, and distracting, to have mixed seating."

Walking down 112th Street to 68th Drive, I turn left. In three blocks, I come to the Arthur Katzman Playground, part of the Yellowstone Municipal Park and situated between 68th Road and Sixty-Eighth Avenue; the entrance is on Yellowstone Boulevard. Small children splash around and enjoy the sprinklers on a hot July day. It's a peaceful, almost idyllic scene. The upper part of the park has benches for adults, and I spot two women lying in the grass and sunbathing. If I didn't know better, I would think of this as merely a lovely place, where one can retreat from urban life and its potential dangers. But even the passage of time does not dull the feeling of horror I had when I read the article in the *New York Times* of February 8, 2008, about how a thirty-four-year-old Bukharian dentist, Dr. Daniel Malakov, was gunned down here in cold blood. The murder reverberated through Forest Hills in ways that would deeply scar it. His estranged thirty-five-year-old wife, Dr. Mazoltuv Borukhova, a physician who was also a member of the Bukharian community, hired a cousin, Mikhail Mallayev, to assassinate him.

I ask people sitting in the park if they know what happened here. One or two do; the others have no knowledge of it. There's no memorial plaque for Malakov. Then again, how could one do it in a playground where small children frolic and enjoy life? Would parents want to bring their children to a place that was the scene of such carnage? Isn't the location a coincidence in a sense, a choice made by the killers? Why make people think about this gruesome murder when it is now a place of happiness?

As we see here, a city is made up of layers and layers of history, each occurring in different periods. What is visible often fails to reveal all. To take another case in point, Long Island City was once a rough-and-tumble community filled with nondescript housing and gritty industrial areas. Today, much of it is being replaced by gleaming towers, upscale residences, and fancy restaurants, visually erasing its own path.

I take a long hike back up Queens Boulevard, perhaps a mile and a half, and turn right at Ascan Avenue to tour the beautiful byways of Forest Hills Gardens. One can walk along its small winding streets for hours and see one elegant home after another, most of them Tudors. Here, as I experienced it, is a suggested route with some highlights:

Turning left onto Greenway North I'm struck by the gigantic oak trees that meet at the top, covering the street with a thick canopy of green. On the left at 72 and 82 Greenway I see two pretty, identical, and spacious homes connected to each other. They have nice tiled roofs, and there are glossy tiles along the front of the home in geometric argyle-like patterns. While such a design is common in clothing such as sweaters or socks, seeing them on a home is unusual. On the right-hand corner of Greenway and Puritan Avenue, there's a very large Tudor home with amazing brick patterns and wooden beams, leaded windows and stained glass, along with an imposing turret.

Walking along Greenway South, I go left and soon turn right onto Greenway Circle and then make a left onto Greenway Terrace. Almost immediately I arrive at the village green, one surrounded by stunning Tudor-style apartment buildings. There's a monument here dedicated to those who fell in World War I. Opposite the memorial off to the left there's what appears, at first, to be a flagpole with a giant American flag. I take note of its height, about six stories, and read the inscription, assuming it will be about fallen heroes, but it's not at all about that. Instead, it reads as follows: "This towering spar was the mainmast of the yacht Columbia which defeated the Shamrock I in 1899 and the Shamrock II in 1901 in the America's Cup race." The America's Cup international competition dates all the way back to 1851. It's the oldest international sports trophy, and the next race is scheduled for the summer of 2021. The yacht that holds the title faces a challenger that must meet certain requirements to be eligible. This is the only distinctive commemoration of this event I've ever seen in the city. It reflects the importance that this race had for those who lived here. In that sense, it perfectly sums up the culture and very comfortable lives of those who resided in the Gardens in the early part of the century.

Today's residents are much more diverse—Jews, Asians, Italians, though, white mainline Protestants still live here as well. For most, I don't think this monument would be a priority. Yet it was so for one of its most famous, or infamous residents, none other than Anthony Wiener. Then-representative Wiener recognized, in a speech to Congress on October 1, 2009, the rededication of the flagpole, remembering the *Columbia*. He noted that the *Columbia* was launched in 1899 by J. P. Morgan for the New York Yacht Club and was the first sloop to win the cup consecutively. Wiener and his wife, Huma Abedin, who are now separated, no longer live in the Gardens, having sold their Ascan Avenue apartment in 2011.

One food joint worth seeing is Eddie's Sweet Shop. I get there by heading south on Seventy-Second Avenue a block away, off Greenway. At Metropolitan Avenue, I turn left, and in a block I'm there, at number 105-29. It's a truly special place. The first thing I notice as I approach is the old original-looking Coke sign above the store. It's mobbed inside. I see gumballs, taffy candy, pixie sticks, sugar babies, jellybeans, some in large glass containers with shiny metal covers, an old white scale, with incomprehensible numbers, that weighs your selections. I wonder if anything here unites the old and the new, and then I see it. Inside an ancient-looking telephone booth, resting on the seat, is a fully functioning ATM machine. It seems to have just been dropped there, not intentionally juxtaposed for effect, because it's hidden away in a back corner.

It's the absolutely quintessential old-style soda fountain emporium, serving up giant sundaes. I walk in and spin around one of the small wooden stools and feel myself going back in time. Looking at the old brands of candies, and watching the kids enjoying themselves with their parents in the booths at 9:45 p.m. on a hot, muggy Tuesday night in July brings back those days in ways that I long ago stopped thinking about—the sounds of happy kids, the easy banter between the soda jerks—yes, that's what they were called—a very long marble counter, the penny tiles, the ceiling made of pressed tin, plus the knowledge that Eddie's has been in existence since 1909, the year my father was born. Eddie's has been there so long that one can't say it reflects what the locals want. But what does speak volumes is how crowded it is night after night, year after year. The magic is clearly still very much there.

Ⓐ Lander College for Men
Ⓑ Meadow Lake (site of the dragon boat races)
Ⓒ Paul Simon's childhood home
Ⓓ Art Garfunkel's childhood home

KEW GARDENS HILLS

THE GENERAL BOUNDARIES OF KEW GARDENS HILLS are Gravett Road
and Melbourne Avenue on the north, Kissena and Parsons Boulevards on the east, Union Turnpike on the south, and Grand Central Parkway on the west. The early history of Kew Gardens Hills
follows the usual patterns of Dutch, British, and American settlement through successive periods that began in the 1600s. As late as
the early twentieth century, the area was called Queens Valley, and
that name still exists in odd ways. For example, there's a synagogue
known as the Young Israel of Queens Valley. By the 1920s most
of the farms had been bought by country clubs looking for space
in which to build golf courses. Until the 1950s, most of the residents were Irish, Italian, and German, with some Jews, who mostly
identified with the Conservative movement. In the 1950s Modern
Orthodox Jews began to move in, and over time they became the
predominant group. By the 1980s the area came to be dominated by
the more rigorously observant Jews, sometimes known as "Strictly
Orthodox," or "Haredi," and today this is the predominant group.
But there have been some new additions, like Bukharian Jews who
have immigrated to Queens from Russia. Because of overcrowding
in adjacent Flushing, Chinese and Koreans have begun moving in,
and to the east, along Kissena Boulevard, Afghanis, Pakistanis, and
Sikhs have also arrived.

Residentially, Kew Gardens Hills is a mix of two-family semi-
attached and attached homes, and detached upscale homes, which
predominate between 141st and 136th Streets, an area known as
"Charm Circle." There are also garden apartments and three-to-
six-story, usually red-brick buildings, most of which were built after
World War II. These are concentrated on both sides of Jewel Avenue
between Main Street and Park Drive East and on both sides of
Seventy-Third Avenue between Main Street, east to Kissena and

Parsons Boulevards. The main commercial thoroughfares are Main Street, Kissena and Parsons, and Union Turnpike. There are small parks and playgrounds in various parts of the community, but the big one is Flushing Meadows Corona Park, with its marinas, lakes, hiking trails, and the usual sports facilities.

To appreciate how overwhelmingly Jewish and Orthodox this community is one need only take a walk along its main commercial thoroughfare, Main Street. As a group, these Orthodox Jews are more rigorous in their observance than the Modern Orthodox who predominate in Fresh Meadows and Jamaica Estates, with many of the men wearing black hats and women covering their hair. Virtually every store that isn't neutral by nature—dry cleaning, pharmacy, flower shop, and the like—is designed to serve this population. Most of them sell kosher food in one form or another, and there are toy stores selling toys with Jewish themes or characters, wig shops for women who cover their hair for religious reasons, and Jewish bookstores. Beginning with the intersection of Sixty-Eighth Avenue and Main, there's Seasons, a large all-purpose supermarket chain along the lines of a Stop and Shop. It carries everything a regular supermarket does, but all its meat, dairy, and other food products are kosher.

Kew Gardens Hills has dozens of fast-food kosher eateries—pizza shops, hamburger and French fry joints, eateries, and the like. This is due, in part, to the fact that it's a community with many children and one where both parents must work to support them. In a nutshell, there isn't enough time to cook meals at home, nor enough money for expensive restaurants. Added to that, there's the fact that Jewish culture is often centered around food. This is reflected in the many holidays and festivals that are anchored around meals that give people a chance to sit and talk and just be together. And it's particularly true among Orthodox Jews, for whom the Sabbath, with its Friday night and daytime Sabbath meals, occurs every single week of the year.[22] Also, Jews are no different than other groups, like Hispanics, blacks, Italians, and Chinese, with a history of poverty and persecution for whom abundance of food is seen as both an achievement and an expression of love and closeness within the group.

Turning left onto Seventy-Fifth Avenue I walk two blocks to 150th Street. Turning right I stand in front of Touro College's Lander College for Men, located at 75-31. It is one branch of a far-flung network of thirty schools in several countries. It deserves mention because it's a small, not especially well-known institution and because so many of its students epitomize the can-do spirit of New York City's residents. It's not exactly a tree-lined campus, consisting, in the main, of functional buildings, many of them small, scattered throughout the city. It was founded in 1970 as a school with an emphasis on Jewish education but quickly grew to encompass other fields. Today, it has law and medical schools, and nursing, social work, and pharmacy programs, and many more divisions. It stands out because it offers its eighteen thousand students, many of whom work full time and live in the poorer communities of the city, a chance to get a bona fide degree. They have a well-deserved reputation for giving a chance to students who didn't do well initially in college, because the school's entrance requirements are not as stringent as those of many other schools.

Heading south on 150th Street, I turn left onto Jewel Avenue. I walk about a mile past blocks of garden apartments to Flushing Meadows Park. My destination is Meadow Lake, where aficionados race dragon boats. I go about half a mile down Jewel Avenue, crossing the Van Wyck Expressway, and continue until about 100 yards before the Grand Central Parkway entrance heading west, turning right and onto a concrete walkway that leads eventually to the Meadow Lake Boathouse, where the races begin. The route's a bit tricky, but there are usually people in this area who know where the boathouse is. This watersport dates back to ancient times in southern China, where people from villages raced against each other. Originally, it was part of the religion and local folkways, but today it's basically a sport. There is, however, a carved dragon head in the front of these boats, which are generally made from carbon fiber and have a tail with yellow scales.

To learn more about this activity, I speak with Karyn Czapnik, a young woman living in Queens, who is an avid participant in the sport. A mechanical engineer by profession, she spends many hours practicing in the park with her friends for the racing season, a high point of which is the festival that takes place in August in Meadow Lake. There are similar festivals held in other parts of the United States and in other countries. I ask Karyn to describe what she does.

"I'm one of the paddlers," she tells me. "It's paddling, like a canoe, not rowing, and I practice for many hours with my friends. Actually, I was born in the Chinese Year of the Dragon."

"Did that play a role in your decision to get involved with this?"

"Who knows? Maybe," she answers, laughing softly. "There's a lot of diversity among the people who go into the sport nationwide and worldwide."

"So how does it work?"

"Usually about six boats compete in a race. There are races of different lengths. There are twenty paddlers, ten on each side, with a drummer who sits in the front facing the back and who determines the cadence. It's not as easy as it looks. You have to learn how hard to paddle, how fast, and how to coordinate with others. We have team names and colors, with mine being black and green. There are cash prizes and trophies for the winners."

"What do you like most about doing this?"

"The feeling of community. As a result, I've met lots of nice people. I met my boyfriend doing this. I also like individual sports, and this is individual, though it's also a team sport. And it's a great way to be in shape. Rain and fog won't stop us, but lightning will. There are hundreds of people who come and enjoy the races, along with lots of food vendors."

Karyn leaves for her practice session and invites me to watch from the shore as she paddles. I do, and it's very poetic, almost musical, to see the synchronized paddlers gliding across the clear blue water. There are all sorts of sports that people play in the city, but this is one of the most unusual and least known.

I save for the end of my walk what I consider the best part—the homes and school of Paul Simon and Art Garfunkel. This is perhaps Kew Gardens Hills' greatest claim to fame. Both Simon and Garfunkel grew up here. Retracing my steps, I walk back up Jewel Avenue to 136th Street, where I turn right, and soon make a left onto 70th Road, where I come to Simon's childhood home at 137-62. It's a modest red-brick rowhouse on a street of many identical attached homes. One wouldn't give it more than a passing glance, and a 1975 photo of the structure reveals it has hardly changed since then.

Today, the block's residents are almost all Orthodox Jews. In Simon's days, the 1950s, the Orthodox population was small, merely a foretaste of what was to come. I continue along 70th Road and go right on 141st Street, making another right onto Seventy-Second Avenue. Art Garfunkel's home is on the left at 136-58 on another overwhelmingly Orthodox block. It's somewhat nicer, at least today, than Simon's, and it's semi-attached, made of red brick. The two met at the age of eleven when they were classmates in the sixth grade at P.S. 164. To get there I turn around on Seventy-Second and soon make a right at 137th, continuing to Seventy-Seventh Avenue, where the school, a still-lovely building, also known as the Queens Valley School, stands. Among the many millions who love their music, this chance meeting was a coincidence with enormous implications. To walk these streets and think about how many times *they* walked them, visiting each other's homes and going to school together, is to take a truly meaningful stroll through musical history.

The childhood homes of Paul Simon (top) and Art Garfunkel (bottom).

KEW GARDENS

BRIARWOOD & JAMAICA HILLS

JAMAICA ESTATES

HOLLISWOOD

FRESH MEADOWS

HOLLIS HILLS

(A) Home of Nobel Prize winner Ralph Bunche

(B) Shaar HaTorah Yeshiva of Grodno

(C) Shaare Tova Persian Synagogue

(D) Site of notorious Kitty Genovese murder

KEW GARDENS

IN AN UNUSUAL TWIST, the history of this charming community was initiated because of the establishment of the nonsectarian Maple Grove Cemetery in 1875, located between Queens Boulevard and Kew Gardens Road. As a result, the Long Island Railroad (LIRR) built a station nearby, and this in turn attracted people to Kew Gardens, so named after the Royal Botanical Gardens in Kew, England, an elegant London suburb. By 1915, private homes, many of them Tudors, as well as six-story and higher apartment buildings, were under construction. The extension of the MTA subway line in 1936 farther east to Kew Gardens, which meant that people could travel from here to Manhattan and elsewhere in the city for a nickel, greatly contributed to the community's rapid growth after that.

Shaped like a triangle, Kew Gardens' general boundaries are Union Turnpike on the north; Queens Boulevard on the east; Eighty-Seventh, Eighty-Fifth, and Eightieth Avenue on the south; and Forest Park Drive on the west. Its main commercial streets are Lefferts and Queens Boulevards and Metropolitan Avenue. The Queens Borough Hall and the Queens Criminal Courts can be found on Queens Boulevard.

Ethnically, the community is quite diverse. Until the late 1950s Kew Gardens was a pretty homogeneous white area. Included in this group were a number of German Jewish refugees who moved in after the Holocaust and whose stories are well told in a book, *New Lives*, by the journalist Dorothy Rabinowitz.[23]

Today, many upper-middle-class Orthodox Jews live here, including Bukharians and Persians, though the latter group is dwindling. Recent trends show more and more Asians, especially Chinese and Koreans, as well as some Hispanics and African Americans, moving in. Many employees from the airlines live here too, as JFK and LaGuardia Airports are nearby. In fact, it has been dubbed, affectionately, "Crew Gardens" by the locals. The community is quite safe, and there's a popular indie multiplex theater at 81-05 Lefferts, the Kew Gardens Cinemas. One great attraction is the large Forest Park, on its western border, where many people can and do jog and hike.

My first foray into Kew Gardens begins with a short walk up Grosvenor Road, where I stop to gaze at 115-24, a beige English Tudor-style home, with exquisitely carved designs etched into a very large window, that sits on a small rise set back from the road. For nineteen years, it was home to Ralph Bunche, a UN diplomat and the first African American to win the Nobel Peace Prize. It was given to honor his successful efforts to bring an armistice to the Middle East between the Arab states and Israel. Bunche, who helped found the UN, had lived before in nearby Parkway Village, a sprawling apartment complex for UN employees. He and his wife used the money from the prize to purchase this home in 1952, where he remained until his death in 1971. The house next door, 115-16, is an interesting-looking colonial, with Romanesque windows and a pair of tall white columns flanking the front entrance.

Grosvenor, and the next two streets running parallel to it, Mayfair and Curzon Roads, have some of the most beautiful homes in Kew Gardens. The house at 115-05 Mayfair has a most unusual round slate roof, shaped like a dome, covering a large balcony on the second story. Next door, at 115-19, is a brand-new structure with a brick-faced chimney in a herringbone style. In fact, every home on this block has interesting aspects. Up the block, Forest Park Drive, between Grosvenor and Mayfair, has several large mansions with front lawns of a size rarely seen anywhere in the city. I head back, downhill, where I see, at 83-15 and 83-19 116th Street, splendid examples of the Tudor-style apartment buildings that predominate throughout Kew Gardens. They are two six-story

The former home of Ralph Bunche.

red-brick structures with Tudor decorative elements on the top floor—beige stucco, with dark-brown half-timber designs and several crenelated towers on the roof. Connecting the two buildings in the front is an elegant brick and fieldstone archway with a pointed slate roof and a small brick tower on the left, topped by a slate-covered spire. Behind is an inner courtyard with a lush garden.

Leaving this small area, I walk down 116th Street to Eighty-Fourth Avenue and go left one block to 117-06, home to the Shaar HaTorah Yeshiva of Grodno, a Jewish, boys-only high school and advanced rabbinical academy, one of many in New York City, which has the largest number of such schools in the country. I decide to speak with Yaakov, a full-time student in the seminary program who's hanging out on the street in front of a building that's on 117th Street, catty-cornered from the school. Wearing a dark jacket and white shirt open at the collar, he's tall and thin, bespectacled, with a friendly smile.

He greets me: "Hello, how are you?"

"Fine, thank you. What is this building you're standing in front of?"

"This is the dormitory where the students live. They're mostly from the metropolitan area, but they live here during the week and often stay for the weekend as well."

"How long have you been studying here?"

"About nine years in all. I came here for high school from Flatbush, Brooklyn, where I grew up, and stayed on for the *beis medrash* [advanced rabbinical program]."

"Is it hard to get into this yeshiva?"

"Yes, because it has an excellent reputation. In the last few years maybe one out of six who applied got in. It also helped that my father and some cousins went here, but if I hadn't been a good student, that alone wouldn't have helped." The school or yeshiva is headed by Rabbis Kalman Epstein and Sholom Spitz, prominent

Talmudic scholars, with excellent reputations. Its antecedents go back to the original Shaar HaTorah Yeshiva in Grodno, Poland, headed by Rabbi Shimon Shkop, Epstein's great-grandfather and one of the greatest Torah scholars of the nineteenth and early twentieth centuries.

From here I head one block up Eighty-Fourth Avenue and turn left onto Lefferts Boulevard. In two blocks, I come to Abingdon Road. There are many synagogues in this area, but Shaare Tova, located on the corner, is unique. It was founded by the Mashadi community, one that lived peacefully in the holy Shiite city of Mashad for several hundred years. In 1839, however, a pogrom, marked by anti-Jewish riots and the murder of thirty-five Jews, ended only after the entire community agreed to convert to Islam. Unlike the Marranos of Spain, who were also forced to convert, albeit to Catholicism, and were largely lost to the Jewish people, the Mashadis secretly continued to live as Jews, while pretending to be devout Muslims. They built and prayed in mosques but also worshiped in synagogues, some of which reportedly existed directly beneath their mosques or homes. They betrothed their children at an early age to other Jews, avoiding marriage with Muslims, and they kept their shops open on the Sabbath but did no business there. They purchased nonkosher meat but discarded it, slaughtering their own animals according to Jewish law, in subterranean tunnels and distant fields.

Some of their neighbors were suspicious about the sincerity and extent of their convictions but looked the other way, with some accepting bribes to buy their silence. Rather than losing their identity, the community was actually strengthened by these tribulations, which made them even more determined to remain true to their beliefs. As a result, they were able to live this way for almost one hundred years. Only in 1926, when Shah Reza Pahlavi granted full rights to Iran's minorities, were the Mashadis able to again openly practice their faith.

The Mashadis came to America en masse in the early 1980s after Ayatollah Ruhollah Khomeini took over their homeland during the 1979 Iranian Revolution. Their first area of settlement was Kew Gardens, and this temple, still in existence, was their first major house of worship. But the true origins of the community go all the way back to the 1940s. At that time, several Mashadi businessmen came to the United States to pursue opportunities here. They were joined in the early 1950s by their wives and children. During this period, a large home on Eighty-Third Avenue, owned by Rahmatollah and Mina Hakimi, became the unofficial welcome center for many Mashadi immigrants. It was where they spent Shabbat and other holidays, ate Persian foods, and maintained their customs.

This tradition continued for decades and served as an inspiration to other immigrants, encouraging them to take care of their fellow coreligionists. This example of a tight-knit group highlights how important it is for communities, especially small ones, to stay together, be aware of their history, and maintain family and cultural ties, if they are to survive in a large country with peoples from many different lands. While most of their community has moved to Long Island to live out the suburban American dream, the Mashadis, about six thousand strong, still have a presence in Kew Gardens.[24]

I walk up Lefferts Boulevard, making a left on the Manhattan side of the LIRR station. Here I trip down a flight of stairs and continue along a walkway. Fifty yards farther is the LIRR, and on the street level there's a café and an upholstery shop that, with the worn gray sofa inside and other old furniture, seems frozen in time. On the right is an entrance for a small, two-story brick, Tudor-style apartment building.

What's frozen in time for me and countless other New Yorkers is the story of the brutal Kitty Genovese murder, which took place in 1964 near her little building at 82-70 Austin Street, a few doors to the right of the café. It was in the vestibule that Winston Moseley stabbed her to death as she tried desperately to fend him off. Moseley served fifty-two years in prison before dying in 2016. The city's murder rate was quite high in 1964, when 636 homicides were reported, compared to fewer than three hundred in 2017. Yet this murder stands out because, according to initial reports in the newspapers, thirty-eight people in the building heard her cries for help and did nothing, didn't even phone the police. These reports later turned out to be either exaggerated or untrue. Most people had no idea of what was going on, though two of them were identified as having ignored clear evidence that something terrible was happening. Some thought it was a quarrel with just a lot of screaming, others thought the shouting came from people who were drunk, and still others heard nothing.

Regardless, the crime reinforced the stereotype of callous New Yorkers who ignored a dying person's screams for help and did absolutely nothing about it. It also spurred research into the reasons why this happened. Studies on this phenomenon, known as "the bystander effect," concluded that the greater the number of people who witness an attack, the *less* likely they are to intervene because responsibility for taking action is diffused. Afraid of becoming victims themselves, each one rationalizes that someone else will step forward and intervene. Conversely, and counter to what people assume, the fewer the people, the *more* apt they are to intervene because they feel that if nothing is done, they will have to shoulder the blame for allowing it to happen. For Kew Gardens residents, the event was very disturbing because it happened in their tranquil, upscale community, but the public often needs a specific location, in addition to a specific event, to enhance its understanding of a tragedy like this.[25]

In search of more clarity on this subject, I ask people now working or living in the immediate vicinity what they remember of or know about the murder. Most weren't around then, but one man was, and he sheds new light on this widely known tale. It's the owner of the upholstery store, Bill Corrado. I begin by asking him his views about it.

"I knew Kitty. She had been coming from work, and she was walking past the apartment building on Austin next to the railroad station, called the Mowbray. Moseley attacked her outside the building, and she tried to get away from him to her house, which was along a walkway behind the stores on Austin around the back of Austin. He ran after her, and she went into the little building near her house at 82-62. But he found her and stabbed her to death in the vestibule. So, she never made it to her own place at 82-70. She died in the arms of her friend, Sophie."

"How do you feel about it after all these years?" I ask.

Bill's eyes water up before he begins speaking. "I was disgusted with how the media treated it. They were only interested in the sensationalist parts. The papers focused on how nobody called the cops, and how nobody cared. But it wasn't true. There were people who called the cops. Others had no idea what was happening. It was 3:00 in the morning. People thought it was a domestic dispute, whatever. But that wouldn't make it so interesting to the public."

We are standing outside a grassy area in front of Kitty's old home, and I see a sign. Thinking it's a memorial to her I read it, but it's an announcement that here, in March of 2014, the Trackside Café opened, which completed the "restoration project," funded and supported by the MTA, the LIRR, Community Board Nine, and the Austin Ale House.

I say, "I'm wondering how come there was never a memorial plaque or something put up in her name. That's often done in such situations."

Bill appears momentarily flustered at the question before blurting out, "You know, that's a great question. In all these years I never was asked that, and I never thought about it."

"That's surprising," I say.

"I guess we were just too busy defending ourselves about what happened, about how we've been seen all these years." I nodded, empathetically. It's a normal response to unpleasant experiences, and this is a perfect example of it.[26]

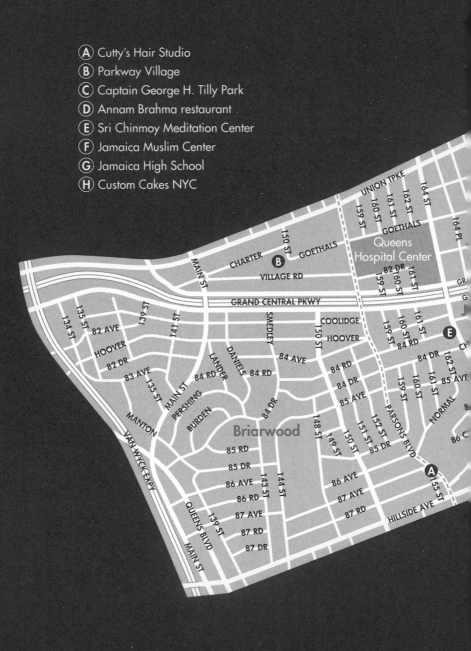

A Cutty's Hair Studio
B Parkway Village
C Captain George H. Tilly Park
D Annam Brahma restaurant .
E Sri Chinmoy Meditation Center
F Jamaica Muslim Center
G Jamaica High School
H Custom Cakes NYC

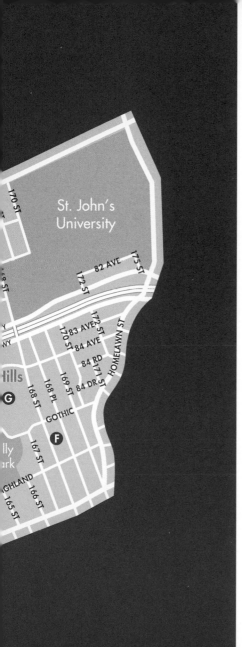

St. John's
University

BRIARWOOD & JAMAICA HILLS

THE WESTERN BORDER OF JAMAICA HILLS, Parsons Boulevard, is also the eastern border of Briarwood, which extends west to the Van Wyck Expressway and Queens Boulevard. As with Jamaica Hills, Hillside Avenue is the southern border of Briarwood, and Union Turnpike the northern boundary. Both areas include followers of the Indian spiritual leader Sri Chinmoy and commercial enterprises established by the group. And Briarwood and Jamaica Hills were developed on empty land in the 1920s. Also, the population of both communities is very diverse and includes Guyanese, South and East Asians, African Americans, Hispanics, Greeks, and Orthodox Jews, many of whom are first-generation Bukharians.

Yet there are one or two differences between Briarwood and Jamaica Hills. In 1947, a huge apartment complex, Parkway Village, was completed in Briarwood, with most of the initial residents UN diplomats. Briarwood also has far more apartment buildings in general, most of them either co-ops or rental units, than does Jamaica Hills. In 1983, following this pattern, Parkway Village became a co-op development.

BRIARWOOD

The primary commercial thoroughfares are Queens and Parsons Boulevards, Hillside Avenue, and Union Turnpike. Subways and buses to the city and elsewhere are within easy reach, adding to the community's popularity, and it has a nice recreational area, namely Hoover Park, about one block from Queens Boulevard. The park is relatively small, about 5 acres, but perfectly adequate, with basketball and handball courts and a playground.

Beginning my walk on Parsons near Eighty-Seventh Avenue, I stop in front of a glass-enclosed porch with lush and large potted plants, followed next door by a barber shop, Cutty's Hair Studio, at 87-14 Parsons. Outside the shop is a tree surrounded on four sides by the familiar stripes that appear on barber poles, only these are made of carved wooden posts, each painted red, white, and blue. I peer inside the salon, and the photos and aquatic tanks look really interesting, so I walk in.

There are chess sets in the sitting area to occupy waiting patrons. There are two bearded dragon lizards inside a tank that looks like a tiny jungle with small rocks on the bottom. The establishment's ceiling is completely covered with road signs—STOP, a yellow street crossing, Interstate 495, some famous subway stops that look authentic. There are photos of Che Guevara and Bob Marley, and uniforms of famous Mets, Yankees, and Knicks players adorn the walls of the shop—Ricky Henderson, John Franco, Anthony Mason, Chris Mullins, Mike Piazza. Next to one uniform I see an old sign from the 1930s, advertising a lotion, called Hall's, that claims to restore a user's hair. There's also a photo of "Ayer's Hair Vigor," with a Venus rising out of a flower, next to a picture of a "Woodie" red roadster, a convertible. There are also old barber tools that I cannot recognize.

Cutty's Hair Studio isn't your typical barber shop!

The shop began attracting celebrities when Fred Avila, who hails from Colombia, began cutting Darryl Strawberry's hair. Fred's obviously a very talented guy, and I'm a bit embarrassed when he casually glances at my fifteen-dollar haircut. There are photos of some of the intricate designs cut into the hair of these players. I think back on my own efforts to get autographs of ballplayers at the stadiums in which they played and the hordes of people who surrounded them. Coming here would have been a much easier way to obtain them!

From here I continue north along Parsons, crossing the Grand Central Parkway and making a left on 82nd Road. At 150th Street, I arrive at Parkway Village, the 35-acre community property that once had hundreds of UN-affiliated residents, but is now a co-op. The green welcome sign in faded gold lettering reads: "A Colonial Village of Distinctive Charm." Unfortunately, I'm surprised to see that the only thing that seems to distinguish these brick, neo-Georgian, two-story residences is how run-down they look. "What a shame," I think, because they have so much potential, with their large grassy areas and lawns that look like they haven't been mowed in ages and which are filled with weeds and scraggly areas of dirt. The paint is peeling off the building entrances, and instead of kids playing outside, no one can be seen on a pleasant weekday afternoon in late May.

A visit to the internet and perusal of the many complaints about the development confirms my impression. Whether it's due to poor management I can't say, but, as a onetime resident of the area many years ago, I do recall how nice it once looked. It was also home to some very prominent leaders in its early days—Betty Friedan, Ralph Bunche, and Roy Wilkins, all of whom were attracted by its openness to people of all nationalities and races. Hopefully, it will be restored one day, surrounded as it is by a thriving community filled with inexpensive but well-maintained residences.

JAMAICA HILLS

Jamaica Hills is also a small community, but one with individuality, and some locations are quite arresting. In the early twentieth century, this was a community for the well-off, who loved the rolling hills and nice views. Today, one can still see some of these homes scattered throughout the area, but most of the housing stock originated with middle-class folks who began coming here in the 1920s once mass transit, namely the Long Island Railroad, became available. By the 1970s it had become one of the most diverse communities in the city, with immigrants from many lands.

The boundaries of Jamaica Hills are Union Turnpike on the north, Homelawn Street on the east, Hillside Avenue on the south, and Parsons Boulevard on the west. The commercial thoroughfares are Parsons Boulevard, Hillside Avenue, 164th Street, and Union Turnpike. There are three high-level public high schools—Jamaica, Hillcrest, and an excellent vocational high school called Thomas A. Edison Vocational and Technical High School, unusual for one small community. Captain George H. Tilly Park is a great place to walk and relax on a bench while watching ducks glide along Goose Pond. My excursion begins in Captain George H. Tilly Park on a fine spring morning, entering on Eighty-Fifth Avenue near 165th

Street. It's a real treasure in the community and almost completely unknown outside of it. The topography is varied, and the landscaping gives one the opportunity to see, from a hill, a well-taken-care-of pond with benches around it. I have a quick lunch and watch a couple of baby ducks following their mother, learning to swim. From there it's on to 165th Street, which features an interesting collection of varied and quaint houses.

Nearby, at 84-43 164th, there's a charming, small Indian vegetarian restaurant, Annam Brahma. The owners are friendly, and the food is reasonably priced and delicious. Inside, lining two of the walls, are hundreds of books, mostly thin paperbacks, most of them penned by Sri Chinmoy, a world-renowned Indian spiritual leader. It feels like I've entered a library, only the books, detailing Chinmoy's philosophy of life, including the unity of all faiths, are for sale. Some of Chinmoy's artworks are displayed here, too, and music he composed is playing in the background. The ceiling consists of mirrored panels, with some potted plants hanging from the ceiling and delicate latticework separating several of the tables to ensure a bit of privacy. There are red tablecloths and artistic drawings, a small library of Chinmoy's writings, and a large photo of Chinmoy, in a flowing blue robe, meditating.

Despite hearing that's it's a private area for the Chinmoy group, I cross the street and walk down a small path. On each side are benches for visitors under cloth coverings to protect people from the rain. At the end on the right is a meditation center with a large photo of Chinmoy beneath a canopy and an exquisitely carved and painted roof, supported by delicate-looking gold and white wooden poles. It's a worthy shrine for this world-famous leader. Another devotee, who graduated from Iona College and who is in charge of some construction taking place here, describes the center and its founder to me.

"Sri Chinmoy, in addition to his spiritual greatness, was also outstanding in sports. He trained with Carl Lewis, the great runner, and used a track here, which was built for his use. He was also a first-rate tennis player. When he was no longer able to play the sport, he turned to weightlifting, where he was also a standout. He was also

A worthy shrine to Sri Chinmoy.

able to pick up baby elephants at the Big Apple Circus, and even a small plane. He lifted weights into his early seventies. His goal was to show that matter and spirit are interrelated part of the oneness of human beings." This is the place to visit for anyone wishing to learn more about Sri Chinmoy, what he stood for, and his legacy in general.

Nearby, at 85-37 168th Street, is the home of the Jamaica Muslim Center. It's one of the first in the city, dating back almost forty-five years. Those who run it are friendly and welcoming. They invite me to attend their prayer services and encourage me to speak with their imam and learn about the Muslim religion. On 168th and Gothic Drive, there's Jamaica High School, founded in 1925, a very imposing-looking school. It's in the traditional style, with large pillars in front of the entrance, high on a hill, overlooking a huge lawn sloping gently toward the street. Among its best-known graduates are director Francis Ford Coppola, science author Stephen Jay Gould, and the noted humorist Art Buchwald.

Walking north on 168th, I come to Custom Cakes NYC, at 80-05 168th Street, just off Union Turnpike. It looks like a pretty small place, a bit cluttered, but in a way that suggests things are happening here. I meet Richard Lee, a retired Metropolitan Transit Authority mechanic, who has been operating this place for the past twelve years together with his wife, Maria. Both hail from the Philippines. Maria is a highly trained baker, who has been making cakes most of her life and has worked under some pretty famous people in the field such as Andrew Beckman, a chef for Martha Stewart, who taught her how to design cakes. I ask Richard, an energetic and voluble gray-haired, bespectacled man with twinkling eyes, if his custom-made cakes are unique in Queens.

"Yes," he says, "in a very important way. Our cakes are made fresh to order. Many bakeries will claim to do that, but they really don't. You'll order a birthday cake; they'll take one that's frozen from the freezer, defrost it, put words you asked for on the cake, and claim it's fresh. You will maybe get sick from it. They'll microwave it and that softens up the cake. You go home, and you say: 'How come that tastes so stale?' Even cheesecake. People think you should refrigerate it, but then it tastes like it's three days old. You should try to eat it fresh." I gaze at a photo of a gigantic multitiered white cake behind the counter and ask how much it cost the customer.

"That's a $2,500 wedding cake. You heard of this place on Bell Boulevard called Elite Pastries? They ordered it for a customer. We deliver all over—Antun's, Crest Hollow Country Club, Leonard's." Richard regales me with stories about his business. One man ordered cakes, paid a lot of money, gave them to friends, and claimed *he* made them. He speaks with enthusiasm, like a man who loves what he's doing, and he does. For many people work is work; for him it's a passion.

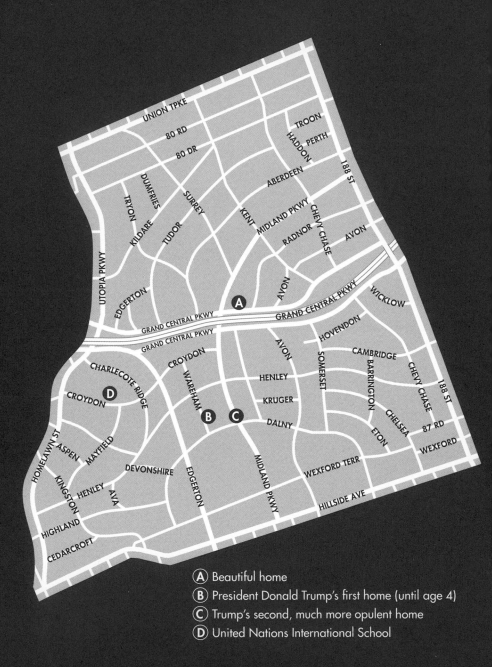

Ⓐ Beautiful home
Ⓑ President Donald Trump's first home (until age 4)
Ⓒ Trump's second, much more opulent home
Ⓓ United Nations International School

JAMAICA ESTATES

THIS IS A SMALL COMMUNITY, yet one that is fascinating and revealing in quite a few ways. It has a long history, metaphorically, in that its developers wanted it to look like the rustic English villages of old with their lush meadows and rolling hills. But its founding goes back only to 1908. It was designed to be an oasis for the wealthy, with winding roads and hills that were not leveled for preordained grids. And when the Grand Central Parkway (GCP) was built, great care was taken in its landscaping to have it blend in with the community. As a reminder of its auspicious beginnings, the place where Midland Parkway begins its journey from Hillside Avenue welcomes the visitor with a stone gatehouse on its grassy mall, dating back to those times.

Today, it's largely an upper-middle-class community, and many of its residents are immigrants or children of immigrants. Of course, it's famous now as the place where President Trump was raised, but there's more to it than that. It has excellent schools, good subway and highway connections to the city, and ample shopping on both Hillside Avenue and Union Turnpike. Its boundaries are Union Turnpike on the north, 188th Street on the east, Hillside Avenue on the south, and Utopia Parkway and Homelawn Street on the west, plus St. John's University, which runs west to 170th Street.

Because they are so beautiful and since some very well-known people, live, or have lived here, the homes are an unusually significant aspect of the area. In addition, many upper-middle-class folks live here in perfect anonymity in gorgeous dwellings. I begin my walk on Midland Parkway. Here, where it intersects with the service road of the Grand Central Parkway, I see, on the northwest corner, at number 181-03, a beautiful stone and stucco home with Roman-style windows. Outdoor lights are turned on in the Christmas season, giving it an ethereal look and feel.

Perhaps the prettiest and most imposing home is on Radnor Road at 182-31, which I reach by walking one block east on the GCP service road and making a left onto Radnor. It sits on a beautifully landscaped lawn with small manicured bushes surrounding a large tree. A Tudor, it has beautiful lines, elaborate stone and brick features, and French windows, and it sports a large circular fountain in the front. Of course, beauty can be a relative term, and one neighbor confides to me that, in her view, while the house is stunning, the fountain "is hideous, so gaudy, especially because they light it up sometimes. It's so ostentatious."

Midland Parkway is, in any case, the Park Avenue of Jamaica Estates, a four-lane road lined with tall overhanging and stately trees, and with a wide grassy median replanted in 2007. If you don't look too carefully, you could almost believe you're in a forest, or at least an urban one. In fact, the developers designed it to have that feel.

I stop in front of President Donald Trump's first home in Jamaica Estates at 85-15 Wareham Place, where he was born and lived in until the age of four, when the family moved to 85-14 Midland Parkway. It's interesting that the two residences have almost identical numbers in the address. Welcome, I presume, to the land of meaningless coincidences. An investor, Michael Davis, purchased the home at auction in December of 2016 for $1.39 million and flipped it in March of 2017, again at auction, for $2.14 million, a very handsome 50 percent profit, taking a page out of Trump's book. After a while it was listed on Airbnb as available for $815 a night. In a very tongue-in-cheek article in the *New York Times*, reporter Andy Newman described the experience of staying there. A brief excerpt reads: "It had been a restless night. I had fallen asleep in the bedroom where, according to a plaque on the wall, 'President Trump was likely conceived.' The place is still a bit shy of five stars. Two of the toilets run unless you jiggle the handles. . . . More troublingly there was no gas, which meant no hot water or stove."[27]

The house was on the market in 2019 for the asking price of 2.9 million. According to two realtors, who requested anonymity, the

Donald Trump's first childhood home.

seller is an unidentified Chinese woman who lives in China. What is known is that Michael X. Tang a Flushing, Queens, lawyer, is representing the seller. The main reason behind the purchase is most likely financial, and, depending on what the future holds, the house is likely to increase in value.

Far more impressive is the stately twenty-three-room Georgian Trump mansion at nearby 85-14 Midland Parkway, a red-brick structure with large white columns. Ironically, the community today is home to many immigrants from all over—China, the Philippines, Israel, India, Pakistan, and Russia. A good number of this last group are Orthodox Bukharian Jews, many of whom supported Trump. But overall, this community can't be compared in any way to the lily-white upper-middle-class population that resided there in the 1950s, when "The Donald" lived there.

Emblematic of Jamaica Estates' diversity is the United Nations International School, which has classes from K through 12, serving hundreds of students of UN employees and is located at 173-53 Croydon Road. There are people of every ethnic background and religion here today, including Muslims, Buddhists, Catholics, Protestants, and Jews. Nearby, St. John's University is an excellent Catholic institution along Union Turnpike, and it has been here for decades, but it welcomes students of all faiths. It may be best known for some of its outstanding men's basketball teams over the years, but it is also highly regarded academically. I speak with Erwin Fried, a businessman and resident of the community, who tells me a most unusual story of outreach to others.

"You see this house here?" he says. "The man is Italian American, and every Christmas he makes a party to which the entire community is invited. It has a large swimming pool and is a really nice house. The whole street is closed off by the police. He brings in two truckloads of snow, and he has it decorated professionally with lights and everything. He sets up grills and serves hot dogs, hamburgers, chicken, and other stuff, and just to show you how considerate he is, there are separate grills just for cooking kosher food for the religious

Jews who live here. He's a great guy who also gives out toys, and expensive ones, to all the kids, anywhere from twenty-five to one hundred dollars. Sometimes he comes out to talk to the people; he's very friendly. Where do you see that? Who's going to know about this great party except the locals? And he's been doing it for the last twenty years."

Along Union Turnpike, I see the usual cavalcade of nail salons, beauty parlors, delis, dry-cleaning establishments, and restaurants, the last with an emphasis on kosher food, both to eat in and to take out. One unusual enterprise, called Glaze-a-riffic, at 180-18, stands out. Here you can learn how to paint and create your own pottery masterpieces. Classes are also offered in canvas painting, glass fusing, glazing, and other art forms. It's a brightly lit, welcoming place. I look at the neatly arranged pottery items as a young, earnest Asian woman explains what is happening at this newly opened business.

"We have classes that mix in traditional art forms with themes like 'outer space,' by making outer-space-related items like space-ships made from cardboard or clay," she tells me. "There are a few, but not many, pottery stores like ours elsewhere in Queens, but we're much roomier and offer lots of material for those who come. If the people make something, we put the clay into the kiln, and it's ready after about ten days." No doubt, a place like this delights young children and their mothers, who love it when such activities are right in their community.

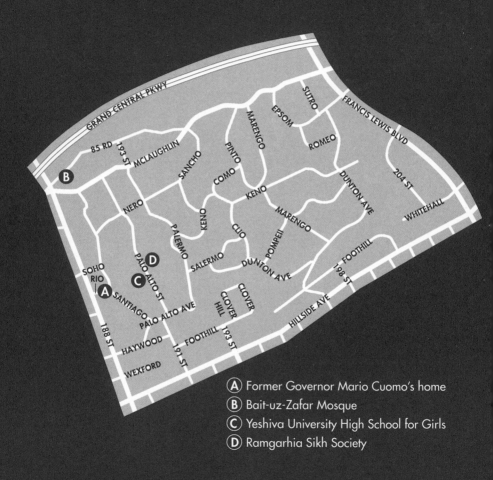

(A) Former Governor Mario Cuomo's home
(B) Bait-uz-Zafar Mosque
(C) Yeshiva University High School for Girls
(D) Ramgarhia Sikh Society

HOLLISWOOD

HOLLISWOOD WAS DEVELOPED in the late nineteenth century by Frederick Dunton. The boundaries of Holliswood are McLaughlin Avenue and 85th Road on the north, Francis Lewis Boulevard on the east, Hillside Avenue on the south, and 188th Street on the west. The minimal shopping available here can be found on Hillside Avenue and Francis Lewis Boulevard, especially where these streets intersect. The winding streets and often charming homes in this postage-stamp-size residential community combine to make it one of the nicest in the city. It has gentle hills, and many of the houses are atop small hills, requiring thirty plus steps to reach the door. Some of the houses are of modest size, most are bigger, and some are very large and even stunning. It's a small area and can be walked in one or two hours. Its population is diverse, encompassing Hispanics, African Americans, Asians, and whites of various backgrounds. Everyone's tastes are different, but most people will find a stroll through Holliswood's leafy environs to be a very pleasant excursion.

Beginning on Palo Alto Avenue just off busy 188th Street, I am immediately transported into a hidden paradise of sorts. It's very quiet, and traffic is minimal, in part because the winding streets make it difficult to use as a shortcut to other communities. As a result, mostly residents use it, which delights the local civic association. I hang a left onto Santiago Street and almost immediately come to Rio Drive. Here, in a Dutch colonial at 188-17, former governor Mario Cuomo lived from the age of seventeen into adulthood. The house across from his, while nice, catches my attention primarily because of a carved expression on a boulder in front of it: "my way villa." How appropriate, I think, for a house at this location![28]

Former Governor Mario Cuomo's family home.

When the Bait-uz-Zafar Mosque opened its doors, local religious leaders came to a dedication and were invited to use the mosque whenever they needed it.

Walking to the end of Santiago, I hang a right onto the south side of McLaughlin Avenue. Immediately across the street is a religious institution with an interesting history, the Bait-uz-Zafar Mosque. In 2008 the group purchased the property from Temple Israel, which merged with another synagogue. It's part of the larger Ahmadiyya Muslim Community, which opposes fanatical Islamic beliefs and is firmly against violence. Its founder, Mirza Ghulam Ahmad, has denounced jihad by the sword and espouses moderation and outreach to other religious communities.

Established in 1889, it has adherents in over two hundred countries and millions of members. When it opened its doors, local religious leaders from the Jewish, Sikh, Christian, and Buddhist communities came to a dedication and were invited to use the mosque whenever they needed it. The mosque has been accepted in the community. This outcome reminds us that there are thousands of positive encounters like this at the grassroots level, which demonstrate the desire for understanding and peace. I peer inside the building and see, in the front lobby, a large American flag and, attached to it, a sign in block capital letters that states: "LOVE FOR ALL. HATRED FOR NONE." How fitting.

I speak with Kenny Wachstock, a resident of Holliswood and father of four. An occupational therapist and an Orthodox Jew, he's very happy about living here. It's not an Orthodox community, but there's a synagogue nearby, the Young Israel of Holliswood on Francis Lewis Boulevard on the border of Queens Village.

"What attracts you most to this community?" I ask.

"To me this is a hidden gem. There's no alternate side of the street parking. Yet I'm still walking distance to the subway, just under a mile. I don't have cars whizzing by, so it feels like suburbia. Also, as an Orthodox Jew it's a one-synagogue town, which is unifying. On the other hand, I have tons of kosher shopping and restaurants nearby on Union Turnpike. It's also about the type of Orthodox synagogue it is. It seems to attract people who are not cookie-cutter types. Some are converts, some are people who became observant as adults and weren't raised that way, and others are from out of town. This made it interesting to us. My wife is also from out of town."

When Kenny first moved here, he lived in one of the very few apartment buildings in Holliswood. Two of his neighbors were a lesbian couple. Because he's a friendly fellow, he made their acquaintance and eventually became friends with them. They also happened not to be Jewish, and it's unusual for the Orthodox to reach out to this extent on a social level. He developed such a close relationship that the couple took care of his kids when Kenny and his wife, Mira, went away on occasion for a weekend. In fact, the couple sometimes took the children with them for minivacations to their own home. One of the women, clearly in jest, but possibly only in half jest, told

Mira with a laugh, "We love your children even more than you do." The degree of trust these people have in each other is quite amazing, considering the cultural differences.

His comments about "suburbia" and being near a subway is something I've heard from many New Yorkers. While there are multitudes of people who revel in being totally urban, in the heart of Manhattan or downtown Brooklyn, there are those who want it both ways. They like to be near the city's amenities and its urban feel, yet they also want to be able to get away from it all. For them places like Holliswood are particularly appealing.

Continuing my walk, I turn right onto Palo Alto Street. I soon come to the Yeshiva University High School for Girls at 86-86. It's been around for decades and has high standards and excellent programs, servicing Modern Orthodox girls in Queens and in Long Island. Many of its students go on to excellent colleges. But before they do so, they are encouraged to study in a religious seminary in Israel for a year after graduation, and most of them do so. In a way, it's seen as a rite of passage by members of the Orthodox community, and boys who study in parallel Orthodox high schools follow the same path. The school's teachers and administrators believe that immersing themselves full time in religious studies will better prepare the students to lead a life centered around religious observance.

Across the street, at number 86-71, is a large home that's actually a small Sikh temple, called Ramgarhia Sikh Gurdwara Sahib. Inside there's a prayer center, called a gurdwara, and a dining area with long rugs for eating vegetarian foods, which are served free of charge to anyone who wants them. Sikhism began over five hundred years ago in the Punjab region of India and was founded by Guru Nanak. He preached equality for all and rejected the caste system of Hinduism. It's a monotheistic religion that believes that there is one god for all religions. It's very progressive in that the sexes receive equal treatment. Sikhism states that men and women are two sides of the same human coin. Both can lead services, and there is no priestly order. Adultery is forbidden as are the consumption of meat, tobacco, alcohol, or drugs and the cutting of one's hair. While peaceful in their orientation they will fight back if attacked and believe in being prepared to do so. They have had violent conflicts with both Hindus and Muslims throughout their history.

Entering the house, I meet Gulzar Singh, the granthi, or caretaker, who maintains this gurdwara and performs the daily services, and his wife, Swaranjit. Gulzar, who sports a luxuriant gray beard and a handlebar mustache, is wearing a long gray robe, and his head is covered with a traditional orange kerchief. His wife is simply dressed, with a soft dark hat perched on her head. Their faces are kind and gentle. They welcome me, and I sense I am in the presence of a serene and very sincere couple. They offer me a seat and bring out some juice and fruits.

"There's a Jewish school across the street. Do you have any contact with them?" I ask.

"No, but we know they are a very good and talented community. They say hello, but we don't see them much because our services are on Sunday and the school is closed on Sunday."

I ask Gulzar if people can join the Sikh religion. He tells me that they are all welcome. In fact, there is a community of converts to Sikhism, popularly known as "Western Sikhs," whose main community is in Espanola, New Mexico. Their origins date back to the 1960s, and today they have provided security services to the US government for many years. As reported in a National Public Radio (NPR) broadcast aired on June 13, 2009, the converts run most of the metal detectors in federal courthouses across the United States, guard many embassies, and work at other federal facilities in Washington, DC. The name of their company is Akal Global. Together with its affiliates, Akal has over a billion dollars in contracts. They aren't recognizable as Sikhs because for security reasons they don't wear turbans at work.

In my conversations with other local residents, I find that little is known about these local Sikhs, not surprising as they are a small group, are recent arrivals, and have adopted a lower public profile than other Sikhs who live in larger communities such as Richmond Hill and Queens Village. Judging from their contacts with their immediate neighbors, the Jewish school across the street, and from the successful adaptation of the larger Sikh community, they are likely to interact more closely with others living here as time goes on and their comfort level with outsiders increases.

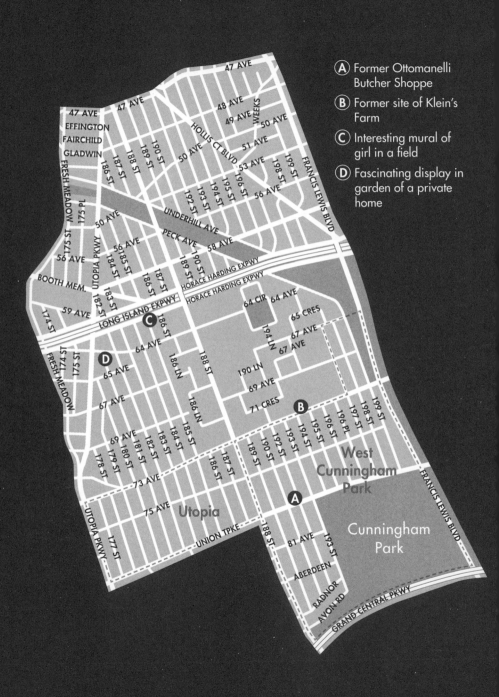

A Former Ottomanelli Butcher Shoppe

B Former site of Klein's Farm

C Interesting mural of girl in a field

D Fascinating display in garden of a private home

FRESH MEADOWS

FRESH MEADOWS OWES ITS NAME to the freshwater streams that flowed through its meadows and farmlands hundreds of years ago. Its boundaries are Forty-Seventh Avenue on the north, Francis Lewis Boulevard on the east, the Grand Central Parkway and Union Turnpike on the south, and Utopia Parkway and Fresh Meadow Lane on the west. The area south of the Long Island Expressway (LIE) consists mostly of detached private homes, and to a lesser but still substantial extent, garden apartments. Several long blocks along Utopia Parkway consist exclusively of two-story, plain-looking, brick attached houses. The Fresh Meadows Housing Development, which runs north along 188th Street from the LIE, is the largest in the community and includes a large shopping center and a multiplex cinema. Built in the post–World War II era on the grounds of what once was the Fresh Meadows Country Club, the development was widely praised by urban experts like Lewis Mumford as a model of urban planning.

The northern side of the LIE down to the Forty-Seventh Avenue border is similarly overwhelmingly residential. The homes, however, while also nice, are generally more modest affairs. The major recreational area is Cunningham Park, which lies partially in neighboring Bayside. A popular indoor/outdoor tennis complex is part of the park, accessible from Union Turnpike, and there are ballfields and wooded areas.

Ethnically, the population is Jewish, Italian, Irish, Korean, Indian, Pakistani, Chinese, black, and Hispanic—a true melting pot. The major commercial streets are Union Turnpike and portions of Francis Lewis Boulevard and the LIE service roads, on both sides of the highway; and sections of Fresh Meadow Lane, 188th Street, and Forty-Seventh Avenue. Union Turnpike, which straddles the border between Fresh Meadows and Jamaica Estates, has many kosher supermarkets, restaurants, and bakeries that service the sizeable Orthodox Jewish community, between about 190th and 179th Streets.

My first stop is at the Ottomanelli Butcher Shoppe at 190-21 Union Turnpike, one of several branches in the city. The chain has been in business for well over a century, but this one is different, specializing as it does in exotic game—partridge, quail, pheasant, alligator, boar, rabbit, buffalo, kangaroo—along with the usual steaks, chops, and chicken. Their meats are reportedly fresh and tasty, and the people behind the counter are very helpful. I walk in and receive a friendly greeting from one of the butchers.

"How much demand is there for the exotic stuff?" I ask.

"A tremendous amount," he says. "People like it because it's leaner and therefore healthier. Others have this meat, but we're the biggest. We sell a lot to restaurants but also to walk-ins. People seem to be buying more of this meat than the regular items." There's nothing about Fresh Meadows that makes it a likely location. People come from all over; they buy on the phone and through the internet. In today's world, location isn't that important, something I've seen many times.

"Has anything weird ever happened in the store?"

"Well, yes. A hunter came in here not long ago and asked if we could butcher his deer for him."

"Did you do it?"

"Hell, no! Maybe forty years ago you could do that. Today, everything has to be done hygienic, according to standards. You can't have meat walking into a shop. Nobody touches it except the guy that cuts it and us when we open it." Ottomanelli's has since closed, but the story of this establishment is worth preserving.

Turning right on Utopia Parkway I turn east onto Seventy-Third Avenue. Ninety years ago, it was called Black Stump Road, after the practice of marking farmland borders with black tree stumps. In fact, that was the previous name of Fresh Meadows until people concluded that the latter name was far more appealing. At 177th Street,

I stroll into the Utopia Playground and referee a footrace between three Indian children. The youngest one wins. The playground boasts several very attractive play spaces with modern equipment that belies its historical importance. At the turn of the twentieth century, this was part of a larger area, consisting of 50 acres purchased by the Utopia Land Company. The plan was to build a cooperative-style Jewish community for Jews looking to escape the poverty and overcrowding of the Lower East Side. The streets were to be named after those on the Lower East Side—Clinton, Rivington, Hester, Ludlow, and so on. Interestingly, American Jews created numerous utopian communities in Louisiana, California, Oregon, Florida, and New York, mostly during the nineteenth and twentieth centuries, but those were agricultural projects, while this one was an urban effort. The company ran out of money, and the project died, but the parkway and the playground are named for the idea.

At 194th Street and Seventy-Third Avenue I arrive at the site of what was once Klein Farm, Queens's last functioning private farm. Located in an urban area—the address was actually 194-15 Seventy-Third Avenue—it sits between a garden apartment development and a school playground. What had been a 200-acre farm in the 1890s is now only 2 acres, but many residents remember having bought vegetables there years ago, especially pumpkins. The Kleins were unable to turn a profit, and so, in 2003, they sold the property for about $4 million. It was leased in 2014, by a day care center. Today, it's still a day care facility, called Ke's Garden. The farmhouse, a handsome, large red-brick building, is still there, as are what looks like the original sheds behind the farmhouse.

Turning around I head west on Seventy-Third, turning right on 185th Street. Just off the southern side of the LIE service road, on 185th Street, I catch a glimpse of a mural, blocked by parked cars. I stand closer to get a better look at a green-painted rural tableau. This is an area with very few murals, so it stands out. On the left, there's a bunch of fruits and vegetables in a pile on a grassy meadow; a waterfall on the right side; a stream, and mountains in the background. There's also a cactus garden in the meadow. Standing in the middle of this is a girl with corn-colored flowing hair. With sturdy legs and wearing a short white dress, she has a stunned and haunted look on her face, almost as though she doesn't understand why she's there. Behind her is a large brown ox. Is she about to be gored by the ox?

On Sixty-Fourth Avenue, which is one block south and parallel to the LIE, I turn west, and at 181-20, I come to a most amazing home. The entire large front yard is literally enveloped by an incredible collection of bric-a-brac, toys, ornaments, flags, signs with quotes from famous poets and writers like William Blake, train sets, a Statue of Liberty, Christmas lights, and figurines. There's an Israeli flag next to a flag of St. John's University. There's a plastic kitchen chair, with an improbably placed basketball hoop resting on it at a crazy angle. The items are laid out right by the side of this fairly busy street. Perhaps people occasionally steal some items, but obviously not often since so many of them are there. There's a disclaimer— "No, not a yard sale, but thanks anyway." In fact, some of the items, like several fake gold coins, are there for the taking. I'm there on February 1, 2017. There's a welcome sign from January 28, five days earlier, commemorating the Chinese New Year of the Rooster. So, we see it's current. The house is owned by a family named Levy. Kurt Levy lived here and was valedictorian of his class at Francis Lewis High School.

The entrance to the walkway leading through the garden to the house is locked, and the home itself looks somewhat dilapidated, with a front porch protected by plastic sheeting, half of which has fallen off. I stop a group of public school students who are passing by, on their way home.

"Does anyone ever take some of these items?" I ask.

"No," says a young boy with jet-black hair. "We respect it because the owner's very nice. Sometimes she comes out and gives us things, little presents. My sister says her husband was a very talented man." The garden is most likely an example of how a family has put together portions of its life, a patchwork quilt of history, as it were. The schools they attended, the values and beliefs they hold, the places they visited. They don't care who knows because they're clearly proud of them. The best way to describe it would be to call it a permanent outdoor eclectic museum.

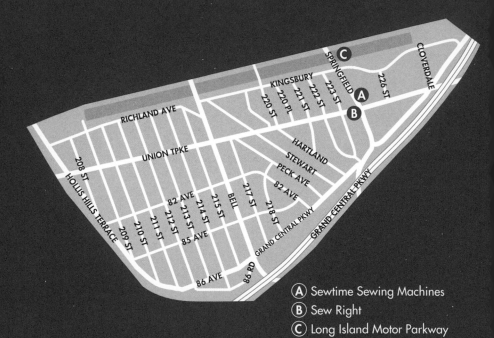

RICHLAND AVE

UNION TPKE

KINGSBURY

SPRINGFIELD

CLOVERDALE

HARTLAND

STEWART

PECK AVE

208 ST

HOLLIS HILLS TERRACE

82 AVE

217 ST

82 AVE

218 ST

GRAND CENTRAL PKWY

GRAND CENTRAL PKWY

220 ST
220 PL
221 ST
222 ST
223 ST
226 ST

82 AVE
212 ST
213 ST
214 ST
215 ST
BELL

209 ST
210 ST
211 ST

85 AVE

86 AVE

86 RD

GRAND CENTRAL PKWY

(A) Sewtime Sewing Machines
(B) Sew Right
(C) Long Island Motor Parkway

HOLLIS HILLS

HOLLIS HILLS IS 90 PERCENT PRIVATE HOMES. They run for many
blocks on both sides of Union Turnpike, from Springfield Boulevard to Hollis Hills Terrace. Most of them were built in the post–
World War II period, and the community is largely white, with
more Asians arriving in the last few years.

The houses are very pretty and well kept, and not terribly interesting, which is the way most of the residents like it. It's not
near a subway or LIRR station, increasing the likelihood that this
will remain a quiet and peaceful, generally upper-middle-class enclave. There is limited bus service to Manhattan on Union Turnpike. The boundaries are Kingsbury and Richland Avenues on the
north, Cloverdale Boulevard on the east, Eighty-Sixth Avenue on
the south, and Hollis Hills Terrace on the west. Shopping is very
limited, with stores on Union Turnpike around Bell and Springfield
Boulevards and several more on Springfield. Geographically, it sits
between two of Queens's largest parks, Alley Pond and Cunningham.

As I near the intersection of Springfield Boulevard and Union
Turnpike, I see something very puzzling. There is not one, but *two*
fairly large sewing machine stores, offering various models, for example, Singer, Pfaaf, and Viking, for sale, as well as fabrics. This is
one of the smallest communities in Queens, and the commercial
shops extend for just two blocks. Sewing machine shops are not
delis, takeout Chinese stores, nail salons, nor even dry-cleaning
places, all of which can be found here. Sewing machines are a dying
industry with very few such stores left. So, what's the deal? I decide
to go into one, Sewtime Sewing Machines, at 78-35 Springfield,
and find out. It's a very nicely laid out emporium, with high ceilings
painted in a light purple, which has a very soothing effect if you
look at it for a moment or two.

One intersection, two large sewing machine stores.

"Hi there. How are you? These are beautiful fabrics you have here."

"Thank you," says the owner, an attractive woman with big eyes, a roundish face, and very straight, dirty-blonde hair. "You looking for something?"

"No, but my wife might be. I'll tell her about your great selection. But hey, I've got to ask you something. Can you explain why there are two stores less than a block apart, selling sewing machines? Couldn't you at least have been in different communities? You can walk through twenty communities in Queens and not see one sewing machine place. Tell me about you and your competition."

"Actually, it's a good thing. When you have a concentration of shops in a specialty area, it brings more business for both of us. He was here first, and we came later because the manufacturers wanted us in one location thinking it would be good for everyone. They felt, if a person doesn't find what they want in one store, they can go into the other one. In fact, so as not to compete too directly, we each sell different brands. At first, the guy was really mad. But after a while, when he saw his business improve, he was happy. We came from Rego Park, and we were on Queens Boulevard. But the rents were too high." As she spoke, I realized it made sense. Given the fact that fewer people are buying machines, consolidating would result in more people coming here. Elaine, the manager of Sew Right, at 223-20 Union Turnpike, a block away, confirms what Susie said. They felt threatened at first, but it ultimately brought more business to both places. It's like I saw on Ninety-Ninth Avenue in Hollis where fifteen or so auto repair shops were clustered together. It doesn't work well with pizza joints, because these are neighborhood outlets and one for each section is probably enough.

Susie continued, "Most people don't sew anymore. My family's been in the business for eighty-nine years. When I was a kid, my father, Leon Fells, had a place in Richmond Hill. When I was a kid we used to go to a section in Manhattan where there were hundreds of sewing machine places. In those days, if you lost your job in the morning you had another one in the afternoon. The money made in these stores built Levittown in Long Island. At one time we had five stores. We did well because I followed in my father's footsteps. He was a happy man, saying, "You can only wear one pair of shoes at a time." He would tell me if you see a poor man coming in, give him a piece of fabric, anything, because you're not poor. He knew. He'd lived in an orphanage for a time growing up because he was one of ten children and the family was poor."

"That's sad to hear. So, how much business is there today?"

"There's only a handful of stores left. The young people don't want to go into the business. My son doesn't. He says: 'Ma, I grew up in a crib in the back of the store.' So, he's studying occupational therapy at Downstate Hospital. He says: 'I want to help people.' And that was because of me in part, because I was always nice to people. He's thirty years old." Susie is lamenting the soon-to-come passing of an era. She was once part of something big and very popular. But today, relatively few people sew. Plus, her son wants to do his own thing.

And now she tells me about another issue: "The main problem is mechanics. A mechanic isn't a mechanic. You can't find people who know how to maintain and repair sewing machines. To fix one you have to have five years of experience at a minimum. And you can't find them. I had to bring one in from England." So maybe the business is dying, but Susie speaks about her products with love and pride. So, it's not surprising that when I tell her I know her Bayside neighborhood and have walked by her house, she suddenly says, "Let me give you a hat as a souvenir. John, can you embroider a hat for him, please?"

John McGlynn, an Irish immigrant and partner in the store, is happy to oblige. He still has a brogue and entertains me with a few off-color and hilarious limericks. In a few minutes I have a navy-blue hat with the letters stitched in green thread: WALKING ALONG, which I thought would be appropriate. It's not often I leave with a memento. It's a fitting end to a great interview.

No book about Queens would be complete without some mention of the Long Island Motor Parkway, and the portion that runs through Hollis Hills is particularly attractive. It was the first road in the country that was built exclusively for auto travel. It functioned as a toll road from 1908 to 1938. Today, it's been incorporated into other existing vehicular roads, but in Queens it's a bicycle and walking trail. At least it is that officially. When I lived for some years in Little Neck, Queens, in the 1970s, I used it as a two-mile shortcut drive to the city when, in the morning, traffic on the Grand Central Parkway was really heavy. I forget how I discovered it, but I was always the only car on it as I traveled through Alley Pond and Cunningham Parks, exiting after about two miles, onto Francis Lewis Boulevard; so maybe it wasn't legal to drive there, something I freely, if belatedly, apologize for now.

WHITESTONE

BEECHHURST

MALBA

BAYSIDE

DOUGLASTON

LITTLE NECK

WHITESTONE

WHITESTONE IS YET ANOTHER MIDDLE-TO UPPER-MIDDLE-CLASS community in northeastern Queens. The boundaries, roughly, are the East River on the north, Utopia Parkway on the east, Willets Point Boulevard and Twenty-Fifth Avenue on the south, and the Whitestone Expressway on the west. The name is believed to have come from the fact that much of the ground in the area consisted of white limestone. It was settled by the Dutch and, later, the English. In the late nineteenth century, large homes were built on what had been farmland. In the twentieth century, apartment buildings and smaller homes were constructed in the area. It has remained a quiet suburban-like community to this very day. Whites make up the majority of the population, with the rest consisting of Asians and Hispanics. The greatest demographic change is the growth of the Korean and Chinese communities.

It's not uncommon in Whitestone to see old, attached Tudors, with nice stucco and stonework fronts, and Spanish tile on the roofs. One such example is a long row of homes between 147th and 148th Streets on Willets Point Boulevard. Another one is on 146th Street between Twenty-Second and

223

Twenty-Third Avenues. In addition, there are thousands of garden apartments populated mostly by small families and elderly couples. The commercial thoroughfares are portions of Francis Lewis Boulevard, 150th Street, Clintonville Street, and Utopia Parkway, as well as some shopping centers along the Cross Island Parkway (CIP).

The area between the CIP and the East River and from 150th Street to the Whitestone Expressway contains homes that typify the entire area—a mix of private homes ranging from elaborate to small in varying styles. These include Tudors, capes, colonials, ranches, Victorians, and Georgians, plus garden apartments, and larger apartment buildings. Walking this area is a good way to appreciate what the entire section has to offer. The streets are quiet and mostly residential. Whitestone south of the CIP has thousands of garden apartments and small, rather modest houses, though there are exceptions of more opulent homes, some of which stand out in an almost garish way. It's almost entirely residential with small stores clustered in a line every few blocks.

Residents of communities and those who study them are familiar with what's known as "community characters." They're people who can lower a community's crime rate simply by being the "eyes and ears of the street," as the urban historian Jane Jacobs called them.[29] They help people in distress, lobby government agencies, and are colorful people. Less well known but equally valuable resources are what I would call "community observers." They are in the community, but not of it.

At Izoid's Barber Shop, on 24-18 149th Street, I ask Robert, a barber from Uzbekistan, with thick, straight hair and a mustache, why so many people from his country are barbers here, a phenomenon I've seen all over the city. His answer is revealing.

"You asking me a very interesting question, and I telling you why," he says. "Young people today from my country, they doesn't want to study; they just want to make money right away. But they doing big mistake because the business nowadays is nothing, too many people in it. That's why I'm here in Whitestone. Here is nothing. I'm the only Uzbek here. Here is all Chinese living here, 90 percent. They go to their own people. It's hard to making a living here. But I stay here because I'm too old to do anything else. I can't go to study. I'm here thirty-three years, before Chinese came." Robert's command of the English language is clearly weak, but not surprisingly so in this city where many immigrant groups establish enclaves where speaking English isn't very important. He lives in such a community elsewhere in Queens, and he doesn't need to speak English to get along. He was also a barber for twenty years in Uzbekistan.

"Why did you choose this occupation in your home country?" I ask him.

"I went to barber school when I was sixteen in Tashkent, where I was born. At the time, my country was very communistic. No money. I went to school for six months. It's quick way to get a trade. I like it. I'm not millionaire, but it's enough to make a living. I not steal money. Even if I want to do business I can't be."

He is critical of the Chinese: "You see, Chinese people, they don't want to learn English. I no study English, but I try to speak it even if not so good. Maybe my accent is not so good. But I speak four languages—Uzbek, Tadzhik, Farsi or Persian, and now English." For him, a main criterion of adjusting in this country is one, not of succeeding, but of trying. Robert believes he should be admired because unlike the Chinese, he makes the effort even if the results are mixed. His daughter is a nurse practitioner. Her husband is a detective.

"What do you like most about your job?" I ask.

"I don't know. For me is everything the best." Like many immigrants Robert considers himself lucky to have gained entry to this country. He is realistic about his situation. He cannot escape the limits of his education, occupational skills, and having come here as an adult. And so, he invests his energies and hopes in his children. It is an experience repeated over and over in New York and elsewhere in the country. Robert has since retired, but the shop is still there with Russian barbers and a new name, Vintage.

On Francis Lewis Boulevard, I head north, and at 1605, I pass Anthony Jerone's, which has a big sign, "Anthony Jerone's Dog Training and Career." Career in this case is what makes it different from the usual places where people take their dogs to be housebroken or for obedience training. "Careers" in this case means teaching people how to be trainers, with certification the goal. It coexists peacefully in the same private home with a yoga center proclaiming "Yoga in Daily Life from Ancient Wisdom for Modern Times. Harmony for Body, Mind and Soul."

Regardless, this place is unique to Queens, the city, and perhaps even the state. It seems to be the only school in New York City that provides certification for professional dog trainers. Jerone received both the Bronze Star and the Silver Cross for starting dog-handling programs for the US Army. He also founded the NYC Transit Authority Canine Unit. He operates nationwide and has many citations attesting to his expertise and success. And he has a universal inclusive message about all dogs: "We make bad dogs good and good dogs better." So, for someone looking into a new career, this might be an option.

Turning around on Francis Lewis, I head south to Twentieth Avenue and go right for about a mile to Harvey Park. It's fairly large, with pretty oak and maple trees and some nice sports fields. The park is named in honor of George Upton Harvey, an Irish-born past borough president from 1928 to 1941, who fiercely opposed the Tammany Hall political machine. Perhaps out of a desire to liven things up or just do something different, a six-foot-high, white-painted, cast-concrete rabbit with huge ears, named Harvey, has been erected as a permanent resident of this nice oasis in a forest of buildings. In this case "Harvey" refers to a 1950 film starring James Stewart as Elwood P. Dowd, an amiable drunk who claims to have an invisible bunny friend. Why here? No particular reason as far as I can tell. I know of no other park with such a denizen.

Leaving the park, I head east to Clintonville Street, turning left and walking to just north of the CIP. Here I gaze on St. Nicholas Russian Orthodox Church, founded in 1916. It has a striking royal-blue onion-shaped dome that's actually visible from miles away if one happens to be in the right spot. The interior, with its large windows and open space, is equally worth visiting. Up front and close, the color is mesmerizing. Outside, five trees are dedicated to the memory of parishioners who died in World War II. The inscription below reads: "Greater love hath no man than this that a man lay down his life for his friends" (John 15:13). It's a somber reminder that religion and patriotism are an integral part of American life and culture.

At 14-30 149th Street, a short distance from the church, an unusual store catches my attention. It's called "Gunsmoke Too: Premium Cigar and Law Enforcement Equipment." What's the connection? I wonder. I've seen a number of business establishments in the city that offer unusual combinations of goods and services, like Maglia Rosa, a Brooklyn store that sells bicycles and has a café; but that makes sense at some level, as both are popular general activities. I walk in and meet an Asian man named Frank, who turns out to be the proprietor.

"Hi there. How are you?" I say. "This is such an interesting combination. Is there a connection between cigars and law enforcement?" At first, Frank sidesteps my question, framing it as a personal preference, but then he comes to the point.

"Well, like I say, it combines two things I really love. I like cigars, and I like law enforcement. I been smoking cigars since the early nineties. But also, a lot of guys in law enforcement smoke cigars."

"Why is that? Is it the look? The image?"

"Well, it could be a lot of things. Like many of them don't smoke cigarettes no more, so now they smoke cigars. You don't inhale cigars, so it's healthier. It could also be their friends smoke cigars. I mean, there is a following. Many people smoke cigars. Not all cops or detectives smoke cigars, but a lot do. Remember Peter Falk? He

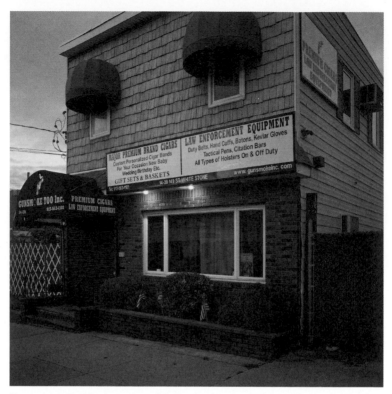

Patrons can find both cigars and law enforcement equipment in Gunsmoke Too.

always had a cigar in his mouth, and he played Lieutenant Columbo, which was on TV forever. Another thing is when you're in retail, you want to sell other things. This is unique. It's unique. It's not a lap of luxury, but this is what I like." Research has, in fact, shown that tobacco use is higher among law enforcement personnel, due, in large part, to the fact that police work is a high-stress occupation.[30]

Frank is an example of a certain type of entrepreneur, people who run a business because they enjoy it, not just to make a profit. I don't see more than two people come in during the forty minutes I'm in the shop. In a way, he's expressing his independence, the right to open a place because it's what he wants to do. It's very well maintained, including a lounge in the back where people can relax on a leather couch with a cigar and what looks like a well-made wooden ceiling fan. The sign outside the room asserts: "What happens in the cave, stays in the cave." Is Frank a happy man? I'd say so. At the very least, he seems content. There are probably other commercial activities that would be more lucrative. Then again, not everyone's willing to spend ten hours a day doing something they don't like.

A few blocks north, at 7-04 149th Street, I walk into the Cascon Baking Company, a bakery and distributor of mostly cheesecakes, their signature offering, but also other cakes and pastries, as well as spumoni, tartufo, and tiramisu. I sit down at a small table and chat with the two owners. Andy, a sixty-five-year-old man with a shock of brown hair, tells me how it all began.

"In 1975 two guys, a liquor salesman and a fireman, decided to open up a bakery. In 2003, my partner, Brian, and I bought the company. We're a hidden treasure. No one really knows us. We're just on this one-block commercial strip."

"Who's your market?"

"Would you believe, and shame on us, everything comes word of mouth. But the business comes to us. I'm a manager in general, and that's the skill that's necessary to make it all happen. We do the cafeteria in the basement of Trump Tower. We have to go through all the security stuff, with the sniffing dogs, but we're not complaining. It's business, and we take the good with the bad. We do Terrace on the Park," a large Queens catering establishment. "We do the Parkside Restaurant in Corona," a famous, top-quality restaurant and sometime mob hangout. "We did Tony Bennett's wedding cake, and he autographed this photo of him we have here."

"But you're on a really quiet street, quiet even for Whitestone. How do you make this happen?"

"We deliver. We just put it in the truck."

Brian jumps in and says, "We also do the Immaculate Conception Seminary out in Douglaston. We take care of God's people."

He smiles, and I say, "Why not? You never know who's eating cheese up in heaven!"

Cheesecakes from Cascon's are made with old-fashioned ingredients—and love.

They both laugh, and Andy adds, "We do a lot of charity works for religious institutions and poor people in general. We were also on NBC. They did a show a couple of years ago about the best cheesecakes in New York."

"So, I guess there must be something special about your cheesecake?"

Brian explains: "It's pure. We don't use cream cheese or make a crust. We use the old-fashioned ingredients—baker's cheese, eggs, milk, flour, and sugar. It's got a gummy kind of texture, the original cheesecake. Not the smooth creamy feel. And it's the love we put into it."

Like Frank with his cigar place, Andy and Brian are happy with what they're doing. But they are large-scale entrepreneurs compared to Frank, and their business is more demanding. Because they're both older, a bit of the enthusiasm is gone, as one would expect. This is evident when Andy says, "I'd rather be with my granddaughters."

As I leave, Andy says, "Hey, wait. Let me give you a cheesecake. That way you can taste what you're writing about." I thank him and leave with the cake and some other goodies. The next morning my wife and I had the cheesecake. It was the best cheesecake we've ever had.

BEECHHURST

BEECHHURST IS A NEIGHBORHOOD IN WHITESTONE that is more up-scale, with many beautiful homes. Its boundaries are Powell's Cove Boulevard on the north, Utopia Parkway on the east, Cryder's Lane on the south, and 154th Street on the west. At the turn of the twentieth century it was a resort area for movie stars of the silent-film era, like Mary Pickford and Charlie Chaplin. Other famous residents included Oscar Hammerstein, Harry Houdini, and Walt Whitman.

Today, there are large apartment complexes here, especially along Powell's Cove Boulevard, where I begin my walk. On Powell's Cove Boulevard, near 160th Street (160-15), there's a beautifully appointed one-block-long building called the Towers. Constructed in 1928, the design is Tudor, with elaborate stonework and brick designs, and a large grassy area in front. It's immaculate and well preserved and worth a look as an example of how pretty these structures can be. A block away a street called Riverside Drive has both apartments and private homes, many of which have stupendous views of the bay. The name, its closeness to the water, and the nearby Ninth, Tenth, and Eleventh Avenues, might cause the unsuspecting to think they were in the Midtown West section of Manhattan.

At 166th Street I turn right off Powell's Cove and then, after a few blocks, make a left onto Cryder's Lane. In a few minutes, when Cryder's ends, I continue straight into Little Bay Park. It lies in the shadow of the Throgs Neck Bridge. There are gorgeous vistas here of the bay, the Bronx, the bridge. In a large grassy area, I see a greyhound running as fast as the wind. My dog Heidi wants to join in, and when the owners see me, I instantly become a possible friend, for we have something in common. I notice a sign on the left admonishing people to keep their dogs on leash. Joe acquaints me with the realities of flexibility in such matters.

"Hi there," he says. "It's okay to let your dog run as long as your leash is in your hands. Then the cops won't bother you. Try throwing this lighted tennis ball. And we also have lasers. You point the laser along the ground, and the dog chases it. Great fun, a lot better than the dog run, where the people are snobby and there's lots of dog poop. The dogs have more fun out here. Anyway, there's lots of ass-holes out there in the run." Clearly there's a "them against us" per-spective among these dog owners. These folks like giving dogs their freedom, and they have a strong feeling of camaraderie, strengthened by their shared dislike for others nearby. Their solidarity also comes from the fact that they, as a group, are allowed to flout the law a little bit. The dog-run folks, as I learn, are more into socializing and sitting around and are seen by these people as having no sense of adventure. It's a subtle insight into the world of dog owners that can be learned only from an insider.

Beechhurst is mostly residential save for a small commercial strip on 154th Street. It has both homes and apartment buildings.

MALBA

THE EXCLUSIVE TINY RESIDENTIAL NEIGHBORHOOD of Malba is another area in Whitestone. Some of the homes here cost upward of $3 million. A good place to see them is on a street called "Boulevard," near the water, and the surrounding area. But Malba has many more modest, though still nice, homes too. The boundaries of Malba, located to the west of the Whitestone Bridge, are, roughly, Powell's Cove on the north, Parsons Boulevard on the east, Thirteenth Avenue on the south, and 138th Street on the west. The population today is mostly Italian, Irish, Jewish, Greek, and Asian. One of the more prominent black residents of Malba, whom I knew personally, was Bill Tatum, long-time publisher of the *Amsterdam News*.

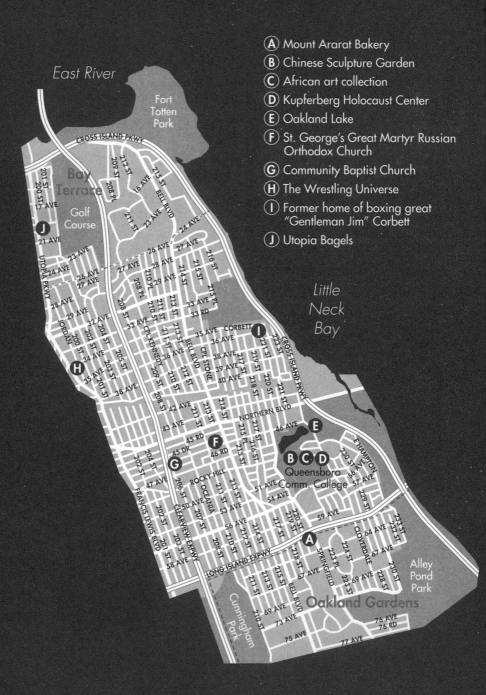

East River

Fort Totten Park

CROSS ISLAND PKWY

Bay Terrace

Golf Course

Little Neck Bay

(A) Mount Ararat Bakery
(B) Chinese Sculpture Garden
(C) African art collection
(D) Kupferberg Holocaust Center
(E) Oakland Lake
(F) St. George's Great Martyr Russian Orthodox Church
(G) Community Baptist Church
(H) The Wrestling Universe
(I) Former home of boxing great "Gentleman Jim" Corbett
(J) Utopia Bagels

Northern Blvd

Queensboro Comm. College

Oakland Gardens

Cunningham Park

Alley Pond Park

Long Island Expwy

BAYSIDE

BAYSIDE WAS ONCE HOME to people from the movie and theater industries, who were attracted by plans to build a large studio there. These included Charlie Chaplin, Gloria Swanson, John Barrymore, Buster Keaton, and Rudolph Valentino. But the studio never became a reality, and when Hollywood emerged as the entertainment center in the 1920s, the stars went to California. Later on, Bayside became a favorite area among some New York Mets stars like Tom Seaver, Nolan Ryan, and Jose Reyes, who liked the quiet and the short commute to Shea Stadium. Its boundaries, generally, are the Cross Island Parkway on the north and east; Seventy-Seventh Avenue on the south; and the Clearview Expressway, Francis Lewis Boulevard, and Utopia Parkway on the west.

Until the early 1990s, this was an overwhelmingly white community with the Irish, Italians, Germans, and Greeks predominating. There was also a small but active Jewish community, as evidenced by a number of synagogues throughout the area. In the past twenty years, the mix has shifted sharply in the direction of Asian newcomers, most of them Koreans and, to a lesser but still significant extent, Chinese. Many have moved here from overcrowded Flushing, seeking more spacious homes. This demographic pattern is likely to continue.

There's also a black community here dating back to the 1920s. Its boundaries, somewhat spread out, are from Forty-Fifth Avenue on the north, Bell Boulevard on the east, Fiftieth Avenue on the south, and 206th Street on the west.

The enclave is shrinking, however, as East Asians buy homes there too. The high prices they are willing to pay because Bayside is very attractive to Asians are seen as irresistible to many home owners who never dreamed their houses could fetch so much money. In addition, the black community has aged out, and the young usually head for either the suburbs or the city.

Bayside has a very eclectic mix of housing, although the majority are single-family detached, semi-attached, and attached homes. The lower-middle-class and middle-class apartments, condos, and co-ops are most likely to be found in the Oakland Gardens section and northward to the Long Island Expressway (LIE). This is followed by older, detached colonial, Tudor, and Cape Cod homes in Bayside Hills, a charming, heavily Catholic neighborhood from the Long Island Expressway to Fiftieth Avenue. Many of the homes along Bell Boulevard and the side streets are Tudors, built by the Gross-Morton Park Corporation. During the holiday season, Queens residents are fond of cruising the streets of Bayside Hills to gaze on the brightly lit Christmas decorations.

Central Bayside, running from Northern Boulevard to Thirty-Fifth Avenue, has hundreds of older, well-constructed, and well-preserved homes on either side of Bell Boulevard, from 221st Street west to the Clearview Expressway. For those into older homes in tranquil neighborhoods this can make for some really rewarding explorations. The area is also Bayside's main commercial hub, running along Bell Boulevard. Francis Lewis Boulevard, to the west, is another main thoroughfare. Below Thirty-Fifth, the area is more varied. The Bay Terrace neighborhood has a large shopping center, and there are private gated communities like Baybridge Commons, the Bay Club, and Bayside Gables near Bay Terrace, along with a mix of private homes and apartment buildings, some of them quite upscale.

Oakland Gardens is the southernmost portion of Bayside, running from Kingsbury and Richland Avenues to the LIE. It's a quiet place with thousands of apartments, co-ops, and condos. Scattered throughout are a sizeable number of private small homes, plus some of the McMansions that have proliferated in nearby Douglaston and Little Neck. Its stability demonstrates that this part of Queens is hugely attractive to middle- and working-class people of all backgrounds. Finally, this very safe community is also home to several beautiful parks, the largest of which is Cunningham Park. The others are Crocheron, with a gorgeous pond, and Clearview, which boasts an excellent golf course.

The story of Queens as a whole is that of the many ethnic groups who have made it their home. While diversity is more pronounced and varied in areas like Elmhurst, Woodside, and Jackson Heights, Bayside is also becoming more diverse. For example, in the shopping area near and on Springfield Boulevard, where I begin my walk, there are Thai, Chinese, Japanese, and Korean eateries, not to mention the well-known Patoug Persian restaurant on the LIE service road. Nearby, at 220-16 Horace Harding Expressway, there's the Mount Ararat Bakery. I step inside and discover hundreds of Armenian products such as baked goods, but also carrots, beans, and chickpeas, all in Armenian-style sauces. I chat with a friendly man behind the counter.

"So, these are mostly Armenian products," I say.

"Yes, yes; the owner is Armenian, and there's a big Armenian church not far away, on Oceania Avenue."

"Are you Armenian?"

"No, I'm from Guatemala. The Armenians are like all other immigrants. They don't want no trouble, but they don't want to lose their culture. And this is one of the biggest Armenian specialty shops, though there are some in Astoria too. We also carry some Lebanese products." This is an example of cross-cultural contact. First, the Guatemalan learns about Armenian products and, by extension, about Armenians in general, through interactions with the customers. Finally, he clearly has a relationship with the Armenian owner, who most likely knows him pretty well and trusts him. But it's only one example. Mexicans work in many pizza shops, many of them still owned by Italians and, more recently Albanians. Jamaicans and Haitians work as nurses in hospitals where they meet physicians, colleagues, and patients from all backgrounds. This is how a dynamic and fluid society enhances cross-cultural fertilization. These contacts and their consequences are ripe for researchers and should be studied and analyzed.

Next, I head north on Springfield to Queensborough Community College (QCC), an excellent institution with many interesting programs, and a very pretty campus serving about fifteen thousand students, many of whom go on to senior colleges. I speak with President Diane Call, who urges me to visit "the relatively unknown but amazing art gallery with some really interesting collections." She's absolutely right, as I soon learn when I take a tour of the gallery, founded in 1967. In fact, the *New York Times* hailed it as "one of the most attractive small museums in the city."[31] My host is the executive director, Faustino Quintanilla, a man with twinkling eyes, a bushy, graying beard, and a great sense of humor. Originally from Spain, he was first a Catholic priest and is now a priest in the Eastern Orthodox Church. I ask him what's special about this place.

"Well, quite a few things, but let me begin with the outdoor sculpture garden outside our building. It contains the works of Professor Wenzhi Zhang of the Guangzhou Academy of Fine Arts. Her specialties are stoneware and lacquer. It's a great spot to bring children to." I walk around the garden, and it's a colorful and dazzling display of cast and fired statues. Many of the sculptures are of females. There are also red figures from the days of the Red Guard, naked, except for their headgear, and carrying Maoist literature. The forty-three sculptures are scattered throughout a beautifully landscaped garden.

"We are also well known for our collection of African art, which is among the three best such collections in New York. The other two are the Metropolitan Museum of Art and the Brooklyn Museum of Art. We opened the museum in 2004, and we're part of the college. When we had the museum exhibition at the time it opened, about four thousand came, but still, the majority of people don't know about what we have. The gallery has more than thirty-five hundred works by modern artists and traditional artists from pre-Columbian South American, Oceanic, and Neolithic Chinese cultures.

The dazzling display of cast and fire statues in the outdoor sculpture garden
at Queensborough Community College.

Another important component of QCC is the Kupferberg Holocaust Center, founded in 1983. It's headed by Dan Leshem, who received his PhD from Emory University under the direction of famed Holocaust historian Deborah Lipstadt. Here I see an award-winning exhibit space, whose variegated glass windows are testament to what happened in Germany on Kristallnacht (the Night of Broken Glass) in 1938, when the Nazis shattered thousands of windows of Jewish-owned stores and synagogues. This event is considered to be the beginning of the physical destruction of European Jewry.

Next to Queensborough, I discover beautiful Oakland Lake. I say "discover" because when I last saw it five years ago, much of it was swampy and neglected. Today, it has been cleaned. The water is crystal clear, and people are even fishing, though the fish must be thrown back in the water. I ask two young Asian men who have just returned a tiny fish to its home if they like fishing here.

"What's the point in doing it if you have to toss them back in?" I ask.

"It's fun to capture them, to meet the challenge." Just then one of the men feels a strong pull on his rod. He reels it in, and it's a large pickerel, at least a foot long. They're excited as they look at it, with evident pleasure at their achievement. Then they return it to the lake, as one says, "This makes my day." I can see why it's enjoyable. I walk around the lake, just under a two-mile walk. It's a Sunday afternoon in mid-November and dog walkers, joggers, and families are taking in the unseasonably warm day.

Heading west I discover, at 211-43 Forty-Sixth Avenue, St. George's Great Martyr Russian Orthodox Church, headed by Father Igor Tarasov. When I look at the church, I can see only the upper part. It appears as though the bottom two-thirds of the building is below ground level, which is, in fact, the case. I see the roof and a bit of the windows. Visually, Gotham's only submerged church is worth a visit. I've never looked down at a church with a tower that's below ground level. I ask Father Tarasov why this is so:

Gotham's only submerged church.

"The parish was founded here in 1923. At that time there was a local community of Russian Orthodox. Eventually, they began constructing a building for the church, but then came the Depression, and everything stopped."

"What about after the Depression ended?"

"Then, during World War II, we had a different problem. There were two factions in the church; one was pro-Hitler, the other anti. The pro-Hitler group lost and left. Unfortunately, they were the rich ones, and the others had no money to finish the church."

"But why does it sit so low?"

"They had only finished the basement level, and so they made the church in the basement, and it's there like this to this day." That cleared it up. Today, the church has about ten to twenty members. It survives because it's funded by the national organization of Russian churches, which is controlled by the Moscow church.

Turning right on 211th Street, I walk two blocks north and hang a left down 45th Road to 206th Street, hang another left, and soon come to the Community Baptist Church at 46-19. It's a small, white-painted church that has served the black community for many years. Generally, the African American population is concentrated in the area north of Forty-Fifth Avenue and east and west of Oceania Street. As I walk in, I'm greeted warmly by a deacon, who invites me to sit in one of the wooden pews. It's a cozy place in a Gothic design with stained-glass windows. In the spirit of the upcoming Thanksgiving Day holiday, some fifty parishioners are standing and swaying to the gospel music, hands waving in the air, loudly proclaiming thanks to the Lord for whatever he has given them, no matter how small. The pastor, C. Omarr Evans, exhorts them, saying, as the organ plays softly, "Give thanks to God every time you can open your eyes; every time you can lift up your hands. Just say: 'Thank you, Lord! Thank you, Jesus!' I don't care how bad you have it. There's got to be something in your life that's good."

The congregation sings, "Thank you, Lord," their faces glowing with the joy of collective appreciation and a common vision. He invites everyone to come forward to the altar and join hands with the others. It feels just like the small Baptist church in Harlem that I visit with my PhD students in sociology every semester. Only it's in a Queens enclave that has a small African American population. In this church, I'm the only white person present. I'm reminded that in this case, a church can truly be a sanctuary. These people's forbears came here in the 1920s and 1930s because there was work here, and they built a community that has lasted for a long time.

At first, they faced discrimination. One woman, Grace Goldsborough, speaks about her school experiences at Bayside High School.

"They never gave the blacks an academic diploma," she says. "I received a general diploma even though I was a B-plus student. They didn't want you to get ahead. . . . Now I look back upon it. It hurts me because I could have gone to college—free." Over time, several church members told me, discrimination lessened, and attitudes changed. Still, they stayed to themselves and built a cohesive community that has lasted a long time. Not far away, though, there's a Korean church, a harbinger of the neighborhood's changing ethnic makeup, and, in a nod to the past, a still-operating Sicilian bakery.

The next day, I pick up my explorations on Bell Boulevard. Between Northern Boulevard and Thirty-Sixth Avenue, it's a happening scene, with many bars, cafés, and restaurants that are frequented by the young, most of them from Queens and Long Island. On the weekends, especially Saturday night, it's packed with revelers who love barhopping and do it until the wee hours of the morning. Most of the people are locals who don't want to bother with traveling to Manhattan. Besides, there are no drink minimums or cover charges. The bartenders are almost always local and know their customers well.

Turning left onto Thirty-Fifth Avenue, I head west, turning right on Francis Lewis Boulevard, Bayside's western boundary. At 34-39 I stumble upon "The Wrestling Universe." The display window is filled with figures of professional wrestlers and videos of bouts. Walking in I meet a young man.

"You have all these wrestling stars," I say. "Let me see if I can remember any from my day—Bruno Sammartino, Haystacks Calhoun, the Hulk . . ."

"Yeah, we've got those guys too, but today's main guys are Seth Rollins, Dean Ambrose, guys like that. People buy these statues and then get them signed by the star."

"Can you make a living selling this stuff?"

"Oh yes. We'll have signings here, and we attract anywhere from twenty-five to one hundred fans then. We did one with the Million Dollar Man, Ted DiBiase, that was huge. He's retired now, but he was a very famous bad guy. Most of our customers are younger people. This is the only place like it in Queens, certainly on this scale, and probably in the city. And we have a lot of figures you won't find anywhere else." My own research suggests he's probably right about its uniqueness.

"Isn't wrestling more like entertainment than knocking guys out?" I ask. "And if so, why do people buy them?"

"They like the entertainment part, and they like to collect things. Kids come in with their parents." I suddenly realize that collectors, from Sotheby's to people who accumulate fake owls, are a huge part of the economy. But why this particular one? Clearly, it's part of the entertainment world, but isn't it just fake?

Bob continues and unwittingly answers my question. "They know it's not real, but they enjoy watching the technique, of seeing how it's made to look real. They enjoy watching them fly through the air. In some ways these people are great to watch because they're great actors. And don't forget, there's real danger here too. Sometimes they slip up and get hurt real bad. You move the wrong way, and you can break a neck." These injuries are the ones that aren't fake and may be an added attraction for some, but even without that, this is just really fun for its own sake. This place, tucked away in eastern Queens, is obviously a mecca for wrestling fans.

One of the most famous figures to live in Bayside was James John "Gentleman Jim" Corbett. A great boxer in the late nineteenth century, Corbett was best known for defeating another boxing giant, John Sullivan. He resided in a three-story house at 221-04 Corbett Road, one of Bayside's nicest areas, from 1902 until his death in 1933. There's a bronze plaque affixed to a small boulder in front of the house today. Corbett got his nickname because he was a classy dresser who was polite and friendly to those who knew him. This was in sharp contrast to the stereotype of boxers as brawlers who often lived on the edges of society. Corbett was also an actor and a writer, and neighborhood kids remembered him as a generous man who gave them nickels.

My last stop is at Utopia Bagels at 19-09 Utopia Parkway. I remember this place from the days, years ago, when my wife worked at a school up the block and went there for lunch. Their bagels are well known throughout Queens, and their tuna fish draws raves from their loyal clientele. Many claim their bagels are the best in the city.

I ask Scott Spellman, the general manager, an enthusiastic friendly man with a bushy mustache, what makes his tuna fish so great.

"It's pretty simple," he says. "We only use solid white tuna, a brand called Premium. And so it looks good and tastes great. And we're just at it every day, working hard."

"You've got all these crazy varieties of bagels here. What's your best seller?"

"Believe it or not, plain bagels."

"And how did you get to be this giant place in such a short period of time?"

"We landed a contract with Fresh Direct, and so we needed to expand." This may sound like a lucky break, and to a certain extent it was. But Utopia has been successful for a long time, thirty-four years, to be exact. And as he said, they work hard. What is luck anyway, if not a combination of being in the right place, at the right time, and, most important, doing something about it? Manhattan- and Brooklyn-centric bagel mavens will include places like famed Barney Greengrass, and Russ and Daughters, on their lists of "the best." Maybe so, but as they say, there's no accounting for taste, and in this instance, namely Queens, the public has spoken, loud and clear.

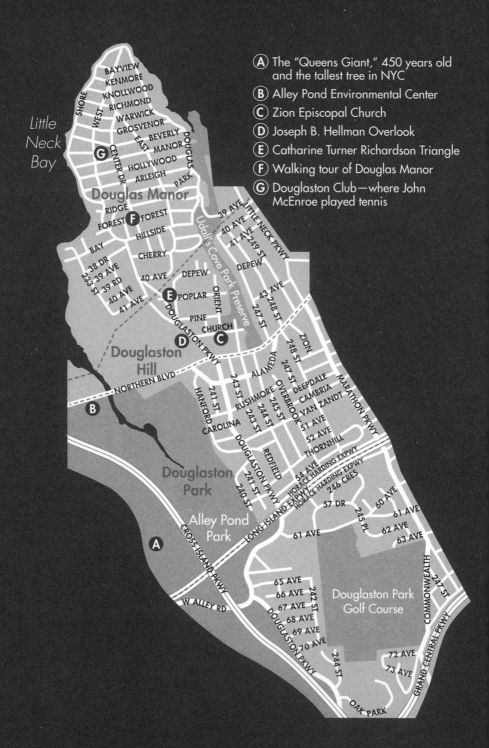

Little
Neck
Bay

A The "Queens Giant," 450 years old and the tallest tree in NYC

B Alley Pond Environmental Center

C Zion Episcopal Church

D Joseph B. Hellman Overlook

E Catharine Turner Richardson Triangle

F Walking tour of Douglas Manor

G Douglaston Club—where John McEnroe played tennis

BAYVIEW
KENMORE
KNOLLWOOD
RICHMOND
WARWICK
GROSVENOR
BEVERLY
MANOR
HOLLYWOOD
ARLEIGH

SHORE
WEST
EAST
CENTER DR.
DOUGLAS
PARK

Douglas Manor

RIDGE
FOREST FOREST
HILLSIDE
BAY
CHERRY
38 DR
39 AVE
233 ST
39 RD
40 AVE
41 AVE
40 AVE
DEPEW
POPLAR
PINE
CHURCH
ORIENT
DOUGLASTON PKWY

Udall's Cove Park Preserve

39 AVE
40 AVE
41 AVE
LITTLE NECK PKWY
249 ST
DEPEW
43 AVE
248 ST
247 ST

Douglaston
Hill

NORTHERN BLVD

ZION
248 ST
247 ST
ALAMEDA
RUSHMORE
OVERBROOK
DEEPDALE
CAMBRIA
VAN ZANDT
51 AVE
52 AVE
THORNHILL
MARATHON PKWY

241 ST
243 ST
244 ST
245 ST
243 ST
HANFORD
CAROLINA
REDFIELD
DOUGLASTON PKWY
241 ST
240 ST
54 AVE

Douglaston
Park

Alley Pond
Park

HORACE HARDING EXPWY
LONG ISLAND EXPWY
HORACE HARDING EXPWY

246 CRES
57 DR
245 PL
60 AVE
61 AVE
62 AVE
63 AVE
61 AVE

CROSS ISLAND PKWY

W. ALLEY RD.

65 AVE
66 AVE
67 AVE
68 AVE
69 AVE
70 AVE
242 ST
DOUGLASTON PKWY
244 ST

Douglaston Park
Golf Course

COMMONWEALTH
247 ST

72 AVE
73 AVE

GRAND CENTRAL PKWY

OAK PARK

DOUGLASTON

ONE OF THE WEALTHIEST COMMUNITIES IN QUEENS, Douglaston has a history that dates back to the 1600s when the Matinecock Indians, part of the Algonquin nation, lived there. Later, it was settled by the Dutch who arrived in the area in 1656. Its boundaries, roughly, are Little Neck Bay on the north; Douglas Road, Little Neck Parkway, and Marathon Parkway on the east; the Grand Central Parkway (GCP) on the south; and the Cross Island Parkway (CIP) on the west.

Douglaston has several subsections, which can be found on the map, the most magnificent of which is Douglas Manor. It is surrounded and, in certain areas, bisected by the various coves, marshes, ponds, streams, and inlets that tend to lead out to Little Neck Bay, and which give the area a very rural feel in many places. Douglas Manor was a predominantly white neighborhood, and blacks and Jews who tried to move here found that agents would try to steer them away from the area, telling them that there were no homes available. In the last two decades Asians, primarily, began moving in. Douglaston Hill, which abuts the Manor, is a mix of smaller homes, apartment buildings, and commercial enterprises. Douglaston Park, farther south, has many nice private homes, predominantly middle and upper middle class, and some that are McMansions. The southernmost part, known simply as Douglaston, includes both a shopping mall and a public golf course, smaller private homes, and a group of four-story condominium homes along Douglaston Parkway. The main commercial thoroughfare is Northern Boulevard.

The area between the Long Island Expressway (LIE) and the GCP contains numerous small streets east of Douglaston Parkway, like Sixty-Fifth to Seventieth Avenues, around the edges of the Douglaston Park Golf Course. The houses are nice but not elaborate, including ranches, splits, capes, and colonials; and there are also several apartment complexes. Don (a pseudonym), an elderly golfer, extolls the golf course's advantages.

"It's mostly Korean, which is all right," he says, "but there are still some of us white folks around. You would like it. They're one of the few golf courses in the city that's open all year. If the temperature's fifty degrees, they'll open, even in the winter. And the price is amazing—just five grand a year. And, you know, it was a private club back in the day. Babe Ruth played here."

For Don, it's apparently okay to make this comment to a stranger. He feels he's creating, or at least emphasizing, a bond between us, by identifying others there, namely Koreans, as outsiders. When he uses the phrase "which is all right," it sounds like he's grudgingly acknowledging that they're okay. Quite possibly a Korean American might say the same things about white Americans. Another man, also elderly, and white, tells me: "The Asians are here, but that's the way it is." He's an avid Mets fan and informs me, falsely, that Asians aren't very interested in baseball. Don also enjoys the status game, as in "Babe Ruth played here."

Walking back along Douglaston Parkway, I pass the eastern boundary of Alley Pond Park, part of which is also in adjacent Bayside. It's the second-biggest park in Queens, the largest being Flushing Meadows Corona Park. It has a tremendous number of activities, as I can easily see when I peruse a bulletin board just off Douglaston Parkway. It lists, among other types of recreation, the "Alley Pond Strivers Program," advertising five-mile walks and other variations on the same theme, showing people walking in heavy rain. No matter what, these seniors are going to walk!

Perhaps the most famous feature of the park is the Queens Giant, an estimated 450-year-old tulip poplar tree, the tallest tree in the entire city, 133.8 feet high. By coincidence, the oldest tree in New York City, and, in fact, on Long Island, was also in Douglaston, at 233 Arleigh Road, in the Douglas Manor section. It was a white oak, estimated to be about six hundred years old, remarkable since

The Queens Giant, an estimated 450-year-old tulip poplar tree.

most white oaks live for about two hundred to three hundred years. Alas, it was cut down about four years ago, a victim of old age.

The Queens Giant isn't easy to locate, but it can be found by looking at online photos of it and comments by others. For those who want to see and appreciate its glory, it's on the Douglaston-Bayside park border at the intersection of East Hampton Boulevard and the LIE. The best way to walk there is through Bayside. Take 223rd Street south off Northern Boulevard, go left on Horatio Parkway, and then go right onto East Hampton Boulevard. Alley Pond Park is on the left as you walk, and in a quarter of a mile just before the LIE, there's a plaque and next to it a small path leading to the tree. The plaque explains the history of the tree and has a description of it. In just a five-minute walk, the amazing-to-behold tree is there, nestled between and above several similar specimens. For help in identifying it, go to the website tmrives.com, where a photo depicts it with the largest limbs curving in distinct ways. It's really amazing to think that the oldest living tree in New York has seen the Matinecock Indians, the Dutch, and the British come and go and can now view, undisturbed, the cars rushing by on the nearby LIE, their drivers oblivious to its presence.

I return the way I came, to Northern Boulevard, and make a right, heading east. In a few minutes I'm at the entrance to the Alley Pond Environmental Center, just east of the CIP's eastern exit. The center acquaints people with the natural environment through tours and educational programs. I continue east on the boulevard for at least a mile and can see, on both sides, high reeds and waterways, which would look more at home in a rural area, yet here they are, within the city. Through its Wetlands Reclamation Project, the center does it's best to preserve the tidal flats, meadows, woods, and both fresh and saltwater wetlands.

At Douglaston Parkway and Northern, I take a left and an immediate right onto Forty-Fourth Avenue (also known as Church Street) and pass, almost immediately, two tall, old, almost identical houses. They have turrets, unusual because they're made of copper, a material more commonly used for church steeples. Their color is green, because of their having oxidized over time. Up the hill I turn right and soon come to Zion Episcopal Church on Northern Boulevard, which dates back to 1829. Thomas Merton's father was an organist at the church in the early 1930s. His son was a renowned theologian, poet, social activist, and author of more than seventy books. Merton later converted to Catholicism and became a Trappist monk, recounting his life in *The Seven Storey Mountain*, published in 1948. Translated into over twenty languages, the book has sold millions of copies. It has had a tremendous influence on its readers, many of whom became fascinated by and even joined monasteries around the world. His comments in this book, his autobiography, make clear that he was not impressed by Zion Church. The family lived nearby at 241-16 Rushmore Avenue, and his autobiography includes some interesting observations of what it was like to live in Douglaston in the 1930s.

A block down from the church, next to an apartment building on Douglaston Parkway, there's a piece of land called the Joseph B. Hellmann Overlook. Someone driving by would be highly unlikely to even notice it because of the sharply sloping downward angle from the sidewalk. There are some nice wooden, gently curved benches where one can relax and enjoy the bucolic view. There's a path that runs through this grassy area between two streets. Those who take the twenty-minute walk to Old Oak Pond will find themselves in what is really unspoiled wilderness, with mallard ducks, blue jays, and robins for company. Very few people have visited except for locals, and I meet no one. It's a winding, easily traversed trail. And at the bottom, I see the pond, with still waters, reflecting the surrounding trees, looking out to Little Neck Bay. On the way back, one can take the only fork to the right and exit, onto Northern Boulevard a bit west of Douglaston Parkway.

Who was Hellmann? An environmentalist, an activist, and a member of Community Board 11. With that pedigree, his family had the connections to name this place after him. But more was involved. Plans had been made to build an apartment house on what was a vacant space. Hellmann fought these plans and succeeded in getting the NYC Parks Department to take it over and preserve it. This is one of many examples of how "the little people," residents in a community, can improve it through their commitment and tenacity. Naming it after him is meant to both honor him and inspire others to care about the place they call home. A city is only as good as its people, whether they're Joe Hellmann or Jane Jacobs.

A bit farther, at the intersection of Poplar Street and Douglaston Parkway, there's a nice triangle-shaped park named after Catharine Turner Richardson. She was the daughter of a United States naval officer, moved to Douglaston in 1932, and was a community activist who worked hard to preserve the residential nature of the community and its wetlands. Like Hellmann, she was appreciated and recognized for her activities and dedication.

I find myself reflecting on how rural some of the eastern communities in Queens are. The many trails and thick woods of Alley Pond Park, the wetlands in the Alley Pond Environmental Center, and the tranquil walks in Hellmann Overlook and Richardson Park, not to mention Oakland Lake in Bayside, all have one thing in common. They are unknown to most New Yorkers, and that's really unfortunate.

For an incredible architectural trip, walk north on West Drive and enter the Douglas Manor section. From here I wander up and down the streets—Hollywood, Beverly, Ridge, Forest, and many more. Some of the styles represented here are Tudor, Victorian, craftsman, colonial, and others. This is probably the most elegant and stately collection of homes in Queens, save for the Forest Hills Gardens area of Forest Hills. What is special perhaps is Shore Road, where there are mansions with magnificent views of Little Neck Bay, and the Throgs Neck and Whitestone Bridges. Along the way I pass the Douglaston Club at 600 West Drive, formerly a privately owned Greek revival mansion. It has a pool and tennis courts and happens to be where tennis great John McEnroe, who grew up nearby, learned the game. Visitors are welcome to enter the mansion, which, with its old furniture, party rooms, and very large wraparound porch, was a popular gathering place for its wealthy residents and their guests in the old days.

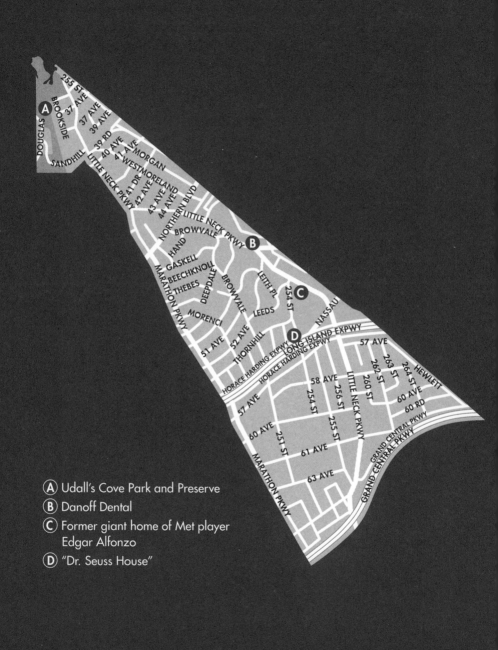

A Udall's Cove Park and Preserve
B Danoff Dental
C Former giant home of Met player
Edgar Alfonzo
D "Dr. Seuss House"

LITTLE NECK

THE BOUNDARIES OF LITTLE NECK are, generally, Thirty-Fourth Avenue on the north; 255th Street, Little Neck Parkway, and Hewlett Street on the east; the service road of the Grand Central Parkway (GCP) on the south; and Douglas Road, Little Neck Parkway, and Marathon Parkway on the west. Centuries ago Little Neck was home to the Matinecock Indians, who lived here in splendid isolation until the English took over the area. By the 1800s the peninsula had become a popular place to gather oysters and clams. In fact, the name for "littleneck" clams is derived from this area, which sits along Little Neck Bay. The railroad that runs here today was built in 1866. A new village consisting of a few homes came into existence in 1873. One structure still there from the old days is P.S. 94, a large yellowish building built in 1915, proudly looking out over Little Neck Parkway. After all, it's part of Queens School District 26, the best academic district in Queens.

Through most of the twentieth century Little Neck was predominantly white. It was a suburban-like enclave with no high-rise structures to be seen anywhere, and that remains true today. The homes gracing the many tree-lined avenues were a mix of traditional and more modern styles. Churches and temples of various faiths served the area; and bars, restaurants, and small supermarkets were easily available to the local inhabitants. Today, the area is increasingly Asian, with many restaurants, supermarkets, and other shops servicing this new population.

I start my walk in Little Neck, which borders Nassau County, at the northernmost beginning of Little Neck Parkway, where it intersects with Thirty-Fourth Avenue. One block to the west is Brookside Street. For anyone who wants peace and privacy, this part of Little Neck is ideal. Thirty-Fourth Avenue borders what is part of Udall's

Wildlife flourishes in Udall's Cove Park and Preserve.

Cove Park and Preserve. I enter the park via a small path near Brookside, which broadens considerably after about ten yards. The area is relatively untamed, with several paths meandering through thick underbrush, poison ivy and other plants, and small trees. I soon come to a body of water with grass along the shoreline taller than my head. It feels and looks like a bayou in Louisiana. Across the way I see another Queens neighborhood, Douglas Manor, which is part of Douglaston. A bit farther a clearing comes into view and, lo and behold, there's a bench. From here I can see Little Neck Bay and, way off in the distance, Co-op City in the Bronx.

Walking to the northern edge, there's an outcropping of rocks, and ahead, off to the right, is Great Neck, in Nassau County. It's 10:00 a.m. on a beautiful Sunday morning. While Riverside and Central Parks are at this hour filled with walkers, joggers, and bench sitters, there isn't a soul to be seen here. The path becomes a fifteen-foot bridge, very well constructed, evidence that people are maintaining the park. Before I'm done, I've crossed over two more bridges. To my left I pass a lone snowy egret that pays no attention to me. Other wildlife flourishes here too, including great blue herons, muskrats, and marsh wrens.

Where Little Neck Parkway crosses the Long Island Railroad (LIRR), there's an Armenian community center and, in fact, Armenian Americans do live in Little Neck as well as elsewhere in Queens. Next door there's a Korean church, not surprising since Korean Americans have a large presence in Queens, from here all the way west to the Flushing area. In fact, one can walk one hundred blocks along Northern Boulevard from 149th Street in Flushing to 254th Street and easily see the hundreds of Korean-owned establishments of every kind. It's a shift that has greatly accelerated in the last decade as the Korean and Chinese populations have found homes in eastern Queens and beyond into northwestern Nassau County. Twenty years ago, this part of the borough was predominately white. Today, whites' presence remains, albeit greatly reduced in numbers.

Walking along Little Neck's main drag, Northern Boulevard, I'm struck by the changes that have occurred here. Korean and Chinese business establishments predominate from Marathon Parkway eastward to 254th Street, the Nassau County border. Gone are some old landmarks, like the Little Neck Theater, on the southern side of the boulevard at Morgan Street, which opened way back in 1929. It closed in 1983, but many area residents, including me, still remember the crowds that went to see the latest films on Friday and Saturday nights. The facade is still in place, as is a handsomely carved sandstone eagle above the entranceway, framed by ionic pilasters.

Sal's Pizzeria, which was nearby, is also gone. Sal was a community character who sponsored little league teams whose members proudly marched up Northern in the Memorial Day parade, reportedly one of the largest community parades in the country. And his pizza, made the old way, with great care taken to have the finest cheeses and sauce, attracted customers from all over the city. A shop that once sold traditional Irish items is now only a distant memory, as is the Scobie Diner on the corner of Northern and Little Neck Parkway. Scobie's was owned at one time by the family of former CIA director George Tenet, who bussed tables there part time. One of the few survivors from the past is the Doyle B. Shaffer Funeral Home, catering mostly to the old-timers who spent their lives in the area.

Spas, nail salons, and places offering body massages are very popular in Asian communities. There are three spas in a two-block area and four nail salons. I wonder how they can all make it. The owners shrug their shoulders when I ask, and one says, "We do okay."

Nearby is Fishing East Coast, which sells fishing equipment of all sorts. I ask the manager why the shop is located here, not next to a waterway, as are places in Sheepshead Bay. The answer is revealing.

"Well," he tells me, "Little Neck Bay isn't that far away. But we have customers from as far away as New Jersey and Connecticut because we have a large variety of excellent supplies, and also because of the internet. Today, it doesn't matter so much where we are because so many people buy online, not on the water." This is emblematic of how the internet has changed life as we know it. I know of a small pharmacy that's always empty because, I initially assumed, of a large CVS across the street. But the owner's explanation was similar: "We survive, even thrive, because we have gotten most of our longtime customers to buy online. They're loyal because we were here before anyone else."

I enter Best Class Carpet at 254-01 Northern. They sell both high-end and low-end carpets, and the machine-made Persian rugs, some as low as $40, are big sellers. For a nonexpert it's easy to believe they're handwoven. A customer in the store tells me, "It's been in my dining room for ten years and still looks great. And because it's synthetic, it doesn't shed." The shop is less than a mile from Great Neck, Long Island, where thousands of Persian Jews live, many in luxurious homes.

I ask Fred, the Persian owner, if they're customers, and he replies, "Oh yes. They buy expensive and cheap rugs. They need cheap ones, not for their living rooms, but less expensive for their kids' rooms, some hallways, like that. Today people want happy colors. One guy bought it for his living room. But fancy carpets are not so much in style because of the economy. Everyone is different. Even rich people, they say that if they drop some tea on a cheap rug, so what? But if it's on a $7,000 rug, then 'Oh no!'"

"What have you learned about life since you came here?"

"Don't make any tension in your life, and be honest." While Fred is Persian, he's not Muslim, Christian, or Jewish, but Zoroastrian, a small ancient religious group dating back thousands of years that keeps a low profile. Before the rise of Islam, Persia was overwhelmingly Zoroastrian. Today, most Zoroastrians live in India.

Fred has a tolerant view on religion as well, telling me, "If you are a good person then you don't need any religion. Everything too much is no good. Like drinking, if you do it too much, then you can't drive home." I ask him about his connection to other Zoroastrians.

"We don't have a center in New York City, but we keep in touch. We don't try to convert others, and we can pray at home." As it happens, a new temple is being built in Pomona, New York, to serve the fifteen hundred or so Zoroastrians who reside in the tri-state area. Fred clearly identifies with his faith and proudly shows me a calendar with color photos of his community. Fred's store has since moved to Long Island, a casualty of a steep rent increase.

I head south on Little Neck Parkway and soon come to Danoff Dental, at 49-33, with the names of four Danoffs outside. Intrigued, I speak with Dr. Kate Danoff Geft, who is one of the dentists.

"I see that there are four dentists here with the same last name," I say. "That seems quite unusual to me."

"All four of the dentists here, my parents, Scott and Laura, and my sister Jaclyn, are Danoffs. We're actually fourth generation. My grandfather was also a dentist, and his father and his father's sister were dentists. In fact, she was one of the first female dentists in

America. And I have at least five cousins that I can think of who are dentists."

"What do you think is the reason why so many people in your family are dentists?"

"In my case, my mom had a home office. I would visit her after school. And I wasn't just watching her fix teeth. I was watching her interactions. Being an orthodontist, you deal a lot with kids. It was a warm and friendly environment, and I enjoyed it. I saw that this was as much about relationships as about doing something technical. Look, it's a great job. You can work forty hours, do well financially, and still have a good home life. When I started dental school at New York University the professor asked us—there were almost two hundred people in the room—'How many of you have parents who are dentists?' And about 50 percent of the class raised their hands. I think lots of those people saw what I saw, that is, a great lifestyle. And it's an especially good job for a woman who has to balance taking care of kids with her job."

Danoff Dental has a division called the Snoring and Sleep Apnea Center of Queens and Nassau. It's the largest such center in Queens. It produces and fits people with oral appliances for sleep apnea and snoring. Research has shown that people with severe sleep apnea have a much higher mortality rate than people without it. The study was based on an eighteen-year follow-up with 1,522 participants.[32] This is the only accredited center in the five boroughs and one of maybe fifty such centers in the United States.

Had I not seen the multiple Danoff names, I might not have walked in. I don't believe there's anything genetic at play when multiple people in a family enter the same profession. In this case, several of the numerous dentists in the extended family were people who had married into the family and had become dentists. For many people, entering a field has to do with the attractiveness of the job, the opportunity to gain entry into a practice, and exposure to people who do and like the work involved. In a competitive world, having an edge is critical, and when people have an "in," namely relatives in the same practice, they will, everything else being equal, take full advantage of it.

There are many interesting homes in Little Neck. One, at 53-27 254th Street, just off Little Neck Parkway, is made of stucco, cement, and various shades of brick. What's remarkable is its size, 12,224 square feet. It's a five-bedroom, five-bath Mediterranean villa with a tiled roof, and columns supporting arched balconies, made of limestone. Even more spectacular is the interior, which, according to realty listings, features a home theater, golf range, batting cage, spa, marble floors, and exquisite mahogany woodwork everywhere. There's also a granite in-ground swimming pool. It would sell today for about $5 million. A "white elephant?" Not at all. Met fans will remember Edgar Alfonzo, a former player (hence the indoor batting cage) who owned the house and put it on the market for $8 million in 2007. It eventually sold for $3.6 million. The immediate area, bordered by Little Neck Parkway, the Long Island Expressway (LIE), Marathon Parkway, and Northern Boulevard, has become a "McMansion center" in Queens, with many custom-built homes that sell for millions of dollars. Many of the residents are wealthy immigrants from countries like Russia, China, and Greece. The 254th Street home may be the most expensive, but it's right at home here.

Walking every street here has its rewards as usual, for at the end of 254th, at 54-17 on the corner of the LIE service road, there's a most peculiar home that doesn't fall into the "elegant" category. I call it the "Dr. Seuss house" because its exterior appears very fanciful, like so many of his drawings. Built in 1930, it's a hodgepodge of so many different building materials and style elements—like a crazy, loopy, brick design along a brick second-story wall—that it defies easy description. There are trapezoidal pieces of colored, mostly purple glass, which look vaguely like leaves on a tree. One tall rectangular turquoise window seems to be made entirely of stained glass. Sporting a tiled roof, it has elements of Tudor styling, along with a glass-enclosed porch. The front has a curving brick shape, which

The "Dr. Seuss house" is a hodgepodge of different building materials and style elements.

has an aperture, inside of which is a hard-to-identify statue. The home is surrounded by heavy, thick underbrush. While no further information is available, it's definitely worth a look as I've never seen a home quite like it.

And then there's a plain, small, brick colonial with black shutters at 53-42 254th that would attract no attention whatsoever. But it has a lurid, well-documented history. In mid-October 1991, forty-seven-year-old Andrew Brooks Jr., who lived in the house and was known locally as an eccentric, went on a killing spree and murdered five people, including his parents; wounded two neighbors; and held several people hostage in another home several blocks away. Besides his father, a retired teacher with whom he lived, Brooks knew all the people he shot with a 22-caliber rifle. He spent the day in the hostages' house, shooting at the police, several homes, and the ground before killing himself. His only demand was a six-pack of Coke. He had no criminal record, but he had been arrested for public lewdness and weapons possession. Nor did he have a medical history of mental problems but had acted strangely for years, talking to himself, following young women, peeking into windows, and frequently swinging a golf club as he walked through the streets. He often wore the same black-and-white plaid shirt, looked messy, and had not worked for almost his entire adult life. In a strange twist, one of the hostages he took was Dr. Paul Gregory, a seventy-one-year-old psychiatrist.[33]

Stories like this are examples of how there's far more to a neighborhood and its residents than can be discovered by simply taking a walk. Every area has its unique history. While beyond the scope of a book of this sort, a story like this raises many questions about the complex relationships that exist in every community and how the way they unfold and are managed by people can have an enormous or minor impact on their lives. In most instances, things like this don't happen, but the mere possibility that they could can increase the wariness with which people thrown together in a big city regard each other.

I thought I knew this part of eastern Queens pretty well in every way. But then, early one summer evening, walking along the back streets behind the pool on the east side of Little Neck Parkway, I found myself wading through and stepping on what seemed like thousands of frogs. As far as the eye could see they were jumping through the air, in gardens, on porches and driveway, and in the street. It reminded me of a visit my wife and I made to Louisiana, where we stayed in the town of Rayne, which billed itself as the "frog capital of the world." The density of these frogs seemed like a plague of, literally, biblical proportions. Residents were looking at this invasion with undisguised horror, and I felt very badly for them. They hadn't a clue as to where the frogs had come from, nor when they would depart.

Despite repeated trips, I never saw them again. I've asked people over the years and have never received an explanation. Yes, there are waterways with frogs in them in Udall's Cove, but that's miles away at the opposite end of this community. Sometimes, I find that I have to accept that things I observe cannot always be explained.

GLEN OAKS

NEW HYDE
PARK &
FLORAL PARK

BELLEROSE

QUEENS
VILLAGE

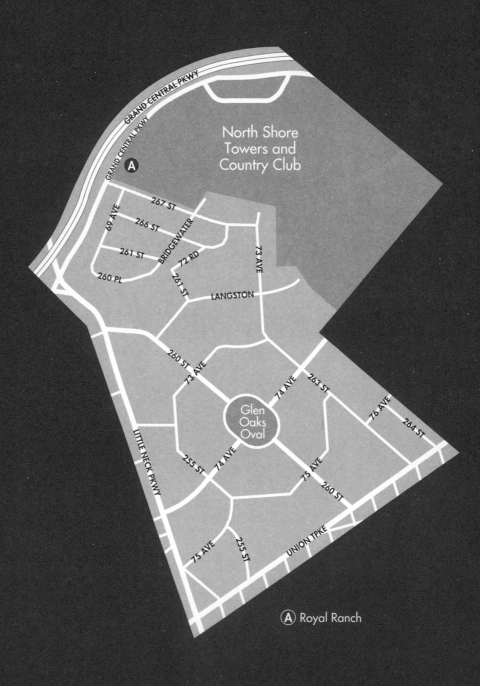

GLEN OAKS

GLEN OAKS IS A TINY COMMUNITY in the easternmost section of Queens. Its general boundaries are the Grand Central Parkway South Service Road on the north; 267th Street, Seventy-Third Avenue, and 263rd Street on the east; Union Turnpike on the south; and Little Neck Parkway on the west. Until the 1920s, the area was home to the William Vanderbilt estate. In 1923, it became the Glen Oaks Golf Club, and in 1944 it was the site for a large rental development of about twenty-nine hundred red-brick garden apartments known to this very day as Glen Oaks Village. Another section of the village is located in the adjacent community of Bellerose. East of the village beyond 263rd Street is where most of Long Island Jewish Hospital (now combined with North Shore Hospital) is located. Up the hill from its northernmost portion there's a development of detached homes, called Royal Ranch, and east of that, beyond 267th Street, is the North Shore Towers luxury apartment cooperative development, which is also in Glen Oaks. The main, and only, commercial thoroughfare is Union Turnpike.

Not surprisingly, given the fact that it was completed in the mid-1940s, Glen Oaks Village attracted thousands of returning World War II veterans. For decades it remained a stable community, with a popular grassy oval, called Tenney Park, where generations of children played ball, frolicked in the playground, and hung out as teenagers. By the 1980s, parts of the development had become somewhat run-down, but in recent years it has been spruced up and is now a very desirable place for a diverse population of young families. The community is extremely quiet and safe, and the public schools, located in District 26, are excellent.

Glen Oaks is also home to a fascinating little community that's relatively unknown to outsiders, despite being located on public streets in Queens. Built in 1954, its informal name is "Royal Ranch," though no one is sure why. Originally, it consisted of about one hundred ranch homes, but today, these now-old homes are being replaced by fancier two-story, mostly brick homes. Some are so large as to have earned the sobriquet of McMansions, dwarfing the remaining one-story ranches. It's four blocks long and four blocks wide, all in all, a speck on the street map of New York City.

It's not only the size that makes it a special community. There are only three ways in and out of Royal Ranch, all of them hard to find or barely noticeable. Cars regularly speed by on the Grand Central Parkway South Service Road, also called Marcus Avenue, past the only northern street entrance, 267th Street. This isolated location gives those who live there a sense of both privacy and solidarity. Until the 1980s it was almost impossible to get a city snowplow to come by and do its job, and even then, it was only when the clamor for city services became very loud that the city paid attention. This is no longer the case. Today, the city is much more responsive to the neighborhood's needs.

But what really unites the residents is their prized swimming pool, built in 1960. It's not a great pool, but it's certainly a good one with a diving board and a small deep-water section. In addition, there's a paddleball court, and a small children's playground. Under the pool deck, there's even an indoor area with showers for guests to use after a relaxing swim. The pool was built as part of the development, and anyone who bought a house received a deed of co-op ownership of the pool entitling them to use it for a small fee. This was the kind of deal you could get in Nassau County, but rarely in the city. Given the fact that the taxes were city taxes, much less than those of the suburbs, it was considered special. In the 1970s property taxes were a mere $1,400, and even today they're only about $6,000, which is still a bargain. The pool is about a block or two away no matter where one lives. During the summers the pool became the place where neighbors met, chatted, shared the facility and socialized, with many becoming good friends who went out to dinner and even took vacations together.

The neighborhood was almost completely white. One day, a black Jamaican couple with children moved in. The family owned a restaurant, and they immediately threw a party to which they invited their neighbors. A longtime resident explained to me what happened.

"At first we wondered why they would want to come here. And we also thought that maybe this was a way in which realtors hoped to cause turnover of homes and the resulting commissions they would make. And some of us were thinking that property values would go down. But none of that happened. The newcomers made a beautiful party. They invited all the neighbors to dinner and served roast chicken, fish, and curried goat. Some of us tried the goat, which was delicious. Others took the conservative approach and ordered the chicken. I remember a Jewish woman who must have thought she was in the Catskills, ordering for their table. She said to the waiters: 'We'll have seven hens,' and I just cracked up. In the end this family lived here for many years; there was no real change in the racial makeup of the community. They were just accepted like everyone. After all, they maintained their house, and they had reached out their hand in friendship."

This attitude wouldn't be surprising to a sociologist because research on intergroup relations strongly supports it. People can always be tolerant of a few neighbors who are "different," sort of like the stereotypical "some of my best friends" claim that people will make to demonstrate how open-minded they are. Sometimes even one is too much, but many of these people were liberal in their thinking. Plus, the catered party broke the ice. In addition, property values rose, and the old ranches go for about $800,000 today, typical of this part of eastern Queens.

"So, what's happened since then? What's it like today?"

"The pool is expensive to run. The older people don't belong anymore. Their kids grew up, and they aged out. So now a lot of members are younger and from outside the area. Also, the ethnic mix is different. There are whites, but also quite a few Indians, Chinese, and Koreans. There's still some bigotry. You're always going to have individuals like that. We still have block parties on some of the streets, and that unites people of different backgrounds and in general. The other thing we have is the Queens County Farm across Little Neck Parkway. And to me what makes it special is that George Washington was supposedly there, and he walked the floorboards of the farmhouse. So, it's like we have a piece of history here. I mean, it was the first president of the United States."

These comments are worth reflecting on. The fact that the pool is now attracting many more outsiders is a pragmatic decision that nevertheless reduces some people's comfort level. On the other hand, it opens up new social opportunities for mixing. A community changes in some way but remains the same in others. The ethnic mix is similar to the makeup of many Queens communities. Finally, the farm, museums, and sports facilities all serve to unite the borough, or at least large sections of it. And that's how residents develop a sense of being Queens residents and residents of a big city.

The George Washington comments are an example of how people create a degree of cachet, something that makes their community stand out. Whether he actually was there I cannot say as I have found no evidence of it. He was in the area nonetheless, and it could have happened. Of far greater importance is that the locals want to believe it. The opportunities for believing in the history of famous people in one's area are much more common in Manhattan, where many famous people live and residents do boast about who lives near them, but the *desire* to believe such things can be just as strong here. So, when one can name-drop a George Washington as having been to the sticks of Queens, it's gold!

The occasional reunion parties made by former residents reflect the feelings many have about their former community, as do their reactions to a brief article about the place on a *New York Times* blog.[34] Most of the writers loved growing up in Royal Ranch. They remembered the camaraderie and the activities. One expressed deep satisfaction at how wonderful it was to visit his childhood home decades later and find it largely unchanged.

Talk about how things don't change. A few years ago, while in New York visiting the old neighborhood, I decided to stop by my home, up on Sixty-Ninth Avenue. I was with my wife, my youngest son, and his fiance. I rang the door-bell, introduced myself and was graciously invited into the home. You won't believe this, but EVERYTHING, was as if I'd never left! Carpet, flooring, furniture, paintings, my desk, my bed, my mirrors, the bathrooms, the basement. My pull-down desk lamp still worked! Both my wife Jackie and I commented on how honored we were to be recipients of this very nostalgic visit. The homeowners, whose names I don't recall, had purchased the home from my mother (about 1980) and stated they loved everything about the home so they wanted to retain it as it was. I guess they weren't kidding. . . . That being said, there is nothing like Royal Ranch. We all are truly fortunate to have grown up with the likes of everything that has been written and will always cherish those moments in time.
Happy and healthy New Year to everyone.

And so, you *can* go home again, at least, sometimes. Millions of people do this every year. And they delight in the ability to be transported through time despite the passage of time. In a way, the less things change, the more pleasure people derive. It's a vindication of how everything was—in this case the carpeting, the furniture, the man's bed, his mirror, even his pull-down desk lamp, which still worked. And it is a paean of praise not only to his own past, but to that of everyone else who lived there.

But things are never perfect in the past. Which brings me to the comments on the blog about a man in Royal Ranch, whom some of the local teenagers knew and viewed as "strange." Children can be cruel, and such a man was an obvious target. The presence of such people in every neighborhood is a fact of life. But people don't always agree about such matters, and some recalled him as "a nice man."

Another blogger observed: "Most of the comments on this blog say that Royal Ranch was a great place to grow up. I grew up there[.] I didn't think it was such a good place. That neighborhood was segregated; not too many minorities lived there. People that lived in the surrounding area, like the Glen Oaks apartments, say it was 'snob hill.' You know, they're right."

This in-depth discussion reveals that communities can be and are very complex places, with people having different opinions about all sorts of things that happened when they lived there. The exchange of views here also demonstrates that the history of a community is subject to interpretation by its residents and that it's often difficult to develop a narrative on which everyone can agree. The sense of insularity on display here at times isn't unique to Royal Ranch. There are many communities like it in the city, places like Gerritsen Beach in Brooklyn and Hamilton Beach and Forest Hills Gardens in Queens. Even a few city blocks, when placed under a microscope, as has been done here, can reveal a great deal. Of course, there are many neighborhoods where there isn't as strong a sense of community, and it's also interesting to explore why that's so.

East of Royal Ranch, up Marcus Avenue, is North Shore Towers, a very large co-op development on the Queens side of the Queens-Nassau border. The towers, all three of them, are so large at thirty-four stories each, that they are visible from the Queens side of the Throgs Neck Bridge, about nine miles away. The first building was opened in 1973, the other two in 1974 and 1975, and the development has been a huge success. With 1,844 apartments, it even has its own postal zip code. There are five swimming pools and five tennis courts, with loads of stores in the interconnected concourse. Here, one can find beauty parlors, clothing stores, a bank, restaurants, a catering hall, food markets, and fitness centers. It sits on 110 acres and boasts a lovely eighteen-hole golf course. Living there is like being in a giant resort hotel all year round. After all, besides the amenities mentioned above, there are also cultural programs, concerts, dinner dances, and walking clubs.

Not surprisingly, most of the residents are elderly retirees, since they are the group that can best take advantage, all day and night, of what the towers have to offer. You never have to leave, and yet you can whenever you want to. Those who can afford it go to Florida for the winter and have the best of all worlds. Unfortunately, it's not open to the public, even for serious walkers and tourists, but it's important for those who want to understand every aspect of Queens to know that such a place both exists and flourishes.

HEWLETT

271 ST
270 ST
269 ST
268 ST
267 ST
266 ST
265 ST
264 ST
263 ST

74 AVE
76 AVE
77 AVE
77 RD
78 AVE

Long Island Jewish Medical Center

New Hyde Park

LANGDALE

UNION TPKE

79 AVE

80 AVE

81 AVE

Floral Park

82 AVE

254 ST
255 ST
256 ST
257 ST
258 ST
259 ST
260 ST
261 ST
262 ST
263 ST
264 ST
265 ST
266 ST
267 ST
268 ST
269 ST

82 RD
82 DR

LITTLE NECK PKWY

83 AVE

83 RD

HILLSIDE AVE

84 RD
84 DR
85 AVE

E WILLISTON

85 AVE

86 AVE

87 AVE

87 RD

JAMAICA AVE

Ⓐ Hans Meatorama
Ⓑ Unusual public library
Ⓒ Usha Foods
Ⓓ Khans Tutorial
Ⓔ Boodram Memorial

NEW HYDE PARK
& FLORAL PARK

BOTH NEW HYDE PARK AND FLORAL PARK are split between Queens and Nassau Counties. The discussion here is devoted to the Queens side. In the nineteenth and early twentieth centuries, this area was mostly farmland. Eventually, it became the William Vanderbilt estate, and after World War II, New Hyde Park and Floral Park became attractive communities for returning war veterans and city residents looking for a place to live that had grass, trees, and fresh air. Thousands of small but quite serviceable three-bedroom Cape Cod houses were built, many of which remain today, albeit with expansions, in many cases. They are augmented by newer colonials that are nice, but modest in size compared to the McMansions in other parts of Queens like Little Neck and Douglaston.

NEW HYDE PARK

The boundaries of New Hyde Park are Seventy-Sixth Avenue on the north, Hewlett Avenue and Langdale Street on the east, one block of Williston Avenue on the south, and 268th Street on the west. The main commercial thoroughfare for New Hyde Park is Union Turnpike.

The major change here has been who lives in these two communities. The initial groups that came were white, with Italians, Irish, Polish, and Jews predominating. In the mid-1970s, South Asians discovered the area, and today the predominant groups are Indians, Sikhs, Bangladeshis, Pakistanis, and Guyanese. The earlier white groups are slowly disappearing. Their children have grown up and moved elsewhere, and the older generation is moving to sunnier climes. As I begin my walk in New Hyde Park—a narrow, mile-long sliver of a mostly residential community—I pass by a small strip of shops along Union Turnpike. Tiny as it is, it's a perfect example of how multiethnic Queens is. Within it are two Indian restaurants, a kosher pizza shop, a Chinese eatery, and a Dominican restaurant. In fact, while there are substantial numbers of Indians living here, the Orthodox Jewish constituency is quite small, and there are very few Dominicans residing in the area. Thus, one can't always know a community's ethnic makeup from the shops that prevail. It simply depends.

The homes in the area are lower middle to middle income, with older capes and newer small colonials predominating. Walking along Seventy-Sixth Avenue near 265th Street, I ask two people unloading some shopping bags from their car why the number of their address reads 98, when it should be something like 265-37.

They laugh as the woman responds: "That's not a house number. That's around the corner on the front entrance. It's just a religious symbol that says God is one."

"What religion does it represent?" I ask.

"No special religion," she says, sounding a bit evasive. As I walk around to the other side of the home, I notice a foot-high symbol, which appears three times on the second-floor balconies, that looks a bit like the sheath to a sword, surrounded by a circle with two swords. Curious, I return to the people, but by now they are no longer in the driveway and have begun driving away. I hail them, and they stop. This second intrusion requires a justification, I feel, so I begin by apologizing.

"I'm sorry to bother you again, but I'm writing a book about Queens, and I noticed these circular symbols on the other side of your house. What do they mean, if you can tell me?"

This time the man answers: "Those are national battle symbols of the Sikh religion. They commemorate that we did serious battle with the Muslims and others who attacked our people several hundred years ago because they were persecuting us." Having learned that they are Sikhs, the woman's answer before no longer seems as evasive. Sikhs are monotheistic and believe that no religion has a monopoly on truth, so it's not surprising that the home has a symbol defining God as a supreme being for all faiths. Was she reluctant to reveal that she's a Sikh? Perhaps. After 9/11, there were numerous instances of vicious physical attacks on Sikhs wearing the traditional garb of a large turban and a full beard. They were mistaken for Muslims, an irony given the history of hostility between the two groups. The trauma of these experiences was long lasting, and it's not surprising that the group would be cautious when encountering strangers asking questions. The man tells me that there are other Sikhs living here, but considerably more in neighboring Floral Park and Bellerose. In the next few blocks, having been alerted to the symbols, I see several more on homes. It's a religious identifier, just like a nativity scene for Catholics, a mezuzah for Jews, or colored prayer flags for Guyanese Hindus.

FLORAL PARK

The boundaries of Floral Park are Union Turnpike on the north and 268th Street on the east. At the intersection of 268th Street and Williston Avenue, the southern boundary runs diagonally west to 257th Street, where Jamaica Avenue becomes the southern boundary until Little Neck Parkway, which is the western boundary. For Floral Park the commercial thoroughfares are both Union Turnpike and Hillside Avenue.

In Floral Park, I start my trip at Little Neck Parkway and Union Turnpike. Here I see "Hans Meatorama: European Prime Cuts— B.B.Q. Chickens—Boar's Head Provisions," at 253-18 Union Turnpike, a place guaranteed to not attract vegetarians. The very name signifies "old-style," and when I walk in it's clear that this is a traditional butcher shop, with a shiny wall of white tiles serving as a backdrop to the glass display of meats. Small statues of cows, chickens, and pigs abound. And why not? That's what's sold here. But the young man who waits on people and is a part owner isn't old-style at all. He's thirty-six and has a very up-to-date stylish haircut. I look around and see plaques of appreciation on the wall commemorating the various birthdays of "Hans," who turns out to be the young man's father, now retired. Hans is from Switzerland, which explains the Swiss national insignias that I see. There are nice but slightly grainy photos of him and his family. What's it like to take over your dad's store, I wonder. I say hello, and we start talking.

"I was born in Switzerland," I say, "and I see you have all these Swiss signs here."

"Yeah, that's where my father's from. He came here when he was twenty-one, and he bought the store from two Italian guys. That was about thirty-five years ago. And they were here for many years, maybe twenty. Now they have a pizza shop on Queens Boulevard called Alba's. That was their name."

From what he tells me as we chat, it's clear that he doesn't see this business as his calling. He's not enthusiastic about it. He admires his father's innovativeness, but he doesn't feel it's what he wants to do. I've seen it on other occasions. The younger generation isn't interested in running a retail operation. They want something more exciting. And, I suspect, many younger people want a business that they started and built on their own.

I walk by the library nearby on 256-04 Union Turnpike and am struck by its sleek ultramodern look. Its exterior is mostly glass, and when I peer through, I see it's a two-story, state-of-the-art atrium, with lots of natural light, featuring spacious reading areas. Designed by the architectural firm of Marble Fairbanks, it has won several environmental and architectural awards. Built in 2013 at a cost of $17 million, it replaced a brick structure that had stood since 1956.

Depending on how the sun hits it, one can see the word "SEARCH" in large letters on the top floor. The word "search" appears in white letters on the wall at ground-floor level in the many languages—Bengali, Hindi, Arabic, Hebrew, Chinese, Spanish, and others—spoken by the library's visitors. It's not just cosmetics, as there are

The sleek, ultramodern Glen Oaks Library.

collections of books and videos in these languages, too. As I walk in, children of seemingly every nationality are there, all excitedly crowding around and using the computers and other equipment. The two librarians with whom I speak, Ann and Scott, are very helpful and professional. While called the Glen Oaks Library, it's geographically in Floral Park, right on its northern border. Its users come from these two communities and from neighboring New Hyde Park and Bellerose.

So, does design really matter? Within weeks after it opened the library's circulation vaulted from twenty-sixth to sixth place among all Queens public libraries. Definitely worth seeing and exploring inside.

I turn right on the next corner and make my way down 257th Street to Hillside Avenue. Here I say hello to a man who turns out to be from India, and we begin a conversation.

"I see people of every nationality living here," I say, "if I can judge from the shops on Hillside Avenue."

"Yes, that's so," he says.

"Would you be friends with a Pakistani?" I ask.

"Of course. I have Pakistani neighbors, and I'm very friendly with them. And I'm also very comfortable with the Pakistanis and Bangladeshis I work with."

"But you wouldn't be if you met them in India, would you?"

"Probably not, but here we are all together, we are all immigrants, and we work for the same thing, to make a better life for our children. You see, it's all politics. The people themselves, they can get along fine."

Hillside Avenue has Indian, Afghani, Bangladeshi, Chinese, and Pakistani shops, and several Hindu temples. Located at 255-03, Usha Foods, a spotless establishment, is a good example. There's a bakery for sweet- and salty-flavored treats, sandwiches, and coffee, in an upscale environment with glass tables and modern chairs. They've won awards for their food, and wi-fi is readily available, just like in any gentrified area. There are people of various nationalities seated at the tables. I think to myself that far away from better known Astoria, Sunnyside, and Jackson Heights, there's a lot happening here.

At 258-11 Hillside, I come across Khans Tutorial, a place where children are given tutorial help in their classes and are also prepared for competitive exams, like the Regents exams, SHSAT (Specialized High School Admissions Test), and SATs that are required to gain admission to the city's top schools.

It's a sunny Sunday afternoon, and the place is packed with young children from grade school as well as high schoolers who pay scant attention to a visitor, sitting at tables writing, reading, and studying together. In the back portion of the center, one of ten Khans locations scattered throughout the city, eighth graders are being taught by an engineering graduate student from the City College of New York, who writes formulas on a blackboard, all the while being peppered with questions from very attentive students. Most of them, according to Shivam Patel, director of this Floral Park branch, are Bangladeshi or Indian.

This is a serious enterprise, very similar to the Kaplan study centers that have performed the same functions for thousands of aspiring students for decades in New York City. Outside, the center proudly displays hundreds of photos of participants who have gained entry to Bronx Science, Stuyvesant, and Brooklyn Tech high schools, the best and most coveted ones in the city, 2,252 to date from all the centers put together. It is widely known that South and East Asians are disproportionately represented in these institutions. It's estimated that Asians are about 13 percent of the city's population. But they account for about 60 percent of the students at the city's specialized high schools, and that percentage continues to rise. Less well known are the places that make it possible for this to happen. In these little centers, students learn how and what to study. They are nurtured and guided by the teachers and administrators, and they can see their futures as they gaze admiringly at the photos of those who preceded them. Shivam tells me more about these students.

"They work very hard, and they come on their own time. They take public transportation to get here, and a good number are here every day. They take a thirty-to-forty-five-minute trip from other parts of Queens and from Long Island, to study here for two hours."

"Where are you from?"

"I'm born here, and my parents are from Bangladesh. I'm studying engineering at New York Institute of Technology. My parents taught me to work hard and study in order to achieve success. It's part of our culture." This has been a hallmark of the Asian immigrants. Work hard at whatever job you can get—driving taxis, selling hot dogs, running small grocery stores. Save money and spend it on your children. Parents see their children as extensions of themselves, and their success is the ultimate achievement for them. Many immigrant business owners, clerks, and cab drivers with whom I spoke on these walks told me that they wanted their children to go into what they saw as higher-status fields like engineering, law, or medicine, even if these professions pay less.

I head south one block on 258th Street and find myself at Williston Avenue, where I spot a large, elegant sign in front of P.S. 191, established in 1954. In large gold letters, it reads: "Donated by The Boodram family in Memory of Ghanwatti Boodram." I was curious as to what the circumstances surrounding this individual's death were. Who was this person, and why is she memorialized by the school? After a little digging I uncover a tragic and interesting story.

Ghanwatti Boodram was actually a forty-one-year-old immigrant from Guyana who worked as a nurse at St. Luke's Roosevelt Hospital and lived in the community, on 260th Street. Tragically, she died in 2009 when her home exploded as a result of a gas leak. To honor her memory a section of the street on which she lived was renamed Ghanwatti Boodram Way. The family had immigrated to the United States in 1988. She was active in the Guyanese community, and hundreds of friends attended the funeral.[35]

The local community in Floral Park united behind the Boodrams, who were also involved in neighborhood groups, and collected more than one thousand gift cards for various stores to help the family rebuild their lives. Their three children attended the local public school, and this handsome sign was one way in which the family expressed its gratitude for the help they received. The children actually attended P.S. 115, and Mr. Boodram donated signs to P.S. 115 and M.S. 172 as well. Noteworthy is the fact that many of those who helped the family were not from the Guyanese community, but were Italians, Irish, Jews, and others who lived here.

A Queens County Farm Museum
B Living Museum at Creedmoor Psychiatric Center
C Preet Super Bazaar
D San Sagar Sikh Temple
E Grand Auction Mart

BELLEROSE

BELLEROSE IS A QUIET AND SAFE COMMUNITY IN NORTH-CENTRAL QUEENS. Its boundaries are the Grand Central Parkway (GCP) on the north; Little Neck Parkway on the east; Jamaica and Braddock Avenues, plus Gettysburg street, on an angle, on the south; and Stronghurst Avenue; plus a portion of the GCP, on the west. It was developed in the early 1900s by real estate developers for residential purposes. The earliest arrivals were Italians, Germans, and Irish, all looking for a way out of the crowded parts of the city. This population was augmented by the arrival of Jews in the 1940s and 1950s.

As is the case with other communities in this part of the borough, there's been a major population shift with more South Asians moving in. Members of this new group retain many aspects of their traditional life even as they Americanize, sending their children to public schools and participating in local community life. The major commercial streets are Jericho Turnpike and its western continuation of Jamaica Avenue, Braddock Avenue, and portions of Hillside Avenue and Union Turnpike.

The Queens County Farm Museum is New York City's only functioning historic farm.

Starting my trip on Little Neck Parkway, I stop in at the Queens County Farm Museum, running from Seventy-First to Seventy-Fourth Avenues and featuring numerous old buildings like barns, sheds, greenhouses, and a farmhouse. But it's much more than a museum. Open all year, seven days a week, it's the Big Apple's only functioning historic farm, growing fruits and vegetables, with goats, sheep, cows, chickens, and even some friendly llamas. In the winter the farmhouse is open, and visitors can learn what it was like to get through a winter without heat and electricity. It's a partially land-marked historic museum on 47 acres with country music, American Indian pow-wows, hayrides, and magic shows, and it has been visited by tens of thousands of schoolchildren over the years.

From here I continue south on Little Neck Parkway, hang a right at Union Turnpike and in half a mile a left onto Winchester Boulevard. Here on my left is the Creedmoor mental health campus. A prevailing view of mental illness in the late nineteenth and early twentieth centuries was that the mentally ill living in crowded cities could benefit from placement in areas that had fresh air and more open spaces, and indeed many did enjoy the country-like setting.

With this in mind a facility known as the Farm Colony was created in 1912. Reflecting the tenor of the times, the agency overseeing this operation was known by the now politically incorrect name of the Lunacy Commission of New York State.

Yet a country-like setting isn't an adequate substitute for high-quality medical treatment and care. Known as Creedmoor after the Creed family, which had farmed the land here in the nineteenth century, the place eventually became one of the many institutions that housed the mentally ill, with more than seven thousand seriously ill people here, many of them spending years, sometimes decades, with little or no improvement in their condition. This hospital and other places like Kings Park Hospital in Long Island came under attack in the 1960s and 1970s as a new movement gathered force and thousands of the mentally ill were eventually discharged and placed in city neighborhoods, where they lived in a group setting inside formerly private homes or were treated as outpatients or both. It's also fair to say that there were quite a few people who got better at Creedmoor. Today, it's much smaller and treats both inpatients and outpatients.

On the positive side and unknown, even to most New Yorkers, is the existence of the Living Museum on the Creedmoor property. The first such museum, it was created over thirty-five years ago, is one of the very few museums in the United States devoted exclusively to displaying paintings, sculptures, and other art by people with mental illness, and is probably the largest of its kind. To learn more, I visited the museum myself. Many of the original buildings are still there. Their worn look, especially on a rainy, foggy day, gave them a surreal appearance, making me wonder what secrets of despair, abuse, and degradation they might hold. I recalled tales of abandonment by family members who warehoused seriously ill relatives there, some of whom were never released. These tales have been substantiated by psychologists and psychiatrists whom I have known for forty years or more, one of whom was a senior administrator at Creedmoor at one time and arranged for me to tour the facility in the 1970s.

The museum is housed in Building 75, deep in the recesses of Creedmoor. It looks almost exactly like the others, a small Roman-style, three-story structure in a faded-beige color, with long and narrow bricks. As I approach the entrance there's a six-foot-high yellow fan on the walkway, which oscillates slowly, intermittently, and needlessly on this raw, cold afternoon in January. In the back above a platform for deliveries, two lights flash on and off every minute for no apparent reason, there being no vehicles in sight. But as I enter, the atmosphere changes completely. I look around the high, open, multistoried space with huge skylights that bring the light of day inside and am literally overwhelmed by what I see. Every inch of this old building, once the Creedmoor kitchen, and never modernized, is occupied by paintings, sculptures, oddly shaped rocks, and other mysterious objects that give full-throated expression to the creativity that can be unleashed when human beings are allowed to fully express themselves. The result is nothing short of a kaleidoscopic treasure house.

In one space is a workshop at which artist and patient John Tursi works. His specialty is fashioning human figures and other creations made entirely out of wire hangers, some of them black, others tan colored, and still others white. What emerges are beautiful sculptures—a giant sunflower of the type Vincent van Gogh drew; a golden-colored guitar made from hanger wire, featuring the guitar itself with a white human arm also made of hangers strumming the chords, and a peace sign dangling from the instrument; an elaborate self-portrait of the artist, with a giant hat perched on his head and emblazoned with capital letters spelling TURSI; and many other items that must be seen to be appreciated. Another artist, Issa Ibrahim, once a patient and now a peer counselor, specializes in paintings about the black civil rights movement of the 1960s, blended with contemporary figures like Barack Obama. One mural has a bright-red background, and in front of it, a black Batman, Superman, and Wonder Woman, the last clad in yellow-and-red bustier and star-studded briefs. In a grim reminder of what the

The Living Museum is devoted exclusively to displaying paintings, sculptures, and other art by people with mental illness.

struggle was about then, streamers coming from these superheroes read: Mammy, Sambo, Negro, and Oreo. Yet another has an American flag with dollar signs superimposed on the stars. A stern-looking Donald Trump, wearing a black suit, his arms folded, stands in front of the flag next to one of the red stripes, which reads: MAKE AMERICA GRATE AGAIN.

To learn more about this museum, I speak with Dr. Janos Marton, a Hungarian-born psychologist and the director of the museum. He was raised in Austria after his parents were expelled to that nation in 1967. He also attended art school and received a major award for his work in the field of art therapy. In his late sixties, with a full head of wavy white hair and wearing rimless glasses, he has a peculiar way about him when he speaks, alternating between serious observations about the place and its inhabitants and wry humor about them and about life in general. Highly intelligent and erudite, he peppers his speech with references to great writers, filmmakers like Fred Wiseman, and artists, as well as insightful observations about Freudian analysis, and more current treatments for mental illness. As we talk, patients wander by and say hello as they pass. Indeed, people are free to walk wherever they wish. There are no closed offices and no secretaries asking what they can do to help you.

"Some of the people have been here since 1983 when we opened," Dr. Marton tells me. "You have to be a patient or former patient to use this facility for creating art. It's not well known, even by those working in the arts and in psychiatry, that mentally ill people are extremely creative. Great art often happens in the asylum."

"Is it possible that all great artists are mad to some extent?

"I think so. The ones not regarded as mentally ill seem normal, but they cheat. They do drugs, they drink, and very few are just regular folks."

"Is doing this work therapeutic?"

"Oh yes. The important thing is identity change. The patient changes from being a patient to the higher status of being an artist. Another important thing to know about the mentally ill is that they have too much time on their hands. As a result, they sit around and watch TV all day. But if you do art, you have art to work on. And that's in addition to the spiritual benefits. And another aspect of the mentally ill is that they are often genuinely nice and generous. They've felt the pain of discrimination."

Marton introduces me to John Tursi, the artist who uses hangers in his work. Tursi tells me, "I'm not interested in selling my work. This is Jesus when he turned into a dove and flew away. The sign says, 'I love my mommy.' Here's a teddy bear I made." John is clearly a highly functioning, if somewhat scripted, individual. Sometimes when he describes something, he goes into a well-rehearsed speech it seems, his voice becoming louder and the words spilling out and sounding as if he has said them many times. Also clear is that he loves his work and that it gives him both great pride and pleasure. Next, I meet a graffiti artist from the days when the subways were covered in graffiti. He admits to having been one of those who spray-painted them. He's also proud of his past and present handiwork. As I walk by, I see an official bus sign, taken from the street, I assume. It has an additional phrase on it: "No Jim Crow." Many of these people function outside the hospital. They have carved out a life for themselves that includes a safe space when they need it.

I leave here feeling that this a unique world within a world. Dr. Marton, a remarkable, sensitive, compassionate, and unassuming man has, in effect, invented it. I am inspired by its innate beauty and hopeful vision.

Leaving Creedmoor, I cross Winchester Boulevard and head east onto Seward Avenue into a very attractive neighborhood called Bellerose Manor. It's bounded by Union Turnpike on the north, Winchester Boulevard and Moline Street on the east, Braddock Avenue on the south, and Stronghurst Avenue on the west. The homes here are more attractive and elaborate than in the rest of Bellerose, but they're not especially large. I would particularly recommend 233rd and 234th Streets between Seward and Hillside Avenues, which have a number of really quaint and well-preserved stucco homes, with multicolored Spanish tiles, some of them one-of-a-kind structures. In a neighborhood known for its cookie-cutter houses these really stand out. Among the nicest are 82-54 233rd Street and 82-31 234th Street. The latter has inset stucco in the shape of a window filled with small tiles of various colors, blue shutters, and blue tiles on the roof. On the right is another gorgeous home with arched windows.

I continue south on Winchester and eventually make a left onto Braddock Avenue. At 236-14 I pass the Preet Super-Bazaar, specializing in South Asian foods. Next to it there's a trailer encased in red, blue, and yellow tassels. Curious, I ask the owner what it's doing there. He's a Sikh, with an orange turban (religious Sikhs do not cut their hair) and a thick black beard. He has bright eyes and an exuberant personality, full of life.

"This is for parades," he tells me, "which we have, here in the community, to celebrate our holidays. On those times, I attach it to a car, and we go through the streets with people playing Sikh music and dancing. You should come next November and see it. It's great, and it's on Hillside Avenue." This is a typical feature of life in the city. Not everyone can do a parade in Manhattan, so they have local versions wherever the community members live. Paramjit invites me into the store, and I get a guided tour of the place. As we stroll up and down the aisles, he shows me an array of bags containing grains and beans of every type, none of them familiar to me. And there's quite a variety of biscuits and all kinds of spices. Of course, Indians, Pakistanis, and especially Punjabis, of whom the Sikhs are part, also buy these products. Some, like uri-dal, a reddish-orange lentil, are used for religious events held in the Sikhs' temple. There's cow ghee, a kind of butter fat made from cow's milk that's similar to an oil.

"Why did you come here from Punjab?"

"Here, I work; I make money and keep it. Over there I have to work much harder and can't keep anything because everything is corrupt. I feel one should not cheat people. If you do God will punish you. And this is my wife and my three children." The children are very friendly, and his three-year-old daughter playfully punches me in the stomach. I take a bottle of water for the road, but Paramjit won't let me pay for it.

"I see you don't cut your hair."

"Never. In India I tried to cut my hair as a teenager, but then my father, he beat me like crazy. When we coming here, from 9/11 on I never cut my hair. Some were afraid because people would think they are Muslim. But I said never cut. I am proud of my religion. You see, I'm playing religious music on the radio in the store because I am proud to be a Sikh."

"But how do you control it? Doesn't it keep growing over, say, fifteen years and then it gets too long?"

"On my head it stops growing after a time. And my beard. I show you. I roll it up. If I take off the roll it is very long, down to my feet," he says, laughing. Observant Sikhs consider hair a gift from God and a sign of love and respect for God. It's an article of faith for them. Today, in the United States, an estimated 50 percent of Sikhs still adhere to this tradition. Centuries ago, Sikhs were even willing to die rather than cut their hair.

A few blocks later, I pay a brief visit to the San Sagar Sikh Temple at 242-25 Braddock. At night, the temple's perimeter is lit up on the outside with bright lights whose red, blue, yellow, and green colors keep changing. Inside, the place is fairly large with a big carpeted space in a high-ceilinged room with several chandeliers. Holy men sit behind a holy book, praying and meditating. Called the Guru Granth Sahib, the book is a compendium of teachings and writing by Guru Nanak and other well-known gurus. The faithful enter and give charity to these priests.

Several blocks east, Braddock meets up with Jamaica Avenue, and I veer left onto it. At 248-51 Jamaica, I find myself in front of a place called Grand Auction Mart, run by Danny Schochet. The door is locked, but he's in there and greets me with a friendly hello. I am his first and only customer of the day, or so he thinks. It's a crowded, even cluttered shop, filled with antiques and stuff of all sorts: vases, statuettes, lamps, an old slot machine, and many other items I can't describe.

"Are you doing retail business here? I mean, hardly anyone's walking down the street here, and I don't see cars stopping."

"No. The retail business here is dead, dead, dead. If I make one retail sale in ten days, I'm lucky. Everything I do, and even that's not much anymore is, eBay."

"How did you adjust to that? Why stay open?"

"The antiques and collectibles markets are a dying business. It was great back in the day. I had ten antiques dealers on Atlantic Avenue in Brooklyn and about forty more in Manhattan. Now, I'm down to zero. As their leases came up, they closed. Couldn't afford the rent. I'm trying to get rid of all this stuff. Thank God, I own this two-story building. I have tenants. That's the smartest thing I did. So, what do I do? I play golf. I have a place in Palm Beach Gardens, Florida. And I live in a nice community on the island. I have fun by doing eBay."

But it isn't really fun. It's more like passing the time because, as Danny explains, "You can't really sell anything because it's global. Where once I had five people competing with me to sell, now there's fifty offering the same thing. So, the prices go down. I used to be able to sell Hummel figurines for ninety bucks each. Now they're five dollars. Too many sellers. So what if I have a Joe DiMaggio card. Everyone else does too."

Danny's a realist. He knows there's nothing he can do, and he has his children, which give him great joy, who are doing fine. Attitude is so important in these cases. These are the casualties of technological change. Many, though by no means all, people, in their fifties or sixties feel they're too young to call it quits, yet too old to start over. The more dramatic stories perhaps, are the auto workers, the old Blockbuster store clerks, those whose jobs were replaced with computers. But people like Danny are, in any case, a significant slice of the tableau of life in the city. Sometimes they just hang on eking out a living, sometimes they have savings or small investments they can live off of. When they close for good, they can retire and do nothing, or they can join the army of volunteers who help out in hospitals, museums, senior citizens' centers. But there's an upside too: without technological change that marginalized them, they might not be available to do the volunteer work that so many organizations and institutions need. How ironic.

Then there are those who can't deal with the hand they've been dealt. I spoke with one man on this walk, whose business became obsolete. He was in his store tinkering around but doing nothing. What he was selling, namely pianos, no one wanted anymore. But his reaction was completely different.

"I really shouldn't be in the business. It's just stubbornness. I feel I was the best in the business. But the best doesn't matter. No one cares about quality anymore."

"What do you regret most?" I asked him.

"That I didn't die five years ago."

"C'mon, you're not serious."

"Not very serious, but, at times, it's how I feel. Five years ago, when I was sixty-five, I still had some customers. Now I have nothing. My wife died six years ago. I have no children, and when I got sick with my back being twisted, I had a nervous breakdown and had to go into a mental institution for a few weeks." This man's story makes clear that the combination of no children, a spouse's death, medical problems, and a failing business defeated him. His setbacks were much greater than Danny's. He defines quality workmanship as a virtue and blames society's changing attitudes for his failed business. At the same time, he accepts some responsibility for not having closed the business sooner. Danny, on the other hand, had other pleasures to cushion the blow—children, grandchildren, a wife, golf, two homes, yet he's still sorry about the business because it's part of who he is.

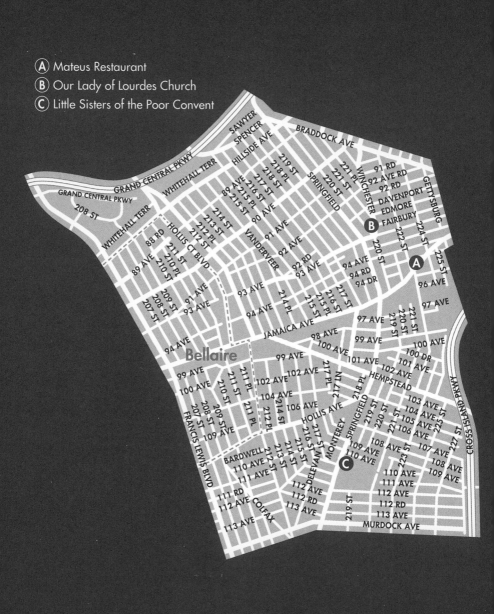

A Mateus Restaurant
B Our Lady of Lourdes Church
C Little Sisters of the Poor Convent

QUEENS VILLAGE

THIS COMMUNITY WAS FOUNDED IN THE 1640s under the name of Little Plains. In 1824, its name was changed to Brushville, after Thomas Brush, a local entrepreneur. In the early twentieth century its name changed once again, becoming Queens Village. In the beginning, white ethnic groups like the Irish, Germans, Italians, and Jews predominated. After World War II, African Americans and Hispanics began to move in. Today, it's home to a very diverse community, including Haitians, West Indians, Guyanese, Hispanics, and African Americans. Its boundaries are, roughly, Grand Central Parkway and Braddock Avenue on the north, Gettysburg Street and the Cross Island Parkway on the east, Murdock Avenue on the south, and Francis Lewis Boulevard on the west.

A very residential and geographically large community, Queens Village has thousands of older, modest detached and semi-attached homes. Walking through many of its quiet, tree-lined streets, I feel as if I've stepped back into the past, perhaps the 1920s, when many of these Tudors and colonial frame houses were much newer. As I look at the sky, its gentle hues of pink, orange, and yellow blending into one another as the sun sets, it seems as though nature's beauty has overtaken the urban sprawl—traffic lights, small shopping centers, buses, highways—that epitomize giant cities like New York. While the housing is fairly uniform throughout, the Bellaire section on the south side of Jamaica Avenue, between One Hundredth and One Hundred Fourth Avenues, is a bit more upscale. The main commercial streets are Jamaica, Hollis, and Hempstead Avenues, plus Springfield Boulevard.

Generally speaking, ethnic stores, especially eateries, can be indicators of which groups live in a community. Certainly, the West Indian shops in Queens Village reflect West Indians' presence in the community, but it's not always the case. Take Mateus, a Portuguese restaurant at 222-07 Jamaica Avenue. There isn't a Portuguese community here, but there once was. I speak with the owner, Ilidio Chaves, a Portuguese immigrant, who tells me more.

"I came here when I was eleven," he says. "At that time there were a couple of hundred Portuguese families here, and we had a community. I went to the local schools and took over the family restaurant. There's also a community near here, in Mineola, Long Island. Senator Jack Martins, whose district includes Mineola, is originally Portuguese. Quite a few of our dishes are Portuguese cuisine, but we have everything here, American dishes, and local favorites for new groups, West Indians, Guyanese, and also Hispanics. So, we adapted, and there was no need to move. People come here because the food is good."

It's almost impossible to know that this was once a Portuguese enclave because the literature about Queens Village makes no mention of it and the major Portuguese Queens community was in Jamaica. Walking is how I discovered this place, as well as a tiny redoubt on the next block, called the Queens Village Portuguese Soccer Club. Ilidio tells me that it was once quite active, but today there are only a few senior citizens who come there.

Turning right on 220th Street, I walk along until I come to Winchester Boulevard. Here I see a long, low building with a blue grotto in the back, off to the side of a chapel. It belongs to Our Lady of Lourdes Church, located a block away on Springfield Boulevard, and established in 1924. The grotto, exquisitely designed, is dedicated to the memory of Bernadette Soubirous, a young woman who, it is believed, had a series of Marian visions. Since that date, February 11, 1858, millions of the faithful have visited Lourdes, France, and Bernadette is venerated as a saint by the Catholic religion. I enter the building in the twilight of a warm Sunday in February. Inside, the church is paneled in dark wood, and wooden beams support the structure. There are bas-reliefs of saints along the walls on both sides. As I listen to the service in French Creole, I realize the worshipers are Haitian. Suddenly my mind goes back to 1969, when I saw a similar looking church in the tiny village of Fermat, Haiti.

My graduate department in sociology and anthropology at Washington University (St. Louis) had sent me to Haiti to do anthropological fieldwork. It was a remarkable, eye-opening experience as I was on my own with no guidance where to go. I decided to try to find a village in the mountains of Haiti near the Dominican border and was fortunate to make the acquaintance of Pastor Wallace Turnbull, who arranged for me to travel to a small village in an area called Nouvelle Touraine. Visiting his Baptist church outside Port au Prince prior to going on my trip, I heard the same soft voicing of devotees singing beautifully in Creole with great fervor.

There are, conservatively speaking, about two hundred thousand people of Haitian origin living in New York City. Some say the number, including undocumented residents, may be double that. In any case, they are a significant presence in the city, especially in Brooklyn and Queens. About thirty-five thousand Haitians reside in Queens, spread throughout several communities, including Queens Village, Cambria Heights, Springfield Gardens, and Laurelton. Their members are generally hardworking and upwardly mobile. Their faith is very important to them, as evidenced by the number of churches here.

Heading back to Jamaica Avenue I see, at 96-59 222nd Street, a sign on a building, "Lincoln Studios." Today's it's the home of the Donnelly Mechanical Corporation, which specializes in heating and air conditioning. Curious about the sign, I speak with the owner, Dan Donnelly.

"I bought the building ten years ago from them," he tells me. "While they did do some productions for TV and plays, their main line of work was building exhibits like for the Javits Convention

Center. But they had a problem with their neighbor, the MTA, whose busses make a lot of noise and who used to block their entrances."

"How do you feel about having this large business in Queens Village?"

"I love it because this is a multiuse community. We have businesses and a lot of private homes, and everyone gets along. There's a low crime rate. I've never been robbed or broken into. There's a Seventh Day Adventist church across the street called the Queensboro Temple, and they give out free food to the hungry and homeless twice a month, on Wednesdays. The line goes around the block. That's what a real community should do. I thank God that I'm not homeless." The fact is that thousands of people and hundreds of New York City institutions care about and help the homeless. And their work is supported by many more people like Dan Donnelly.

On Springfield Boulevard and Jamaica, I turn left and eventually come to the Little Sisters of the Poor Convent and St. Ann's Novitiate. On the day that I visit, most of the nuns are away, caring for senior citizens at their nursing home nearby, Queen of Peace. The convent is at 110-39 Springfield near One-Hundred-Tenth Avenue. It is surrounded by a light-gray concrete wall about ten feet high. The tall gates happened to be open, for a delivery as it turned out, so I decided to take a peek. The grounds are lovely, with benches and statues along curving byways that run through a grassy lawn. Perhaps it's because of the location, but it definitely feels very tranquil as I walk through it, pausing for a few moments to sit on a concrete bench. I go up the steps of the large red-brick, tile-roof, Italianate-style building and am greeted by a seamstress from Europe who works there. She tells me, with a trace of sadness, that currently there are only two novitiates in residence. This is hardly shocking, as the number of nuns in the United States has fallen from about 180,000 in 1965 to about 50,000 in 2014, a drop of about 72 percent.[36]

The Little Sisters of the Poor Convent has been in existence here since 1902.

The convent, founded in France in 1839, has been in existence here since 1902, fulfilling the order's mission to care for people and, especially, the aged and infirm. Nowhere else, perhaps, do I feel the contrast between the sacred and profane more sharply than when I walk out and look at the nail salons, video shops, auto body places, and delis and take note of the traffic going by on the boulevard. These nuns have chosen to dwell in the city even though they are definitely not of the city. At the same time this small order, of twenty-three hundred members in this country, has been involved in a controversial case, heard by the US Supreme Court in 2016, related to whether or not employers are required to provide free contraceptives to employees. The Little Sisters argued that they should not be compelled to provide free insurance coverage for contraceptives. The Supreme Court sent the case back to the lower courts along with some comments. And so, we see that the outside world can intrude on those who retreat from it in all sorts of unanticipated ways.

The convent serves as a reminder that this was once a white community with a very strong Catholic presence. I spoke with Marjorie Burnside, a former New York Police Department officer who grew up in Queens Village.

"Our family moved to Queens Village in 1969," she tells me, "when I was four years old. We lived on 215th Place and Ninety-Third Avenue. We were raised not only by our families, but our community. We volunteered as candy stripers at Little Sisters of the Poor on weekends. We also put on Broadway plays to raise money for Our Lady of Lourdes Church. Our little village got bigger as we got older and started hanging out in the parks with kids from adjoining parishes. In high school, we were working alongside of them in fast-food places and at Antun's Catering Hall." What is clear here is that this community was centered around the church and that social relationships with friends and family were intertwined with it. Today, the convent is mostly what's left of the community; that and the nostalgia for what once was by former residents. Marjorie reminisces about that too as she places it in what she knows of the community's history.

"From my front stoop you could see clear up to Jamaica Avenue through the canopy of trees," she says. "At the intersection was the Community Movie Theatre and what was once the Community Gardens building. There they used to have live bands and dance socials in the forties and fifties, and teenagers went to dances there through the 1960s. In the other direction was Mr. Sugarman's Deli, who knew everyone on a first-name basis. My brother and I would often walk here to pick up bread and milk for my mom, and if there was change, we'd go next door to Helen's Candy Store and buy penny candy. Woolworth's had a luncheonette counter where you could get an old-fashioned egg cream with your platter. And there were no play dates then, or video games. To see our friends, we rode our bikes and walked to school."

Marjorie lovingly identifies all these places that gave her a feeling of closeness to others and of being recognized as an individual even if she was just a kid. The storeowner knew her and her friends "on a first-name basis." She observes that there were no "play dates" or "video games." The feeling one gets is that people interacted and communicated with each other in a less structured and more intimate way. One had to make the connections on one's own. There's both a sense of loss as she speaks, yet also an appreciation of what she had as a child. Those memories are for her a source of comfort, even joy, as she thinks about them.

Surely, the children growing up in Queens Village today will also have memories of their own one day, but the content will be different, a product of the modern age. Perhaps they'll recall the video games that Marjorie didn't have, the home theaters in their basements, the amusement parks they went to, the way they communicated with their friends on their iPads or iPhones. Thus, when one walks through a community today it's important to treat it as a snapshot suspended in time. What it means today to its residents may differ in some ways from what it means to those who lived there in the past. Yet what it means to be a part of a community is not that different.

CAMBRIA HEIGHTS

HOLLIS

ST. ALBANS

LAURELTON

ROSEDALE

SPRINGFIELD GARDENS

JAMAICA

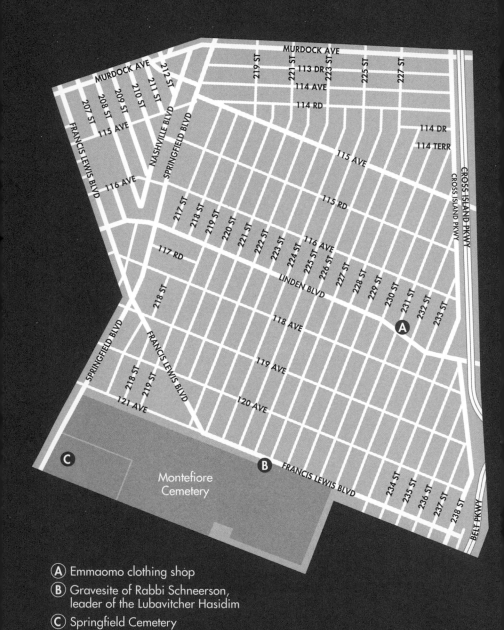

Ⓐ Emmaomo clothing shop
Ⓑ Gravesite of Rabbi Schneerson,
   leader of the Lubavitcher Hasidim
Ⓒ Springfield Cemetery

CAMBRIA HEIGHTS

A SMALL COMMUNITY IN SOUTHEASTERN QUEENS, Cambria Heights is bounded by Murdock Avenue on the north; the Cross Island Parkway on the east; Francis Lewis Boulevard, One Hundred Twenty-First Avenue, and Montefiore Cemetery, alongside and beyond it, on the south; and Francis Lewis and Springfield Boulevards on the west. It was founded in 1923, and its population, almost all white then, consisted of Irish, Italians, Germans, and Jews. In the 1960s, black families in search of the American dream began moving here.

Today, Cambria Heights is a very nice, middle class black community with many people from the Caribbean, especially from Haiti, and also a sizeable number of Guyanese. It doesn't have jazz greats, hip-hop personalities, or sports figures, like St. Albans, its neighbor to the west. But it's very safe, with miles and miles of small but beautifully maintained homes, the vast majority of them Cape Cods. There isn't much nightlife either and no abundant shopping, but most of the residents seem to like it that way because they're home owners who wanted suburban living with lower city taxes than was the case in the suburbs. Its main commercial thoroughfare is Linden Boulevard.

In Cambria Heights, which is overwhelmingly black, and heavily Caribbean, African Americans and West Indians may, like in many other communities, have ambivalent feelings about each other. To learn more about this issue I spoke with Marie Adam-Ovide, district manager of Queens Community Board number 8 and got an interesting response.

"These were mostly my parents' concerns," she tells me. "They put certain people in a box: 'Don't get into trouble with the Jamaicans because of this or that, nor with African Americans because of this or that.' But then you go to school, where you meet kids and find that some of them are not getting into trouble. And I find that the African American kids get the same stuff from their parents for similar reasons: 'Don't hang out with the Haitians, because they're stuck up'; and they called them 'Frenchie' because they went to school and they dressed a certain way. In Haiti, you went to school in uniforms. So here I had slacks and skirts but not jeans, and that did not go over well in school. Pretty soon I convinced my parents to let me wear the jeans, because I told them if I didn't, I was going to get beat up."

Every immigrant group must adapt somewhat to the culture of the receiving country, and the Caribbeans do that, as can be seen from this story. Adam-Ovide's comments also remind us not to stereotype when walking through communities. What may seem like a monolithic black community is often quite varied. There are differences not only between African Americans and Caribbean-origin people, but also within immigrant groups. People from Haiti are different culturally from those who hail from the West Indies, and Africans are culturally distinct from all the other groups.

The importance of this last group is highlighted as I pass the Emmaomo clothing shop at 231-01 Linden Boulevard, specializing in traditional African clothing. There are many such shops in the city, and this one is pretty typical. Among the items offered are robes, dresses, suits, beads, jewelry, pocketbooks, and gift baskets. I decide to take a look and am greeted by Emma Omotade, the proprietor. She's African American, and her husband is a Nigerian from the Yoruba tribal group.

"Hello. How are you?" she asks in a very friendly voice.

"Great." Seeing a $100 bill scotch-taped to the back of the cash register I ask Emma, "What's this bill doing here? And what do the words: 'The first and last, in Jesus' name,' mean?"

"It means that I pray this is the last counterfeit bill I ever get."

"Do your clothes come from a specific African country?"

"Oh yes. And we even know what tribe they come from. Every group is trying to relate to their history and culture, and this is what

The Emmaomo clothing shop specializes in traditional African clothing.

Emmaomo is trying to bring into the community. My husband and I have done some research on who comes from where. Most of the Jamaicans are actually Nigerians of the Ibo tribe. The Haitians are mostly from Guinea, Togo, and Benin. Of course, this can't be precisely determined for an individual, but establishing a connection clearly helps with sales because folks believed to come from these lands will feel a concrete connection to clothes they buy that were produced there. They can say: 'I'm wearing traditional clothing from my homeland.'"

"Are people coming in a lot and expressing a desire to make this connection?"

"Actually, it's something I'm trying to promote. I had people come in from South Africa wanting African clothing from there, and I didn't have any from their tribes. We sold these dresses here to the church that are made from a cotton material called "Ankara," and we sold them for $65 each. They were very popular."

On the surface this looks like an entrepreneurial effort to promote sales through culture, but it's actually far more important than that. As the only group that came from another country and was enslaved, blacks were oppressed in ways that had far-reaching consequences for their identity. The plantation masters tried to obliterate their history so as to demoralize them and reduce the likelihood of rebellion. In many cases slaves were separated from those who came from their land. The emphasis on African culture by blacks in this country—in books and TV series, like Alex Haley's *Roots*; by celebrating Kwanzaa; by taking trips to Africa; through DNA testing to determine country of origin; and, in this case, by wearing African garb—is part of a general movement to engender pride.

I continue my walk down Linden, but there isn't that much to see. Most of the stores are restaurants, nail salons, and barber shops, with lots of nice-looking, small storefront churches, as well as some large ones. A few indicate the ethnicity of their adherents—West Indian, Haitian, and so on. One sign does catch my eye. It's a driving school called "Moses the Patient." A very unusual name, to be sure, and also a reminder that patience is a crucial qualification when it comes to teaching people how to drive. To get a flavor for what it's like to live here I take detours onto a number of side streets on either side of Linden. It's as quiet and peaceful a community as any I've seen.

In another section of Cambria Heights, where One Hundred Twenty-First Avenue intersects with Francis Lewis Boulevard, I have a totally different experience. Inside the Jewish Montefiore Cemetery is the grave of Rabbi Menachem Mendel Schneerson, the leader of the Lubavitcher Hasidim, a group with hundreds of thousands of adherents around the world. Hasidim are devout Orthodox Jews with an emphasis on spirituality, rather than Talmudic scholarship. They wear distinctive black clothing and hat and are extremely devoted to their chief rabbi, in this case Rabbi Schneerson. Their group is not insular at all. They are dedicated to reaching out to Jews and increasing their level of religious observance. I go through the entrance on One Hundred Twenty-First Avenue at 228th Street, turn right, and soon come to the welcome center. I see a member of the Lubavitcher Hasidic sect and ask: "Why is his grave all the way out here instead of in an easier place to get to, like Brooklyn?"

"The Rebbe's father-in-law was buried here in 1950, and the Rebbe [the popular name for Rabbi Schneerson] used to visit his grave here a lot. He was close to him and wanted to be buried here."

I speak with a middle-aged man originally from England, Rabbi Abba, who welcomes visitors. He has a warm voice and a neatly trimmed brown beard, wears a black hat, and has twinkling, brown eyes that exude warmth.

"What an interesting coincidence," I say. "Crown Heights, where your headquarters are, is a largely black community, and so is Cambria Heights, where the cemetery's located."

"Yes, and quite a few of the locals here were apprehensive about us coming here. I mean, around the holidays, like Rosh Hashanah, we get thousands of visitors. But over the years we've worked out a relationship with them. Some are anti-Semitic; many aren't. Some are fine with us being here. They appreciate that it's a spiritual experience. Some of these blacks even have a photo of the Rebbe in their homes. Others are apathetic about it. By the way, this welcome center was once a home bordering the cemetery that we bought and changed into the welcome center."

"What makes the grave of the Rebbe holy?"

"Partly that when a person is buried, we believe that a part of the soul stays with the body. According to the Kabbalah [a mystical Jewish work] the body is the vehicle by which people actually do good deeds. So as a token of appreciation part of the soul remains with the body."

"Do you believe, as I've heard, that the Rebbe is possibly the Messiah and will come back as such one day?"

"We believe that the Messiah will be a very special and spiritual person. And the Rebbe would be an excellent candidate for it." It's an indirect response, and I decide not to push it. The Rebbe was childless, and no successor has been appointed. However, the movement has continued to thrive through its many local leaders around the world and the influence of his teachings, which are continually studied by his followers. One of his teachings was the importance of outreach, and I mention this.

"It's not only that it's important," Rabbi Abba tells me. "It's a privilege to do so. The Rebbe said never to judge by outward appearances. Everyone has a spark of holiness in them."

At this point, Rabbi Abba takes me to the actual grave (it's called "the Ohel," or tent) of the Rebbe. I'm asked to write the name of my mother on a slip of paper and express a wish. One doesn't have to be Jewish to do this. Victor Espinoza, the jockey who rode American Pharaoh to become the first Triple Crown winner in thirty-seven years, prayed at the gravesite before the race. I also recall meeting a woman who was a devotee of the Russian Orthodox Church who told me she regularly visits the grave of the Rebbe.

"But you're not Jewish?" I asked her.

"Yes," she responded. "But he was a holy man."

Rabbi Abba is a man whose whole life revolves around religion. But more than that he wants to share his beliefs with others. There's no price that can measure his happiness when he touches a human being's soul. One sees it on his face. One hears it in his voice.

Adjacent to Montefiore, on Springfield Boulevard, there's a non-sectarian cemetery called the Springfield Cemetery. Cars speed by, never slowing down on this quiet stretch. It's really old, one of the oldest in the city, having been established in 1670. The oldest remaining gravestone is that of Jean Cornell, who died in 1761.[37] As I wander among the graves, I see the variety of types buried here. There are the old Dutch names like Nostrand and, also, modern gravestones of Russians, who place large portraits of the dead on the surface of the headstone.

People place all sorts of things here, plastic flowers, children's toys. A red-and-white pinwheel flutters in the breeze as a robin lands nearby, chirping its own song of spring, heralding a new season of life for everything that grows. Amid all the stones, many of them faded, crooked, and broken, are new sections featuring the stones, set into the ground, of people who died five or ten years ago, or even last year. I find myself wondering how many of these people have not had a visitor in many, many years, perhaps even a century? Yet they all believed or hoped they would be remembered. Perhaps it's just as well that they don't know. It's a humbling thought.

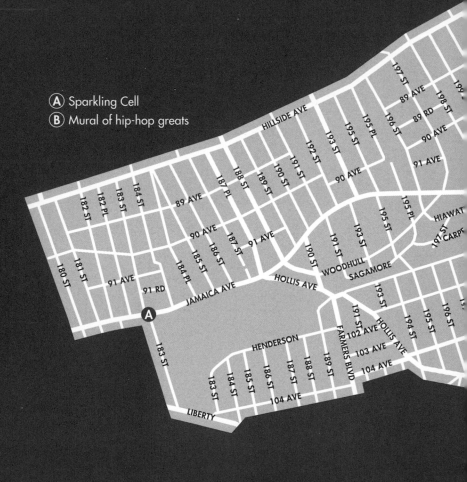

(A) Sparkling Cell
(B) Mural of hip-hop greats

HILLSIDE AVE

197 ST
89 AVE
198 ST
89 RD
90 AVE
195 ST
195 PL
196 ST
91 AVE
193 ST
192 ST
191 ST
190 ST
189 ST
188 ST
187 PL
90 AVE
184 ST
183 ST
182 PL
182 ST
89 AVE
90 AVE
90 AVE
91 AVE
195 ST
195 PL
HIAWAT
191 CARPE
195 PL
195 ST
193 ST
191 AVE
187 ST
90 AVE
91 AVE
185 ST
186 ST
184 PL
190 ST
191 AVE
WOODHULL
SAGAMORE
181 ST
180 ST
91 AVE
91 RD
184 PL
JAMAICA AVE
HOLLIS AVE
(A)
193 ST
183 ST
HENDERSON
FARMERS BLVD
102 AVE
HOLLIS AVE
194 ST
195 ST
196 ST
183 ST
184 ST
185 ST
186 ST
187 ST
188 ST
189 ST
191 ST
103 AVE
104 AVE
104 AVE
LIBERTY

HOLLIS

HOLLIS WAS DEVELOPED FOR RESIDENTIAL LIVING near the end of the nineteenth century after having been farmland from the seventeenth century on. Until the early 1950s it was a mostly white community, changing over by the early 1960s to a predominantly African American working- and middle-class community. Today, the population has been augmented by influxes of Guyanese, South Asians, and Latinos. At first glance, Hollis seems to be an extension of Queens Village. Many of the homes look similar to those in Queens Village, and Hollis borders it on the east, separated by Francis Lewis Boulevard. However, culturally and historically, it's really closer to St. Albans, which begins at Hollis Avenue, its southern border, and this is how many of its residents see it.

Hollis's boundaries, roughly, are Hillside Avenue on the north, Francis Lewis Boulevard on the east, Hollis Avenue on the south, and 180th and 183rd Streets on the west. The homes in the Hollis Gardens Park section and the homes between Ninety-Ninth and One Hundred Fourth Avenues are, in many cases, worth seeing for their attractiveness. One fine example of this is 100-50 199th

Street, a spacious Dutch colonial on a corner lot, where Reverend Al Sharpton lived at one time. The main commercial thoroughfares are Jamaica and Hillside Avenues.

I begin my exploration of Hollis at Hollis Avenue and 205th Street, where hip-hop began. Generally defined, hip-hop is a cultural form of expression consisting of breakdancing, graffiti art, DJ performance, and rapping. I begin my trip, appropriately enough, at 205th Street, renamed Run-DMC, JMJ Way, after hip-hop artists Darryl "DMC" McDaniels, Joseph "DJ Run" Simmons, and JMJ, Jason "Jam Master Jay" Mizell, right where it intersects with Hollis Avenue. Among the best-known hit hip-hop singles are "Christmas in Hollis" (Run-DMC) and "Hollis to Hollywood" (LL Cool J).[38]

Joseph and his brother, Russell, founder of Def Jam Records, grew up at 104-16 One Hundred Ninth Avenue, and Jam Master Jay was raised at 109-81 203rd Street (the house number isn't on the house entrance, but 109-79 and 109-85 are on each side of it). Their success put them and other hip-hop artists in a position to advocate for racial justice, which they did through their music and public comments. These groups had millions of followers, and their success demonstrated to the black community that people can succeed if they're talented and ambitious. Of course, people evolve over time, and while Darryl McDaniels still performs, Joey Simmons is now a Pentecostal minister, known colloquially as "Reverend Run." But Run-DMC has achieved immortality, having been inducted into the Rock and Roll Hall of Fame. I speak with Ralph McDaniels, the hip-hop coordinator for the Queens Library, to get an idea of what it was like to live here in the early days.

"I'm fifty-eight," he says, "and when I first moved out here in the early 1970s, we lived in Queens Village. We were like, maybe the second black family on the block on 212th and Murdock, just a few blocks from St. Albans. That was the first time I ever heard the word nigger. Coming from Brooklyn, I didn't know what that word meant. But I knew it wasn't good. I told my mother, and she looked

Jam Master Jay wears his trademark black hat in this mural on 205th street.

at me like, 'We came from Brooklyn looking for a nicer place to live, and now this? Some people are just not nice.' Welcome to the real world. And today, it's all changed. And the hip-hop scene was very important, and it's critical that people get an understanding of how significant this scene was to the black communities around here."

It does matter indeed. The 1980s were wracked by the violence and despair that prevailed during the crack epidemic of that decade. And hip-hop, while it too was associated with violence, guns, and drugs, was also a movement of great creativity as exemplified by the music that flowered during that era.

On 205th, corner of Hollis, there's a mural, *The Best DJ in the U.S. of A.* It shows a very well-done image of JMJ wearing his trademark round black hat and leather jacket and a cool-looking pair of sneakers next to it. This location is not accidental, as quite a few hip-hop greats lived in the immediate vicinity, including Jam Master Jay, whose house was 203-81 203rd Street, and Run, who resided on 205th Street, also near Hollis Avenue. Q-Tip (the "Q" stands for Queens) from the group a Tribe Called Quest, once lived not far from here, on Linden Boulevard. A mural of the group, whose members also include Phife Dawg Way, can be found on 192nd Street near the corner of Hollis. To find out more about these artists and to speak with those who grew up with them, I walk into the In the Chair Barber Shop at 203-5A Hollis and speak with Jah-Jah, a master haircutter, and others. While people are careful in what they say because some of these artists died violent deaths, I still learn quite a bit about who these people were in terms of their work and the almost worshipful way in which they are viewed by the locals.

Hollis Playground, known locally as 192 Park, is on the corner of 205th and Hollis. It's another important location because hip-hop artists used to jam there. They often used an outlet on a lamppost at 205th to broadcast the music to teenagers in the playground. The police would come and remove the extension cord because no permit had been issued. But more often than not, an extension cord would be plugged in again a day or two later. In truth, the entire community is infused with local lore about this musical movement that went national in the 1980s.

I enter the St. Albans branch of the Queens Public Library system a few blocks west on Hollis Avenue. The manager, Kacper Jarecki, is very attentive to those using the computers, most of them elderly black people, asking them repeatedly if they need assistance and patiently answering their questions. Suddenly, I hear the sounds of Ping-Pong, a sport I love. Sure enough, in the back of the main room there are two adults enjoying a game. I've never seen this in any of the many city libraries I've visited. I ask one of the players what this is doing in a library.

"I mean, isn't the noise distracting here?" I ask. "And isn't a library mainly devoted to books?"

One of the players, also an employee there, gives me an interesting answer. "This library is in a community with lots of poor people. Maybe because of their problems, lots of them don't read much. But they do like Ping-Pong, and we use it to draw them into the library, and then, hopefully, we can interest them in the books we have." A library is there to serve the community and needs to adjust to its members.

Walking along Jamaica Avenue on a Friday afternoon, I spot a group of Mexicans playing Mariachi music near 201st Street. They are wearing the sombreros and colorful shirts associated with their trade. They tell me they're practicing and getting ready to do their thing in the subway stations of Manhattan. They live nearby, part of this ethnically polyglot community. Speaking of which, I also notice that many of the small private detached homes between Francis Lewis and 180th Place have flags clustered together outside the front of their houses. Called *jhandis* and resting on mats of bamboo poles, they are commonly displayed among Hindus from Caribbean lands like Guyana as a symbol of pride and religious faith. The custom, not practiced by all Hindus, comes from a part of central India known as Bhojpuri Belt, where *jhandis* are very popular. It is where many of the Guyanese came from in the nineteenth century.

At 195th Street on Hillside Avenue are two brick pillars, topped by large stone urns. Etched in concrete is "Fairmount Avenue" (the street's former name) and a carving beneath it identifying this section as Hollis Park Gardens, a residential development. On 195th between Hillside and Ninetieth Avenue, I spy several really nice colonial homes, all worth seeing. The next street west is 193rd Street, a broad thoroughfare with a grassy divider. The homes along 193rd are also quite handsome, as are those on 192nd and 191st Streets. It's a great area to walk through and explore.

At 182-07 Jamaica Avenue I meet Honnette Goodluck, the owner of Sparkling Cell, "where the prices are too low to say no." A native of Guyana, he's standing outside, a merchant with a ready smile for everyone. He's dressed casually, but neatly, wearing a green Ralph Lauren sweater, jeans, and a cool-looking pair of sneakers. Middle-aged and energetic, he gives the impression of someone who's been around and knows what he's doing. His small shop, like others I've gone into, carries a little bit of everything. There's coffee, toiletries, Tide detergent, women's handbags, coats, jackets, t-shirts with names like Tupac Shakur emblazoned on them, and expensive perfume sold at a substantial discount. He shares the space with his wife, who runs a salon, with several chairs. It's a logical decision because in these outlying communities, there aren't department stores within easy reach. And the hours are long—the store is open from morning until 9:00 p.m.

"Are these Michael Kors handbags real?" I ask.

"Oh, yes."

"You're kidding."

"Oh no. Out here you don't want to risk a fine for doing that. It's not worth it. And you want to do it the right way. We buy them at high volume, together with six or seven others, and we get a good price for them. And we don't have the overhead of a Macy's. We're doing a men's cologne drive at half price if you're interested." I don't bite and change the subject.

"What did you do in Guyana?"

"I worked for a while in a family-run gold mine. You take the sand and put it into a batel [the prospector's gold pan] to extract the gold. My uncle owned the machinery we used. You get paid well for it. I left there in 1987 at age nineteen." Gold has become important to Guyana's economy, but it's also a risky proposition, with robberies and theft not uncommon as the price of gold remains high.

"What made you decide to come here?"

"America's a great country. I had always loved technology, and what better place than America to be involved in that. Before I came here, I was given a How and Why Wonder book about technology, and I really got turned on. They talked about electricity, mechanics, to get young people to choose a trade." The How and Why Wonder books were a series of illustrated volumes, released in the 1960s and 1970s, whose audience was children and teenagers.

Honnette's story is yet another example of what it means to be an immigrant. He works hard, tries to find something he likes, and has dreams about working at what he loves. Clearly, he's not doing major things in technology, but he's connected to it in some way, selling technology products. And he's proud of his children, who are doing well, typical of so many immigrants I've encountered. If they can't completely achieve their goals, then at least their children may.

Perhaps the most unusual aspect of Honnette's life is that his wife is a Guyanese Indian and he is a Guyanese from Africa. This is both a racial and a cultural divide. The population is divided about 50/50 between the two groups, and they have a long and bitter history of disliking each other. In New York, the Guyanese Africans reside primarily in Brooklyn, in communities like East Flatbush, and the Guyanese Indians are concentrated mostly in Richmond Hill, Queens. I asked Honnette how this marriage came about.

"A friend of mine who was married introduced me to her," he tells me. "We each thought it would be interesting to have a relationship with someone from a group we'd been taught to dislike. And it worked out well because I'm not a typical black person, largely because I own and operate my own business. Most black people are in the civil service—bus drivers, teachers, government workers."

In a sense, this may have been Honnette's biggest achievement, at least on a personal level. He was able to bridge the gap between two hostile cultures and thereby reveal the true promise of America, an America that gives people the opportunity to get to know each other on neutral territory, that is, away from the tensions that prevail in their homeland. In so doing he and his wife set an example for openness and tolerance for their children and others around them.

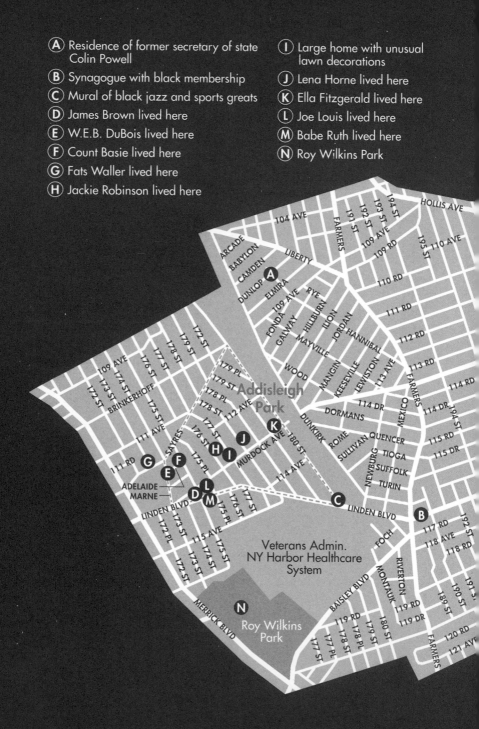

Ⓐ Residence of former secretary of state Colin Powell
Ⓑ Synagogue with black membership
Ⓒ Mural of black jazz and sports greats
Ⓓ James Brown lived here
Ⓔ W.E.B. DuBois lived here
Ⓕ Count Basie lived here
Ⓖ Fats Waller lived here
Ⓗ Jackie Robinson lived here
Ⓘ Large home with unusual lawn decorations
Ⓙ Lena Horne lived here
Ⓚ Ella Fitzgerald lived here
Ⓛ Joe Louis lived here
Ⓜ Babe Ruth lived here
Ⓝ Roy Wilkins Park

ST. ALBANS

ST. ALBANS HAS A RICH AND STORIED HISTORY AS A BLACK COMMUNITY. It was considered *the* place in Queens for upwardly mobile African Americans, and many well-known personalities were attracted to it and contributed greatly to its reputation. While it doesn't have the glory of the old days when it was considered *the community* in which to live by most people in the black community, it remains a very viable area with many hardworking and stable families. Its boundaries, generally, are Hollis and One Hundred Ninth Avenues on the north; Francis Lewis Boulevard on the east; Springfield Boulevard, One Hundred Twenty-First Avenue, and One Hundred Twentieth Avenue on the south; and Merrick Boulevard on the west. The main commercial streets are Hollis Avenue, Farmers Boulevard, and Linden Boulevard. It has one major recreational area, Roy Wilkins Park.

St. Albans has a wide mix of homes—colonials, Tudors, capes, some attached, some not. It has better-built housing stock overall than Queens Village and about the same as Hollis. The homes between Hollis and One Hundred Fourth Avenues are well constructed, but the most beautiful area by far is the historic district of Addisleigh Park, which was where wealthier folks, including many show business personalities, lived. When first developed in the early twentieth century, it was a white community with restrictive covenants designed to keep out other groups. But that all changed in the early 1940s when blacks began moving in. Today, it's overwhelmingly black, with many residents of Caribbean heritage, and has retained much of its charm and beauty. This triangle-shaped area is bounded by Linden Boulevard, Sayres Avenue, and 180th Street.

I begin my trip through St. Albans at 183-68 Elmira Avenue, where former secretary of state Colin Powell moved from the Bronx in 1955. To find it, head west on Hollis Avenue until it meets up with One Hundred Ninth Avenue. Continue west on Liberty Avenue, make a quick right and then a quick left, and you're on Elmira. It's a small, charming, and well-maintained Cape Cod. Most of the homes are identical, and it could be a street in any quiet suburb of America. In his case it literally was a dream come true, courtesy of Powell's father. Powell's parents regularly played the numbers in the Bronx, and one night he had a dream in which a number appeared. When he went to church the next day, the same number appeared on the hymn board. Seeing this as a divine sign, Luther Powell bet $25 on it, a lot for a family earning $100 a week, and hit the jackpot of $10,000. He used that money to buy the Queens house for $17,500. Many people see the numbers as just a racket, but for others it was seen as a path to the promised land, whatever the odds. Colin Powell describes what it meant to live in this part of Queens, a veritable gold coast for the black middle class. "Our new home was ivy-covered, well-kept and comfortable, and had a family room and a bar in the finished basement. Pop was now a property owner, eager to mow his postage stamp lawn and prune his fruit trees. Luther Powell had joined the gentry."[39] But his mother was a worrier, concerned that they wouldn't be able to carry the mortgage. It took years for her to feel they wouldn't have to move back to the Bronx.

Walking west to the corner of Elmira, I turn left onto Dunkirk Avenue, take it all the way, past Murdock to Farmers Boulevard. Turning right I go one block, hang a left onto Linden Boulevard, and a few doors down, on my left, I'm standing at 189-31 Linden Boulevard under the canopy of Beth Elohim Hebrew Congregation. It's an unusual house of worship in this area because the overwhelming majority of black people in this country, be they from the United States, the West Indies, or Africa, are either Christians or Muslims. Black Jews are a rarity. I pick up a flier with the headline "Let My People Go," which proclaims the imminent arrival of the Passover holiday in early April. It's basically a form for those who wish to attend a *seder*, or meal on the holiday.[40] Next door on the left is the Scriptural Baptist Church.

Three blocks farther in the other direction, right under the St. Albans Long Island Railroad Station, I come to a very important memorial to the great black music and sports figures who lived in or near the Addisleigh Park enclave of St. Albans. The large blue-and-orange mural has well-drawn lifelike versions of some of these people including James Brown, Fats Waller, Count Basie, Ella Fitzgerald, and others. They're all depicted here singing or playing on musical instruments or both. For example, Count Basie is playing the piano, and Billie Holiday is singing her lungs out. Three sports heroes portrayed here are Roy "Campy" Campanella, Jackie Robinson, and the boxer Tommy "Hurricane" Jackson. While the mural has not been defaced, there's one scrawled query about Robinson. With an arrow pointing to a rendering of Robinson's midcentury sneakers, the question reads: "What are Those?"

Besides the music and sports people, there were other very important folks who lived here. I decide to create my own minitour of some of these people.[41] First, I pass the home of James Brown at 175-19 Linden Boulevard. Known as "the Godfather of Soul," he was a singer, musician, and songwriter who reached the pinnacle of success in the 1960s and 1970s. It's a gray stucco medieval revival house with a striking brick turret made of all kinds of stone, with

A memorial to the great black music and sports figures who lived in or near

different colors—beige, gold, gray, black—pieced together in a very intricate fashion. Brown lived here from about 1962 until the early 1970s. I turn right on Marne Place and walk along Addisleigh Park itself, a very nicely laid out park, with lovely paths and greenery, as well as an up-to-date playground with modern equipment.

Turning right on One Hundred Thirteenth Avenue, I come to an important but almost unknown historic site, a home where W.E.B. DuBois—among the greatest leaders of the black community worldwide, a prolific author, social scientist, and the founder of Pan-Africanism—and his second wife, Shirley Graham DuBois, lived from 1946 to 1951. She moved there in 1947, and he joined her in 1951–52. The house, at 173-19 on this one-block street, is an arts-and-crafts-style home in fair condition, in desperate need of a paint job. In fact, it's the only home on the block that's not well

the Addisleigh Park enclave of St. Albans.

taken care of. As of 2017, it wasn't landmarked. Perhaps it will be in the future, if only to prevent it from being razed to the ground one day.

The home of Count Basie, a world-famous jazz musician, composer, and bandleader, is next, around the corner, on the left, at 174-27 Adelaide Road, though the entrance is actually on 175th Street. It's a large medieval revival edifice with a nice sunroom. When Count Basie lived there it had a tennis court and a swimming pool. He probably set a record for longevity in the neighborhood, staying in that house from 1940 until 1982. Nearby, at 173-19 Sayres Avenue, is the landmarked home of Fats Waller, a small, pretty semi-attached brick Tudor revival. According to the Landmarks Preservation Committee, he lived there from 1940 to 1943, though the plaque on the house says he lived there for a year.

Jackie Robinson's home from 1949 to 1956, at the height of his career with the Dodgers.

Heading north on Sayres to 177th Street, I turn right and stop at 112-40, a substantial yellow Tudor revival home that belonged to Jackie Robinson. Standing here, looking at the very large lawn, I wonder if Robinson played baseball here with his family. The period in which he resided at this address was from 1949 to 1956, a time when he was at the height of his career with the Dodgers. Addisleigh Park was a cohesive neighborhood, with parties, clubs, and much fraternizing between families. The backbone was the large numbers of regular people who raised families and were solid citizens, but there was also an elite group of marquee players who knew each other. The home, with no identifying plaque, stands in stark contrast to the one at 2254 Tilden Avenue in East Flatbush, Brooklyn, which is landmarked but had literally fallen into rack and ruin. About two years ago someone purchased the house with the intention of rehabilitating it.

A half block away, on the corner of Murdock Avenue and 177th, on the left, stands a large, rambling shingle-and-white-stucco home with a very old stone wall running along it framed by a country-style white picket fence. The owner has seemingly strong religious sentiments, as attested to by what is clearly a stone tablet for the Ten Commandments, reading "Believe." Another sign nailed to a tree proclaims: "As for me and my house we will serve the Lord." The yard has various nautical symbols, too: a ship's steering wheel, a life preserver, and a masthead. The front porch has gauze curtains flanked by small lanterns, giving it a cozy feel.

I go one block east along Murdock, turn onto 178th Street, and there I see the residence of Lena Horne, a great singer and actor, at 112-45, a gathering place for the cognoscenti of Addisleigh Park. Built in the arts and crafts style, it features wide timbers, French windows, and a small peak above the center windows on the second floor. Horne resided there between 1946 and 1962. It's a handsome black-and-white Tudor-style colonial in excellent condition, it seems, on a very nice residential block

Throughout this structured walk, looking for the homes of the great, I pass many gorgeous, well-maintained homes, like an elegant gray-and-white Tudor on the corner of 178th Place and Murdock, and 177-15 Murdock, which alone would justify this walk. But I have a different goal in mind and soon arrive at 179-07 Murdock, former home of Ella Fitzgerald. It's a well-cared-for neocolonial home, made from fieldstone, with a slate roof and blue trim around the windows, and she lived there from 1949 to 1967.

Turning around, I head back down Murdock and soon arrive at boxing great Joe Louis's abode, a medieval revival, where he lived from 1955 to 1958. Located at 175-12, it's a very large and deep property, extending for about two-thirds of the block. It's a yellow-painted, tall, peaked Tudor-style residence with stucco and brick, like so many others here. I turn left at the corner, onto 114-07 175th Street, where Babe Ruth once lived, or at least spent summers. According to various sources, the Babe, who lived in Manhattan at the time, wanted to be near the St. Albans Country Club, where he played golf on its eighteen-hole championship course. It's an unusual colonial revival house with tall Corinthian columns, a very large wrought-iron fence, and a slate roof. Ron Marzlock, vice president of the Central Queens Historical Society, researched this question and found newspaper articles about the home stating that Ruth rented space in this house in the late 1940s.[42]

This may be the most iconic and, in a way, diverse corner in the city when it comes to famous people. For adjacent to Ruth's home, there's the residence of Joe Louis, and behind Louis's home, on the corner of 175th Place and Linden, there's James Brown's home. Thus, all three greats, one a champion boxer, another a baseball slugger, and the third a tremendously gifted singer and dancer, lived next to one another. True, the time frames are totally different—James Brown from 1961 to 1971; Joe Louis in the mid-1950s; and Babe Ruth in the late 1940s. Still, it's all hallowed ground.

The last leg of my jaunt through St. Albans includes a separate visit on another day to Roy Wilkins Park, about 53 acres of fields, filled with activities of every type. It can be accessed from Baisley and Merrick Boulevards. It's a full-service recreational facility with baseball, basketball, indoor and outdoor tennis, cricket, an indoor pool, and an excellent 4-acre vegetable garden. It also has pickle-ball tournaments for all ages. This is a game where paddles are used to hit a perforated plastic ball over a net. It's also home to the Black Spectrum Theater, which has regular performances, mostly by black artists. It's a hidden gem in that most Queens residents, not to mention people from elsewhere in the city, are unaware of its many offerings. For me, what was really special were the many outstanding framed mosaic pictures done by senior citizens, in the park's main building.

A few weeks later, in May, I attend a performance of the Universoul Circus at Roy Wilkins Park. Over the years the circus has been seen in many locations, and it has been coming to this park for a number of years. The audience, almost all of whose members were black, was very welcoming to the relatively few whites, Hispanics, and Asians who showed up. Whenever there's this type of numerical disparity, those in the minority tend to take note of how they are treated by the majority. It's a scene I've witnessed over and over wherever I've gone in this city. My friends and I were mesmerized by the high-quality acts. It has the usual assortment of elephants, zebras, horses, and camels, the last of which perform a very intricate version of do-si-do square dancing. To see camels pass each other back-to-back and then return to their original positions is really something!

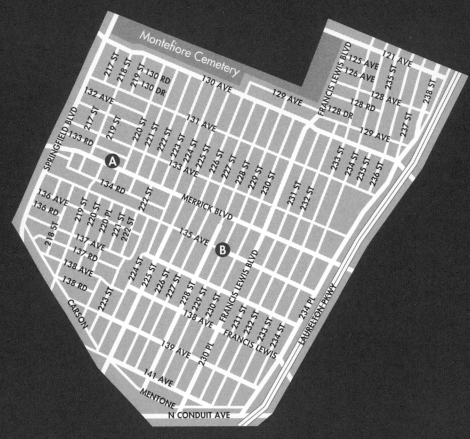

Ⓐ Chi Eta Sorority
Ⓑ Former home of Young Israel of Laurelton synagogue

LAURELTON

LAURELTON, A MOSTLY BLACK COMMUNITY, is next to Cambria Heights and Springfield Gardens but considerably more upscale. Many of the homes are detached and more substantial. The attached homes are sometimes elaborate, and the income levels of people living in the community are generally higher. Laurelton has long prided itself on its Garden Club, which sponsors annual competitions for the best flowers in the community. In keeping with the emphasis on beautification, many of its wide streets are enhanced by grassy dividers in the middle of the street.

In recent years the population has become more heavily Caribbean, part of the general trend in southern Queens. The boundaries are One Hundred Thirtieth, One Hundred Twenty-Ninth, and One Hundred Twenty-First Avenues on the north; 239th and 237th Streets and Laurelton Parkway on the east; North Conduit Avenue on the south; and Carson Street and Springfield Boulevard on the west. The main commercial thoroughfare is Merrick Boulevard, with some shopping outlets on Springfield Boulevard as well.

I begin my journey through this area by walking west on Merrick. The vibe and feel of a community can often be captured by looking at the shops and the shoppers, as well as those who are just hanging out on the corner. At 234-04, I pass a store called African Market. They're selling grocery items, cosmetics, and clothing. In communities where large supermarkets and department stores are not in the immediate area, small stores must carry a variety of products to serve local customers. At 231-32 there's Health Conscious. In the window, a large beige drum from Nigeria is advertised for sale. Besides the usual attributes, the store claims to have products that will "increase a woman's desires and passion and stamina." Inside, Rastafarian hats are also offered for sale.

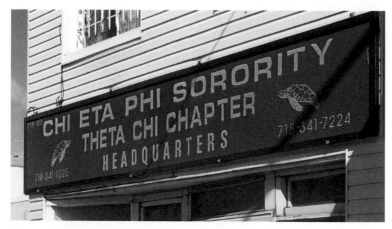

The nurses of Chi Eta Sorority focus on helping to combat cancer, strokes, and other illnesses.

Most of the stores are fairly typical—barber shops, beauty and nail salons, grocery stores, and small restaurants serving up Jamaican food, along with a number of preschools. Thus, the following place stands out. It's the Chi Eta Sorority, established in 1932 and located at 219-03 Merrick. With 122 chapters nationwide and more than eight thousand nurses who are members, it's a substantial organization. The focus is on helping to combat cancer, strokes, and other illnesses. But a subtext is to provide fellowship and networking through social activities and events. An elderly woman, Rosalyn Moore, who currently heads the group, opens the door and lets me in. Inside are dozens of photos of the chapter members at events and on trips, mostly to Africa, indicating their commitment to these countries—Senegal, Ghana, Kenya, and other nations. Societies like these are the lifeblood of the black community. Fraternal organizations, church groups, and the like have always served as a place where blacks can get together and feel truly at home. Blacks can feel uncomfortable in settings where they feel they might be looked down on or judged by outsiders.[43]

At 224th Street I make a left and walk to One Hundred Thirty-Ninth Avenue, one of the nicest streets in Laurelton. Turning left on

One Hundred Thirty-Ninth I stroll down to 228th Street, passing many gracious homes. The avenue is wide with a grassy divider. At 227-05 One Hundred Thirty-Ninth there's a very large, three-story, red and white stucco home with thick round pillars spaced along a wraparound porch. Most striking are two large, very handsome, gold-colored lions seemingly standing guard on each of the two railings along the steps leading up to the house. There's also a graceful white swan statue to the right of the home.

Next to it, at 227-15, is another home with an unusual feature. To the right of the garage and above it are hundreds of small, roundish yellow, gold, red, gray, brown, black, and white stones pressed into the cement backing. Their size, shape, and smoothness remind me of the stones people see at the bottom of the water when they walk through a shallow stream. Placed flush against the wall, extending the length of this large house, they are very impressive in appearance, and I don't recall having seen them elsewhere on a home. I also notice that quite a few homes are using solar panels, something I hadn't seen as much in other nearby areas.

Another street of Laurelton homes worth seeing is on 229th Street from One Hundred Thirtieth to One Hundred Thirty-First Avenues. It's one house after another of tall red-brick homes with Tudor elements and mostly red tile or blue and gray slate roofs. There are decorative half timbers and diamond-shaped patterns on the stucco sections, with fieldstone around the doorways and the windows, as well as on archways and balconies. Lions and eagles grace some of the entranceways.

On One Hundred Thirty-Eighth Avenue near 219th Street, I meet Jeff, a forty-nine-year-old African American who has lived in Laurelton his entire life. Dressed in jeans, a lightweight gray jacket, and a baseball cap, he speaks with pride and love about his community.

"I was born and raised here, and it was a great place to live in. In those days I knew every person on the block, and they all knew us. If you acted up any one of my neighbors could grab me by the ear and bring me to my mother. And my mother would deal with me.

Now if you do that, the parent will come out and bite you. Today, people don't even know who their neighbors are.

"So, you liked growing up here?"

"Yeah. Whites were living here with blacks, and we knew them all, loved them all. I could go into their homes and play with my white friends. I knew which house I could get the best candy from on Halloween, who I could ask for help in fixing my fishing pole. On the other hand, you take Rosedale, the next community over; that's where I had my first experience with racism. There's a park, Brookville Park, where blacks couldn't walk through it without getting hurt. It's well known that the first family that moved in there, they blew up the house. I don't know who moved in first here, but no one blew up anyone's house. It wasn't the older folks who pulled this kind of stuff. It was the younger ones, their children. But when the whites came over here from Rosedale, we couldn't do nothing to them because they were buying drugs, and the black dealers had them under their protection. In those days the drugs were sold in the park by Conduit Avenue. Today, everything's done with cars by delivery. The whites moved out because they wanted to go to the suburbs and have bigger houses. Today, you have break-ins sometimes, but you can still walk around at night."

Jeff talks about the old days in a tone of nostalgia, about how idyllic things were then. He reflects about how everyone knew everyone and how people took responsibility for your welfare and also how they took you to your parents if you misbehaved. He inveighs against today's people who aren't friendly and don't want to be. I often hear this view expressed, about how things were better and simpler in the old days. Perhaps they really were, but quite possibly this idea is rooted in the fact that people become comfortable with what they know and fear the unknown. The old times may represent to them an environment that they could comprehend and deal with.

Black and white residents have much more contact today, but for Jeff the point is that the old-time whites, at least in Laurelton, were friendly. He describes them as people who simply went to the suburbs looking for a bigger house. Perhaps he doesn't like the implied question: If everyone got along so well, why did they leave?

Then again, perhaps there's no real contradiction since blockbusting prevailed throughout Laurelton, and declining home values was something all whites, as home owners, were afraid of even if they got along fine with blacks. Perhaps his explanation of voluntary departures is one that he feels more comfortable with as opposed to one that implies that whites, his friends, were running away from him. Or, quite possibly, he believed it because it was the excuse that guilt-ridden whites gave him.

This is an African American's perspective on the community. It's also interesting to see how someone white sees the same community. Daniel grew up in Laurelton around the same time. He takes me on a tour of his old 'hood and begins by showing me where his Orthodox Jewish synagogue, the Young Israel of Laurelton, was located. The building, on the corner of 228th Street and One Hundred Thirty-Fifth Avenue, still stands. Even the large Star of David on the second floor and the cornerstone are still there. But today, there are few white residents, the temple has closed, and in its place there's the Jamaica, Queens, Wesleyan Church.

"What goes through your mind when you look at it?"

"It got smaller. Then again, *I* was smaller, and everything around me looked bigger then. Also, our community was more spread out in a large radius. It wasn't like everyone was Jewish. We lived among Italians, Germans, Irish, and later, blacks."

"How did you get along with the other groups?"

"The white kids made fun of me sometimes because I wore a kippah. And I sort of went along with it. I remember an Italian kid whose dog was barking at me, and he said: 'The dog doesn't like people who wear hats.' The community was already changing to a black area by the early 1970s. In those days, blockbusting was not illegal, and agents made the people afraid. No one wanted to be the last one left and be forced to sell their house at a big loss. So, they panicked. I remember coming to play basketball on our outdoor court inside the synagogue yard when I was about thirteen. It was ours, but black kids took it over, and they were annoyed when I showed up. They saw it as their turf even if it was synagogue property. There was no one at the synagogue to stop them. There was no security. I just came there and said, 'Can I play with you?' I didn't say, 'This my court.' And before I knew it, they were cursing me and throwing rocks at me. I had to run inside the shul to protect myself. I called the police, and my father came to pick me up. It was literally a gang. Their view was who am I to say, 'Let's play'?"

Let's look at Jeff and Daniel's narrative a little more carefully. Jeff talks about the great relationship whites and blacks had together, and Daniel recounts how black kids attacked him. Both are valid statements based on personal experiences. In Jeff's case, the whites lived on his block or very nearby. They were in each other's homes. But one key difference was that Daniel was Orthodox and attended a yeshiva. Therefore, he didn't attend public school, a missed opportunity to have something in common with other kids and to cement a relationship. Second, as he explained to me, he was limited by not being able to eat in their homes and hang out in nonkosher fast-food places where teenagers often congregate. He also couldn't go to the movies or baseball games on a Saturday or on a Friday night since he was a Sabbath observer.

Differences can create distance, and these were not, in any event, the days when diversity and ethnic identity enjoyed a great degree of respect. This was not the case, however, with most of Jeff's white friends, who seemed to be more socially integrated with black kids. The fact that the synagogue basketball court was little used by synagogue kids or whites in general but that it was also in an area that was becoming black may have heightened the teenagers' view that it was their court. They could see how it stood empty, and so they used it, and that meant it belonged to them.

But Daniel's Orthodox community did not go quietly into the night. Nor did Daniel. There was a man living in his community who was to become the national and international face of militant defense against anti-Semitism—Rabbi Meir Kahane, who lived at 222-13 One Hundred Thirty-Third Avenue. Kahane had written a book, *Never Again*, that was a clarion call for Jews to rise up against those who hated and discriminated against them. At that time, he was an inspiration to Jews living in changing communities, be it Laurelton or Crown Heights in New York, or Roxbury, Mattapan, and Dorchester in Boston. Later on, Kahane became much more extreme in his views and moved to Israel, where he ran for and won a seat in the Israeli parliament. He was denounced for his radical views about the Arabs and was ultimately assassinated. And here he was, a member of Daniel's own synagogue. In fact, Kahane's organization, the JDL (Jewish Defense League), was founded in Laurelton. He and those influenced by his views played a role in the development of Daniel's views. Daniel had felt the sting of anti-Semitism as a youth, and it no doubt contributed to his perspective on life.

"At the time there was a large movement of people willing to engage in sometimes violent demonstrations," he told me. "In those days many Jewish activists were intensely focused on demonstrations and other activities aimed at freeing Soviet Jewry so that they could emigrate. In fact, I went to all the protests, even got arrested, though I didn't do anything except dance the hora."

This is a graphic example of how, if people hadn't given in to their fears, the mass exodus, stoked by avaricious real estate agents, could perhaps have been avoided. This was happening in many neighborhoods then. But not everywhere. Jamaica, Queens; Mariners Harbor, Staten Island; and parts of Flatbush, Brooklyn, were three exceptions to the rule. By contrast, today, most people don't run. It's the opposite in the city now. They flock to areas even if there's poverty there, and then they invest. Attitudes have changed, crime is down, and the cities have become far more attractive. How this happened is complex and beyond the scope of this book. But exploring the past reminds us that it wasn't always this way.[44]

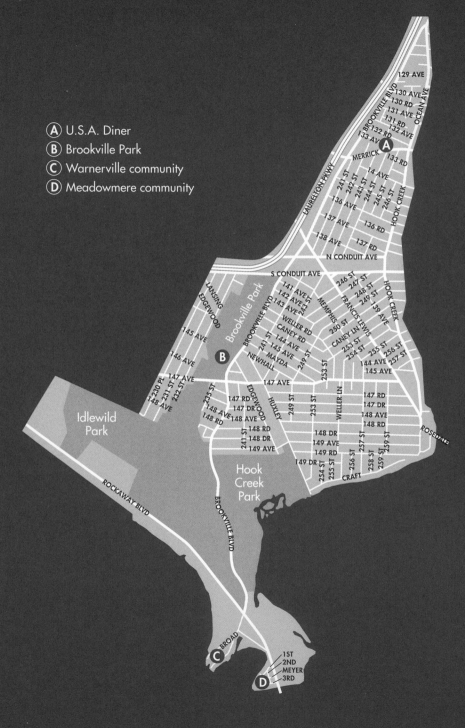

Ⓐ U.S.A. Diner
Ⓑ Brookville Park
Ⓒ Warnerville community
Ⓓ Meadowmere community

ROSEDALE

ROSEDALE IS A COMMUNITY IN SOUTHEASTERN QUEENS. Its boundaries are One Hundred Twenty-Eighth Avenue on the north, where Brookville and Hook Creek Boulevards intersect; Hook Creek Road, the eastern border that divides Queens from Nassau County; One Hundred Forty-Ninth Avenue and Craft Avenue on the south; and Brookville Boulevard, 230th Place, and Laurelton Parkway on the west. Its beginnings date all the way back to 1647, when it was known as Foster's Meadow after two brothers who settled there. It became a village called Rosedale in 1892 and was a largely rural area until developers built it up in the 1930s. Until the mid-1970s it was a mostly Irish, Italian, German, and, to a lesser extent, Jewish community. Then, blacks began moving in, and tensions flared. The changeover was gradual and accompanied at times by outright racism, including vandalism, cross burnings, and even the bombing of a home owned by a black family. Eventually, things quieted down, as residents, most of them lower-middle- or middle-class home owners, learned to live with each other through contact and support from local community organizations.

Today, it's a mostly black community, with many Caribbean residents. Hispanics also live there, and occasionally one can see holdovers, mostly elderly, whites who still remain. The homes are a mix of attached, semi-attached, and detached neocolonials, ranches, splits, and Cape Cods. Public transportation to the city is available via buses or the Long Island Railroad. It's a heavily residential community, with commercial thoroughfares that include small portions of Merrick and Francis Lewis Boulevards, about a mile of Sunrise Highway, and a small portion of 243rd Street.

The small northern tip of Rosedale is a very quiet pretty area that runs along Brookville Boulevard and, just beyond it, the Belt Parkway.

On the eastern side there's Hook Creek Boulevard and on the eastern side of the street the Nassau County town of Valley Stream. On the corner of Merrick and 243rd Street, there's the U.S.A. Diner, whose exterior is covered with a combination of gleaming silver metal, like so many diners, but with the added attraction of shiny, multicolored mosaic tiles—red, yellow, orange, and white. The large, nicely painted American bald eagle matches up nicely with the U.S.A. name. It all looks so nice that I walk in, curious to learn what the inside offers. I am not disappointed. The menu is pretty straightforward and fairly inexpensive for this twenty-four-hour place, with breakfast, lunch, and dinner available.

But it's the gaily, even wildly designed murals that stand out. One is a tropical scene with palm trees, almost surely meant to evoke some idyllic place in the Caribbean. A portrait of the superstar Bob Marley also livens up the scene, as do several renderings of jungle animals. A sign by the cashier admonishes: "Pull your pants up or don't come in, Have some decency and respect for others. No one wants to see your underwear."

I say to the manager, "That's a pretty interesting sign for a diner."

"Well, you never know who might come in, though most people are respectful. We have to have some decorum here even if people come in to relax and have a good meal."

About a mile down, at 243rd, at 143-29, on the corner of Mayda Road, I take a peek at the lawn of a house on the corner. It has a large white stone fountain that isn't currently being used. All around are statues of cupids, what looks like a statue of a Greek goddess, statuettes of small animals, a broken TV, and a tree adorned with broken pieces from a satellite dish. It's not a thing of beauty, but it reflects a common practice of New Yorkers, and people in general, to "decorate" their front yards in ways that please them, though not necessarily others.

From there I walk two blocks west to Brookville Park. This is a really special place, and it doesn't hurt to have an organization like Friends of Brookville Park that supports it. They teach youth volunteers about planting flowers, equipment used to maintain the park, painting benches, and other pursuits. The 90-acre expanse has many activities—tennis, bocce, basketball, handball, cycling, jogging, and barbecuing facilities. One of the real attractions of the park is Conselyea's Pond, a relatively large body of water where people can fish and just enjoy looking at the water.

Around the park area are some wilder-looking, marshy sections, where reeds sway gently in the wind, beckoning to those who like rugged, natural beauty. There are many vantage points that provide wide-range views of the waters that flow through here. One way to appreciate it is to hang a right on nearby One Hundred Forty-Seventh Avenue and then a quick left onto 235th Street. Walk a few blocks until it dead-ends, and enjoy the vistas. A similar view is available for 232nd and 231st Streets, and 230th Place.

I return to Brookville, walking toward Rockaway Boulevard, about a mile away. The tall grass sways gently from side to side, and as it does, I can glimpse Kennedy Airport on the right, in the distance. Crossing busy Rockaway, I enter the tiny, and I mean tiny, neighborhood of Warnerville. It has about a dozen houses along Broad Street and Bayville Avenue, surrounded on three sides by water and marshland. But stand in the street, and you will be thrust into the maelstrom of modern civilization. Every two minutes, as I stood there on a clear Sunday afternoon in April, a plane went by on its descent into Kennedy. The sound reminded me of the title of Jonathan Safran Foer's novel *Extremely Loud and Incredibly Close*. It looked like a giant silver bird of prey, ready to pounce and snatch up its victim. As it went over my head, I could see every detail of the aircraft's underbelly, a few hundred yards above my head, very clearly. And then it was gone, and the silence and tranquility returned, only to be broken once again, 120 seconds later.

Yet peace and quiet isn't everything. A neighborhood also needs basic services to flourish. Warnerville has finally gotten its sewage system hookup from the city, a $37.5 million undertaking, completed in 2010. Requests made for decades by residents had fallen on

The tiny neighborhood of Warnerville.

deaf ears, but the complaining finally helped. This community, whose residents includes firemen, cops, delivery truck drivers, plumbers, and other working-class types, is virtually unknown to outsiders. But way back when, it was a summer getaway for Hollywood's Warner brothers, after whom it is named. Visitors will feel they've stepped into a time warp but will be pleasantly surprised by the Bayhouse Bar, a friendly and inviting place with both atmosphere and really good eats.

From here, it's a short walk back to Rockaway Boulevard. Heading toward the Nassau County border, I turn right onto narrow 1st Street, nestled between a store called Customer's Kitchen and Bath and a boat shop and enter Meadowmere, a small six-block neighborhood with rutted, puddle-prone streets separated by a narrow body of water. A footbridge over the water separates it from its wealthier neighbor, Meadowmere Park, a part of Lawrence, Long Island, where roads are better paved, the homes are spacious, and there's a fire department, and other services, many of them paid for by their higher taxes. But for their sister town in Queens, Meadowmere Park is a place you can visit yet can't benefit from. Interestingly, a Meadowmere Park resident acknowledges that Meadowmere isn't beautiful but adds, "Their taxes are so low, they're laughing all the way to the bank. Overall, it's a mostly white neighborhood, for the time being that is, and I'm hoping it stays that way." It's not uncommon in New York for people to feel secure making such comments when the other person is of the same race. And since I'm trying to find out what folks really think, I say nothing, though I feel a bit guilty about it. The planes here are almost as noisy as in Warnerville, and I ask the lady how she feels about that.

"Well, it's like they say: 'If you live by the railroad station and the milk train doesn't run, that's when you notice it.'"

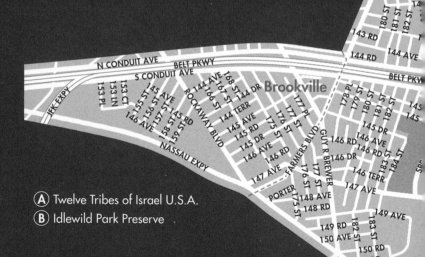

FARMERS

BENN
DENIS
CHE
135 AVE
136 A
WESTGA
BEDELL
182 ST
14

180 ST
181 ST
182 ST

143 RD
144 AVE
144 RD

N CONDUIT AVE
BELT PKWY
S CONDUIT AVE
BELT PKW
144 RD

Brookville

178 PL
179 ST
180 ST
181 ST
182 ST
145
145

JFK EXPY
153 CT
153 LN
153 PL
145 AVE
155 ST
156 ST
157 ST
158 ST
159 ST
144 AVE
166 ST
167 ST
168 ST
ROCKAWAY BLVD
144 TERR
144 DR

146 AVE
145 AVE
144 RD
145 RD
145 DR
146 AVE
146 RD
147 AVE
145 DR
146 AVE
146 RD
146 DR
146 RD
181 ST
183 ST
146 TERR
147 AVE

NASSAU EXPY

GUY R BREWER
FARMERS BLVD
177 ST
176 ST
175 ST

176 ST
177 ST
175 ST

PORTER
148 AVE
148 RD

149 AVE

149 RD
150 AVE
182 ST
183 ST

150 RD
150 DR

ROCKAWAY BLVD

(A) Twelve Tribes of Israel U.S.A.
(B) Idlewild Park Preserve

SPRINGFIELD GARDENS

SPRINGFIELD GARDENS WAS FIRST SETTLED, ALBEIT SPARSELY, in the mid-1600s and remained a rural area for over two centuries. Anyone wishing to see what a home looked like in the 1700s can walk by the Samuel A. Higbie home at 141-31 Springfield Boulevard. Built around 1770, it's been modified a bit since then and has been well preserved. In 1906, a housing development called Springfield Gardens was constructed, and people began moving here. The community soon became a popular destination, mostly for people fleeing the more crowded precincts of nearby Brooklyn. Despite its location near the wetlands area of Jamaica Bay, which caused massive flooding at various times, the area didn't have storm sewer systems until the beginning of the twenty-first century.

This is yet another mostly middle-class black area in southeastern Queens. Much of the population is West Indian, Haitian, and Guyanese, a trend that accelerated in the 1980s. Its boundaries, generally, are One Hundred Twenty-First and One Hundred Twenty-Second Avenues on the north; Springfield

Boulevard, the Long Island Railroad tracks on a diagonal path, and 230th Place, on the east; Rockaway Boulevard and Nassau Expressway on the south, and beyond it, JFK Airport; and Farmers Boulevard and the JFK Expressway on the west.

The homes in this middle-class area are nice, but not fancy. They are well tended with the usual assortment of attached, semi-attached, and detached capes, ranches, "high ranches," colonials, and Tudors. The area is very quiet, especially the section between South Conduit Avenue and Idlewild Park Preserve/Brookville Park, as well as the residential subsection of Brookville near the southwestern border of the community. The portion south of One Hundred Forty-Seventh Avenue to the southern border is mostly industrial. The primary commercial thoroughfares are Farmers, Rockaway, Merrick, and Springfield Boulevards. The main shopping hub in Springfield Gardens is the area where Springfield and Merrick Boulevards intersect. Recreational areas include Springfield Park on Springfield Boulevard and One Hundred Forty-Seventh Avenue, with a picturesque pond; nearby Idlewild Preserve on One Hundred Forty-Ninth Avenue; and Baisley Pond Park, just over the western border, in Jamaica.

On Farmers Boulevard near One Hundred Twenty-First Avenue, I walk along a fairly high wrought-iron fence distinguished by several, yellow-painted Stars of David that have been placed within the fence itself. At first, I think there must have been a synagogue or Jewish school here long ago, but a quick glance at the large white-painted private home behind the fence disabuses me of this notion. A large sign above the entrance at 121-17 reads "The Twelve Tribes of Israel, U.S.A." They fly two flags, one American, the other Jamaican. I notice a man entering the home and wave to him, calling out "Hi!" as I do so. He sees me but says nothing. A moment later a heavyset black man, who I'll call Robert, emerges, unlocks the gate, shoots me a suspicious look, and asks me what I want. I tell him I'm writing a book about Queens.

"Oh yeah. What's it about?" he asks, not sounding very convinced. "It's about all the unknown interesting things about Queens. What's your group about?"

"It's about Rastafarians who support Ethiopia as the place of our ancestors, and Haile Selassie the Lion of Judah, the man who was the emperor of Ethiopia. You can come through later on if you want to when we meet. We been here since thirty years. We have art rooms, eating rooms, everything else. We have about one hundred members here, but we're all over the world. We're not wild like the Israelites. That's a different group. They be standing on the streets everywhere, preaching and yelling in Times Square about how everyone's sinning. Real aggressive. Rastas aren't like that. We're mellow." Throughout the conversation another man, resplendent in a bright-red and black robe has been standing there warily eyeing me, his face hard but rather devoid of expression. I get the feeling he doesn't trust me.

I tell Robert I teach at City College. He seems to more or less accept that after examining my college ID, but the Rastas here probably don't see white professors coming by their headquarters very often. Thus, a white person stopping, asking them questions, and declaring that he was writing a book about Queens naturally struck him as being highly unusual. A joke he made about my being a cop could have been serious or simply a form of banter.

Heading south on Farmers, I swing left onto Bennett Court and then left again on Crandall Avenue, near One Hundred Thirty-Fourth Avenue. Here I meet Mike Flythe, a trim, mustachioed man who's a professional drummer and who both performs and gives drumming lessons. He's wearing a red, black, and white running suit and tells me he runs two to three miles a day to stay in shape. He's with a man named Mike Taggart, who's a realtor in the area. We're standing in front of his house at 178-54 Crandall.

"He's really bad," Taggart remarks, referring to Mike's musical talents." We both laugh at how newcomers to the United States can be confused if they don't realize that "bad" can mean "good." He tells me that homes here go for around $350,000 on the average. Mike's flyer refers to him as "The Atomic Drummer." He has worked with some big-name people including Dizzy Gillespie and has been a musician for almost half a century. He was also a drummer for a show that featured Audrey Hepburn and Neil Diamond, and he performed on TV over a period of about six years for the United Negro College Fund. Raised in Queens, he explains that many musicians came from there. He played in Count Basie's house as a child and knew Roy Haynes, probably the greatest jazz drummer alive today. The atmosphere is relaxed, not at all with the edge present in my previous conversation with Robert.

After a five-mile walk through this largely middle-class black community, I come home and write up my notes. It isn't until the next day that it dawns on me that I didn't see one white person during the walk. I went into playgrounds, schools, a Stop and Shop, clothing stores, and strolled up and down large boulevards like Merrick, Springfield, and Farmers, and encountered only black people.

The larger truth here is that New York City remains quite segregated, but it's much more likely to be voluntary today. And this self-segregation is equally true of predominantly white communities like Douglaston, Beechhurst, and Throgs Neck, or mainly East Asian sections like Flushing, and large swathes of Sunset Park, Brooklyn, and of middle- to upper-middle-class black communities like Cambria Heights or Laurelton.

The very fact that people choose to reside where they do may be out of lack of choice, like economic factors, or fears of encountering prejudice and discrimination. But it may also suggest that this is their preference. They can live where they wish today, as opposed to thirty years ago, but for largely social and practical reasons they may decide to be with each other. These reasons can range from feeling socially comfortable with people who have similar backgrounds, to the convenience of having stores that have markets and restaurants catering to their tastes and needs, to having churches they prefer to worship in. Nevertheless, it's important to them to know that they *can* live in any white, Hispanic, or Asian area if they so desire. Except for some isolated pockets in the city, the only color that matters is green.

Near one Hundred Forty-Seventh Avenue, I see a secondary road leading into the Idlewild Park Preserve, one of several parcels of Idlewild scattered throughout extreme southeastern Queens, in Springfield Gardens and in Rosedale. Idlewild Preserve is about 346 acres in size, a Forever Wild wetlands site, near Jamaica Bay and Kennedy Airport, and is known to have more than a few rare species like fiddler crabs, ospreys, and diamond-back terrapins.

I walk down the road and see that I have entered a very undeveloped wooded area with trees and trails going off on both sides, without visible markers or anything except for several blue wheelbarrows implausibly scattered in the underbrush off the road. Blue jays, robins, and sparrows are plentiful, not to mention a pair of snowy egrets standing in a small pond, and I even spy a brown snake slithering across the road. One sign of civilization is a fire hydrant poking out of the ground, but beyond that, nothing. It is definitely the most isolated spot I've ever seen in New York, except for a few portions of the Staten Island Greenway.

And yet in this city you can find people in the strangest places, including here in Idlewild Preserve. A man dressed in an official orange-and-yellow jacket is standing in the middle of a meadow, peering into a surveyor's tripod. Eugene is a tall, slim, very friendly, bespectacled black man, with a hearty laugh. I hail him, and he responds with a friendly wave.

"What are you doing here?" I ask.

"I'm surveying the area for the airport authority. The land is owned by the NYC Parks Department, but we were asked to do this by the airport. We're doing an inventory of every tree here, marking the type and height because it's on the approach to some runways and there are regulations about how high the trees can be."

I look around at this very large, unearthly moonscape, with no one else in sight, complete with odd-shaped boulders, large craters made

Trails and walkways wind through the 346 acres of the Idlewild Park Preserve.

of earth dug into the ground, and tall grass, as well as creeks and streams, and I feel like Christopher Columbus.

"Tell me," I say, "do you ever see anyone here?"

"Rarely. There's a guy who bikes through here, but I've never talked to him, and then there's a middle-aged fellow who walks across here over to, I guess, Rockaway Boulevard, where he buys groceries. He comes back with all these packages. He looks real poor, and I guess he found a place where he can save money." At this he breaks into laughter, thinking about, he tells me, how far the man must walk, miles perhaps, to realize his goal. "Is it really worth it to walk that far?" he asks. "He'll go by, and then he returns hours later with all this stuff in shopping bags."

"Is this a public place?"

"Yes. It's part of the preserve, open to the public, though hardly anyone ever comes here except to play cricket on the field. Last Saturday was an exception. They celebrated Earth Day and put wood chips along the side of a trail to mark it off for hikers." So, there are activities going on here, but it's only happening in a tiny portion of the area, which stretches as far as the eye can see. For naturalists and outdoor types, a visit here will reap rich dividends.

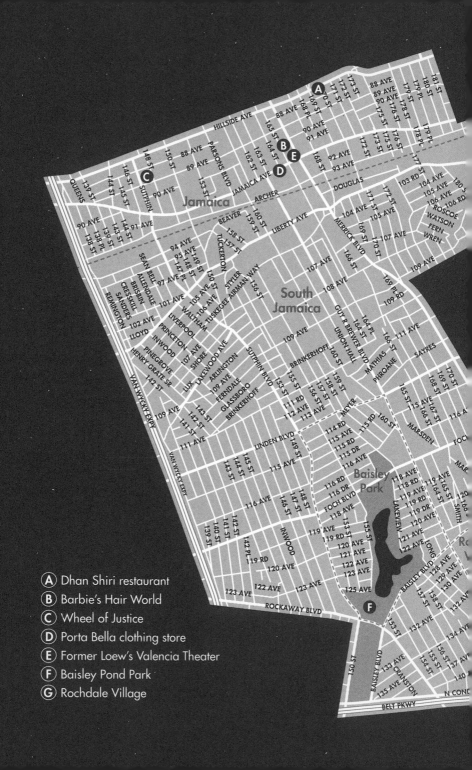

(A) Dhan Shiri restaurant
(B) Barbie's Hair World
(C) Wheel of Justice
(D) Porta Bella clothing store
(E) Former Loew's Valencia Theater
(F) Baisley Pond Park
(G) Rochdale Village

JAMAICA

JAMAICA HAS BEEN THE ADMINISTRATIVE CENTER OF QUEENS from the time of the Dutch and, later, the British. The subways were completed in the early twentieth century, and Jamaica is as far east as the subways go to this very day except for the Rockaways area. It covers a large area, and the general borders are Hillside Avenue on the north; 181st, 183rd, and Dunkirk Streets and Merrick Boulevard on the east; North Conduit Avenue on the south; and the Van Wyck Expressway on the west. It has several neighborhoods of interest, namely South Jamaica, Baisley Park, Rochdale Village, and Locust Manor. The housing stock is very varied, including all styles of architecture.

Jamaica was a mainly white, especially Irish, area from the nineteenth century until the late 1950s, when white flight turned it into a predominantly black, initially middle-class community. In the 1970s, 1980s, and 1990s, economic decline, lower property values, and high crime rates resulted in lower-income people, including immigrant Hispanics, taking advantage of lower rents and moving in, especially in Jamaica proper and South Jamaica. After 2000, Jamaica began to improve economically, with higher-income people settling in Rochdale Village and Baisley Park. The area has a very substantial West Indian population, most of them from Jamaica. The rest of South Jamaica has actually gotten a lot better from the days in the 1970s and 1980s, when visitors and residents felt it was like the notorious Fort Apache police precinct in the Bronx. It still has a relatively high crime rate compared to the rest of the borough, but there are many quiet and safe streets.

The major commercial thoroughfares are Hillside, Jamaica, Archer, and Liberty Avenues, and Guy R. Brewer, Parsons, Merrick, Sutphin, and Rockaway Boulevards. Jamaica also possesses excellent railroad, subway, and bus service since it is a major hub of Queens, with courts, department stores, federal offices, and the borough's central library. The major institution of higher education is CUNY's York College, and the nicest park is Baisley Pond, which has good sports facilities and a stunning pond that people love to stroll around.

At 169-28 Hillside Avenue, where I begin my walk, my attention is drawn to the Dhan Shiri Restaurant, which specializes in a mix of Indian, Chinese, Thai, and Malaysian dishes. It's spotless and very attractively laid out, and the dark-red napkins are cloth, generally a sign of a more upscale place. The décor, with shiny wooden chairs, as well as bamboo-covered walls and a replica of the roof of a thatched hut over the cashier area, creates a delightful atmosphere—warm, friendly, and inviting.

The owners are Bangladeshi, not surprising, as this part of Jamaica, from 178th Street down to Merrick Boulevard, has a fairly substantial Bangladeshi community, and there are many Bangladeshi shops along Hillside in this vicinity. The owner, Noor, takes his work seriously and holds an MBA from Queens College. I also meet Saadia, a pretty, dark-haired young waitress from Bangladesh with large, almond-shaped, soulful eyes, who tells me an interesting life story.

"I grew up in the Middle East," she says, "where my father owned a business. When that ended, we went back home, but I wanted to come to America so, on my own, I used the internet to apply to

American colleges. I was accepted at Monroe College and did a three-year BA there."

"What was that like?"

"You have no idea how hard it was. I worked thirteen hours a day as a waitress to pay my $7,000 a year tuition at Monroe. Whatever little time I had I used to take classes, study, and sleep."

"Do you have any family here?"

"My father died a few years ago, and my mother is very sick in Bangladesh in an ICU. My brother, my only relative here, lives in Canada, but he went home to take care of my mom."

"Do you have any friends here?

"Not really. How can I make friends when I'm so busy?"

"I guess you could always marry somebody," I say, thinking this would help her financial situation. She looks startled by this comment, and I don't blame her:

"Well, it would be easier to become a citizen if I married an American citizen, but I'm not going to get married just for the sake of being married. You have to be in love with someone, and then you can marry them." Her attitude reveals an acceptance of marriage and love as seen by most Americans, rather than very common practice of arranged marriages in Bangladesh.

"I guess you live in the area."

"Actually not. I live in Flushing and have since I came here several years ago."

"But that's a Chinese and Korean area, where you wouldn't have other Bangladeshis who might help you."

"And that's why I moved there. I didn't want to live in a Bangladeshi ghetto. I wanted to meet totally new and different people, which I thought would be more interesting. And it is. I love it there. Plus, my landlady, who's Chinese, is so nice. She kept me at the $400 a month rent. Put it this way. I want to succeed here, not just live here." We tend to stereotype immigrants as wanting to be with other coethnics, but this isn't always the case. These are individuals who may opt not to live among other people from their homeland.

Saadia chose to strike out on her own, and her life experiences point to that: She grew up in the Middle East, where she became fluent in English. She arranged to get a student visa to the United States by gaining entrance on her own to an American college. She's also here by herself with no family and no real friends. In short, she's a very determined individual. This fall she begins an MBA program. She's not a hard person. In fact, she's very sweet, but, at the same time, very determined. I have no doubt she'll do very well in life.

Nearby, I come to Barbie's Hair World at 89-23 165th Street, located just off Hillside Avenue. Is this another beauty parlor of which there are so many here, at least one on every block? Absolutely not, because another sign reads: "100% human hair sold." I walk in and see that this is really another world. A white woman is standing behind the counter and weighing some hair, presumably human, on a scale.

I ask her, "What's this all about?"

"We import human hair, mostly from China and India, we process it into different textures, and then we sell it by the ounce. Then people go somewhere else and can have it made into a wig. We're the only ones in Queens who do this. There are other places in other boroughs, but it's all people who are in our family. We live in Queens. We've been in this line of work for decades. My husband has been here for thirty-three years, and his family has been in the business for close to sixty years. His father started out selling human hair in a train station. Sure, you can purchase a bit of hair, like a human hair wig, but we're the only ones who sell it by the ounce or pound. The people who make the wigs buy from us."

"Can people sell their hair here to you?"

"No, we don't buy it. People may also give their hair away to, say, cancer victims, but that's not what we do."

"Who are your customers?"

"It varies. People who want to get good-looking, very smooth, shiny hair, or they want to extend it. For some women it's just to look good all the time. For others it's for a special occasion, like a wedding. They'll buy extensions." As I'm standing there, a Chinese importer is opening bags of hair and weighing them. Genevieve produces a card with different samples of hair, some of them wavy, some straight. People can make their purchasing selections from the card.

Seeing the hair lying on the scale makes me think of a cut of meat being weighed in a butcher shop. Actually, this is one of the only parts of the body that can be offered for purchase so casually. You can get a heart or kidney transplant, but this is much more commercial and casual. One can sell one's hair, let it grow, and sell it again. I'm also reminded of how different folkways are from one culture to another, even in the same country. Indians sell their hair, but Sikhs, who also live in India, aren't even allowed to cut their hair, much less sell it. It's also an example of an offbeat occupation, one we don't think about very often.

From here I go one block east to Merrick Boulevard. At 90-11 there's a nondescript two-story building next to the bus terminal. There are shops on the first floor and offices on the second floor. Opposite the offices of the Jamaica Realty Company, there's a studio. It happens to be the place where hip-hop legend Jam Master Jay was murdered on October 30, 2002. The murder remains unsolved.

I head back to Hillside Avenue and continue walking south. Much of it has gradually transformed from a predominantly black commercial thoroughfare to one dominated by South Asians, not only Bangladeshis, but Sri Lankans, Nepalese, Guyanese, and other groups. In a further sign of adaptation, South Asian lawyers and physicians have also hung out their shingles, often with ads aimed at attracting their own people whose language, culture, and needs they are more apt to understand. The lower portion of Jamaica, from the 150s to the upper 130s, is dominated by new and used car dealerships.

I turn left on Sutphin Boulevard, one of Jamaica's major commercial streets. On the plaza in front of the landmarked Queens County Supreme Court Building, at 88-11, there's what's called "The Wheel of Justice," a twelve-foot-high cast-bronze wheel with

"The Wheel of Justice" tells the story of the court process.

intricate carvings encircling the wheel itself. It was created in 1998 by the artists Claudia DeMonte and Ed McGowin and tells the story of the court process, depicting the judges and juries involved in it. Around the "wheel," scattered throughout the plaza, are eighteen round stone benches with room for one or two people to sit. Each one is engraved with the names of different Queens communities— Laurelton, Astoria, Jackson Heights, Bellerose, and so on. As I inspect the wheel close up on a Sunday morning in April, I can make out the inscription from former US Supreme Court justice Benjamin Cardozo: "Danger invites rescue. The cry of distress is the summons to relief." Looking at the sculpture, I see a telephone, books, people in uniform, someone's hands clasped in prayer, chains, and more.

If any community in Queens could be thought of as a downtown, this area would qualify. The office buildings, courts, administrative centers, CUNY's York College, and newly built apartment buildings for those wishing to live near work are clear evidence of it. And small wonder, for this is also a major transportation hub with convenient LIRR trains, subways, and express buses going to Manhattan and Brooklyn as well as every part of the borough and Long Island. Among the stores on Jamaica Avenue are the Children's Place, Navy Yard, Bolton's, Modell's, Sprint, Verizon, and many others. Here, as opposed to Hillside, are many African American and West Indian shoppers, who tend to reside in the large residential sections south of Jamaica and Archer Avenues, though South Asians are creating a presence here too. A tastefully designed outdoor shopping mall on 165th Street, off Jamaica, adds to the allure of this section.

One store, Porta Bella, at 164-08 Jamaica, claims to be celebrating its grand opening in April 2017 and offers an incredible three men's suits for a mere $69. A recorded come-on blares out—"From Madison Avenue to Jamaica, these suits are great!" I can't resist this pitch and enter the store to see what they look like and am amazed to discover that they're made from polyester and wool, certainly legitimate materials. But most important, they look presentable, have nice colors, and are available in checked patterns, pinstripes, and solids. In fact, they would likely fool a casual observer if they were told that they cost, say, $120 or even more.

Another interesting find in the cultural area is what remains of the Loew's Valencia Theater at 165-11 Jamaica Avenue. It was once one of the grand movie theaters of old, just like the Loew's 175th Street in Upper Manhattan and the Loew's Paradise in the Bronx. Like these, the Valencia was taken over by a church, the Tabernacle of Prayer for All People. With their high ceilings, more than ample seating space, stages, and elaborate baroque designs, they can, with appropriate modifications, become hugely inspiring places for spiritual experiences. And what are those modifications? Well, the naked human statues need to be covered, and religious ornamentation, paintings, and the like must be added. The exterior facade of terracotta and brick in a Spanish style above the marquee has been landmarked and is definitely worth seeing, especially the seashells and cherubs. Along with Brooklyn's Loew's Kings, which has become an entertainment venue, the Valencia reminds us that there was a time, way before anyone ever heard of multiplexes, when going to a movie in a big theater was a truly special experience.

The next day I begin my walk in the southern part of Jamaica on Foch Boulevard and 155th Street. Nearby, is the entrance to Baisley Pond Park, a truly beautiful and bucolic place. It's quite large and dominated by a big expansive pond. Near the shore, the water is covered by floating lilies. Walking along its 155th Street border is a great vantage point from which to view the landscape, one with beautiful vistas, large trees that provide ample shade, and tall grass. What makes this park special is that its documented history dates back 10,000 years, after the Ice Age ended 11,700 years ago. When the Parks Department took over the area, they discovered the remains of an American in the pond: mastodon remains, including several large teeth and a piece of bone. To memorialize this, a sculpture of a mastodon sits in the park's Sutphin Playground. A park employee tells me that storks and swans are often here, as well as snapping and musk turtles that swim around and under the lilies.

Baisley Boulevard is also a good location in the park, if you don't mind sharing the space with lots of students who attend August Martin High School, which overlooks the park. The park also has well-maintained basketball and tennis courts.

A woman walking her dog in Baisley Pond Park informs me, "I wouldn't walk in the park after 9:00 p.m. But that's true of many parks. Anyway, it's a lot safer than the area around South Road and 160th Street, near the projects, about three miles away." Safety is a relative issue in this mostly black neighborhood. In a period of a little over an hour, I counted thirteen separate patrol cars driving by. Knots of hard-looking young men hang out in front of houses in the daytime, and at night, a good number of houses have pit bulls on chains or behind fences. This is based on my visual impressions and comments made to me by several people sitting on the park benches.

The homes in the area, many of them attached, are fairly modest. Nonetheless, quite a few of them reveal pride in ownership. For example, one, at 154-12 One Hundred Nineteenth Avenue, has five gold-painted lions, and a gold-painted water fountain in the front yard, which is well cared for. Walking around here and exploring the backways off nearby 154th Street, with their narrow, grassy, public paths wide enough for a car, reminds me of the way some of the small towns I've seen in Louisiana and Mississippi look. Sutphin Boulevard is fairly close and, along with Linden and Guy Brewer Boulevards, provides for the shopping needs of the local residents.

I head down Guy Brewer, two blocks east, make a left onto it, and come to a safer, middle-class area, Rochdale Village, a cooperative development. Residents with whom I spoke say they feel safe here, in part, because it is 100 percent owner occupied, which makes for stability. In addition to the New York Police Department, the area is also patrolled by the co-op's own security guards. When first completed in 1963 as a housing development for low- and middle-income families, it was about 90 percent white. Today it's a 100 percent owner-occupied development, and most of the residents are middle-class black families. The apartments are of good quality, with parquet floors and terraces, and there's parking for residents. I walk through a small shopping mall in the village with a pharmacy, a Dunkin Donuts, and a small restaurant. People saunter along the concrete paths of the complex, socializing, and sit on chairs, taking in the sun. All in all, it seems like an attractive space, which is its reputation.

Immediately south of Rochdale Village, from One Hundred Thirty-Seventh to about One Hundred Forty-Fourth Avenue, is a small neighborhood of primarily private homes, known as Locust Manor. The houses here are somewhat nicer than the housing stock in Baisley Park.

In Jamaica, Jamaicans are the single largest ethnic group residing here. (The name probably comes from the Jameco, or Yamecah Indians, who first lived here.) It's not surprising that the Door, at 163-07 Baisley Boulevard, is one of the best, if not the best, Jamaica food eateries in the borough. It serves fine Jamaican food in an elegant setting. For those in search of authentic dishes this is the go-to place in New York, according to insiders and food critics. Here you can get escovitched chicken, a poached or fried dish served in a marinated, somewhat acidic sauce; callaloo, spinach-like leaves from a tropical plant often served in soup; and other delicacies not well known to those outside the community.

My last stop is a Catholic church called St. Pius V at 106-12 Liverpool Street between Tuskegee Airmen Way and One Hundred Sixth Avenue. It has services in Spanish, Portuguese, and English. The design features beautiful, clay-colored terra-cotta on a beige and bright-red stucco building. There are Corinthian pilasters on either side of the building. The designs on either side of the entranceway have crosses, shields, grapes, musical instruments, jugs, lanterns, and helmets, all jumbled together. Several statues stand on the second floor. The complex ornamentation and the building as a whole are well worth seeing as is the rest of this varied and fascinating community.

SOUTH
OZONE PARK

OZONE PARK

RICHMOND
HILL

WOODHAVEN

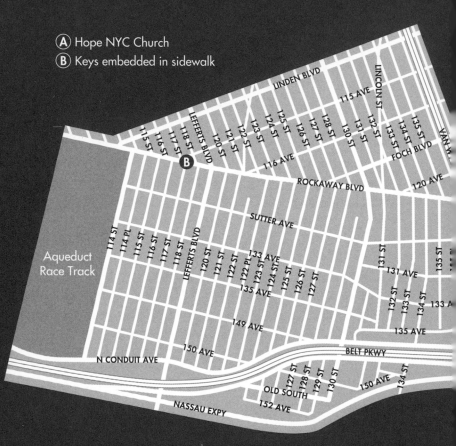

Ⓐ Hope NYC Church
Ⓑ Keys embedded in sidewalk

LINDEN BLVD

LINCOLN ST
115 AVE
132 ST
131 ST
130 ST
133 ST
134 ST
135 ST
FOCH BLVD
VAN W

125 ST
126 ST
127 ST
128 ST
123 ST
124 ST
122 ST
121 ST
120 ST
LEFFERTS BLVD
118 ST
117 ST
116 ST
115 ST

116 AVE
Ⓑ
ROCKAWAY BLVD
120 AVE

SUTTER AVE

131 ST
135 ST
131 AVE

114 ST
114 PL
115 ST
116 ST
117 ST
118 ST
LEFFERTS BLVD
120 ST
121 ST
122 ST
122 PL
123 ST
124 ST
125 ST
126 ST
127 ST
133 AVE
135 AVE

132 ST
133 ST
134 ST
133 A

Aqueduct
Race Track

149 AVE

135 AVE

150 AVE

N CONDUIT AVE

BELT PKWY

127 ST
128 ST
129 ST
130 ST
OLD SOUTH
150 AVE
134 ST

NASSAU EXPY
152 AVE

SOUTH OZONE PARK

SOUTH OZONE PARK'S BOUNDARIES are Linden and Rockaway Boulevards on the north, the Van Wyck Expressway and 150th Street to the east, North Conduit Avenue and the Nassau Expressway on the south, and 114th Street on the west. This community was first built in the early twentieth century, when developers put up inexpensive private homes. The early residents were primarily Irish and Italian. Aqueduct Race Track opened in 1894 and has been there ever since. Its racing seasons are during the fall and winter, and it is home to a large flea market during the off-season. One of its biggest events had nothing to do with racing. On October 6, 1995, Pope John Paul II celebrated Mass here before an estimated seventy-five thousand persons. Aqueduct is also where New York City's only casino is located, operated by Resorts World. Of course, as a community right next to Kennedy Airport, similar to Rosedale, Springfield Gardens, and Howard Beach, airplane noise is a problem that residents struggle to deal with.

The major groups residing in South Ozone Park are African Americans,

Hispanics from various countries, and immigrants from Guyana (the largest group), Trinidad and Tobago, Jamaica, and Haiti. Religion is a powerful presence in this community, with many churches, temples, and mosques, large and small, serving its inhabitants. While the area is predominantly Christian, Hindus and Muslims are strongly represented as well.

Today, it's an overwhelmingly residential area with Rockaway Boulevard and small portions of Lefferts Boulevard as the main commercial thoroughfares. While most of the homes are modest colonials, the more recent and often upwardly mobile arrivals have found the community much to their liking. As a result, more and more new homes of impressive size are being built here.

I begin my trip walking down Rockaway Boulevard from 150th Street through the 140s and 130s. It's a broad street, and there are many stores, most of them small—liquor shops, groceries, hair parlors, and eateries, along with many storefront churches, sometimes as many as four to a block. Many of the storefront churches have grandiose-sounding names, something I've seen all over the city. But there are many with more down-to-earth signs, like the Morris Brown Church, AME.

At 142-82 Rockaway and 143rd Street, I pass by a large church in a red-brick building. The ground floor has a few bays, which makes it look like an auto repair place, which, in fact, it once was. It's festooned with bright, multicolored signs, one of which proclaims: "YES THIS IS A CHURCH." To the left is another large sign: "Welcome to HOPE NYC Church. Not just church. It's home. Sundays 10:30 a.m. . . . free gift for new guests." To the left is the Compass Café, which turns out to be owned and operated by this Pentecostal church. To the right of it there's another storefront—a Hindu house of prayer.

Intrigued by the church, I cross over to investigate and meet Brent, a tall, good-looking young man who's stacking boxes inside one of the bays while enjoying some Caribbean music. It's actually a warehouse for the church.

"What are you doing here?" I ask.

"We're getting things in order for the church. I belong to the church."

"Are you doing anything for the summer?"

"Well, one of our fun activities is we build a forty-foot ice cream sundae with bananas, cherries, sprinkles, and chocolate fudge sauce. People take a few bites, and then they start this big ice cream fight, sort of like a snowball fight. When we stop, we try to eat the sundae wherever possible, and then we wash up with soap to get everything off ourselves." At Brian's suggestion, I go inside the Compass Café.

It's a really nicely laid out place, spotless and attractively designed, with small tables, comfortable chairs, and a wide array of desserts and coffee selections from Haiti, Jamaica, Guatemala, and other lands. There are gift items on various shelves—ceramic cupcakes and decorative boxes—and wallpaper that's an old-fashioned-looking map of the world. The employees, all young people who belong to the church, are a very friendly group. I purchase a caramel white chocolate chip cookie and a Haitian coffee. As I do so, the chief operating officer of the church, a pretty woman named Ruthie who was born in Guyana, invites me to sit down and speak with her. She has a winsome smile and sparkling, almond-shaped eyes, soft yet full of life at the same time. She's a true CUNY product, an immigrant who worked her way through school, and who had a challenging childhood with all sorts of family issues. She was a teenage mother and had to do work-study to get through college. It wasn't easy, yet she prevailed and went on to become a senior administrator at Goldman Sachs after obtaining a BS from Baruch College and a master's in management from NYU, with an emphasis on operations.

"How many people come to the church on Sunday?"

"Anywhere between four hundred and seven hundred people." Ruthie proceeds to tell me an interesting story about why and how the church's current pastors came here.

"Our pastors, Sharon and Curtis Ramkhelawan, came to New York in a most unusual way. They had been ministers in Texas for about sixteen years, where they were part of a bigger church, the Church of God. Then, one day, Pastor Sharon had a dream in which God said to her: 'You're leaving for New York City.' But they were settled in Texas, so she didn't tell Curtis the dream. Not long after, on her husband's fortieth birthday, he too had this immense dream that he was heading a church in New York, that he was also a doctor. And so they decided that this was a divine message, rented a U-Haul, and moved to New York."

"How did they manage to relocate?"

"At first, they rented space in a storefront farther down on Rockaway Boulevard, actually in a Buddhist temple. When I became a member in 2008, they were on Liberty Avenue and were growing."

"Are your members Guyanese?

"They're from all over—Sikhs, Trinidadians, Jamaicans, Guyanese, even Hispanics. It's like Queens, which is a real melting pot. Every year we fast and pray for twenty-one days. We do this to express our commitment to God. It's biblical because Jesus fasted for forty days before he went into ministry. One of the most important things was getting this building, which is huge. But we didn't know how we could raise the money. And that year the fast was dedicated to finding a way to raise enough money, $2 million, to buy this huge location."

"You must have thought this would never happen."

"Well, yes. But then one night, Pastor Sharon woke up in the middle of the night and took a phone call. It was someone from Texas she hadn't heard from in many years. The person said: 'Will you have dinner with me?' So they had dinner, and the person said: 'I had a dream in which the Lord told me to give you this check for $5 million. I kid you not.' At first, she couldn't believe it, but it was true. We tell our people the story because we believe you can't grow if you don't understand how the Lord has helped us."

"How did you become involved in the church?"

"I was a person who sat in the back and thought that was enough to do in the church. But I was looking to get my little kid into a good private summer program, and I saw a flyer from Hope right near my house. My son went there and loved it so much. And it's all built around the Bible. They were so nice, and I fell in love with the hearts of the people. They had the kind of smile that you just don't often see in New York. And it was a time when I needed that. The pastor was so endearing and poignant to me. So I became a member, and that was it. I grew so much spiritually. I was putting my hand "into the kingdom," as they say. I prayed to God and someone gave them the money to hire me. And that was also a miracle. I could have continued at Goldman, but God had a higher purpose for me. Every year we have a parade on Christmas, the only one in Queens, and we march down Rockaway Boulevard. Mayor de Blasio has been here too."

This experience exemplifies the major role that religion plays in the lives of so many New Yorkers, rich and poor. For Ruthie, her faith is the most important part of her life. The dreams that her pastors had can't be proven, but in the end, it doesn't matter. What counts is that the pastors believed in and acted on them. For the followers, the stories inspire and motivate them. Ruthie received love from the church at a time when she needed emotional support. As she put it: "I fell in love with the heart of the people." That it happened at that moment solidified her belief in God. Ruthie shows me around the complex and then leaves me with the following message: "In our future plans, the church will resemble an ark, after Noah's ark, because the ark represented hope, and that's one of our central messages. At the end of the day, everything is God's will. That's the story of the world."

Ambling along Rockaway, I reach 117th Street, just where it intersects with Rockaway and with One Hundred Fifteenth Avenue. I turn right onto 117th and begin walking toward Linden Boulevard, a block away. After about two hundred feet, my eye catches something glinting in the afternoon sun. I look down and am amazed

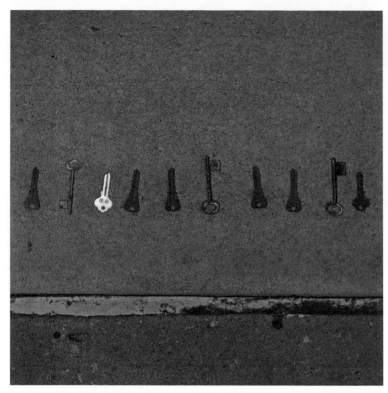

A striking and delightful work of art in the sidewalk.

to discover an interesting, almost mesmerizing pattern made entirely from keys of every sort—very old-looking skeleton keys, car keys, regular keys of every shape, all of them in either a gold or a silver color. There are literally hundreds of them spread out over two large sidewalk squares. I deduce, correctly as it turns out, that someone had new sidewalk squares placed here and put the keys in the squares when the cement was first poured onto the surface and it was still soft. It's the first time I've seen this anywhere in the city, and the effect is striking, almost like a work of art. It had to be done very painstakingly and precisely, as each key is placed exactly next to the other and it must have taken a very long time to do. These sidewalk blocks sit in front of a metal, shuttered door behind which is a two-car garage. There's no sign indicating to whom it belongs, but I assume it might have been the handiwork of the owner of S&S Locksmiths, located on the corner at 117-01 One Hundred Fifteenth Avenue. As I'm about to leave, who should come by to open the garage but the owner. It's my lucky day, I decide. Jim Shubert is a tall, very handsome man, with richly textured brown hair and piercing blue-gray eyes. I introduce myself, we shake hands, and I ask him, "How did this happen?"

"The city people came by with a steamroller about two years ago, so I asked them if they would mind going over these squares so I could put some keys in. They said 'Sure.' I had all these extra keys in the store just lying around and thought it would look good." As I leave, I'm suddenly struck by the realization that if I had driven by this place, I would never have discovered this display. It happened only because I walked and decided to look down at the ground.

At the corner of 117th, I turn left onto Linden Boulevard, and at 114-11, I chance upon a most visually interesting house. The walls are made of white stone pieces of every shape, and there's black cement between each stone. This makes for an interesting color contrast. On the second floor, above the door, two small windows sit below a very unusually shaped wall. The wall is rounded off at the top of the home, and the sides, which contain Spanish design features, resemble pieces of a puzzle. In fact, the entire house reminds me of a giant jigsaw puzzle. The same is true of the garage on the side. The front entrance is flanked by two black-and-white columns whose colors match the rest of the structure and which support a portico. It's a Guyanese-owned home, as evidenced by several prayer flags. It's certainly a one-of-a-kind house.

Some blocks away I say hello to an elderly white man. Many communities have whites who remained here rather than join the majority of whites who left, and I'm curious as to why these particular individuals didn't join the others when the area changed demographically. I also want to learn how they feel about their new and different neighbors, who are now the majority as opposed to the old days. Glenn is a brown-eyed, stocky man with close-cropped hair who appears to be about seventy. Sporting a dark-gray North Face sweatshirt and holding a straw broom in his hand, he's standing outside his immaculate, split-level home. He is wearing a cap that says "Duck-Hunting," though I learn later that while he owns a rifle, he does not hunt.

"Your place looks beautiful, and everything's swept clean."

"Always, always."

"Is this a safe community?"

"Safe? It's safer than it ever was. I'm here fifty-three years. I was born here. It went through its times. It was once Irish, Italian. There was robberies later on, in the eighties and nineties. Now, it's mostly Indians from Guyana. They're building mansions all over. I mean there are still some whites here. My friends, Lenny and Larry. But nobody bothers nobody here."

"But can you be friends with the Guyanese? I mean, do you have enough in common with them?"

"Yeah, they're all working people here."

"You have them over to your house for a beer?"

"Naw, I don't get too friendly with anybody like that. More 'Hi.'"

"How do you feel about so many of your friends moving away?"

"What am I going to do? I mean the houses' value went up."

"How come you didn't sell?"

"Because I had put in new windows and things. Like I got bow windows; I got underground and solo lights, like botanical gardens back there."

"And you got a nice flag."

"Yeah, that's the only flag I fly." (This may be an indirect reference to the ubiquitous prayer flags in so many yards here.).

"Here's where you're good, not near Rockaway?" I say.

Glenn's a holdover. He's got one foot out the door because he doesn't have a real social life here. He claims that it's possible to be friends with the Guyanese, but his definition of friendship is a bit narrow. He will not have them over for a beer, stating plainly: "I don't get friendly with anybody like that." He's clearly not into diversity, and the comfort level of sameness just isn't there. But he does appreciate the way they did their houses up. I also ponder, briefly, how he perceives me. In an earlier time in the area's history, when it was mostly white, he might not have spoken so freely. I would be an outsider, despite my white skin. Today, however, with so few whites left, I'm in *his* group, even though he's just met me.

ATLANTIC AVE
96 ST
97 ST
95 AVE
97 AVE
99 AVE
ROCKAWAY BLVD
89 ST
83 ST
85 ST
87 ST
WOODHAVEN
94 ST
93 ST
95 ST
97 ST
98 ST
103 AV
FORBELL
ELDERT
82 ST
83 ST
81 ST
80 ST
78 ST
77 ST
76 ST
75 ST
DREW
84 ST
85 ST
86 ST
88 ST
89 ST
90 ST
91 ST
92 ST
102 AVE
102 RD
103 AVE
LIBERTY AVE
GLENMORE
75 ST
Acacia,
Bayside and
Mokom
Sholom
Cemeteries
106 AVE
107 AVE
108 AVE
109 AVE
84 ST
87 ST
80 ST
PITKIN
84 ST
SUTTER
76 ST
77 ST
78 ST
79 ST
SUTTER
81 ST
82 ST
83 ST
84 ST
85 ST
86 ST
87 ST
88 ST
86 ST
133 AVE
SPRITZ
N CONDUIT AVE
PITKIN
ALBERT
WHITELAW
ARION
LAFAYETTE
REDDING
RICO
CHICOT
SITKA
GOLD
SILVER
DESARC
PLATT
133
13
96 ST
95 ST
108 AVE
109 AVE
SUTTE
CROSS BAY BLVD

Ⓐ Bolla Market
Ⓑ Former location of mobster John Gotti's Bergin Hunt & Fish Club
Ⓒ Fantastic mural of kitchen interior

OZONE PARK

THE BORDERS OF OZONE PARK ARE AT-LANTIC AVENUE ON THE NORTH, 108th Street and Aqueduct Road on the east, North Conduit Avenue and the Nassau Expressway on the south, and a combination of 75th Street, Drew Street, and Eldert Lane on the west. The community was first created in the 1840s in the southeastern portion of the community near Centerville Street. Developers began constructing houses relatively early, in the 1870s. With railroad and subway lines up and running, building accelerated in the 1920s, and the population increased almost threefold, from around 40,000 to almost 120,000. The homes built then were mostly semi-attached or detached, nice, but certainly not luxurious.

Today, it's still a thriving community, not far from Manhattan, with good transportation, and decent schools. The main commercial thoroughfares are Cross Bay, Woodhaven, and Rockaway Boulevards, along with Liberty and Atlantic Avenues. The major recreational area here is the 24-acre Tudor Park, located along North Conduit Avenue and running west from 81st to 78th Streets. It's next to Joseph Addabbo Playground, named after the former congressman, whose district included Ozone Park. There are also some nice base-ball fields at the intersection of Cross Bay Boulevard and North Conduit Avenue, plus the well-maintained London Planetree Playground near 88th Street and Atlantic Avenue.

The major development in this community has been demographic. In the last twenty years, it has changed from an area that was predominantly white, mostly Italian, along with smaller groups of Poles, Germans, and Irish, into a South Asian and, to a lesser degree, Hispanic population. One easy way to chart this is to note the number of commercial establishments serving these groups along Rockaway Boulevard and One Hundred First Avenue. The newcomers are primarily working and middle class, and the homes are well maintained. One pocket that still has a white, largely Italian presence is the area east of Cross Bay Boulevard and just north of North Conduit Avenue.

Like most people, I often go into convenience stores attached to gas stations when I'm driving. They are generally of varying quality, with most in the so-so or good category. Nothing prepared me for the one in Ozone Park, adjoining a Sunoco station at the intersection of Pitkin Avenue and Cross Bay Boulevard. Called Bolla Markets, it's part of a fast-growing chain. What's special about it is the quality of the place—spotless, with wide, spacious aisles and outstanding design and signage, high-quality fast food, gourmet coffee, milk shakes of every flavor, and highly professional service. The bathrooms are clean and roomy, with marble floors and walls. The shelved items are perfectly arranged, with nothing out of place. If a customer messes it up, an employee immediately straightens it out. The man behind this brainchild was Harry Singh, who came to New York City from Punjab, India, in 1984 and began his career as a busboy and cab driver. Eventually he went into business, and by 2011 he owned fifty-five stores and forty-five gas stations around the country. Singh described his vision best: "Bolla pledges to provide our customers with unexpected luxury and elegance not normally found in a convenience store." He's right. This level of professionalism is truly unknown in Queens and in general, and definitely worth noting.

A little farther north on Cross Bay, I pass the San Pasquale Society club, founded in 1917. There's a five-foot-high color photo of the leaning Tower of Pisa on the door, clear evidence that an Italian presence remains. These clubs can be found in other New York communities like Bensonhurst and Carroll Gardens, Brooklyn. They are there for the elderly who remained behind as the younger people moved out to greener suburban pastures. Once they were centers of activity, but what's amazing is that they are still vibrant places for those who care about their history and culture. Here they sit and reminisce about the "old country," play cards, eat Italian delicacies that they bring from home to eat, and watch television shows beamed from Italy. But these societies are slowly fading away, including San Pasquale. It closed shortly before this book appeared.

I turn right on One Hundred Thirty-Fourth Avenue and soon make another right onto 96th Street. It's a very quiet enclave within Ozone Park, bounded by Rockaway Parkway on the north, Aqueduct Racetrack on the east, North Conduit Boulevard on the south, with Cross Bay and Woodhaven Boulevards on the west. While there are Guyanese and others living here, there's still a sizeable white, mostly Italian presence, as evidenced by the nativity scenes on the front lawns, the fig trees, and the names on the doors of the homes. I head left on Pitkin Avenue and right on 97th Street to Bristol Avenue, where I make a left. Bristol is actually a one-block, dead-end affair. Most of the homes are old, but a huge new home with a brick exterior and tiled roof is being built on the block. It's on a forty-by-eighty-foot lot, and the height on just the first floor is twenty-one feet. The man has four children and comes from South Ozone Park. This will be his palace, according to the neighbors. It's a very quiet location, but about 500 yards away the A train rumbles by every few minutes.

This area is more mixed ethnically and has both ordinary and nice homes. As I head west and return along Pitkin Avenue I'm reminded when I pass the homes that, as opposed to Queens, Pitkin becomes a major commercial thoroughfare in Brooklyn servicing the Brownsville and East New York communities. Many homes in this area are colonials but look more like saltbox-shaped houses; and they're much closer together with smaller lots.

One major exception to this is a subsection called Tudor Village that runs, generally, from 86th to 81st Streets between Pitkin and North Conduit Avenues. Built in 1929, the homes, attached, semi-attached, and detached, are built in a Tudor style with several peaks, in the center and on each side of the roof. They are entirely made of brick with hardly any stucco, few slate roofs, and no half timbers on the facing, nor the distinctive lines that typify most Tudors. And they are not very large. On the other hand, the lawns and homes are, for the most part, in excellent condition, and many, if not most of them, proudly display a metal sign near the front entrance in block letters that reads "TUDOR VILLAGE."

From here I travel north along 84th Street to One Hundred First Avenue and turn right. The street is no longer filled with stores catering to Italian Americans. All that's left of that community are a few churches and funeral parlors, and some pizza shops, plus medical offices. In their place are temples, mosques, and shops catering to the South Asian and Hispanic population that predominates today in Ozone Park.

At 98-04 I come to the building that was previously home to the truly legendary club of Mafia mobster John Gotti and of the Gambino family; it was known as the Bergin Hunt and Fish Club. Its name is now Lords of Stitch and Print. I enter and find out that the store stitches anything you want on baseball-style caps. Before this it was an ice cream shop, according to the present owner, Dereck Singh. He and his associate are members of families who immigrated here from Guyana.

"Do you realize that this place has a history?" I ask.

"Sure. People tell us this all the time."

"Is anything left that was here when Gotti ran the club?"

"The only thing is a stall shower in the back." They don't have any special feeling about this but kind of like the idea that it isn't just your average address and that it might even attract some business from curious visitors. For such people, coming here is like being in touch with Mafia history, one that has become a very large slice of American history, the subject of innumerable films, TV shows, and books.

Heading north on 98th Street to Atlantic Avenue, which parallels 101st, I turn left and walk down this mostly industrial street. It's here, between 90th and 89th Streets, on the south side of Atlantic, that I come to a rather remarkable and extremely colorful wall mural divided in two panels that meet at ninety-degree angles. It covers two adjoining sides that meet at a right angle. In other words, it's a half square of walls, and what I'm gazing at is the inside of a kitchen, and what a kitchen it is! It's clearly very chaotic and messy. The first panel has two windows with venetian blinds and a light fixture, and the rest of the panel is very complicated. A pigeon is perched on a windowsill, looking in. There are proportionally small helicopters on each side of the light fixture, one of them engulfed in flames.

On the countertop, I see a gigantic cup of tea and an unidentified can of something in a corner. There are military tanks, driven by rabbits wearing gas masks. On the left are several discarded cigarette butts near a box of Newport cigarettes. In the air, there's a splash of blue paint consisting largely of bubbles twirling around the light fixture. A cowboy figure standing on the counter has lassoed this bubble mass with a rope. Moving to the panel on the right, which faces Atlantic Avenue, I glance at a large bowl of cereal with alphabets floating in milk, alongside a watery Captain Crunch. Nearby, standing on the counter, is Roger Rabbit. It's basically a 1950s kitchen, with a Formica table around which are turquoise-colored vinyl chairs so popular during this period. The cabinets are painted in 1950s colors, turquoise and yellow, and the countertop

The remarkable, creative—and chaotic—kitchen mural.

is bright red. On the left side of the counter is Bugs Bunny near a can of Spam. There's also a blender with what looks like Franken-stein, seemingly imprisoned in the blender and perhaps awaiting his demise.

I chance upon an elderly man who's getting into his car and who has just come from the building on whose exterior the mural has been painted. I introduce myself and ask him what this is all about. Abe, who turns out to be the owner, enlightens me.

"About ten years ago," he tells me, "two teenagers began painting the wall. They didn't ask for permission, but I was fine with it. They did it over several weeks." I wonder what was behind this mural choice—whimsy or a carefully thought out decision? Regardless, this is a tribute to both human creativity and the importance of carefully exploring cities on foot where the walker will notice something like this.

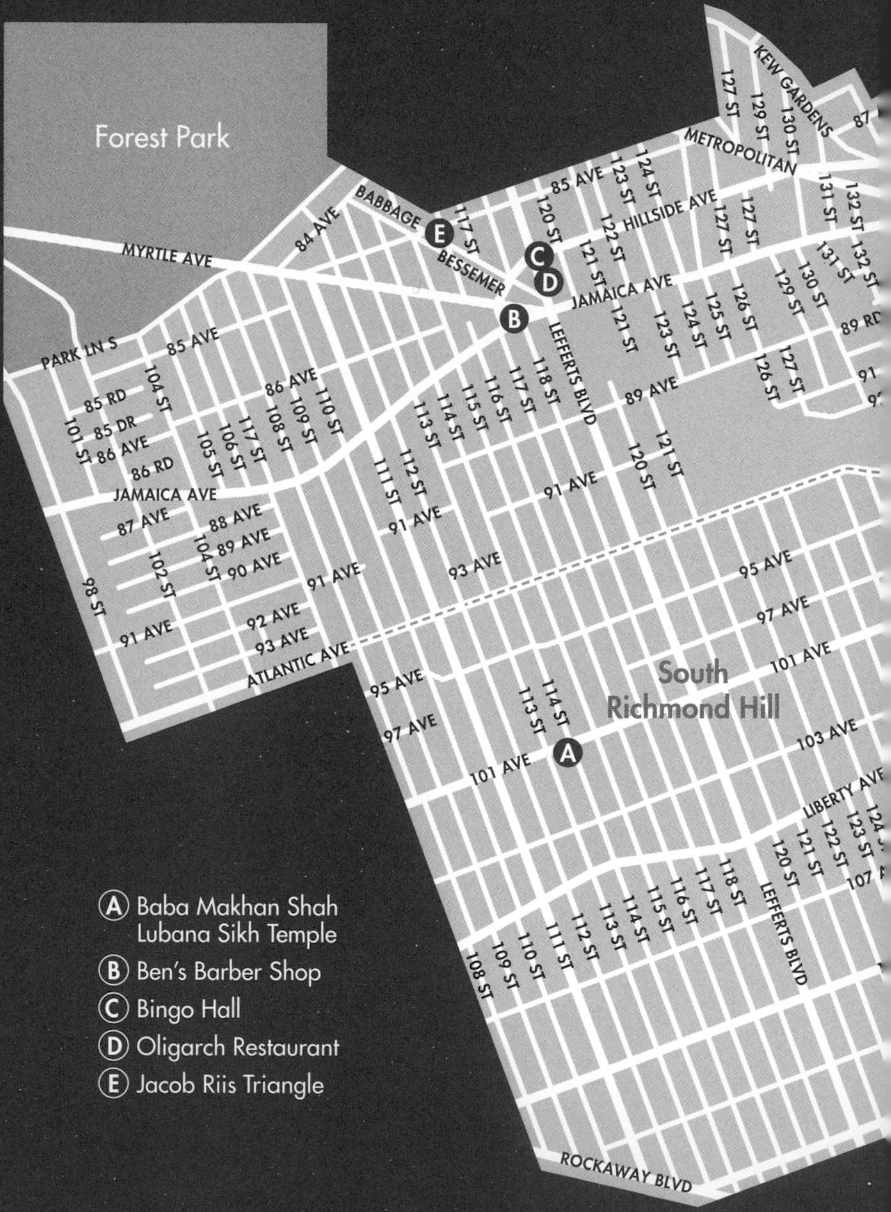
Forest Park
South Richmond Hill
KEW GARDENS
METROPOLITAN
MYRTLE AVE
BABBAGE
BESSEMER
JAMAICA AVE
HILLSIDE AVE
LEFFERTS BLVD
PARK LN S
ATLANTIC AVE
LIBERTY AVE
ROCKAWAY BLVD
84 AVE
85 AVE
85 RD
85 DR
86 AVE
86 RD
87 AVE
88 AVE
89 AVE
89 RD
90 AVE
91 AVE
92 AVE
93 AVE
95 AVE
97 AVE
101 AVE
103 AVE
107 AVE
98 ST
101 ST
102 ST
104 ST
105 ST
106 ST
108 ST
109 ST
110 ST
111 ST
112 ST
113 ST
114 ST
115 ST
116 ST
117 ST
118 ST
120 ST
121 ST
122 ST
123 ST
124 ST
125 ST
126 ST
127 ST
129 ST
130 ST
131 ST
132 ST
A Baba Makhan Shah Lubana Sikh Temple
B Ben's Barber Shop
C Bingo Hall
D Oligarch Restaurant
E Jacob Riis Triangle

RICHMOND HILL

RICHMOND HILL WAS ESTABLISHED AS A RESIDENTIAL COMMUNITY IN 1867. It attracted wealthy people from Manhattan, who built large homes here. Its boundaries, roughly, are Myrtle Avenue, Park Lane, Babbage Street, and Eighty-Fifth Avenue on the north; the Van Wyck Expressway on the east; Linden and Rockaway Boulevards on the south; and 108th and 98th Streets on the west. With the establishment of subway service in 1915, the community grew rapidly, with the number of smaller houses and apartment buildings increasing dramatically to accommodate the new residents. The main commercial thoroughfares are Jamaica and Atlantic Avenues, along with small portions of Myrtle and Hillside Avenues, and Lefferts Boulevard. The main recreational area is Forest Park, which borders the community on the north.

Myrtle Avenue is a very long avenue that traverses two boroughs. It begins in Queens, where Myrtle and Jamaica Avenues meet, and ends, a little over eight miles later, at Duffield Street in Brooklyn. Its name stems from the myrtle trees that were once there in the days when it was a plank road, which charged a toll to the stagecoaches that used it.

Until the early 1970s, the predominant groups living here were Irish, German, and Italian, along with a smattering of Jews. Then, slowly, Hispanic and Indians from Caribbean lands began moving in. Today, the community is a true amalgam of ethnic groups and includes Guyanese and Trinidadians of Indian heritage, Sikhs, Pakistanis, Mexicans, Dominicans, Colombians, and Peruvians. The northern part, between Eighty-Fifth Avenue and Jamaica Avenue, still has clusters of Irish, Italians, and Jews.

South Richmond Hill, a subsection of Richmond Hill, is bounded by Atlantic Avenue on the north, the Van Wyck on the east, Linden and Rockaway on the south, and 108th Street on the west. Population density here is far higher, and the residents are a mix of Sikhs, Guyanese, Mexicans, and other Latino groups. The houses in South Richmond Hill are much closer together and have a certain sameness, as they are tall and thin Dutch colonials. But interspersed among them are some 120-year-old survivors from the era when Balthasar Kreischer, a German immigrant who built a brick factory based in Staten Island, built two- and three-story, mostly yellow-brick homes with bow and bay windows.

My own journey begins on Jamaica Avenue and 110th Street with the goal of exploring the streets between Jamaica and Myrtle. It's a lovely residential area with large, old, gracious homes. In general, the part between Eighty-Sixth and Myrtle Avenues has some of the nicest homes—Victorians, regular colonials, and Tudors. At 85-42 110th Street, there's a rather unique green-and-beige home, with fish-scale shingles over the entrance and on top of the third floor. There's wooden cutout scrollwork above the porch and the front door that resembles a vine. The wraparound porch with spindles running along the perimeters has old-fashioned ceiling lights and two equally charming ceiling fans, plus numerous hanging plants, all of which make it look very inviting. Across the street is a very attractive Tudor, with French windows and half timbers, though not as special as this one. At 84-16, we have a remarkable house with black stone winged griffins guarding the walkway, and large flowered-filled metal urns above their heads. On the left side of the front lawn there's an old-looking willow tree and a small tree with potted plants hanging from its branches. A large open porch has a pointed roof with a flowering vine that has orange flowers.

This street, 110th, is just one example of the pleasures awaiting those who stroll up and down these blocks. I turn right onto Myrtle Avenue, which is residential in these parts, featuring old homes that are, for the most part, quite well preserved, and then stop at 114th Street and Myrtle Avenue to gaze at something quite unusual.

There are instances where a structure may be deliberately designed so that it will go unnoticed. This building is only a few blocks away from the border for Kew Gardens, an area that's heavily Jewish, but the location is definitely not a Jewish area and, in effect, crosses a border into a section, south of Myrtle Avenue, that has many Muslims, Hindus, and Christians. The synagogue here is a one-story affair that has almost no markings to identify it as a Jewish house of worship—not even a mezuzah—even though it is an Orthodox synagogue. The building's art moderne glass blocks make it virtually impossible to see inside, and there are no windows. The entrance has a combination lock and a small sign with English letters above a door of plain heavy metal identifying it as Khal Nachlas Avos. But those letters would not give away what it is except to a knowledgeable observer. Most startling, there's no address on the door, no Star of David, or any of the usual markers of temples. I ask a member who happens to be leaving the synagogue if the congregants have removed the identifying markers out of fear that the building might be bombed.

"We just don't want any trouble, no rocks thrown by kids. We try to keep a low profile. It's not a Jewish neighborhood, and we were advised that it's best to not make waves. It's also right in front of a bus stop so people are always standing here, waiting for it, or getting off." This is clearly a beachhead, since young Jewish families have been moving into other parts of Richmond Hill in search of less expensive housing for their growing families. This place means a shorter walk to a synagogue. I ask a Sikh neighbor, owner of the house next door, and he corroborates the member's explanation for its low profile. I notice that there is a camera aimed at the building, and the neighbor informs me that, at the congregation's request, he keeps a close eye on it.

Turning right on 114th, I walk past more pretty homes, eventually crossing Atlantic Avenue, the northern border of largely Indian South Richmond Hill, to One Hundred First Avenue. This intersection at 114th Street is home to the Baba Makhan Shah Lubana, which I have visited numerous times with my graduate students on our forays throughout the city. Removing my shoes, placing them in a cubbyhole, and donning a bright-orange kerchief, I step into the sanctuary, a large room with seating on the carpeted floor for men on the right side and women on the left. There is no partition between the sexes, and people sometimes cross over and chat for a few moments.

I'm greeted cordially. It's a very laid-back kind of place. Each time I've visited, they have invited me in and let me know they were available to answer any questions about their faith, which was founded in Punjab, India, in the fifteenth century. Their religion is neither Hindu nor Islamic, nor an offshoot of either. It's a monotheistic faith and one that adheres to the teachings of its ten gurus. Many of the men wear the traditional turbans and refrain from cutting their hair. It's one of the key tenets of their faith. Hair is considered holy, and the Sikhs have many stories of people who were tortured and even lost their lives because they refused demands to cut their hair. In their view, the more they suffer for their beliefs, the more they can prove the strength of their devotion.[45]

The younger generation is more liberal, yet many of them still attend services on a regular basis. Often there is singing and music along with the prayers. A religious figure sits in a separate room and will offer specific prayers for you. Food is served in another room

The Baba Makhan Shah Lubana sanctuary.

any time of the day or night and is offered to all who come, residents or visitors. This consists of tea, rice, pita bread, and vegetarian soup (everything is vegetarian).

Resuming my walk, I continue south along 114th Street and turn left onto Liberty Avenue, the commercial nerve center of the Indian community, for both Sikhs and Guyanese. The Guyanese are one of New York's largest ethnic groups, perhaps 140,000 strong. Among the Indians, the vast majority, including the Guyanese, are Hindu, though there are also many Muslims and even a number of Christians among them. I speak with Gary Girdhari, publisher of the *Guyana Journal*, an online publication. He explains that "under the British, many Guyanese became Christians so they could get ahead in the schools, in business, and in general. Thus, Christianity became an expression of nationalism, not religion. As a result, you have syncretism, with people celebrating Christmas and Hindu holidays."

In the nineteenth century, indentured servants from lower castes in India came to Guyana, then a British colony, and intermarried with indigenous tribe members. Today, they make up 50 percent of the Guyanese population. The other half consists of Africans originally brought here by the British as slaves to work on plantations and who were replaced by the Indian workers. Although geographically part of the South American mainland, Guyana is also regarded as belonging to the Caribbean region because its people, historically, politically, and culturally, are part of the Caribbean islands. Like the Guyanese, who live mostly in Queens, the African population also came to New York City and resides mostly in the Flatbush, East Flatbush, and Canarsie communities of Brooklyn. The two groups have competed for power in Guyana and are not especially friendly with one another, although a small number have intermarried over the years.

To walk up Liberty is almost like entering another country. I've always said, only half-jokingly, that if one lives in New York, it isn't necessary to go abroad. In Flushing, one can feel one is in China or Korea; in Jackson Heights and Elmhurst, Latin America; and so on. The stores, entertainment centers, and houses of worship here reflect the culture of the residents—stores featuring West Indian imports; Guyanese bakeries and restaurants specializing in roti and curry dishes; clothes selling traditional Indian garb; Guyanese nightclubs, some specializing in "chutney music," a mix of sounds from Mauritius, Fiji, and the Caribbean; shops selling so much jewelry of the bright-yellow gold favored by the Guyanese; and temples, mosques, and churches. There's a carnival-like atmosphere on the avenue, and the sidewalks are filled with vendors of every kind.

I return down Liberty to Lefferts Boulevard and go right until I arrive at Jamaica Avenue again, entering Ben's Barber Shop at 117-21 Jamaica. Much of the talk about communities takes place in barber shops, bars, bodegas, and local hangouts, where residents gather to chat and pass the time. And this Bukharian barber shop, featuring a large drawing of a mustachioed Ben, seems like a good place to get a sense of the community.

I ask a barber taking a break, "How's business?"

"Good," he says. "We have people from everywhere coming into the shop—from Guyana, Punjab, Sikhs, Moslem, Jews. We Jewish, but we don't care. It's not good for business. Everyone the same. God is one in the barbershop." Unsaid is the fact that the shop is only ten minutes by car from the Bukharian-dominated communities of Forest Hills and Rego Park, thus making him feel comfortable here. The Bukharians have taken over the barbering industry in much of New York City. It's a real change from the days when this was an Italian-dominated profession. In truth, barbering is a popular choice for immigrants, just like laundries, shoemaking, small restaurants. All these require low capital investment—a barbershop costs about $10,000 to set up. They can also employ numerous family members, and many feel it's not that important to be educated or even know English. They're cash businesses, and, if one is willing to work long hours, they can be fairly lucrative.

But there are reasons why they, the Bukharians, and not the Chinese or Mexicans, became barbers, reasons specific to their culture and history. Under Soviet rule in central Asia, many Jews went into this trade, and one owner of a business brought in the other. That's usually how it happens. Coming here, without capital resources or higher education, they continued doing what they knew best— watch repair, shoemaking, jewelry, and cutting hair.

Yet there are differences between them and their Italian predecessors. As one Bukharian barber put it, "The Italian guys are very slow and precise. We have a little less attention to detail." But they have the same sense of the barber shop as a community center.

Nearby, at 117-33 Myrtle Avenue, is the home of the Classic Diner. It has been there for seventy years, with several changes in ownership and name, but it's always been a diner. It's a very nice-looking place, with the usual extensive menu. Besides good food, the diner boasts the only diner bathroom (that I know of) that becomes a disco, with blinking lights in many different colors, and with great music to boot.

A bit farther east, I turn left onto Hillside Avenue, pass one of the numerous bodegas in this section, and enter a building that used to be a cavernous movie theater. It was called RKO Keith's and closed in 1968, though there are still folks around today who remember it. It's missing the 2,234 seats it once had, but it could once again become a movie theater if an entrepreneur cared to create one. Today, it's a bingo hall that I've visited several times where enthusiasts gather on a regular basis.[46]

Like bocce, bingo has Italian antecedents. The original version was invented in Italy in 1530 and was called Lo Giuoco del Lotto D'Italia (meaning "The Clearance of the Lot in Italy"). It entered the United States in the 1920s and was first called beano, after the beans that players used to mark their cards.

Bingo is a sedentary game, but the players, the venues, and its dependence on luck make it a whole different ball game, from, say, chess or checkers. It's very popular among members of a specific group—senior citizens, mostly working-class women—and the game helps bring them closer together. Their conversations focus on health, politics, and the economy, as well as on the changing community. Several avidly discussed stock tips that panned out, as well as some that didn't.[47]

These are the same people who get on a bus to Atlantic City bound for the casinos, but in this case, they don't even have to do that since they mostly live in the city. For many of these old-timers, bingo is almost a religion. Their lives revolve around it—the playing, the camaraderie, the possibility of a thousand dollars or more in winnings—and a good number of them were invested in the game many years before they retired. But now it has the additional value of filling the long days that stretch before them.

From political parties to wedding parties: that's the story of the Republican Club at 86-15 Lefferts Boulevard, where Lefferts, Myrtle, and Jamaica Avenues all meet. It was first opened in 1908. Its interior has beautiful oak columns and sliding doors, a tin ceiling, and thick cushioned leather chairs. The lower level was once a bowling alley for members and their guests. Arrayed on the walls were signed photos of former presidents Teddy Roosevelt, Warren Harding, and Calvin Coolidge. The community, in those days was staunchly Republican. Today, it's heavily Democratic.

In 2002, the exterior of the structure received landmark status, and a few years ago it began a new life as a catering hall aimed at the

Bukharian Jewish market and called the Oligarch. It's an amazing-looking place.

I spoke with the owner, who gave me a tour and said, "Welcome to paradise. It's kosher, but everybody comes, Jewish, not Jewish. Look at this incredible chandelier. It has 110,000 lightbulbs. From the outside, with the words Republican Club, you would never know what's inside here." The style is Russian, with flashing lights, lavish decorations, colors that aren't at all ashamed to be seen and appreciated, and comfortable seating.

Leaving here, I walk two blocks north from Myrtle Avenue along 116th Street to Eighty-Fifth Avenue. Here I turn right and in two blocks come to my last stop in this incredibly rich and diverse community. It's a little grassy area called the Jacob Riis Triangle, at 118th Street and Eighty-Fifth. It's dedicated to this great Danish American crusader for the poor and destitute immigrants who came to this city from the mid- to late nineteenth century. Riis himself was poor when he came here and worked at menial jobs, sometimes sleeping outdoors when he had no money. Eventually, he became a journalist and photographer and chronicled the lives of New York's impoverished masses, writing a classic book, *How the Other Half Lives*, published in 1890.

The book aroused the interest and concern of former president Teddy Roosevelt, who was then police commissioner of New York City. Riis and Roosevelt became good friends and would travel through the communities, uncovering injustices and fighting to eradicate them. The memorial is here because Riis resided in Richmond Hill on 120th Street (the house is long gone) from 1886 to 1912. When Riis's daughter was married in 1900 at the Church of the Resurrection at 85-09 118th Street, Roosevelt was there. Riis obviously had no idea that Richmond Hill, home to many white European immigrants, would remain a melting pot for immigrants who today hail from many South American and Caribbean nations, but there's no doubt he would have taken up their cause. It's a fitting end to the story of this polyglot community.

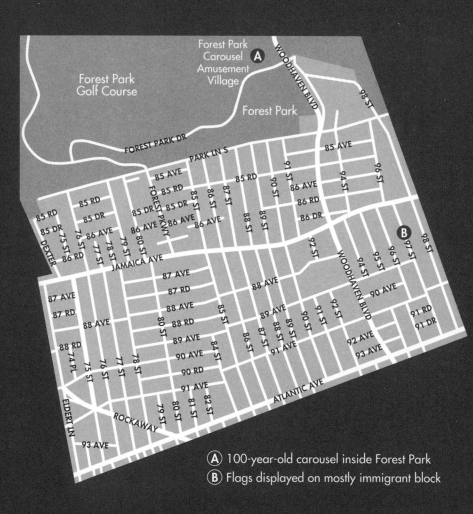

Ⓐ 100-year-old carousel inside Forest Park
Ⓑ Flags displayed on mostly immigrant block

WOODHAVEN

THE BOUNDARIES OF WOODHAVEN are Park Lane South on the north, behind which is Forest Park; 98th Street on the east; Atlantic Avenue on the south; and Eldert Lane and Dexter Court on the west. Dutch farmers first settled this area in the 1700s. It remained farmland until the early twentieth century, when the elevated subway lines attracted thousands of largely working-class Italians, Germans, Irish, and eastern Europeans, mostly Poles. It had a small-town feel right up to the 1980s. While there are some large homes, generally Victorians, and some scattered small apartment buildings, most of the homes are small, detached, semi-attached, and attached. Many blocks have old brownstones, some in excellent shape, the rest in so-so condition.

Ethnic change began to make itself felt in the 1970s, when immigrants from the West Indies, those from Latin American lands, and, a bit later on, Guyanese, spilled over from Ozone Park, South Ozone Park, and South Richmond Hill. The community is relatively safe and close to the city with easy access by subway. It's also near the Rockaways (a straight car or bus ride south on Woodhaven Boulevard), making it accessible to the beaches. Forest Park offers a multitude of recreational activities for sports enthusiasts of all types, including walkers, joggers, and cyclists, and as well as for picnickers. It also features a rich array of free cultural programs for those who visit. Shopping is available on the commercial thoroughfares of Jamaica Avenue and parts of Atlantic Avenue and Woodhaven Boulevard.

I begin my walk on 91st Street, heading toward Forest Park. It's an old community in terms of the housing stock, which consists mainly of colonials and Victorians of varying sizes, many of them more than a century old. This is true of much of Woodhaven. At Park Lane South, I climb up several flights of stone steps and go left, walking along some permanently closed tennis courts before coming to some that are open and in use. At 543 acres, Forest Park is one of the largest in Queens.

I pass by some homes, mostly Victorians that are outstanding in their design, here on this street, which is covered by a canopy of trees, most of them London plane trees, which are actually a hybrid version of the American sycamore tree. At 84-32, there's a closed porch on top, which is in a decorative crisscross pattern I've not seen in many years, a design dating back to my childhood. A number of the houses feature beautiful, oval-shaped stained-glass windows with fleur-des-lis patterns in the middle of the window.

I return up the hill to the park, along 86th Street, to see the concert. Passing by the tennis courts, I see an object flying about three hundred feet from the ground. These are drones, which have become very popular in recent years among young people. I ask Don, who's flying one with his friend, what this is all about.

"It can go up about five hundred feet," he tells me. "It costs about $800, and, believe it or not, you can get them at Best Buy. With this one you can get the highest resolution photos with its camera. Of course, you have to register and get a license from the FAA [Federal Aviation Administration]. This basically lets them track all your flights, and they know then that you're not doing crazy stuff. And if it ever gets disconnected or whatever, it comes back automatically to where you are." There are at least three other people here flying drones.

From here I head over to the bandshell about ten minutes east, following the sound of the music from the Rat Pack group. It's a free concert, one of many presented by parks throughout the city. There's a huge crowd of people, perhaps two thousand, from many backgrounds, most of them white. Many have driven here. I sit down, and the Dean Martin imitator warms up the audience with some slightly off-color jokes, which are greeted with laughter from the mostly older crowd. Everyone seems to be having a good time, with many couples dancing in the aisle, enjoying the oldies selections. In this way, I learn, on the scene, another way in which this park is enjoyed.

Moving on, I soon come to a classic-looking carousel from the old days that has a special history. It's a landmark, the only carousel in the city to receive such a designation. The majority of wood figures on the carousel are horses, but there are also a few tigers, lions, and chariots, all of which were created early in 1903. They were designed by D. C. Muller, who learned his craft in Germany. A member of the Philadelphia school of carousel carvers, Muller also studied at the Pennsylvania Academy. Besides the animals, he made the swords, buckles, and other military fittings that are on the carousel, all of them very intricate and detailed. Whirling around on top of the animals, the entire length of the carousel, is a collage with photos and drawings of roads, racetracks, and homes in this area, dating back to the turn of the twentieth century and before. It's one of only two of his creations still in existence and absolutely worth seeing. The other one is in Cedar Point, Ohio.

Nearby are a few other rides like the Frog Hop and a small train ride. According to Daeshawn, an employee, "The children's rides attract people to the carousel. Part of what makes it different is that it's original and it has faster action." Another worker tells me, "Nostalgia buffs come here all the time. They took their grand-kids here, and now they're bringing their great-grandkids."

The Greenhouse Playground has the usual equipment, sprinklers, and benches for children and their caregivers, but it also has skateboarding, one of six playgrounds in the borough with this activity. I ask the skateboarders, all teenagers, how they would rate this place. They indicate that it's "okay," but especially good for beginners.

This part of Forest Park runs along Woodhaven Boulevard, near where it intersects with Myrtle Avenue. I turn right onto Woodhaven and walk south to Jamaica Avenue. There, I turn left and then right down 97th Street. It is here, between Jamaica and Eighty-Ninth Avenues, that I encounter a remarkable sight that, at first, looks rather unremarkable. It's a street with a plethora of large American flags. This would not be unusual in parts of Staten Island or Brooklyn. The flags are often seen as a giveaway that it's a white, politically right-of-center

Thirty-six of the thirty-nine homes on the block have an American flag out front.

community. That these flags are not nearly as numerous in liberal communities like, say Brooklyn's Ditmas Park, or the Chelsea section of Manhattan, isn't necessarily a sign that the residents care any less about this country. More likely it's a reaction to the stereotype and a desire not to be associated with what the flag seems to represent.

What makes it so unusual is that another category of people lives here—immigrants from South Asian and Hispanic lands and their children. This population is not known for flags in front of their homes, but thirty-six of the thirty-nine homes on the block have one. What's the reason? It's the work of one resident who individually approached his neighbors and asked them if they would be willing to put it in front their houses. He offered to give them a flag and take care of the upkeep. The response was clearly enthusiastic and verified by conversations with individuals.

Approaching two Guyanese men I asked them, "How come there are so many American flags on this block?"

"Because a man, I think he's Irish, gave us the flags and asked us if we would put them in front of the houses, and we thought it would look nice."

"This is pretty unusual, so many."

"Why not? You got a problem with that?"

"Not at all."

I ask another man, a Bangladeshi in the restaurant business about the flags.

"I was very happy to do it," he says. "The man is very nice. He'll do anything for you."

A third resident, a middle-aged man from Honduras, says, "He's a great guy, and I was happy to do it. He checks on everything. Besides, why shouldn't I do it? I've been in the US since I was seven, and I'm proud to be an American."

The architect of this idea is Paul Michael Kazas, and he lives on the block. He turns out to be easy enough to find on the internet, and he's quite a guy, having been honored by Congress for his community service. He belongs to more than twenty community groups, cleaning up malls and other areas in the community, and doing good works in places besides his own block. He even became a certified tree pruner so the community could receive a state government grant. I decide to speak with Kazas about his activities. He's a fifty-nine-year-old attorney who has devoted himself to this cause. Of Lithuanian descent, he's active in that community, as well, and has been honored by the Lithuanian consul in New York.

"What prompted your decision to get involved?" I ask him.

"I've been doing this for years, and I've lived on this block all my life. Symbols are important, and the American flag represents, among other things, the idea of diversity because Americans come from so many countries in every part of the world. Of course, these flags aren't cheap. They cost $15 each, but I love doing it. I don't force anyone to do it, but I tell them that the flag unites us all, and they relate to that."

"How do they relate to it?"

"It gives them pride in being an American, the idea that the flag belongs to them and everyone else in this nation. I tell them 'It doesn't matter who you are, Democrat, Republican, Independent, liberal, moderate, conservative.' No one disagrees. I also fix and replace the flags. Two of the people who didn't have flags when you walked by are having them replaced, and the third one didn't want it because of something about the duct tape I used to affix it, but he was very friendly and polite about it. You see, you can't do this in European countries. There they want you to assimilate totally, to be French or German."

This man has changed the stereotype of who puts up flags by publicly putting every group into the category of those who appreciate and even love America. He has also increased these immigrants' own feeling of really belonging, especially because he's a white, native-born American and wants to do it. Kazas also demonstrates the importance of what I've called "community characters" in the city. It isn't enough to have social workers, legislators, or community relations experts because the "characters" are true volunteers, and they come from the communities themselves.

As I continue down Jamaica, I see the usual assortment of meat markets, mattress stores, physicians' and dental offices, bodegas, dry cleaners, 99¢ stores, and a lone Irish-sounding bar from the old days, with an Irish name.

Almost all the faded brick structures—they are apartments—along Jamaica Avenue are really old. Looking at the second and third floors above the stores is a great way to visualize what this area looked like one hundred years ago. Yet the trains that rumble by overhead every few minutes also bring me to the present because they are the J and Z trains, the name adopted by the rapper, Jay-Z, also known as Shawn Corey Carter.

But my reverie about that is interrupted when I chance upon Schmidt's Candy, at 94-15 Jamaica Avenue, where above the entrance are the words "HOME MADE," along with a drawing of a glass jar filled with gumballs. They are closed during July and August because the hot weather isn't conducive to candy making. Schmidt's has been around since 1927, serving treats like gooey caramels, chocolate-covered cherries, buttercrunch, and mint patties, mostly from time-tested German recipes.

HOWARD BEACH

BROAD CHANNEL

THE ROCKAWAYS

Ⓐ New Park Pizza
Ⓑ NYFAC autistic
children's center

157 AVE

103 ST
102 ST
101 ST
100 ST
99 ST

CHURCH
BAYVIEW
BROADWAY

RUSSELL

1 ST

DUNTON
RAU
DAVENPORT
163 RD
JAMES
164 AVE
164 RD
164 DR
165 AVE

104 ST

lton
ch

AVE

4 AVE

98 ST

165 AVE

98 ST

Hawtree Creek

*Grassy
Bay*

HOWARD
BEACH

THE BEGINNINGS OF HOWARD BEACH
can be traced back to William Howard,
an entrepreneur who raised goats on a
farm near Ozone Park and had a glove
factory in Brooklyn. In 1897, he bought
land in what is now Hamilton Beach
and soon opened a hotel near the water,
hoping to attract wealthy guests from
Manhattan. The hotel had a casino,
which sat on land that is now Charles
Memorial Park. The hotel burned
down in 1907. In 1909, Howard built
streets and small homes in the community, which went for about $3,000 each.
After the railroad was opened in 1913,
growth accelerated, and many more
people settled in the area. When a subway station opened in Howard Beach,
the population increased even more,
with the dominant groups being Italians and, somewhat later, Jews.

The general boundaries of Howard
Beach are North and South Conduit
Avenues on the north; 102nd, 103rd,
and 104th Streets on the east; One
Hundred Sixty-Fifth and One Hundred Sixty-First Avenues on the south;
and 78th Street on the west. There's one
major commercial thoroughfare, Cross

Bay Boulevard. Transportation to the city takes about an hour by express bus, and there's the A train at One Hundred Fifty-Ninth Avenue and 103rd Street. The community is far away from the center of Queens, and its location, surrounded as it is by the Belt Parkway, Jamaica Bay, and JFK airport, has resulted in a close-knit community. Today's dominant groups are Italians and smaller groups of Jews, Irish, Hispanics, Asians, and some African Americans. The area is safe, the homes are nice, and there are parks, good fishing spots, restaurants, and easy access to the beaches of the Rockaways. It should be noted that the presence of Mafia members, especially the well-known John Gotti and Joey Massino, and some highly publicized racial incidents, have given the area a somewhat unsavory reputation.

My excursion through Howard Beach begins, appropriately enough, on its main and only commercial thoroughfare, Cross Bay Boulevard. The first stop is New Park Pizza, at 156-71 Cross Bay, literally an institution in this community. There are two entrances. The first leads to a counter where you order pies and other things to go. The second brings you to a small rectangular area with an old tin ceiling that's divided into small squares. The walls are a bright-yellow stucco with some wainscoting and paneling. There are framed pictures on the wall, mostly of employees and also various cityscapes.

New Park has been there for more than sixty-two years, and for as long as I can remember it's almost always been packed with people of all ages—teenagers with their spiked haircuts and tattoos; seniors wearing shorts, t-shirts, and Yankee caps, and looking fit and trim for their age; grandmas, with their grandchildren trailing behind them; and just plain folks taking a lunch break from their jobs as steamfitters, electricians, bank employees, and the myriad of occupations that make this community tick. I talk to a manager, a short fellow, with small, alert eyes that immediately size me up.

"So, tell me," I begin, "what's your secret? Why do so many people come here?"

New Park Pizza is an institution in this community.

"No secret," he says in that twangy, staccato, "New Yawk" way of speaking. "We just have good pizza, and the people like it."

"But that's true of lots of places, isn't it?"

"Yeah, but ours is *really* good. I mean we have all sorts of well-known, really knowledgeable sophisticated people who come in here. Take the actor Adrien Brody. He's here at least once a month. He visits his mother, I'm told." To me that's impressive because Adrien is a real New Yorker and one who identifies with Queens. He was also the youngest person, at age twenty-nine, to win a Best Actor Oscar, for his role in *The Pianist*. He grew up in the nearby Woodhaven community, on 85th Road, and attended Queens College. My informant tells me another vignette.

"I don't want to make a big deal, but one of the major Hollywood studios orders a hundred pies a month through FedEx. They freeze them and send them out."

"Who there wants them?" I ask.

"I don't know. We just send them, and they pay for them."

"Do you have a website?"

"Nope. Everything is just word of mouth. I guess we don't need one." I have to agree.

I speak with Dr. Chaim Anfang, a gastroenterologist who has been treating patients in Howard Beach since 1983 and ask him about the community and its people.

"This is actually a very interesting and unique community. It's a very insulated place. The people in Howard Beach don't go anyplace else as a rule. They like the shops, they like the community, they like their doctors, and they just stay here. They'll go to hospitals in Manhattan or Long Island Jewish Hospital in New Hyde Park if they're told to go, but otherwise they'll just stay local. It's such a family-oriented place. They raised their kids here, some of whom even live here now, or visit a lot. It was a third Italian, a third Jewish, and the rest, other groups. The Jews have mostly left, but the Italians are still here."

"What else is special about the community?"

"Howard Beach used to be known for the mobsters who live here. I used to drive around here at Christmastime with my family. The houses were huge, and the decorations were amazing. But two things devastated Howard Beach's reputation as a nice, desirable, family-oriented place. The first was with the black kid that was killed when local kids attacked him and his friends and one of them was hit by a car and killed. The other was Hurricane Sandy. The water actually came all the way up Cross Bay and stopped a few blocks away up the hill by the Belt. It had to be a foot of water. All the first-floor places on the street were inundated with water. People were walking around in shock. They were standing on the streets, bewildered, with all their possessions. They just didn't know what to do."

"What about Gotti? Didn't he also affect the community?"

"Yes, he did, but actually in one sense, in a good way, from the residents' point of view. He was respected because he kept the community safe."

This last comment has a certain measure of truth, and I've heard it from people in other parts of the city where the mob prevailed. Their attitude doesn't mean they approve of everything the mob does or did—killing and torturing people, extorting money, racketeering, and the like—but the peace they bring to the community is seen as a side benefit.

There's no question, in any event, that Howard Beach is associated by many with the mob. John Gotti, who lived at 160-11 85th Street, headed the Gambino crime family, was convicted of thirteen murders, and died in prison in 2002. And then there's the story about John Favara, Gotti's backyard neighbor, who accidentally ran over Gotti's son in 1980. Favara apologized profusely, and Gotti told him it was okay, that he realized it was an accident. Five months later, Favara disappeared, reportedly shot and killed by a hitman, who had the body dissolved in acid. No one was ever charged with the murder.

I continue walking on Cross Bay, and at 164-14, I see a small, very sleek-looking glass building with the letters NYFAC on it. On the walls are several large puzzle pieces in red, yellow, and pink, facing in different directions. It turns out to be the home of New York Families for Autistic Children. Outside, painted on the sidewalk squares, are many more puzzle pieces. I go inside and speak with Leo Compton, the program director. As I suspected, the puzzle pieces symbolize the puzzle of autism, its causes, and treatment. The center was started four years ago to help autistic children in the Queens area. They are also dedicated to educating the public. In April 2017, the CEO, Andrew Baumann, gave a training session to 675 police cadets about autism and how to recognize it.

Lindenwood, just north of the Belt Parkway, is considered to be in "New Howard Beach," which is the part west of Cross Bay Boulevard, from about One Hundred Fifty-Seventh to One Hundred Forty-Ninth Avenues. It's a mix of two-family homes, garden apartments, and apartments in six-story brick buildings. Most are co-ops or condos, with very few rentals. It has always had a strong sense of community, and back in the day there were two swimming pools, which fostered friendships. I speak with Barry Mitchell, a longtime resident and a TV producer, about the development. His mother, the first school crossing guard at local P.S. 232, also lives here.

"What's the population makeup here?" I ask him.

"There's still a large population of Italians, and now, Hispanics, Poles, Russians, and Asians, but most of the Jews have left. My mom, who is ninety-two, looks out the window at Hanukah time and sadly observes: 'We're the only ones who still display a menorah.' There's also been a renaissance of young people here. Not yuppies, but blue-collar strivers. They're very nice—cops, clerical people, sanitation engineers, and the like—Greeks, Poles, Italians. For many of the young this is a starter apartment. It's a self-contained community, with shopping centers frequented by the residents."

On another day I explore Hamilton Beach, one of the most isolated and unknown neighborhoods in the city, which has no connection to Hamilton Beach blenders, and Old Howard Beach, both located on the eastern side of Cross Bay. I make a left off Cross Bay, heading east on One Hundred Fifty-Seventh Avenue and turn right onto 102nd Street, crossing One Hundred Sixtieth Avenue, the beginning of Hamilton Beach.

Until about ten years ago, this was an isolated neighborhood without even a sewer system. The houses are mostly small, sometimes ramshackle affairs, with largely unpaved side streets that often dead-end into canals where people keep boats for fishing. Change has come, and small apartment buildings have been built, some of whose residents participate in the Housing Choice Voucher Program as well. Now, most of the area has sewers, and the roads have been paved. After Hurricane Sandy devastated the area, new homes were built to replace the destroyed ones. Nonetheless, it still has a very quaint feel.

Soon, 102nd Street winds a bit to the left and becomes, first, 103rd Street, and then 104th Street, dead-ending into Hamilton Beach Park at One Hundred Sixty-Fifth Avenue. This is literally the end of the road in Queens, since One Hundred Sixty-Fifth is the highest numbered avenue in the borough. On the right, there's a small property containing many chickens, roosters (some of them huge), ducks, geese, and even a few rabbits. The park is small and has a somewhat run-down handball court, a playground, and a little beach, from which I gaze at Jamaica Bay.

I return via 104th and explore some of the one-block streets on my left. The locals tell me that more Hispanics and South Asians are moving in, a significant change from when this area was almost all white ethnics, especially Irish and Italians. I hang a left on Davenport Court and cross over a footbridge at the end, which leads into Old Howard Beach. Turning left, I travel down 99th Street. Economically and visually, Old Howard Beach is a bit more upscale than Hamilton Beach. The houses are mostly colonials, capes, high ranches of moderate size.

I return and cross the footbridge again to Hamilton Beach and turn left on 104th Street. At Broadway, which isn't on any map I've seen, not even the normally very thorough Hagstrom map, I turn left. Just after Russell Street, it's, maybe, two city blocks long and has to be the most obscure Broadway in the city. There are some boulders alongside a half-block-long grassy area plus several smaller homes. Just for the record, this Broadway has no connection to the much longer Broadway in Queens that runs through Elmhurst, Jackson Heights, Woodside, and Astoria. It dead-ends into Bayview Avenue. Here I meet Tom. He's a tough-looking guy, who speaks in a rough manner. He has close-cropped hair, a broad face, big shoulders, and numerous tattoos. He's very friendly and tells me about the area:

"I'm fourth generation. My family goes back forever. I live in my great-grandfather's house, here on the canal. Originally, they came from East New York, and before that Ireland. Everything's changing. You got all these Section 8 people coming. No criminals, but they're changing the whole friggin neighborhood here. We used to have the whole place to ourselves. Everybody knew everybody. Now it's all being developed, and I don't like it." In a sense, Tom mirrors the view of many people who don't like change. He also is a living link to the people who were the original pioneers in Hamilton Beach and who lived in the fishing bungalows that dotted this immediate area in the 1890s. Who could have known, one hundred years ago, what the area would become—far more built up, and while still a bit isolated, a completely different world.

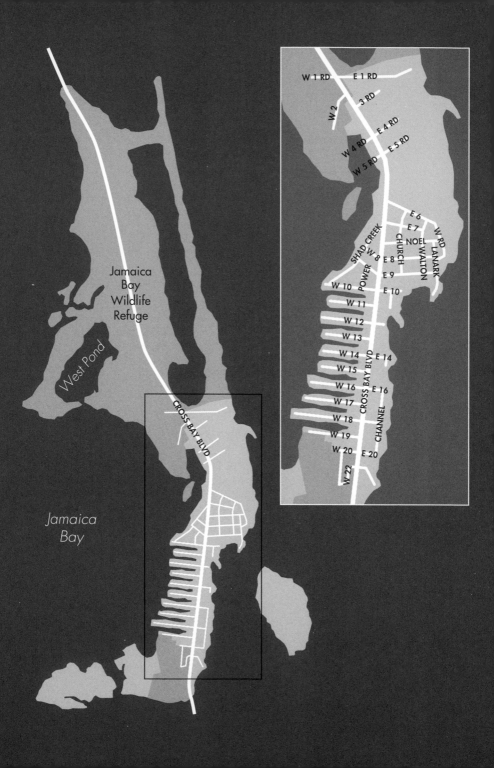

BROAD CHANNEL

THIS IS A MILE-LONG, LARGELY WORKING-CLASS COMMUNITY, actually more like a village, where people, often referred to as "Channelers," have lived in splendid isolation from the rest of New York, including Queens, for decades. The boundaries, roughly, are 1st Road on the north, 22nd Road on the south, and Jamaica Bay on the eastern and western sides. It was originally home to Dutch settlers who earned their livelihood from fishing in the local waters. In the early part of the twentieth century it attracted mostly fishermen and birdwatchers, along with a few summer guests who mostly stayed in local hotels.

Broad Channel is actually an island, which also encompasses the Jamaica Bay Wildlife Refuge and is within walking distance of the A train. Although many of the three thousand residents work in and for the city, mostly for the police and fire departments, they consider this their little paradise, as it were. Most of the population, many of whose members have lived here for generations, are of Irish descent, with large representations of German- and Italian-heritage residents as well.

The vast majority of people driving between the Queens mainland and the Rockaways don't stop here because they have no reason to do so. The main and only thoroughfare is Cross Bay Boulevard, which opened in 1924. Until then it wasn't possible to reach the island by car. The island was owned by the city, and people could build their homes but couldn't own them or the land under them. In 1982, the policy changed, with residents permitted to purchase their homes and the land from the city. The community did not even have sewers until 1988.

Broad Channel has basically one main street running through it from north to south—Cross Bay Boulevard. On each side are streets extending for a few blocks and some short avenues, several blocks long. In 1998, a Labor Day parade held there was condemned as racist because some marchers wore blackface. One black resident of the nearby Rockaways said: "I don't even go to Broad Channel. None of the black people do, because we know we are not welcome."[48]

Thinking it would be a good idea to see how much, if anything, has changed in the past twenty years, I attended the annual Memorial Day parade on a Sunday. While not Labor Day, I thought it would give me an idea of what things were like now, and I was not disappointed. Four black men, members of a Broad Channel volunteer group, marched in the parade. They bantered with the war veterans as they gathered for the start of the event and then walked near the head of the parade route. As I traversed the streets, I also saw that some black families live here. Attitudes have changed here.

As I wander the streets here, I notice many homes that are being "raised." What this means is that to prevent the terrible flooding that damaged so many homes here, the first floors, including their entranceways, are being moved to the second-floor levels, with concrete placed underneath to support the rest of the structure. One man says to me, "Of course, Sandy was a once-in-one-hundred-years affair, but if it happened to you, you'd never forget it. My basement had seven feet of water."

Near one of these homes, between 540 and 536 Cross Bay Boulevard, there's a man-made pond with exquisitely colored goldfish swimming in it. An American flag flies overhead. Number 540, like many houses here, was once a simple bungalow, and today it, like many others, is quite elaborate. It, and other homes in the area have been expanded into multilevel single-family homes.

I turn left down E. 6th Road, then right onto Walton Road, and I am struck by how quiet and quaint everything looks—nautical designs on the homes, seagulls swooping down, boats in the driveway. It feels as if I've landed in a New England fishing village. And yet it's relatively easy to get here via the A train, which stops in Broad Channel. Back on Cross Bay, there's a two-block shopping strip with a couple of delis, a liquor store, a 99¢ store, and an ice cream shop. People I pass greet me with a cheery hello at the slightest eye contact, just the way they would in a small town.

Walton Road almost feels like a New England fishing village.

I come to E. 17th Road, where the parade participants have gathered in a small park with a marina right behind it, for a small ceremony. There are several brief speeches, with one speaker somberly summing up the theme: "We're here today because of those who gave up their tomorrows." This is followed by the playing of taps and the singing of "The Star-Spangled Banner." It's a small crowd, perhaps one hundred strong, and everyone seems to know each other. There aren't many onlookers, but the marchers pay no heed, moving crisply along to the music from a sound truck, with the veterans, in their neatly pressed uniforms, leading the way and followed closely by a blonde-haired woman wearing a flowing poncho designed as an American flag.

Broad Channel is the only inhabited island in Jamaica Bay, and if you want to get to the Rockaways from Queens you must drive through it. From Howard Beach, Queens, you continue for several miles with the Jamaica Bay Wildlife Refuge on both sides of the mini-highway. The entrance to the refuge is on the right, shortly before the beginning of Broad Channel. I've often taken my graduate students here, and it's one of the best places to explore as it is home to more than three hundred species of birds and sixty or more varieties of butterflies, not to mention many small mammals and amphibians. It's a very well-run place with hiking trails, trips, boat outings, and lectures. As soon as one passes the last home, it's on to the Cross-Bay Veterans Memorial Bridge, and in two minutes you're in Rockaway Beach.

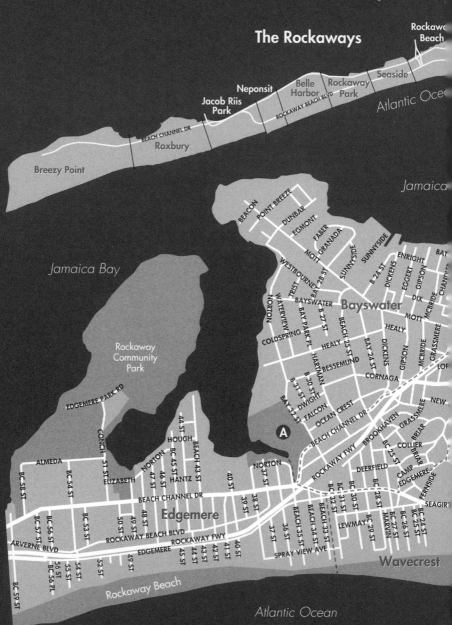

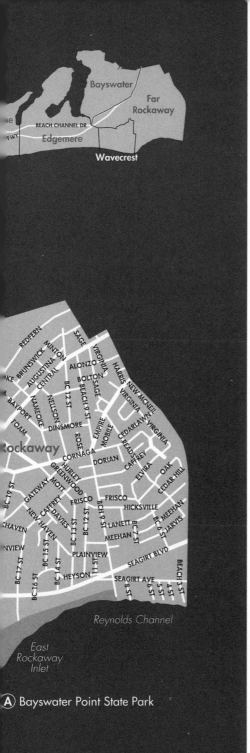

East
Rockaway
Inlet

Ⓐ Bayswater Point State Park

THE ROCKAWAYS

THIS ELEVEN-MILE PENINSULA, KNOWN AS "THE ROCKAWAYS," consists of nine distinct communities, each of which will be discussed here. Its only land border, to the east, is Nassau County, and it's the most southeastern part of the five boroughs. It's somewhat out of the way, but a fascinating place to explore, with lots of variety and many miles of beautiful beaches and a world-class boardwalk, rebuilt after Hurricane Sandy wreaked havoc on the area. Its isolation makes it perhaps the least known part of the city. Beginning with the 1830s and continuing on into the early 1960s it was an important resort area, at first for the wealthy and then later for working-class people as well. The creation of bridges leading to the Rockaways and the A subway line made getting to the beaches much easier. Every summer thousands of New Yorkers would gather up their belongings and migrate for the summer to the Rockaways, staying, for the most part, in simple bungalows. Because of urban renewal and the building of much public housing, especially in the 1950s, 1960s, and 1970s, most of these bungalows were eventually torn down.

Today, the Rockaways has both safe and unsafe areas, with a variety of residential options—public housing, co-ops, and condos, plus private homes, all in a broad price range. Public transportation is mostly by bus and subway, and many people use their cars to get around. There are parks, but the main attraction is the beach. Commercial streets include Beach Channel Drive and Rockaway Beach Boulevard, as well as Mott Avenue. Interspersed throughout the peninsula are numerous smaller shopping strips that run anywhere from one to three blocks.

FAR ROCKAWAY

Far Rockaway is the easternmost and largest community in the Rockaways. It began as a resort area, and many vacationers frequented it until the early 1960s. From the 1960s through the 1990s, the area declined as low-income housing attracted a larger number of poor people than the community could absorb. But it has changed dramatically over the years, with crime declining significantly. The boundaries of Far Rockaway are Beach Channel Drive on the north; Nassau County on the east, or, if you will, the 878 Highway; the Atlantic Ocean on the south; and Beach 32nd Street on the west.

For many people above the age of sixty, the Rockaways evoke fond memories of inexpensive yet delightful and memorable summer vacations. People by the thousands rented small bungalows for the summer, swam in the ocean, relaxed on the beach, and made lifelong friends. It was sort of like an urban Catskills, and many, if not most, of the summer residents came from the five boroughs. With the advent of easy travel by air and changing tastes in recreation in the 1960s, the Rockaways began to decline in popularity. The city took the easy fix and decided to place poor people, many of whom had migrated northward from the Deep South, into public housing that had been erected in the area.[49]

Sometimes the power of a place is so great that people are attracted to it even if it's not a community that they would otherwise be drawn to. There is something intrinsic to the community that turns them on to it in an almost irrational sense. Take the case of Susan Anderson, who reconstructed one of the thousands of bungalows that used to dot the streets of Far Rockaway. It's clear that she wanted to recapture the ambience as well. As Constance Rosenblum writes in a *New York Times* piece: "Painstakingly restored, studded with unusual found objects and glowing with an almost unearthly light, in its mood and spare décor, this house seems a throwback to an idyllic era."

Anderson did not grow up here, according to the *Times*. She came to New York in the early 1980s, attending college there, and happened to visit Far Rockaway in 1984. She fell in love with a bungalow she saw there on Beach 26th Street, but the crime-ridden area deterred her. Now that it's safer, she has returned, spending six figures to fix it up and herself becoming a strong advocate for these modest structures that were once attractive, not for artists, but for those who wanted live, or spend their summers at least, near the beach and the ocean. But make no mistake. She loves the ocean and says that when it rains heavily, the "rain pelts the walls so violently that she feels as if she were in the heart of the storm." For her it's not the community. She has a cat, and there are squirrels, rabbits, and possums nearby. Plus, she can hop on the A train or drive to see friends in Manhattan. Her community is not tied to where she lives, and this is true of many New Yorkers. They live in one place and hang out in another.[50]

On Beach 20th Street, just beyond Cornaga Avenue, I pass by what's left of the Strand Theater, an off-white building. One of its claims to fame is that Al Jolson, Sophie Tucker, and other headliners used to perform there. When it was part of the RKO chain, they played popular movies like *A Yank in the R.A.F.*, starring Betty Grable and Tyrone Power.

The area between Beach Channel Drive and Beach 20th and from Edgemere Avenue to Virginia Street is a mostly black and Hispanic area, and the people are generally lower income. The surrounding neighborhood from about Central Avenue to Seagirt Boulevard and from Virginia Street to Plainview Avenue is where the Orthodox Jewish community is located, and many of the homes are nice, though it too has its share of poor people living in substandard housing. The eastern part of the neighborhood is called Reads Lane after one of the streets there. But there are many blocks that are mixed as Orthodox Jews continue to move into the community.

I continue along Seagirt Avenue and soon arrive at the Wavecrest section and cross over to Beach 24th Street to see what's left of the bungalows. Many are abandoned and shuttered, but here and there they've been reclaimed and rebuilt, boasting wind chimes, flowerpots, and flags. This is by no means a safe area just yet. A white man sporting a bushy brown beard, large gold earring, and a bandanna is standing on his porch. He informs me, "Most of these people are renters and only come here on weekends."

"Are you afraid here?"

"You can walk at night on this block, but don't go on 26th Street. They got illegal three-family houses with drug dealers. They rent to Section 8 people and don't check their backgrounds. But they don't come on my block. I was born and bred in 'Bed-Stuy, live or die,' back in the eighties. That's why this place is a piece a cake for me." One can't rely on this respondent's words because many voucher holders are law-abiding citizens. I check out 26th, and it appears that they do have a drug problem on that and other nearby blocks. I witness open dealing and see discarded needles on the ground. If intrepid folks are the only people willing to live here, then Wavecrest still has a way to go. But there are others here too, families with young children, so perhaps there's hope. Time will tell.

Overall, Far Rockaway is becoming more and more Orthodox. They are looking for affordable housing, and because the infrastructure is already in place, it is likely that the community will continue to grow.

BAYSWATER

This is a charming community, a throwback almost to the days when the Rockaways were much quieter and more residential. It's not really a beach community because its location on Jamaica Bay is either rocky or swampy, or the beach areas have not been properly maintained. Like Far Rockaway, it was a resort area as well as an elegant address for the mansions that once proliferated here. It's a bit hard to define geographically because its shape is, more or less, a triangle. Its boundaries are, roughly, Jamaica Bay and Mott Basin on the north, Beach Channel Drive on the east, and Beach Channel Drive on the south; then there's Norton Basin and Beach 32nd Street on the west. It's a racially diverse middle-class community, and there are many Orthodox Jews residing there. The main commercial street is Beach Channel Drive,

In the old days, Mott Avenue had opulent homes. Today only traces of them remain, and those that are still standing are run-down, mere shadows of what they once were. Examples are some old Victorians and colonials at 2259, 2263, 2267, and 2279 near Beach Channel Drive. Farther down on Mott, near the water, the mansions have been replaced by new and quite pretty homes. Along the way I explore the surrounding streets—Granada Place, Dunbar Street, Waterloo Place, and others. All of them have either well-maintained large older homes or new attractive domiciles. The most impressive street in terms of homes is Westbourne Avenue. I turn right on Point Breeze Place. Here's where quite a few of the mansions were, but not much remains.

Entering Bayswater Point State Park at the foot of Mott Avenue, I see a garden dedicated to various varieties of butterflies common to the area, the American lady, the eastern tiger swallowtail, and the endangered monarch butterfly. Some of them can be spied amid the bushes, spreading their wings and daintily fluttering about, their wings rendered iridescent by the afternoon sun. I walk another hundred yards to the crest of a small hilly knob in a meadow and look out over the water. A giant dark bird appears out of nowhere and slowly, soundlessly glides over the water, disappearing gradually in the distance as it ascends to a lofty height. There's no one here. The vistas are stupendous—magnificent trees, tall grass waving in the wind, and pathways that cut right through it. If it's serenity and landscapes you're searching for, look no further.

EDGEMERE

Edgemere is a lower income community bounded on the north by Jamaica Bay and the Norton Basin, on the east by Beach 32nd Street, on the south by the Atlantic Ocean, and on the west by Beach 59th Street. At the turn of the century, this now run-down area was a very popular seaside resort community with nice hotels that had bands and other entertainment and, of course, beautiful oceanfront views. Its decline began in the 1950s and 1960s, when, as part of urban renewal, low-income housing was built here. In the 1980s, during the height of the crack epidemic, things got so bad that people from the projects were known to occasionally take potshots at the nurses leaving the building at Peninsula Hospital on Beach Channel Drive near Beach 51st Street. A man who used to live in Far Rockaway recounted to me how it was.

"When my parents drove through the area from Far Rockaway it was so bad that they wouldn't even stop for red lights and the police looked the other way. If you stopped, hoodlums would sometimes throw a large drop cloth or blanket over the car, giving you the feeling of being trapped in a dark cave. People would panic, since they couldn't see, and jump out of their cars, run away, and then their car would be hijacked. They considered themselves lucky to still be alive." The community lay forgotten and forlorn until the late 1990s, when there was a lot of noise about rebuilding the Rockaways, but progress stalled when the 2008 recession arrived.

The community is still blighted, as evidenced by boarded-up homes and windows with bars. The rot and neglect are present not only on the streets, but also along the abandoned lots that front out to the beach, strewn with mattresses whose springs jut out through the stuffing, rusted shopping carts, and abandoned automobiles, and with high weeds and swampy areas. This contrasts with the spanking-new beautiful boardwalk that runs here and pretty much the length of the Rockaways. It's a delight to traverse, a haven for roller skaters, joggers, and sunbathers. It's also well patrolled. The approaches to the boardwalk from the streets are another story, with caution advised.

ARVERNE

This adjacent area is bounded on the north by Jamaica Bay, on the east by 59th Street, on the south by the Atlantic Ocean, and on the west by Beach 77th Street, and it may offer a glimpse into the future of Edgemere. It was a summer resort area too, and it also deteriorated in midcentury as the homes succumbed to neglect and public housing like the Ocean Bay Apartments became a breeding ground for crime and drugs. Most of the existing housing was torn down, and nothing was built to replace it. The oceanfront portion of Arverne looked like a debris-strewn lunar landscape. But then came Arverne by the Sea, a private condominium development for middle-income families. It extends generally from Beach 62nd to Beach 81st Streets and between the Atlantic Ocean and Jamaica Bay. A good number of the units can be purchased as two-family homes, with one unit that can be rented out. This has changed the face of the community as the development is highly attractive and very well designed. It's near the A train, and commuters can also get to the Rockaways from Manhattan by ferry. Many young people have been attracted to the developments, including those who love surfing, as nearby Beach 67th Street is a highly popular surfing location.

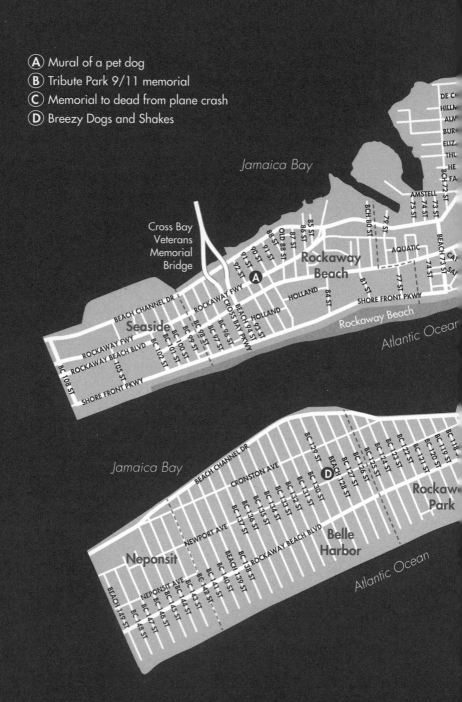

Ⓐ Mural of a pet dog
Ⓑ Tribute Park 9/11 memorial
Ⓒ Memorial to dead from plane crash
Ⓓ Breezy Dogs and Shakes

Jamaica Bay

DE C
HILLM
ALM
BUR
ELIZ
THL
HE
FA

Cross Bay
Veterans
Memorial
Bridge

AMSTELL

BCH 72 ST
BCH 73 ST
74 ST
73 ST
75 ST
79 ST
BEACH 73 ST
CA
SAI

BCH 80 ST

85 ST
86 ST
87 ST
OLD 88 ST
88 ST
91 ST
90 ST
91 ST
92 ST

AQUATIC

Ⓐ

Rockaway
Beach

81 ST
77 ST
74 ST
84 ST

HOLLAND

SHORE FRONT PKWY

BEACH CHANNEL DR

ROCKAWAY FWY

BEACH 92 ST
CROSS BAY PKWY

HOLLAND
HOLLAND

Rockaway Beach

Seaside

BC 98 ST
BC 99 ST
BC 100 ST
BC 101 ST
BC 102 ST

BC 96 ST
BC 97 ST

93 ST

Atlantic Ocean

ROCKAWAY FWY
ROCKAWAY BEACH BLVD

BC 105 ST

BC 108 ST

SHORE FRONT PKWY

Jamaica Bay

BEACH CHANNEL DR

CRONSTON AVE

NEWPORT AVE

Neponsit

NEPONSIT AVE

BEACH 149 ST
BC 148 ST

BC 146 ST
BC 147 ST
BC 144 ST
BC 145 ST
BC 143 ST
BC 142 ST
BC 141 ST
BEACH 140 ST
BEACH 139 ST
BC 138 ST
ROCKAWAY BEACH BLVD
BC 137 ST
BC 136 ST
BC 135 ST
BC 134 ST
BC 133 ST
BC 132 ST
BC 131 ST
BEACH 130 ST
Ⓓ
BEACH 128 ST
BC 127 ST
BC 126 ST
BC 125 ST
BC 124 ST
BC 123 ST
BC 122 ST
BC 121 ST
BC 120 ST
BC 119 ST
BC 118 ST
BC 129 ST

Belle
Harbor

Rockaw
Park

Atlantic Ocean

Walking through Arverne by the Sea is almost surreal. It feels as though one has entered a lovely suburb somewhere in America complete with nice cars, manicured lawns, and the like. The nearby sound of the ocean waves beating against the craggy rocks makes me think I'm somewhere in New England. There aren't many people around on a weekday afternoon except for schoolchildren returning home. I assume everyone is at work.

A mailman, always a good source of information, tells me, "The apartments are really nice inside, and many hipster types are coming here since they're priced out of Williamsburg and here they can get a lot more space for less money. It's also quite safe even though there are poor areas not far away. The cops patrol it pretty regularly." Conversations with residents and my own observations tend to confirm his appraisal. On a weekend morning one can see large numbers of people getting off the A train and heading for the beach. There's not much nightlife, nor are there many upscale restaurants now, but those are surely coming because the demand is here.

ROCKAWAY BEACH

This area, immediately to the west of Arverne, goes from about Beach 77th to Beach 109th Streets, with Jamaica Bay on one side and the Atlantic Ocean on the other. It's a mostly white area, with a large number of Irish-heritage residents. It features many older, charming, and well-maintained homes, quite a few of them large colonials with wraparound porches. There's some public housing, namely Hammel Houses, from about Beach 81st to Beach 86th Streets, between the Rockaway Freeway and Rockaway Beach Boulevard. This area has had some problems with crime over the years, notwithstanding cameras and increased patrols. Rockaway Beach was once a resort area and still bears the original name by which it was known, Seaside. Rockaways Playland, an amusement park with a famous roller coaster, was located on 97th Street and Rockaway Beach Boulevard. It operated from 1901 to 1985, attracting over 175 million visitors through the years.

Wandering the streets here I come across a larger-than-life wall mural of a lovely-looking French bulldog on Beach 91st Street, just off Rockaway Beach Boulevard, the main commercial drag here. It's very rare to see a mural of a dog anywhere in the city, and this one also happens to be a community resident. The owner, a civic leader who lives nearby, reportedly had it commissioned by an artist because he so loved his pet.

Many of the homes have replicas of ships in their windows, lighthouses on the front lawn, and other signs that this is an oceanfront community, but one in particular catches my attention. It's a white cube in the window of 326 Beach 91st Street that proclaims, "I need Vitamin Sea."

Finally, I come across two eateries in the shadow of the Cross-Bay Veterans Memorial Bridge near Beach 94th Street. One is the Bungalow Bar and Restaurant, serving standard American fare with an emphasis on seafood, and the other is a place called Thai Rock, which, not surprisingly, features Thai food. It also has live music on the weekends, mostly jazz and blues. Both are among the few lively nightspots in this relatively quiet area, and their views of the bay from the deck are spectacular.

The bungalows of Rockaway Park.

ROCKAWAY PARK

Rockaway Park runs west from Beach 109th to Beach 125th Streets, with the ocean to the south and the bay to the north. It's home to scattered bungalows that were once very common in the Rockaways. Some of these have been nicely preserved, and I visited a group of them on the west side of Beach 109th Street. Spying an elderly, yet quite fit man, with the words "American Patriot" emblazoned on his navy-blue cap, and carefully watering a small grassy space on the sidewalk, I say, "Hey, you're doing a great job watering these plants."

"Yeah, well I'm retired, and I have the time. Glad you like it. You see these round green plants? They're going to grow to four times this size."

I remark on how up-to-date and beautiful the bungalows here look, and he says, "I bought my bungalow in 1973 for $7,000. It was built in 1913. Now it's worth a couple of hundred grand. It's right by the ocean. Originally, these were rentals, but then the owner decided to sell them, so I bought one. Now I have other family members who have places here. There's about twenty bungalows in this area. Come, I'll show you." And with that, he takes me, a total stranger, on an impromptu tour. He shows me his in-laws' very nicely furnished bungalow, and then his own lair. I meet his wife, son-in-law, and daughter, none of whom seem surprised to see me. The home has been expanded and has a little basement. It's nothing like the original simple rustic bungalows, but it's still a bungalow. And to him it's a place he's very proud of.

At Beach Channel Drive and 116th Street, I enter the 9/11 memorial, called Tribute Park. The names of those from the Rockaways who were killed are inscribed on bricks in the ground and on benches. People saw the towers burning from here. There's an award-winning gazebo with colored glass and the names of many victims. Nearby, a twisted piece of brownish-black metal from the towers sits in the middle of the grassy area, serving as a stark reminder. There's also a nicely sculpted rock with the names of all 343 firemen who died. A number of people are strolling through the memorial area on this weekday afternoon. It's been close to twenty years since 9/11 happened, and I'm convinced that it will be a long time before it fades from people's minds.

At the end of 116th Street in front of the ocean I come face to face with the memorial to the people, most of them Dominicans, who perished in the crash of an American Airlines plane on Beach 131st Street on November 12, 2001, just two months after 9/11, killing all 260 people on board, plus five people on the ground. With bricks and names inscribed on them in a semicircle, it looks similar to the one for 9/11 victims, if not as elaborate. The memorial has a doorway and two windows looking out on the Atlantic Ocean in the general direction of the Dominican Republic. A sign in Spanish is etched into the stone, which, translated into English, reads, "Afterward I want only peace." The names of the countries the victims

A memorial to those who were killed in the crash of American Airlines Flight 587 on November 12, 2001.

came from are also listed—Taiwan, France, Israel, the Dominican Republic, and others.

BELLE HARBOR

Belle Harbor is a middle- to upper-middle-class community. It's bounded on the east by Beach 125th Street and on the west by Beach 142nd Street. It was founded in 1900, and today the population is predominantly Irish, with smaller numbers of Italians and Jews. As with its neighbors to the west, Neponsit and Breezy Point, there are many American flags in front of the homes. The only commercial street is a one block strip on Beach 129th Street, from Cronston to Newport Avenues. The beach is open to the public, but local zoning ordinances limit parking by nonresidents.

All in all, the Rockaways, counting former and summer residents, lost more than seventy people in the 9/11 tragedy, along with those 265 people two months later in the crash of the American Airlines flight bound for the Dominican Republic. These tragedies were followed by the devastation of Hurricane Sandy a decade later on October 29, 2012. There's something about the Rockaways in general, especially in the quieter sections, a feeling of isolation, of being at the end of the city, that makes people see it in an almost mythical, sometimes even cataclysmic way. Stuart Feintuch, a dentist practicing in Great Neck, Long Island, recalled how his father viewed living there.

"When my parents moved there in 1975," he tells me, "from Bensonhurst, Brooklyn, my mother said, 'We're moving to "utopia."'" What she meant was that Belle Harbor feels like a small semirural town. It's all one- and two-family homes. If you were to blindfold someone and take them to Belle Harbor, say, by plane, you could convince them they were anywhere, and certainly not in New York. And my father said to me as he looked out over the ocean near his home in Belle Harbor: 'Mark my words. One day the ocean on the east side of the community will meet the bay on the western side.' And, when Hurricane Sandy hit, that's exactly what happened in the streets. I never forgot his comment."

To understand the magnitude of Hurricane Sandy in the Rockaways one needs to listen to how those affected describe it. Shirley Siegel, who has worked in a private school in Belle Harbor for many years and still does, reflected on the past.

"I lived in Belle Harbor from 1956 until 2013, but Sandy did me in. You had storms periodically, but this was a tsunami. I had six feet of water. I lived three blocks from the ocean. It's strange. I knew someone who lived three *homes* from the ocean, and she only had two inches of water. Another friend of mine had sand in her basement. She said: 'I always wanted to live on the beach. Now I do.'"

A funny line—unless it was your house. I then asked Shirley if she could think of anything else of interest that had happened to her in Belle Harbor in the fifty-seven years she had lived there. Nothing came to mind, so I thanked her for her time. And that was it, or so I thought.

Two days later I bumped into her with her daughter Janet, a physician, and told Janet how much I enjoyed my conversation with her mother.

"Mom," she said, turning to her mother, "Did you tell him about how the plane crashed right on your block and while you were there?"

A somewhat perplexed look spread across Shirley's face as she said, "No."

"What exactly happened?" I asked.

"Well, I was on the block when I suddenly heard a loud noise, a sound I'd never heard before. So I ran outside, then back in because I wasn't dressed, and then I came out again. There was smoke everywhere, and there were body parts."

"How close to the plane were you?"

"It was just a few houses away from me on Beach 131st Street, where I live, near the intersection of Newport Avenue. I was just totally shocked."

"Then how come you didn't tell me that when I asked if anything of note had happened in all the years you lived there?"

She gave me a bemused look and said, "I have no idea. I must have blocked it out from my memory. And five people on the ground were killed."

The homes here are nice enough, and one can spend a pleasant day walking the quiet blocks, with interludes strolling along the beach. There's a quality of sameness to it, but the sameness is certainly nice enough.

On Beach 130th Street and Cronston Avenue, I come across an advanced Jewish seminary called Mercaz haTorah. The students come from different parts of the New York metropolitan area. Here they study intensively the Talmud, a sixty-three-volume compendium of oral Jewish law that seeks to discover and interpret the Old Testament. The students, of both high school and college age, live on the premises, going home to their families for a weekend every few weeks or months. They are dressed in white shirts, open at the collar, and dark slacks. When they pray, they don a dark sports jacket and replace their black skullcaps with a black hat.

A block away on Cronston I turn right and go up Beach 129th Street. It's a one-block shopping strip ending at Newport Avenue.

It has the usual stores—a liquor shop run by a friendly Sikh couple; three taverns with Irish-sounding names; nail salons; Mr. Giuseppe's Barber Shop, which has that old-time elegant feel; and Breezy Dogs and Shakes. This last place is like a Carvel and a Nathan's rolled into one. One can buy a hot dog, knish, and other fast-food fare, but the real draw is the 170 varieties of milk shakes, which must be a record. They get rave reviews all over the internet, and there are indoor and outdoor sitting areas. Alas, they have closed, but their story serves as a history lesson for what once was a major attraction in this still vibrant community.

I speak with Jeff Gold, a Jewish past resident of the area. He's a longtime administrator at Long Island University in Brooklyn, and a brilliant man. Jeff is the quintessential New Yorker. He runs conferences on everything from science fiction and UFOs, to the Brooklyn Dodgers, bungalow colonies in the Catskills, basketball leagues, and more. Although he's pushing seventy, he has the energy of a twenty-five-year-old.

"When I grew up in the mid-fifties and sixties," he tells me, "the area was much more Jewish, and the other, even more dominant group was the Irish. In both cases these people had made it, as Belle Harbor was an upscale area."

"And so even though it was an affluent community there were, as I've been told, physical fights? Why?" I ask.

"I guess it was that to each group the other was 'the other,' and we Jews were the only 'other.' We fought back even though the Irish were probably tougher, though not as tough as the Irish from Breezy Point, where no Jews lived. But these were not the really vicious fights on display in *West Side Story*. It was more like pounding each other for the workout. In the end many of us bonded with each other because we had things in common—the beach, sports, and public schools. I certainly had Irish friends on my block. I also had friends in the black community from the Hammel Houses in Rockaway Beach, who I would ride with on my bike."

On Rockaway Beach Boulevard, at the corner of Beach 137th Street, there's a private home with an unusual history. The largest Hasidic sect in New York is the Satmarer group, headquartered in Williamsburg. Interestingly, Rabbi Yoel Teitelbaum, their rebbe or leader, used to spend his vacations in this home. To help him observe the laws more punctiliously, a mikveh, or ritual bath, was built here. Today, the rebbe's successors no longer summer here, but the building is still functional as the students in the yeshiva use it.

NEPONSIT

This is a small community with a fairly large Jewish population. It runs west from Beach 142nd Street to Beach 149th, with the ocean on the south and Jamaica Bay on the north. The homes are striking and often expensive, though there are moderately priced houses here as well. One example of a pretty home is at 146-16 Rockaway Beach, which has beautifully carved statues gracing its front lawn. Another is at 144-03 Neponsit Avenue, an elegant brick structure. As in Belle Harbor, all the homes on the Jamaica Bay side have terrific vistas, most notably of the Manhattan skyline.

One almost jarring place in this community is a large brick building with a faded exterior and an uninhabited interior, located on Rockaway Beach Boulevard near Beach 149th Street. Until 1998, this was the Neponsit Home for the Aged. Then, literally in the middle of the night, its 280 residents were spirited away and relocated in various city hospitals. It seems the home had been damaged by a storm, and former Mayor Giuliani ordered it evacuated immediately. This 6-acre parcel is exceedingly valuable, but there has been controversy about what to do with it. Many home owners favor a park. Others lean toward a health facility, and developers, of course, want to build expensive homes there.

There's definitely history here, as the great muckraker and advocate of the poor Jacob Riis established a home on the site a century

ago for tubercular children. Financial support came from Jacob Schiff, Andrew Carnegie, and John D. Rockefeller. Signs of a previous life can be discerned from two entrances on the boulevard. One says, "SOCIAL HALL," the other, "CRAFT HOBBY," both in large silver lettering. Some of the people here may well have had a good life here before they were whisked away without, as generally required by law, any prior notice given to their families.[51]

BREEZY POINT

The beginnings of Breezy Point go all the way back to 1911 when about 900 acres on the western edge of the Rockaways became a summer resort. By 1920, about two thousand bungalows had been built there. In addition, there were hotels for guests looking for respite from the summer heat. The bungalows were purchased by individuals, most of them Irish Americans. Plans to erect a large number of high-rise apartment buildings were shelved as the owners of the bungalows resisted them, forming a cooperative to preserve their community, one that also includes a tiny neighborhood to the east, known as Roxbury, with an almost identical ethnic population.

Perhaps nowhere else in New York City does a community feel, at first sight, more removed from the city than in Breezy Point. Its broad expanse of beach, its seclusion at the very end of the Rockaways, its many walkways where one would normally find narrow roads for vehicular traffic all combine to give the walker a feeling of having come, as they say, "to the end of the road." In part, this is a conscious decision by the founders, who established it as a gated, cooperative community, with strict regulations for prospective home owners. Generations of families have lived here, and people look out for each other; doors are frequently left unlocked, just as if the people lived in a small town anywhere in the United States.

Despite its relative isolation, Breezy Point, with three thousand or so homes, and a population of approximately four thousand souls, is, nonetheless, very much tied into New York in certain ways. There is ferry service at Beach 106th Street from the area to Manhattan, and by driving over the Marine Parkway Gil Hodges Memorial Bridge you can be in Brooklyn in about twenty-five minutes. In addition, this is a community made up mostly of NYC firefighters and policemen, many of them from south Brooklyn communities like Marine Park, Gravesend, and Sheepshead Bay. Whether they are active or retired, their lives are therefore very much intertwined with that of the city, a place that they have been ready to sacrifice their own safety for.

The boundaries of Breezy Point proper are the Rockaway Inlet/ Jamaica Bay waterway on the north, Beach 201st Street on the east, the Atlantic Ocean on the south, and Beach 222nd Street on the west. Ethnically and racially, it's a virtually all-white community made up of mostly Irish-descent residents, along with a smaller number of Italians, Germans, and some Jews. A good number of these people are married to Irish folks. So, it's no surprise that the community is also referred to as "the Irish Riviera." There are no public or parochial schools in Breezy Point, with most children attending schools in nearby Belle Harbor.

I walked Breezy Point, a cooperative community, street by street and found it be a place that guards its privacy. There is a small commercial area on Rockaway Point Boulevard, which runs the length of Breezy Point, including a coffee shop, supermarket, bank, and tavern.

Many of the homes, ranging in price from about $500,000 to more than a million dollars, sport American flags, some quite large and all of them in excellent condition. The houses, almost all winterized for year-round living, are well kept, and I notice that virtually all the names on the mailboxes are Irish sounding. I see a sign on one of the few automobile-access streets to the homes, exhorting drivers: "Drive like your kids live here. Speed Limit 10 M.P.H." There's considerable variation in the styles thus making the homes more interesting to look at. Many of the folks walking around seem to be retirees. One such individual told me, "Many, if not most people, keep their doors unlocked. It's very safe." Almost everyone I pass says, "Hi," as I stroll down these quiet lanes, much as they would in a village.

The beach here is very wide, and it's a fairly long distance to the water. One can see for miles up and down the Rockaways coastline. I sit on a bench dedicated to the memory of a resident, and the plaque on it concludes with a quote from the deceased woman: "Breezy Point. It doesn't get better than this." Numerous other plaques are in memory of 9/11 victims.

The rest of the area immediately east of Breezy Point and Roxbury became part of the Gateway National Recreation Area, which includes Fort Tilden and Jacob Riis Park. The fort was built during World War I to protect against any invasion via New York Harbor. It was also the site where the *Golden Venture*, a decrepit vessel carrying hundreds of undocumented Chinese immigrants, washed ashore.[52] The park has the usual sports facilities, as well as trails, plus a golf course. It begins at the base of the Marine Park Bridge, and as one goes east, there's a truly distinctive art deco bathhouse dating back to 1932. Its two octagonal brick towers rise into the sky with the beach and the Atlantic Ocean as a backdrop. While visually stunning, the interior was neglected and boarded up for many years.

In 2016, the parks department began efforts to restore it, but when I was there in June 2017 nothing had been done. Touring the large interior courtyard I had the feeling of being inside a haunted castle. The only visible sign of life was the equipment for the lifeguards, including seven very tall chairs that allow the guards to scan the area along the beach.

The octagonal towers are still pretty intact with bricks arranged in neat geometric designs. It's deserted, and no one asks me why I'm here. It's really a shame since it could be a really fun place. As I leave, I bump into a lifeguard wearing a large straw hat. Victor, a man in his sixties, I'd guess, and in great shape, greets me cheerfully.

"Hey, how are you? Can I help you?" he asks.

"Is anything happening with this place? Have they raised the money to refurbish it?"

"Not that I know of. You should cruise by Bay Nine, where the hipsters are. This is Bay Three. They're looking to move down here. Hopefully, the federal government, which is in charge here, can raise some money from them."

"How long have you been a lifeguard here?"

"Since 1976. During the year I was an airline steward."

"Wow! That long? You must know everything about the Rockaways."

"I grew up here. On weekends this beach is packed." I look at this upbeat man and realize he has apparently had a pretty good life. What could be better and healthier than a job where you hang out at the beach, stay in shape, and just enjoy life?

ACKNOWLEDGMENTS

I want to thank, first and foremost, my editor, Meagan Levinson, who is talented, thorough, professional, and a pleasure to work with; second, Christie Henry, director of Princeton University Press (PUP), for her keen interest in this project and wise counsel. Others who were very helpful at PUP are Christopher Holewski, my photographer; Mark Bellis, in production; Laurie Schlesinger, in sales; Julia Haav, in publicity; and all the other people at PUP whom I don't know but who make it all happen. They're a great team in every way.

Also, many thanks to Bill Kornblum and to Paul and Irene Marcus, who read the manuscript and made many helpful suggestions. Others who read and commented on portions of the manuscript include Joseph Helmreich, Jeff Helmreich, Deborah Halpern, Deni Kolatch, Jeff Wiesenfeld, Jack Nass, and Norman Rutta. Colleagues who shaped my thinking on these issues include Elijah Anderson, Mitchell Duneier, Ruben Rumbaut, Roger Waldinger, Parmatma Saran, Marta Tienda, Richard Alba, Pyong Gap Min, Philip Kasinitz, and Lynn Chancer.

Then there are those who helped me in various ways that only they know. Among them are Kenneth Cohen, Colin Powell, Andy Rich, Baruch and Pam Toldedano, Russell Warren, Paul Kazas, Lance Grieff, Josh Halpern, Esther Friedman, Ronnie and David Weprin, Rob Katz, Itzhak Haimovic, Kane Noel, David Rothenberg, Chaim Anfang, Howard Zimmerman, Susie Tanenbaum, Diane Rein, Karyn Czapnik, Avi Hadar, Alan Helmreich, Vince Boudreau, Maris and Stu Blechner, Melissa Castillo, Charlie Papia, Elisabeth De Bourbon, Ed and Sudha Gilroy, Danny Vitow, Steve and Joan Goldberg, Janos Marton, Barry Mitchell, Ben Lunzer, Susie Blumstein, Manes Kogan, Erwin Fried, Marjorie Burnside, Eric Schwartz, Jessica Schwartz, Peter Dougherty, Nina Johnson-Mende, Laura Bowman, Mary Curtis, Ralph McDaniel, Kenny and

Mira Wachstock, Jeff Gottlieb, Shirley Siegel, Kacper Jarecki, Brian Levinson, Josh Rothman, Diane Call, Peter Moskos, Marty Sokol, Joyce Levine, Xiang Lu, Robert Wilson, Jana Helmrich, Bob Berger, Anthony Gilroy, Monica Lynch, and finally, my dog Heidi, who walked several hundred miles of Queens with me.

Last, and most important of all, I want to thank my wife, Helaine. As we celebrate our fiftieth year of a wonderful marriage, I am aware, more than ever, of how truly lucky I am to have her as my best friend, reader, confidant, and adviser. I'm very grateful to her for reading every word of this book and for the hundreds of insightful and stimulating observations she made. As the author of eleven books ranging from history, to biography, to fiction, she knows what it takes to write a book. And I was blessed to have her on many of my meanderings through this wonderful borough, which she fell in love with.

APPENDIX

Except for a small portion of Jamaica, and some of the eastern sections of the Rockaways, Queens is a perfectly safe place to walk provided you exercise caution and are reasonably familiar with large cities, and with New York City in particular. The statistical risk of being attacked in any neighborhood is actually quite low in absolute terms. The vast majority of residents are honest, hardworking folks who will be friendly if approached the way you would approach anyone else. It's fair to say that in the many talks I gave after *The New York Nobody Knows* appeared, this was by far the question I was most often asked. So, if you decide to "go for it," I offer the following tips:

1. Be alert at all times.
2. Dress innocuously and not very well—no loud colors, especially gang ones—bright blue or red. Because they don't wish to be easily identified by the police, many gang members have stopped wearing gang colors in the past ten years, opting instead for large white t-shirts. Some still do, however, so why take a chance?
3. Never stare at anyone, but if you should make eye contact, and the person isn't looking at you in a hostile manner, smile and say "Hi." It's a counterintuitive, disarming approach that has served me well, though gauging this can sometimes be tricky.
4. Avoid groups of people congregating on the street, especially teenagers, but do not cross the street if you feel they've already seen you approaching. You don't want to look nervous or fearful. This is obviously not easy to determine with certainty.

5. Walking at night, on weekends, and in the summer is riskier than at other times.
6. Do not walk with more than one person since you don't want to attract attention.
7. Avoid areas where it's difficult to exit, such as neighborhoods without nearby transportation.
8. Avoid deserted areas.
9. Don't carry a lot of cash, but do have some. Having nothing on you may increase the likelihood of physical attack from a disappointed assailant. Never fight back unless all else is lost.
10. Be careful about giving money to panhandlers. Generosity can lead to trouble, especially if others take notice.
11. Always be respectful. If someone is walking toward you be ready to give way, as you are not in your own community.
12. Never try to project an image of toughness. It won't work, and, in fact, people may judge you as insecure if you try it.

These are not hard-and-fast rules. Circumstances may dictate a different response or approach. Each situation is, by definition, unique, and you need to be flexible and adapt. Having and using common sense is an essential quality, but it cannot be easily taught.

Women, as a rule, should exercise more caution and should not walk in reportedly unsafe areas alone. Older people, provided they are physically fit and can walk at a reasonable pace and without using a cane, are actually at less risk than those who are younger. A younger person who looks like an outsider, meaning of a different race or ethnicity, may be seen as a challenge to a resident of similar age. People who look like they could be a cop or a worker in the area—for example, a teacher, social worker, delivery person, or store employee—are at less risk.

On a personal note, I walked 8,607 miles of city streets at all times of the day and night and was never harmed. Why? I grew up in a rough area of the city and was familiar with life there. I hung out on the streets and developed the usual sixth sense about danger. Even more important perhaps, I was just plain lucky. One incident brought this home to me. I once walked into a public housing project in Brooklyn at midday. As I passed a teenager who glanced at me, I said, "How you doing?" His face was expressionless as he said something in Spanish into a walkie-talkie. I looked around and saw seven heads go up about fifteen yards away. Without any hesitation, I said, "Have a nice day," and walked out, not quickly or slowly, toward the street, never looking back. My goal was to indicate that I wasn't a threat to what they were doing.

Nothing happened to me. I was fortunate.

NOTES

1. In drawing these maps, I relied on my own walks, on Kenneth Jackson's *The Encyclopedia of New York City*, and on the book by Claudia Copquin *The Neighborhoods of Queens*. Because the maps are designed for walkers, canals, creeks, basins, etc. are not generally demarcated as boundaries. Instead, the appropriate streets are given. In Queens, "avenues" run east/west and "streets" north/south. "Roads" and "drives" are between the "avenues," while "lanes" and "places" are between the "streets." Also, a good number of major thoroughfares run at angles. For more on this see, https://untappedcities.com/2014/04/03/cities-101-how-to-navigate-queens-street-grid.
2. Howard 2018.
3. Pesantez 2019; Jackson 2019.
4. Simmel 1900, 412–13.
5. Tonnelat and Kornblum 2017.
6. Constantine 2017, 21.
7. Sanjek 1998, 223.
8. For more information by an insider about the South Asian communities here, see Ojha 2017.
9. Gregory 1998.
10. Berger 2011; Gregory 1998, 63–65.
11. Thomas and Thomas 1928, 572.
12. Tonnelat and Kornblum 2017.
13. Rosenberg 2011.
14. Lelyveld 1964.
15. Tonnelat and Kornblum 2017.
16. Min 1992; Lu 2017.
17. Min 2010.
18. Khandelwal 2002; Barnard 2009b.
19. Sax 2009.
20. Semple 2008.
21. Semple 2008.
22. Zborowski and Herzog 1962, 365–97.
23. Rabinowitz 1976.
24. Ungar 1995, 304–30.
25. Darley and Latane 1968.

26. Festinger, Riecken, and Schachter 1956. There's a scientific name, *cognitive dissonance*, for this response. Simply put, the theory says that when people feel that things are out of order with the way they would like to see them, they rearrange them in a way that makes it easier for them to deal with reality. The term was first coined in 1956, based on a book about how people dealt with their failed prediction that the world would end. The concept is as true today as it ever was.
27. Newman 2017.
28. Roberts 2015.
29. Jacobs 1961, 36, 42.
30. Zimmerman 2012.
31. Cotter 2005.
32. Young et al. 2008.
33. McFadden 1991.
34. Barnard 2009a.
35. Pereira 2009.
36. Mencimer 2016.
37. Seyfried and Asadorian 1991.
38. Copquin 2007, 84.
39. Powell 1995, 30–31.
40. For more on these groups and their relationships with Jews see Brotz 1970; and A. Helmreich and Marcus 1998.
41. There are sometimes conflicting dates in the sources for when these people lived here. The dates given and the architectural styles noted are based on the New York City Landmarks Preservation Commission report. See Noonan 2011.
42. Hershon 2008. The Landmarks Preservation Commission report says that Ruth "possibly lived here." Noonan 2011, 96.
43. Frazier 1957, 23; Bennett 1966, 240.
44. Helmreich 2013, 231–95.
45. Sikh Missionary Center 2008.
46. Kleinfeld 2010.
47. Kleinfeld 2010.
48. Breen, Donohue, Goldiner, and Lombardy 1998.
49. This was a common citywide policy. See, for example, Pritchett 2002. Poor whites also lived in the projects. See Naomi Ragen's fascinating 2003 novel *Chains around the Grass*.
50. Rosenblum 2010.
51. Rosen 1998.
52. Keefe 2009.

BIBLIOGRAPHY

Alba, Richard D. 2009. *Blurring the Color Line: The New Chance for a More Integrated America*. Cambridge, MA: Harvard University Press.

Alba, Richard D., and Victor Nee. 2003. *Remaking the American Mainstream: Assimilation and Contemporary Immigration*. Cambridge, MA: Harvard University Press.

Barnard, Anne. 2009a. *New York Times*, City Room Blogs. November 23. https://cityroom.blogs.nytimes.com/2009/11/23/recession-siphons-a -small-town-vibe/.

———. 2009b. "Reconsecration with Bells, Saffron, and Elephant." *New York Times*, July 14. https://www.nytimes.com/2009/07/14/nyregion /14temple.html.

———. 2009c. "Two Get Life without Parole for Paid Killing in Queens." *New York Times*, April 21. https://www.nytimes.com/2009/04/22/ny region/22dentist.html.

Barron, James. 2018. "City's Allure Grows Stronger: Analysis of Census Figures Shows a Record Population, Reminiscent of a Century Ago." *New York Times*, March 23.

Bennett, Lerone, Jr. 1966. *Before the Mayflower: A History of the Negro in America 1619–1966*. Rev. ed. Baltimore: Penguin Books.

Berger, Joseph. 2007. *The World in a City: Traveling the Globe through the Neighborhoods of the New New York*. New York: Ballantine Books.

———. 2010. "An Old Synagogue Downsizes in a Desperate Bid to Keep Itself Alive." *New York Times*, January 8. https://www.nytimes .com/2010/01/09/nyregion/09metjournal.html.

———. 2011. "There Stays the Neighborhood." *New York Times*, January 8. https://www.nytimes.com/2011/01/08/nyregion/08elmhurst.html.

Breen, Virginia, Peter Donohue, David Goldiner, and Frank Lombardi. 1998. "Racist Parade Shocker; 2 Cops, 2 Firemen on Float." *New York Daily News*, September 11. https://www.newspapers.com/newspage /478424629/.

Brotz, Howard. 1970. *The Black Jews of Harlem: Negro Nationalism and the Dilemmas of Negro Leadership*. New York: Schocken Books.

Constantine, Dahlia Hamza. 2017. "Snapshots of a Changing Woodside." Research paper. Department of Sociology, City University of New York Graduate Center.

Copquin, Claudia Gryvatz. 2007. *The Neighborhoods of Queens*. New Haven, CT: Yale University Press.

Cotter, Holland. 2005. "Giving African Art an Example of What It Is Due." *New York Times*, August 19, E34.

————. 2013. "Shangaa: Art of Tanzania." *New York Times*, May 10. https://www.nytimes.com/2013/05/10/arts/design/shangaa-art-of -tanzania.html.

Darley, John M., and Bibb Latane. 1968. "Bystander Intervention in Emergencies: Diffusion of Responsibility." *Journal of Personality and Social Psychology* 8:377–83.

Festinger, Leon, Henry Riecken, and Stanley Schachter. 1956. *When Prophecy Fails*. New York: Harper and Row.

Feuer, Alan. 2017. "At Core of 5Pointz Trial: Is Graffiti Art Protected by Law?" *New York Times*, October 17. https://www.nytimes .com/2017/10/17/nyregion/at-core-of-5pointz-trial-is-graffiti-art -protected-by-law.html.

Foner, Nancy. 2005. *In a New Land: A Comparative View of Immigration*. New York: New York University Press.

Frase, Peter. 2005. "The Next Neighborhood: Hunters Point/Long Island City." Research paper. Department of Sociology, City University of New York Graduate Center.

Frazier, E. Franklin. 1957. *Black Bourgeoisie: The Rise of a New Middle Class in the United States*. Glencoe, IL: Free Press.

Goodman, Peter. 2004. "Immigrants Bring Dreams and Combs to N.Y. Shop." *Newsday*, July 24.

Gregory, Steven. 1998. *Black Corona: Race and the Politics of Place in an Urban Community*. Princeton, NJ: Princeton University Press.

Helmreich, Alan, and Paul Marcus, eds. 1998. *Blacks and Jews on the Couch: Psychoanalytic Reflections on Black-Jewish Conflict*. Westport, CT: Praeger.

Helmreich, William B. 1982. *The Things They Say behind Your Back: Stereotypes and the Myths behind Them*. New York: Doubleday; New Brunswick, NJ: Transaction Books.

————. 2013. *The New York Nobody Knows: Walking 6,000 Miles in the City*. Princeton, NJ: Princeton University Press.

————. 2014. "I Was on Your Block: Here's What I learned." *New York Daily News*, February 7.

————. 2016. *The Brooklyn Nobody Knows: An Urban Walking Guide*. Princeton, NJ: Princeton University Press.

Hershon, Nicholas. 2008. "Is This Really the House Where Ruth Slept?" *New York Daily News,* January 12.

Horowitz, Jason. 2015. "Donald Trump's Old Queens Neighborhood Contrasts with the Diverse Area around It." *New York Times,* September 22. https://www.nytimes.com/2015/09/23/us/politics/donald -trumps-old-queens-neighborhood-now-a-melting-pot-was-seen -as-a-cloister.html.

Howard, Greg. 2018. "Graffiti Artists Find Validation in Judge's Ruling." *New York Times,* February 21. https://www.nytimes.com/2018/02/20 /nyregion/graffiti-artists-5pointz.html.

Jackson, Kenneth T., ed. 2010. *The Encyclopedia of New York City.* Rev. ed. New Haven, CT: Yale University Press.

———. 2019. "New York Needs Amazon." *New York Times,* February 12. https://www.nytimes.com/2019/02/12/opinion/amazon-hq2-new -york.html.

Jacobs, Jane. 1961. *The Death and Life of Great American Cities.* New York: Vintage Books.

Kasinitz, Philip, John H. Mollenkopf, Mary C. Waters, and Jennifer Holdaway. 2008. *Inheriting the City: The Children of Immigrants Come of Age.* New York: Russell Sage Foundation.

Keefe, Patrick Radden. 2009. *The Snakehead: An Epic Tale of the Chinatown Underworld and the American Dream.* New York: Random House.

Khandelwal, Madhulika S. 2002. *Becoming American, Being Indian: An Immigrant Community in New York City.* Ithaca, NY: Cornell University Press.

Kilgannon, Corey. 2017. "Who Needs Manhattan? Hanging with the Locals on Bell Boulevard." *New York Times,* March 10. https://www .nytimes.com/2017/03/10/nyregion/saturday-night-in-new-york-bell -boulevard-bayside-queens.html.

Kleinfeld, N. R. 2010. "Bingo in the Blood." *New York Times,* November 28, Metropolitan section. https://www.nytimes.com/2010/11/28 /nyregion/28bingo.html.

Lehrer, Warren, and Judith Sloan. 2003. *Crossing the Blvd: Strangers, Neighbors, and Aliens in a New America.* New York: W. W. Norton.

Lelyveld, Joseph. 1964. "Former Nazi Camp Guard Is Now a Housewife in Queens." *New York Times,* July 14. http://www.nytimes.com/images /promos/magazine/20050306braunsteiner.pdf.

Lu, Xiang. 2017. "People Who Bridge the Chinese and Korean Communities: Korean-Chinese Immigrants in Flushing." Research paper.

Department of Sociology, City University of New York Graduate Center.

Marwell, Nicole P. 2004. "Ethnic and Post-ethnic Politics in New York City: The Dominican Second Generation." In Philip Kasinitz, John H. Mollenkopf, and Mary C. Waters, eds., *Becoming New Yorkers: Ethnographies of the New Second Generation*, 227–56.

McFadden, Robert D. 1991. "4 Killed and 2 Are Wounded in Queens Rampage." *New York Times*, October 14. https://www.nytimes.com/1991/10/14/nyregion/4-killed-and-2-are-wounded-in-queens-rampage.html.

McGeehan, Patrick. 2017. "To Rockaways Residents, New Ferry Service Is a Promise Kept." *New York Times*, May 1. https://www.nytimes.com/2017/05/01/nyregion/rockaways-ferry-new-york-city.html.

Mencimer, Stephanie. 2016. "Sometimes Nuns Need Contraception." *Mother Jones*, March 22. https://www.motherjones.com/politics/2016/03/supreme-court-little-sisters-contraception-obamacare-religious-freedom/.

Min, Pyong Gap. 1992. "A Comparison of the Korean Minorities in China and Japan." *International Migration Review* 26:4–21.

———. 2010. *Preserving Religion through Ethnicity in America: Korean Protestants and Indian Hindus across Generations*. New York: New York University Press.

Newman, Andy. 2017. "In Search of Donald Trump at His Boyhood Home." *New York Times*, August 21. https://www.nytimes.com/2017/08/21/nyregion/trump-childhood-home-queens.html.

Noonan, Theresa. 2011. *Addisleigh Park Historic Designation Report*. New York: New York City Landmarks Preservation Commission.

Ojha, Abin. 2017. "Jackson Heights: An Exploration of Diversity." Research paper. Department of Sociology, City University of New Graduate Center.

Onofri, Adrienne. 2014. *Walking Queens*. Birmingham, AL: Wilderness.

Pereira, Ivan. 2009. "City Renames Street after Mother Killed in Floral Park Blast." *New York Post*, December 23. https://nypost.com/2009/12/23/city-renames-street-after-mother-killed-in-floral-park-blast/.

Pesantez, Nathalie. 2019. "Reactions Pour in after Amazon's Stunning Decision to Drop Long Island City Campus. *Long Island City Post*, February 14.

Powell, Colin, with Joseph E. Persico. 1995. *My American Journey*. New York: Random House.

Powell, Colin, with Tony Koltz. 2012. *It Worked for Me in Life and Leadership*. New York: HarperCollins.

Pritchett, Wendell. 2002. *Brownsville, Brooklyn: Blacks, Jews, and the Changing Face of the Ghetto*. Chicago: University of Chicago Press.

Queens Chronicle. 2009. "Car Crashes into Blockbuster." December 31. https://www.qchron.com/editions/south/car-crashes-into-blockbuster/article_f08d057b-6602-5677-bc09-3bd31c8779a5.htmlhttps://www.qchron.com/editions/south/car-crashes-into-blockbuster/article_f08d057b-6602-5677-bc09-3bd31c8779a5.html.

Rabinowitz, Dorothy. 1976. *New Lives: Survivors of the Holocaust Living in America*. New York: Random House.

Ragen, Naomi. 2003. *Chains around the Grass*. New Milford, CT: Toby.

Roberts, Sam. 2015. "An Outsider's Borough Shaped a Politician Who Helped Shape It." *New York Times*, January 2. https://www.nytimes.com/2015/01/03/nyregion/mario-cuomo-rose-from-queens-the-outsiders-borough-.html.

Rosen, Marty. 1998. "Nursing Home Moves Stun Patients. *New York Daily News*, September 22.

Rosenberg, Noah. 2011. "Ice Cold, 42 Flavors of Nostalgia." *New York Times*, August 7, Metropolitan section. https://www.nytimes.com/2011/08/07/nyregion/at-lemon-ice-king-nostalgia-is-served-ice-cold.html.

Rosenblum, Constance. 2010. "A Beach Bungalow with a Magnetic Pull." *New York Times*, October 22. https://www.nytimes.com/2010/10/24/realestate/24habi.html.

Sanjek, Roger. 1998. *The Future of Us All: Race and Neighborhood Politics in New York City*. Ithaca, NY: Cornell University Press.

Sax, David. 2009. *Save the Deli*. New York: Houghton-Mifflin.

Semple, Kirk. 2008. "Questions of Size and Taste for Queens Houses." *New York Times*, July 5. https://www.nytimes.com/2008/07/05/nyregion/05forest.html.

Seyfried, Vincent F., and William Asadorian. 1991. *Old Queens, NY, in Early Photographs*. New York: Dover.

Shack, William. 1956. "Modern Art in the Synagogue, II: Artist, Architect, and Building Committee Collaborate." *Commentary*, October.

Sikh Missionary Center. 2008. *Pearls of Sikhism: Peace, Justice, and Equality*. Phoenix, AZ: Sikh Missionary Center.

Silberman, Charles. 1985. *A Certain People: American Jews and Their Lives Today*. New York: Summit Books.

Simmel, Georg. 1900. "The Metropolis and Mental Life." In *The Sociology of Georg Simmel* translated, edited, and with introduction by Kurt H. Wolff, 409–24. New York: Free Press, 1950.

Smith, Betty. 1943. *A Tree Grows in Brooklyn*. New York: Harper and Brothers.

Thomas, William I., and Dorothy S. Thomas. 1928. *The Child in America: Behavior Problems and Programs*. New York: Knopf.

Tonnelat, Stephane, and William Kornblum. 2017. *International Express: New Yorkers on the 7 Train*. New York: Columbia University Press.

Ungar, Sanford J. 1995. *Fresh Blood: The New American Immigrants*. New York: Simon and Schuster.

Young, Terry, et al. 2008. "Sleep Disordered Breathing and Mortality: Eighteen-Year Follow-Up of the Wisconsin Sleep Cohort." *Sleep* 31, no. 8:1071–78.

Zborowski, Mark, and Elizabeth Herzog. 1962. Life Is with People: The Culture of the Shtetl. New York: Schocken Books.

Zimmerman, F. H. 2012. "Cardiovascular Disease and Risk Factors in Law Enforcement Personnel: A Comprehensive Review." *Cardiology Review* 20:159–66.

Zukin, Sharon. 2010. *Naked City: The Death and Life of Authentic Urban Places*. New York: Oxford University Press.

INDEX

Note: Page numbers in italic type indicate illustrations.

Hillcrest, Flushing, 151–53
Hinduism, 207, 368
Hindus, 144, 319
Hindu temples, xii, 148, *149*, 280
Hindu Temple Society of North America, xii, 148, *149*
hip-hop, 316–18, 359
Hispanics, xvi, 4, 18, 35, 45, 55–58, 72, 76, 79, 91–92, 102, 106, 115, 126, 135, 157, 164, 179, 189, 203, 211, 223, 297, 315, 341, 355, 368, 378, 380, 386, 395, 398, 404, 408, 409, 418. *See also specific Hispanic populations*
historic districts, 36
Hitchcock, Benjamin, 45
Hitler, Adolf, 241
Holder, Eric, 76
Holiday, Billie, 325
Hollis, 315–21; arts and culture, 316–18; ethnic groups, 315; famous people, 316–18; history, 315; housing, 315–16, 319; map, *314–15*
Hollis Hills, *216*, 217–20
Hollis Playground, 318
Holliswood, 203–9; ethnic groups, xiii, 203; famous people, 203; history, 203; housing, 203; map, *202*; religious life, 205–8
Holmes, New York, artist retreat, 141
Holocaust, 108, 179, 240
homelessness, 300
Homer, *Odyssey*, 28
Hoover Park, 190
Hope, Bob, 23
Hope NYC Church, 368–71
Horne, Lena, xi, 329
Horowitz, Vladimir, 24
horses, 111, *112*
Hot Tuna, 153
Houdini, Harry, xiii, 130–32, 231
Housing Choice Voucher Program (Section 8), 408, 409, 418
Howard, Ebenezer, 163
Howard, William, 403
Howard Beach, 403–9; community sense, 404, 406–7; ethnic groups, 404, 408, 409; famous people, 405–7; history,

403; housing, 407, 408; map, *402–3*; parks, 403, 408
Hua-lian Tsu-Hi Temple, 138, *139*, 140
Huguenots, 35
Hulk (wrestler), 243
Hunter, George, 6
Hunters Point, Long Island City, xv, 5–11
Hurricane Sandy, xv, 406, 408, 412, 415, 427–28

Ibrahim, Issa, 288
i-COOK Restaurant, 59–60
Idlewild Park Preserve, x–xi, 348, 351, *352*, 353
Iglesia Ni Cristo (Church of Christ), 49, 166
I Love Paraguay, 41, *42*, 43
Immaculate Conception Seminary, 229
immigrants, xiii, 3–4, 17–18, 41, 43, 45, 46–47, 53, 55, 63–64, 79, 91–92, 102, 112, 126, 144–45, 152, 154, 183–84, 192, 197, 200, 225, 235, 237, 261, 275–76, 282, 285, 308, 320–21, 355, 356–58, 368, 391, 393, 395, 398–400, 435
Indians, x, xi, xiii, 63, 64, 144, 200, 211, 270, 275–76, 280, 281, 292, 388–89
Indo-Guyanese, xii
Indonesians, 53
Intermediate School 227, 72–73, *73*
internet shopping. *See* online shopping
In the Chair Barber Shop, 318
Irish, xi, 3, 9–10, 18, 35, 38, 45, 46–47, 53, 79, 106, 115, 125, 135, 144, 157, 171, 211, 233, 235, 275, 283, 285, 297, 307, 337, 341, 355, 367, 374, 378, 386, 395, 404, 409, 411, 424, 427, 430, 433–35
Isamu Noguchi Garden Museum, 4
Israel, 339
Israelis, 164, 200
Italians, xi, 3, 7–8, 18, 35, 45, 53, 79, 82–84, 91, 106, 115, 116, 126, 144, 157, 163, 168, 171, 211, 233, 235, 275, 283, 285, 297, 307, 337, 341, 367, 374, 378–80, 386, 391, 395, 403, 404, 406, 408, 409, 411, 427, 434
Izoid's Barber Shop, 224–26

ALSO BY
WILLIAM B. HELMREICH

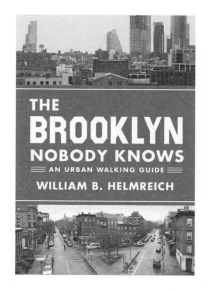

PRINCETON UNIVERSITY PRESS

**AVAILABLE WHEREVER BOOKS ARE SOLD
FOR MORE INFORMATION VISIT PRESS.PRINCETON.EDU**